WOMEN

AND

UNIONS

FORGING A PARTNERSHIP

Dorothy Sue Cobble,
Editor

ILR Press
Ithaca, New York

Library of Congress Cataloging-in-Publication Data

Women and unions: forging a partnership / Dorothy Sue Cobble, editor.

p. cm.

Includes bibliographical references and index.

ISBN 0-87546-300-2—ISBN 0-87546-301-0 (pbk.)

1. Women in trade-unions—United States—History—20th century.

2. Women in the labor movement—United States—History—20th
century. I. Cobble, Dorothy Sue.

HD6079.2.U5W63   1993

331.4'78'0973—dc20   92-38599

Copies may be ordered through bookstores or directly from

ILR Press
School of Industrial and Labor Relations
Cornell University
Ithaca, NY 14853-3901

Printed on acid-free paper in the United States of America

5 4 3 2 1

To Jack Olsen, who lived his belief in equality between men and women.

And to Ida Kellems Cobble, whose hillbilly fierceness and pride helped me speak my piece.

Contents

Acknowledgments

I salute the forty authors who contributed to *Women and Unions: Forging a Partnership*. Their patience, intelligence, and good humor kept the manuscript afloat during its six-year voyage from a three-page proposal to a three hundred-page anthology. I hope each realizes how critical her or his particular piece is to the overall impact and insight of this volume.

But some crucial contributors to the production of this volume are not listed in the table of contents. Let me name them here. Mary Paige Lang, my research assistant and a graduate student in the Labor and Industrial Relations Master's Program, served as communications liaison to the corps of authors assembled for *Women and Unions* when she wasn't waiting tables, writing seminar papers in labor studies, or tracking down obscure data (which at times I wrongly insisted *did* really exist). Sarah Ryan, another talented graduate student, joined the effort in its final stages, spotting errors my wearied eyes had overlooked. Irene Bouton, administrative assistant in the labor studies department, ably assisted me by keeping the incredible paper flow between editor, author, and publisher from overwhelming us all. Thanks go as well to Gail Allen, former administrative assistant in the labor studies department, for her diligent transcriptions of the 1987 Women and Labor Colloquia Series at the Institute of Management and Industrial Relations, Rutgers University, that provided the basis for chapter 2.

The staff of Cornell University's ILR Press deserve the highest accolades. Fran Benson, director of the press, believed in the book from the beginning and helped shape it in fundamental ways. She was consistently enthusiastic about the anthology despite missed deadlines and the emergence every six months or so of dramatically revised book outlines. She craftily lured me and the book toward the finish line by recounting what I later realized were the same arguments I'd made to her four years earlier about the value of the project. Patty Peltekos edited the entire manuscript in superb fashion, managing to be both painstaking and imaginative.

Lastly, I want to thank the unions to which I've belonged—the International Longshore and Warehouse Union, the American Federation of Teachers, and the American Association of University Professors—and the many unions and union members with whom I've worked since the early 1970s. They taught me that virtually every generalization about "organized labor" breaks apart when confronted with the complex, daily realities of individual unions and individual lives. It is also their wisdom that, although union membership continues to decline in the United States, the necessity and desire for collective power in the workplace is as great as ever.

WOMEN
AND
UNIONS

"They'd think they got the union crushed, but just like putting out a fire, you stomp on it and leave a few sparks, and here come a wind and it's going to spread again."
                                        —Southern worker

Introduction

Remaking Unions for the New Majority

Dorothy Sue Cobble

It has become the fashion to bemoan the stalled march toward women's economic equality and the decline of organized labor (for example, Hewlett 1986; Lipset 1986). Much of this commentary tends to premature death pronouncements. Social movements can be dormant for extended periods without losing their ability to blossom forth. This volume assumes such capacity for regeneration; it also assumes that intelligent and persistent horticultural care can hasten the spring.

The potential for forging a creative, productive partnership between working women and unions is greater now than at any other historic moment. Many of the historic barriers to cooperation have fallen: women make up close to a majority of the work force, the adherence to rigid gender roles has crumbled, and the permanent character of women's work force participation is widely acknowledged. Of equal importance, fundamental economic and social transformations have catapulted women onto the front lines of social change. Women are the new proletariat worldwide and it is the contradictions women are articulating and experiencing (as well as those experienced by men who do "women's work" in the service sector and take on "women's dual burden" of work and family) that are driving workplace reform. It is the needs of these workers that will in large part inform the agenda of any successful labor movement of the future. And in part it is the ability of organized labor to recognize these discontinuities and transform itself to attract this new work

The author would like to thank Ruth Milkman, Michael Merrill, Joyce Miller, Alice Kessler-Harris, Barbara Tischler, and those who participated in the February 1992 roundtable "Women, Feminism, and Unions" (organized by the Michael Harrington Center, Queens College, New York) for their trenchant and useful comments on this essay.

force that will determine whether workers opt for paternalistic, individualistic, or collective solutions to their workplace dilemmas.

The beginning steps in forging such a partnership must of necessity involve the two parties taking a fresh look at one another. Certain myths and biases have fogged the viewing lens of both groups. The feminist dismissal of unions as male-dominated institutions inherently antagonistic to women's interests has only recently come under reconsideration. A new, more open perspective is emerging among feminist scholars, one that asks under what conditions can unions represent the aspirations of women. Unions are being reconceived as more flexible, gender-neutral institutions—ones that, depending on the leadership or the will of the rank and file, can be more or less open to women's concerns. Feminist scholars also are questioning the class-biased scholarship (from both the right and the left) that assumes unions have unlimited power to enact their agendas (the myth of "big labor") and that holds unionists to standards of self-sacrifice and heroism that are never demanded of other classes (for example, Milkman 1990; Baron 1991).

Similarly, the women's movement itself has moved away from an exclusive focus on the needs of career women and a reliance on affirmative action, equal opportunity law, and access to professional training. The economic problems facing the majority of working women—low pay, job segregation, the added burden of a "second shift" at home—are now central to the feminist agenda. This shift in constituency and in tactics has evoked a new, more sympathetic stance toward unions and their viability as mechanisms for advancing the collective economic needs of working women (for example, Blum 1991; Fiorito and Greer 1986).

The labor movement for its part no longer automatically privileges the needs of white, male workers over those of others, and it has begun numerous initiatives aimed at strengthening its ties with women and minority workers. Yet labor needs to take a closer look at the transformations occurring in the world of work—transformations that primarily but not exclusively affect women—and the implications of these changes for the very nature and structure of unionism. Women (and the new work force generally) occupy jobs that are quite different from those held by labor's traditional constituency, the blue-collar hard hat. The new majority tends to be found in service jobs, in decentralized workplaces with under fifty employees, and in jobs with less of a permanent, continuous attachment to a single employer.

The majority of unions, however, remain wedded to an industrial model of employee representation. The industrial model of unionism emerged in the 1930s and 1940s primarily in response to the needs of blue-collar male workers toiling in large industrial worksites; it is a model that is increasingly outmoded for today's transformed work force (Kochan, Katz, and McKersie 1986; Heckscher 1988). Obviously, industrial unionism should not be abandoned wholesale. Manufacturing itself is not going to disappear, and many of the practices of industrial unionism may continue to be appealing and advantageous to a wide variety of workers. But just as industrial unionism developed alongside craft unionism in the early twentieth century as technological change and economic restructuring transformed the workplace, so too must other new forms of unionism evolve to meet the changed circumstances of the present. The labor movement must once again think in terms of multiple and competing models of unionism and, in particular, of devising approaches suitable for organizing and representing the growing female, service, and contingent work force.

This volume is designed to extend these emerging intellectual reformulations and hence to stimulate more informed and pointed policy and practice. What, in fact, has organized labor accomplished for working women? This volume documents the oft-ignored triumphs as well as the better known defeats. And what about the future? Are unions the institutional vehicle that can break the logjam on such longstanding issues as pay equity and child care? As the work world transforms and other issues, such as part-time and contingent work, work flexibility, and shorter hours, emerge, can unions meet these new needs as well as continue to serve their traditional constituency? The essays collected here attempt to address these questions and raise others. In so doing, the book aims to formulate the basis upon which a new, more productive partnership between working women and unions can be built—one that will energize labor's current membership as well as address the needs of those outside its ranks.

Why the Decades Ahead May Be Different

Historically, working women and unions have been at odds. The majority of international unions in the nineteenth century, for example, forbade female membership in their written constitutions. Formal barriers fell in the early twentieth century, but many unions remained skeptical or at best indifferent to the organization of women (Wertheimer 1975; Kessler-Harris 1975). In the 1930s and 1940s, women were swept into the newly emerging CIO unions—in large measure because of "the logic of industrial unionism" that included all workers at a particular worksite regardless of job title, race, or gender—but, even so, the primary objective of the CIO remained organizing the male-dominated mass production industries (auto, steel, rubber) (Brody

1980). Moreover, gender prejudice at times triumphed over industrial inclu-
siveness: Sharon Strom (1985), for example, has documented instances in
which every occupational group within an industry organized with the exception of the clerical sector, the one female-dominated unit. When the dust
settled in the late 1940s, virtually every major industry had unionized, boosting
the proportion of organized workers to a high-water mark of one in every
three workers in 1954 (Estey 1981:2–4). Nonetheless, until the last decade,
the male work force consistently enjoyed unionization rates more than double
those of female: in 1920, 26 percent of men were organized, 7 percent of
women. In the late 1970s, 29 percent of men and 12 percent of women
belonged to unions (Milkman 1980:96, 120–21). Only in the 1980s did the
gender gap in union membership close significantly. By 1990, unions represented 21.4 percent of men and 14.5 percent of women (USDOL 1991:228).

The record of union action and inaction toward women workers partially
reflected the economic competition between men and women, competition
fostered by employers concerned with boosting their profitability and authority at the workplace. Male unionists as well sought the exclusion of women
from their trades and the continuation of sex-segregated workplaces in order
to secure better jobs and working conditions. Psychological concerns, however,
undergirded the economic. Frequently, men desired separation from women
to retain their status in the eyes of a society that devalued jobs held by women
and to sustain their sense of masculinity—an identity that, Nancy Chodorow
and others have argued, rested in large part on the definition of women as
other and as inferior (Chodorow 1978; Williams 1989; Baron 1991). Lastly,
male unionists viewed women as marginal, temporary interlopers in the waged
work world and sought (often with the support of women) to enhance the
earning capacities of men so that women could return to their duties in the
domestic sphere.

The attitudes and actions of women also shaped the nature of their relationship with organized labor. As soon as they entered wage work, women
began to form separate-sex unions as well as demand access to the existing
male-dominated labor institutions (see, for example, Dublin 1979:86–107;
Blewett 1988; Cobble 1991a). Yet even in the instances in which the doors
of unionism swung open, fewer women (proportionately) than men crossed
the threshold. The poor bargaining position of women as "unskilled" workers
and the intense opposition they faced from employers dependent on their low
wages inhibited union formation and longevity among women. Union membership also lagged because women themselves made other choices. Some
wage-earning women viewed their labor force participation as temporary or
as secondary to the problems they faced fulfilling their home responsibilities.

Instead of joining workplace-based organizations directed toward improving their lives as waged workers, some wage-earning women devised alternative vehicles of collective protest. They initiated consumer boycotts, engaged in legislative reforms, and at times supported male struggles to unionize and maintain the family wage (Kessler-Harris 1982; Tentler 1979; Kaplan 1982; Frank 1991; Blewett 1988). Women spent more of their work lives within the family realm than did men and their protest activities historically have reflected this reality.[1]

Long-term economic and social changes have now dramatically altered the situation of both women and unions and created the basis for a new relationship. Women can no longer be considered a supplemental, temporary work force. In 1992, three out of four women between the ages of twenty-five and fifty-four were in the work force (USDOL 1992), women work nearly as many years as men, and the pattern of women's labor force participation increasingly resembles that of men. They begin work early, drop out for only a few years at most, and work into their sixties and seventies (Rix 1990:374–85).

In addition, by the 1990s, fewer women qualified as "secondary" workers in an economic sense. The rise of single female-headed families and the overall decline in real wages since 1973 have increased the economic pressures on women wage earners. The majority of U.S. families in the 1990s *require* at least two incomes to maintain what they perceive as an adequate standard of living; only one family in five has an adult devoted full-time to unwaged household tasks. Indeed, the living standards of American families would have plummeted further had not more and more women taken on the dual burdens of wage earning and housework (Nussbaum and Sweeney 1989:5–34, 103–26). The increased economic pressures on women also are evident in the skyrocketing poverty rates for women and children. Single-parent, female-headed families make up over half of all poor families, and one-fifth of all children live below the poverty line (Kamerman 1986:42–43).

Attitudinal shifts among women have been equally dramatic. The women's movement of the 1960s and 1970s helped move U.S. society toward a new consensus regarding the status of wage-earning women. It became legitimate for married women and even women with children to work outside the home and to expect equal treatment while on the job. The longstanding division of the work world into men's jobs and women's jobs also appeared increasingly indefensible both legally and in the eyes of the public.

---

[1]It is important to note that if labor activism is reconceived as encompassing reform efforts in relation to both waged and unwaged work, then women's participation in the labor movement (broadly defined) may have matched that of men.

In particular, women rejected the notion that their identity and sense of fulfillment should come solely (and in some cases primarily) from the domestic sphere. Despite the historic reality that the majority of wage-earning women always worked out of economic necessity (and not for "pin money"), the myth of women as nonessential earners had persisted among women themselves as well as in society at large. As late as the 1960s and early 1970s, sociological studies reported that married blue-collar women often characterized themselves as "supplemental" and "secondary" workers regardless of the essential or nonessential nature of their economic contribution (Komarovsky 1962; Rubin 1976). Only in the last two decades have the majority of women come to define their relation to work differently. Married working-class women as well as "career women" and single heads of household now talk about waged work as central to their identity and essential to the economic well-being of their family (Ferree 1980).

By the 1980s, it was clear that women would not be returning to the home and that the 1950s ideal of the family would never again be the dominant reality. Yet what kind of family structure and what status in the waged sphere did women want? How would the competing demands of work and family be resolved? Rather than choose between them as in the past—aspiring to become either a full-time housewife or deciding to give up all for one's career—most women now found themselves, by choice and by necessity, trying to "have it all," to be both the equal of men at work and the primary caretaker at home. Access to waged work and to the best-paying, highest-status jobs were important rights, and the freedom to define one's womanhood in ways other than the domestic was an equally critical achievement. Yet the pleasures of the private sphere, of emotional relationships, of child rearing, of noncommercially defined productive labor were also compelling.

It is this dual commitment and dual burden that has propelled the women's movement and women in general to place renewed emphasis on economic issues and the resolution of the tension between work and family. Whether an individual woman aspires to the highest career plateau, desires to work at a decent part-time job and raise a family, or simply seeks the option of spending less time at work and more time with her family, she faces almost insurmountable barriers. The top echelons of the work world are still closed to women; few good part-time jobs are available; and the fall in real wages since 1973 means that fewer women have the option of being at home (Schor 1991:80). Most women must resort to juggling full-time work with household responsibilities. They cope by curtailing their career ambitions and by demanding more support services in the family realm—increased household labor from other family members and/or paying for some of the traditional household tasks of child care, cleaning, and food preparation.

Yet many of these individual solutions are becoming increasingly problematic. Despite access to professional training and increased educational achievements, the gender wage gap and occupational segregation persist. The hours spent at work are lengthening. As real wages continue to fall, women must work ever longer hours to provide economically for their families. Family and leisure time is shrinking. Simultaneously, the neighborhood and extended family ties that once supported parents are frayed, if not severed. Grandparents live thousands of miles away; other relatives and even the once-dependable next-door neighbor are working as well. Indeed, if grandparents or other relatives *are* nearby, they are often cared for by an adult child (usually a daughter) who is simultaneously caring for her own children.

In the face of these heightened pressures, some women simply have lowered their expectations. They have given up their careers; or they have (partially) reconciled themselves to raising children with whom they hardly ever spend time. But most women do not see these compromises as permanent or desirable. They are looking for other options and would be the first to tell you that change is necessary.

Despite the overworked media phrase, "post-feminist," most women continue to believe that discrimination exists in the work world. Survey research inevitably reveals that the majority of women still identify with the historic goals of the feminist movement for job equality and equal opportunity (see, for example, *New York Times* 1989). In addition, however, they want their desires for a life outside of work to be an important part of that movement. *Newsweek,* for example, found in 1986 that most of the women they polled wanted *neither* full-time jobs *nor* full-time housework; they wanted a reasonable balance—an alternative our society has yet to offer (March 31, 1986:51). The new generation of women demands not only "equal treatment" and "opportunity," but a work world responsive to their desires for family, community, and leisure (*Time* 1990; Friedan 1981; Schor 1991).

Thus, women are concerned with creating new workplace options, and increasingly, I would argue, they are recognizing that these changes will only come about through collective power, whether it be political or economic. Significantly, there is now a gender gap in union sentiment paralleling the oft-cited gender gap in political attitudes. Countering the conventional wisdom that women are less "organizable" than men, research in the last decade consistently has shown that women workers are more interested in unions than men and, when given the actual choice, are more likely to vote for unionization. Thomas Kochan's 1979 findings that 40 percent of women would vote for a union if given the chance (as compared to only 33 percent for all nonunion workers) have been confirmed by Freeman and Medoff (1984) as well as others (Freeman and Leonard 1987; Kruse and Schur 1992). Indeed, AFL-CIO organizing survey data for 1986–87 revealed that unions won 57 percent of all campaigns conducted in female-dominated workplaces (units with 75 percent or more women) as compared to 33 percent in those with a majority of men (AFL-CIO Organizing Department 1989:6; see also Bronfenbrenner n.d.).

In part, women are more responsive to unions because the labor movement itself has changed. The feminization of the work force and the unionization in the 1960s and 1970s of female-dominated sectors of the economy—education; federal, state, and municipal government; the health care industry—altered the gender composition of organized labor. In 1954, 17 percent of organized workers were women; by 1988, the figure had climbed to 37 percent (Milkman 1990:4). By 1990, women constituted a majority (or close to a majority) of members in the newer international unions that had emerged in the 1960s—the American Federation of State, County and Municipal Employees (AFSCME), the Service Employees International Union (SEIU), and the teacher unions. Women also numerically dominated in such older internationals as the United Food and Commercial Workers (UFCW), The Communications Workers of America (CWA), and the garment unions (see table 1). Women moved into leadership positions as well. Although a "glass ceiling" blocks the rise of women into the top executive positions in the labor movement as it does in every institution in society (see table 1), the emergence of women as local union officers, heads of central labor councils, and as paid staff on the local and international level has been impressive (Needleman 1989; Gray this volume).

Many of the most powerful and vocal internationals within the labor movement are now unions with large female constituencies. As many of the contributors to this volume will demonstrate, it has been these unions that have provided national leadership on a wide range of women's concerns, from pay equity to parental leave, devising what sociologist Ruth Milkman has called a new "gender politics" (Milkman 1991). They have also pioneered more democratic, participatory approaches to organizing and representation—approaches that appear to be more in line with "female styles" of leadership and conflict resolution (Lerner 1991; Gilligan 1982; Hurd this volume). Their sensitivity toward and surprisingly successful advocacy of women's issues have gone a long way toward undermining the longstanding feminist critique of unions as bastions of male power and privilege.

Table 1. Female Membership and Leadership in Selected Labor
Organizations, 1978–1990

Labor organization	Year	Women members (thousands)	Women as percent of all members	Women officers and board members	Women as percent of all officers and board members
National Education	1978	1,240	75	5	55
Association	1985	1,000	60	3	33
	1990	1,600	72	4	45
International	1978	481	25	0	0
Brotherhood of	1985	485	26	0	0
Teamsters	1990	400	25	0	0
United Food and	1978	480	39	2	3
Commercial	1990	663	51	3	8
Workers					
American Federation	1978	408	40	1	3
of State, County	1985	450	45	4	4
& Municipal	1990	600	50	5	17
Employees					
Service Employees'	1978	312	50	7	15
International Union	1985	435	50	9	18
	1990	420	45	13	34
American Federation	1978	300	60	8	25
of Teachers	1985	366	60	11	32
	1990	455	65	11	32
Communications	1978	259	51	0	0
Workers of America	1985	338	52	1	6
	1990	338	52	1	6
International	1978	304	30	0	0
Brotherhood of	1985	330	30	0	0
Electrical Workers	1990	240	30	0	0
Amalgamated	1978	331	66	6	15
Clothing and	1985	228	65	3	9
Textile Workers	1990	160	61	5	20
International Ladies'	1978	279	80	2	7
Garment Workers'	1983	219	85	3	13
Union	1990	145	83	4	22
Hotel and Restaurant	1978	181	42	1	4
Employees	1985	200	50	2	8
	1990	143	48	1	4

Sources: 1978 data are from CLUW 1980: tables 3 and 5; 1983–85 data are from Baden 1986:236, 238; 1990 data are from a survey of unions conducted by Dorothy Sue Cobble with the help of Joyce Miller and Sandy Pope of the Coalition of Labor Union Women. The author thanks Ruth Milkman, who designed this table. See Milkman 1993 for further interpretation of the data.

Significantly, the increased power of women in certain sectors of the labor movement may even be responsible for the enhanced economic dividends women are now reaping from unions. Union membership has always offered women higher earnings. In 1988, for example, median weekly earnings of women union members were over $100 higher than for nonunion women workers (USDOL 1989). But in the public sector and in white-collar jobs where women have achieved the most power within their unions, the union premium (or the amount unionization raises wages) is now higher for women than for men (Freeman and Leonard 1987).

In addition, although some sectors of the labor movement remain wedded to tradition and appear bogged down in institutional protectionism, others—whether female-dominated or not—have shown considerable interest in reaching out to the new work force and in experimenting with new initiatives on the political and economic front. The AFL-CIO itself published a thoughtful and surprisingly candid document calling for concrete institutional reforms as well as for a recognition that the current generation of workers has needs that differ from those of the past (AFL-CIO 1985). In 1988 SEIU sponsored a major conference—"Solutions for the New Work Force"—in which some 250 scholars, policy analysts, and practitioners gathered to forge new policy and tactics (Nussbaum and Sweeney 1989). SEIU, the United Food and Commercial Workers, and the International Ladies' Garment Workers' Union, in particular, have turned successfully to "community-based" organizing and realized substantial union victories among Black and Hispanic low-wage service workers, many of whom are female (McMahon, Finkel-Shimshon, and Fujimoto 1991; Bronfenbrenner n.d.; Lerner 1991; Kelleher 1986).

Given these positive developments on the part of women and of unions, what keeps them apart? Why did 9 to 5 founder Karen Nussbaum's prediction that the 1980s would see a resurgence of labor activism among wage-earning women that would rival the great organizing campaigns of the 1930s fail to materialize? (Plotke 1980). Most obviously, the potential for collective action among women remains unrealized because of adverse external forces—hostile employers, restrictive labor laws, a new competitive global economy, technological transformations—all of which at times appear beyond the immediate control of women or of unions (Strauss, Gallagher, and Fiorito 1991). Yet despite these hostile forces, I would argue that the potential for organizing the new work force remains unfulfilled in part because the reforms occurring within the labor movement have not gone far enough. A new work force has arisen whose collective power will remain dormant until new forms of unionism are devised.

But who is this new work force and what kind of union representation do they desire? The work force of the 1990s is new because for the first time the majority of workers are female and minority: in the 1980s, the white, male worker lost his majority status. Women currently make up 46 percent of waged workers and may be half by the close of the century. In 1991, minorities constituted 20 percent of the work force; by the year 2000, they will comprise 25 percent, with the greatest increases posted by Hispanics and Asians (*Business Week,* July 8, 1991; AFL-CIO 1990). Black women will outnumber black men in the work force (Johnston 1987). Clearly, the changing gender and racial composition of the work force has significant implications for employee representation; of equal importance, however, are the transformations occurring in the work environment itself. The typical jobs of the postindustrial work force are ones whose very nature and structure differ profoundly from the blue-collar industrial world of labor's historic constituency. If the work force of the future is to be organized, the work lives and work needs of this new majority must be seen not as deviant or as a "special interest" group but as the norm, as expressive of the dominant reality.

The New Service Work Force

But what is so different about the work lives of the new majority? Aren't the problems plaguing them largely the same ones that have always troubled workers? Hasn't the proposition that the postindustrial work force would be a radical departure from the old—that it would mean the disappearance of the working class and the emergence of a bright new work world comprised of white-collar technicians and professionals—been thoroughly discredited? (Bell 1973). Well, yes and no.

Currently, the fastest growing occupations are not the highly skilled and well-paid knowledge workers but jobs such as janitor, food server, retail salesperson—jobs that are low-paid, lack promotional opportunities and benefits coverage, and exhibit high turnover (Silvestri and Lukasiewicz 1985; Nussbaum and Sweeney 1989). Given this new working poor, the wisdom has been that the primary implications for unions of the rise of the service sector are obvious. Workers need the basics unions have always provided: wages, benefits, improved working conditions, and job security. I agree. These issues will remain central for the new work force just as they are for the old. Yet there are discontinuities as well as continuities that warrant attention. It is to these discontinuities and their implications for labor that I now turn.

At least four fundamental transformations are reshaping the world of work. First of all, 90 percent of all new jobs in the last decade have been created in the service sector. Many of these jobs—low-level and professional—often involve personal service or interaction with a client, customer, or patient. The employment relationship is not the classic one described by Marx nor even the conventional adversarial one. A new third party, the customer, complicates and transforms the old dyad. Some service workers, for example, perceive the customer as more important in determining their wages and/or working conditions than the employer (for example, Cobble 1991a:44–48; Hochschild 1983:174–84). This attitude may prevail regardless of whether the worker's income is derived wholly from the customer (the professional in private practice or the home cleaner or handyman listed in the newspaper), only partially so (the waiter, bartender, or cab driver), or not at all (the nurse or salesclerk). The customer, described by saleswomen as "our friend the enemy," may also engender more strong emotion—usually anger, sometimes affection—than the employer (Benson 1986:258; Woods 1979). The quality of service provided and controlling the interaction with the client is central to service worker dignity. A union campaign based merely on an antiboss message may have little relevance to these workers.

Second, the relationship between employer and employee is changing in other fundamental ways, affecting service and nonservice employment. The dominant employment arrangement (at least since World War II) consisted of a continuous forty-hour week and the expectation of long-term tenure, benefits, and promotional opportunities. This traditional relationship—with its defined boundaries and its progressively deepening mutual obligations as employees accumulated seniority, pension contributions, and presumably increased their skills and productivity—is now eroding. Roughly one-quarter or more of all workers in the United States are part-time employees; are hired on a "temporary," subcontracted, or leased basis; or are defined as "independent contractors." Their numbers also are predicted to grow at a much faster pace than the total labor force for the rest of this century (Belous 1989). Few put in a nine-to-five workweek at the office, shop, or factory, and fewer still have long-term continuous relations with a single employer (Plewes 1988; Christensen and Murphree 1988). This "casualized" work force may not see the employer as either friend or enemy: their relationship with individual employers is brief, distant, and often mediated by a subcontractor or temporary agency.[2]

[2]Historically, women have been more likely than men to reside in the "casualized" sector of the economy, and this trend persists. What is changing, however, is that this typical female work status is now more widely shared by men. A similar point was made earlier in regard to men taking on "women's work" in the service sector and experiencing increasing tension between work and family.

Moreover, even in the so-called "core" sector of full-time, permanent, high-wage employment, the traditional reciprocal loyalty between employer and employee has slackened. Job turnover has increased in the face of employer reluctance to expend capital on human resources and lower employee commitment to an individual firm (Leinberger and Tucker 1991; Howes 1990).

Third, work sites themselves are changing. Economic restructuring and the growth of service work has meant the proliferation of smaller workplaces and the decentralization of production. Even industrial workplaces have followed this pattern (Nussbaum and Sweeney 1989). The seamstresses, legal transcribers, and business consultants toiling alone in home work sites scattered across the decentralized residential landscape represent but the furthest extreme of this trend (Boris and Daniels 1989).

Fourth, the long-standing separation between home and work is being challenged. With the continuing entry of women into the waged sphere beyond the home, the dissolution of the traditional family, and the aging of the work force, the problems of household production and human reproduction have become business concerns. Those juggling work and family—primarily women but some men as well—are demanding family support services such as child care and family leave. They are also calling for a "new work ethic" and asking that the workplace adjust to family needs rather than vice versa. Why, for example, should waged work be structured along the traditional male model of a nine-to-five, five-day (or more) week?[3] Why should intermittent, noncontinuous, and part-time work be penalized? Why should productivity gains be taken in the form of higher wages rather than shorter hours? Why should leisure or retirement years all be taken in one's sixties—a time when many women are still quite healthy and are free of child care responsibilities? Why not, as Swedish economist Gösta Rehn suggests, provide paid time off from wage work in one's early and middle years when household responsibilities are the greatest? (AFL-CIO 1990; Howe 1977; Hochschild 1989; Schor 1991; BNA *Daily Labor Report* May 1, 1992; Deutsch 1991; Kerr 1991; Brandt 1990; see Ratner 1979, pp. 427–28, for Rehn's ideas).

Partially in response to these demands, employers have implemented so-called flexible work arrangements: flextime, job sharing, temporary and part-time jobs, and "mommy tracks" for women professionals. The question is,

---

[3]When *Newsweek* asked working mothers in 1986 what work arrangement they would prefer if "they had a choice and finances were not a problem," only 13 percent stated they wanted full-time, regular hours while 16 percent preferred "not to be employed at all." A whopping 69 percent wanted to continue working but in a restructured work environment: 34 percent wanted part-time work; 23 percent wanted full-time, flexible hours; and 12 percent wanted to work from their home.

Are there union forms of flexibility and contingency that could be advocated—ones that would provide workers with increased leisure, autonomy, and choice without undermining job security and income? When the *New York Times* can report that 59 percent of women and 32 percent of men would give up a day's pay for a day of free time, clearly "the politics of time" must be given more attention (Sirianni 1988; Kerr 1991).

In sum, then, the new majority breaks with the past in that it is predominantly female and minority; it is also a work force whose daily realities have been radically transformed. Economic restructuring has fundamentally altered the nature of work, the employment relation, and the separation between work and family.

Hastening the Spring

The implications of these and other changes for employee representation are profound, and those concerned with organizing and representing the new work force have just begun to sketch out possible new approaches. Clearly, an openness to new issues is required. But, simply adding work and family issues to the collective bargaining agenda will not be enough. Fundamentally new forms of organizing and representation may be necessary to empower the new service occupations and the more mobile, contingent work force. The issue is not just how to organize women and minorities but how to organize the jobs they hold and the industries in which they work. In 1985, the AFL-CIO itself asserted that "unions must develop and put into effect multiple models for representing workers tailored to the needs and concerns of different groups." Charles Heckscher, in *The New Unionism,* has called for an "associational unionism" that would be suitable primarily for semiprofessional and managerial workers. I've argued for a reformulated "occupational unionism" and advocated the use of "worker-run temporary agencies" and "peer management"—two approaches historically relied upon by craft unions (Heckscher 1988; Cobble 1991a and 1991b; see also Sockell 1990). Others insist on new organizational styles and a "union culture" more amenable to women and minorities (Kessler-Harris 1985; Feldberg 1987). No consensus has emerged, however, on which changes should be given priority or which specific approaches would be best for particular workplaces and particular kinds of workers. But the dialogue has begun.

It is the aim of this volume to further that dialogue and help lay the basis for a reinvigorated labor movement. The volume is unique in that it combines an informed, sympathetic yet critical assessment of the labor movement with a feminist analysis. There are many excellent policy-oriented critiques of the labor movement (see, for example, Kochan 1985 or Strauss, Gallagher, and Fiorito 1991), as well as a growing number of feminist studies that reassess particular aspects of social policy affecting women workers (see, for example, Christensen 1988). Yet rarely are the two projects joined. Moreover, numerous studies are now in print that dissect the historic relation of women and the labor movement (Milkman 1985; Gabin 1990), and a flood of work has appeared on the current dilemmas of working women (Brown and Pechman 1987; Koziara, Moskow, and Tanner 1987). The need remains, however, for a volume that places both organized labor and working women at the center of its analysis, that explores not only the concerns of the new generation of women workers but the oft-overlooked potential for those concerns to be realized through collective organization at the work site.

Women and Unions: Forging a Partnership does not seek to provide definitive answers; it seeks to stimulate controversy and debate. The contributors to the volume represent a range of voices and backgrounds. They are university professors, international and local union officers and staff, labor educators, community activists, government policy makers, graduate students, and independent policy analysts. They are minority women and nonminority women; industrial, white-collar, and service workers; scholars, activists, or some combination of the two. Their opinions are diverse and sometimes at odds. Taken as a whole, the perspectives emerging from this book are those honed from the best of recent scholarship and then tested against the hard realities of life on the front lines of organizing, bargaining, and public policy-making.

The volume is structured as a series of conversations, in part to encourage maximum reader participation and responsibility. Following the foreword, the essayists present their views on six broad themes. Commentators respond to the arguments in the essays and to the larger topic under consideration. They ask, How convincing are the essays? What policy and research implications do they raise? What other aspects of the topic need attention? It is hoped that the reader will become part of the conversation, interacting with the authors and, along with the commentators, attempting to reconcile contradictions in the text and push the discussion forward to the next plateau.

The first two sections of the book reexamine the concerns that have preoccupied labor and women's activists in the last decade. Part 1 looks at the historic commitment of labor to closing the wage gap; part 2 assesses the new policies that have emerged from the labor movement to meet the family needs of workers. What progress has been made toward these goals? What strategies have proven effective? Which should be discarded? Which retained? How compelling will these issues be as rallying points for the work force of the future?

Parts 3 and 4 detail the rise of new forms of work and attempt to spin out the implications of these changes for workers and workplace representation. Is organized labor's historic commitment to retaining traditional on-site, full-time, and permanent forms of employment still desirable in an economy rapidly moving toward more part-time, home-based, and "flexible" job assignments? Should these workers be organized into unions? Can they be? In the eyes of many, management appears to be taking the lead in responding to the needs of the new work force. To what degree is this judgment warranted? What has been the impact on workers of the implementation of employer forms of "flexibility"? What alternatives has labor presented?

The essays in parts 5 and 6 assess the current state of union organizing and the degree to which union women are reshaping labor institutions to meet their needs. The essays reveal potential new models for organizing and representing workers—models that are being forged largely by women union leaders and activists. Whether it is mobilizing Chinese immigrant women to demand day care centers, organizing Harvard clerical employees, or handling grievances in a public sector bureaucracy, women union leaders emphasize the importance of worker involvement, of the necessity of democracy and participation. Can these new approaches organize men as well as women? Will the culture and structures of unions alter as more and more women enter their ranks? Can we speak of female "ways of knowing"? What about black female "ways of knowing," as one commentator suggests? Is the feminization of labor a positive development or simply another case of "male flight" from a devalued and weakened enterprise?

This volume is committed to furthering economic justice for working women. It assumes such a task requires collective as well as individual initiatives. It also assumes that social movements can only achieve their goals of democracy, human dignity, and individual liberty when they are committed to a process that reflects those goals. Tolerance for difference and encouragement of intellectual debate and study must be at the heart of that process. Only then can the participants realize their own potential. Only then will the movement remain a vehicle for progress rather than an end in itself.

References to the Introduction

AFL-CIO. 1985. *The Changing Situation of Workers and Their Unions: A Report by the AFL-CIO Committee on the Evolution of Work.* Washington, D.C.: AFL-CIO. February.

————. Department of Economic Research. 1990. *American Workers in the 1990s: Who We Are . . . How Our Jobs Will Change.* Washington, D.C.: AFL-CIO.

————. Department of Organization and Field Services. 1989. *AFL-CIO Organizing Survey: 1986–87 NLRB Elections.* Washington, D.C.: AFL-CIO. Mimeo. February.

Baden, Naomi. 1986. "Developing an Agenda: Expanding the Role of Women in Unions." *Labor Studies Journal* (Winter):229–49.

Baron, Ava, ed. 1991. *Work Engendered: Toward a New History of American Labor.* Ithaca, N.Y.: Cornell University Press.

Bell, Daniel. 1973. *The Coming of Post-Industrial Society: A Venture in Social Forecasting.* New York: Basic Books.

Belous, Richard. 1989. *The Contingent Economy: The Growth of the Temporary, Part-Time, and Subcontracted Work Force.* Washington, D.C.: National Planning Association.

Benson, Susan Porter. 1986. *Counter Cultures: Saleswomen, Managers, and Customers in American Department Stores, 1890–1940.* Urbana: University of Illinois Press.

Blewett, Mary. 1988. *Men, Women, and Work: Class, Gender, and Protest in the New England Shoe Industry, 1780–1910.* Urbana: University of Illinois Press.

Blum, Linda. 1991. *Between Feminism and Labor: The Significance of the Comparable Worth Movement.* Berkeley: University of California Press.

Boris, Eileen, and Cynthia Daniels, eds. 1989. *Homework: Historical and Contemporary Perspectives on Paid Labor at Home.* Urbana: University of Illinois Press.

Brandt, Barbara. 1990. "If We Just Had More Time: Why We Need a Thirty-Hour Work Week." *Dollars and Sense* (October): 16–18.

Brody, David. 1980. *Workers in Industrial America: Essays on the Twentieth-Century Struggle.* New York: Oxford University Press.

Bronfenbrenner, Kate. n.d. "Successful Union Strategies for Winning Certification

Elections and First Contracts: Report to Union Participants, Part 1: Organizing
Survey Results." Unpublished paper available from Bronfenbrenner, Dept. of Labor
Studies, Penn State University, New Kensington, PA 15068.

Brown, Clair, and Joseph Pechman, eds. 1987. *Gender in the Workplace.* Washington,
D.C.: Brookings Institution.

Business Week. July 8, 1991, 62.

Chodorow, Nancy. 1978. *The Reproduction of Mothering: Psychoanalysis and the Sociology of Gender.* Berkeley: University of California Press.

Christensen, Kathleen. 1988. *Women and Home-based Work: The Unspoken Contract.*
New York: Henry Holt.

Christensen, Kathleen, and Mary Murphree. 1988. "Introduction." In *Flexible Workstyles: A Look at Contingent Labor.* Conference summary. Washington, D.C.: U.S.
Department of Labor, Women's Bureau.

Coalition of Labor Union Women. 1980. *Absent from the Agenda: A Report on
the Role of Women in American Unions.* New York: Coalition of Labor Union
Women.

Cobble, Dorothy Sue. 1991a. *Dishing It Out: Waitresses and Their Unions in the
Twentieth Century.* Urbana: University of Illinois Press.

———. 1991b. "Organizing the Postindustrial Work Force: Lessons from the History of Waitress Unionism." *Industrial and Labor Relations Review* 44 (April):419–
36.

Deutsch, Claudia. 1991. "The Fast Track's Diminished Lure." *New York Times*
(October 6).

Dublin, Thomas. 1979. *Women at Work: The Transformation of Work and Community
in Lowell, Massachusetts, 1826–1860.* New York: Columbia University Press.

Estey, Marten. 1981. *The Unions: Structure, Development, and Management.* New
York: Harcourt Brace Jovanovich.

Feldberg, Roslyn. 1987. "Women and Unions: Are We Asking the Right Questions?"
In *Hidden Aspects of Women's Work,* edited by Christine Bose, Roslyn Feldberg,
and Natalie Sokoloff, 299–322. New York: Praeger.

Ferree, Myra Marx. 1980. "Working-Class Feminism: A Consideration of the Consequences of Employment." *Sociological Quarterly* 21:173–84.

Fiorito, Jack, and Charles Greer. 1986. "Gender Differences in Union Membership,
Preferences, and Beliefs." *Journal of Labor Research* 7 (Spring):145–64.

Frank, Dana. 1991. "Gender, Consumer Organizing, and the Seattle Labor Movement, 1919–29." In *Work Engendered: Toward a New History of American Labor,*
edited by Ava Baron, 273–95. Ithaca, N.Y.: Cornell University Press.

Freeman, Richard B., and Jonathan S. Leonard. 1987. "Union Maids: Unions and
the Female Work Force." In *Gender in the Workplace,* edited by Clair Brown and
Joseph Pechman, 189–212. Washington, D.C.: Brookings Institution.

Freeman, Richard B., and James Medoff. 1984. *What Do Unions Do?* New York:
Basic Books.

Friedan, Betty. 1981. *The Second Stage.* New York: Summit Books.

Gabin, Nancy. 1990. *Feminism in the Labor Movement: Women and the United Auto
Workers, 1935–1975.* Ithaca, N.Y.: Cornell University Press.

Gilligan, Carol. 1982. *In a Different Voice: Psychological Theory and Women's Development.* Cambridge: Harvard University Press.

Gray, Lois. 1993. "The Route to the Top: Female Union Leaders and Union Policy." In this volume.

Heckscher, Charles. 1988. *The New Unionism: Employee Involvement in the Changing Corporation.* New York: Basic Books.

Hewlett, Sylvia. 1986. *A Lesser Life: The Myth of Women's Liberation in America.* New York: William Morrow.

Hochschild, Arlie. 1983. *The Managed Heart: Commercialization of Human Feeling.* Berkeley: University of California Press.

———. 1989. *The Second Shift: Working Parents and the Revolution at Home.* New York: Avon.

Howe, Louise. 1977. *Pink Collar Workers: Inside the World of Women's Work.* New York: G. P. Putnam.

Howes, Candace. Forthcoming. "The Cost of Maturity: Foreign Direct Investment in the Auto Industry." Washington, D.C.: Economic Policy Institute.

Hurd, Richard. 1993. "Organizing and Representing Clerical Workers: The Harvard Model." In this volume.

Johnston, William. 1987. *Work Force 2000: Work and Workers for the Twenty-First Century.* Indianapolis: Hudson Institute. June.

Kamerman, Sheila. 1986. "Women, Children, and Poverty: Public Policies and Female-headed Families in Industrialized Countries." In *Women and Poverty,* edited by Barbara Gelpi et al., 41–64. Chicago: University of Chicago Press.

Kaplan, Temma. 1982. "Feminist Consciousness and Collective Action: The Case of Barcelona, 1910–18." *Signs* 7 (Spring):545–66.

Kelleher, Keith. 1986. "Acorn Organizing and Chicago Homecare Workers." *Labor Research Review* 8 (Spring):33–45.

Kerr, Peter. 1991. "Tempus Fugit, but You Can Buy It." *New York Times* (October 10): D8–D10.

Kessler-Harris, Alice. 1975. "Where Are the Organized Women Workers?" *Feminist Studies* 3:92–110.

———. 1982. *Out to Work: A History of Wage-earning Women in the United States.* New York: Oxford University Press.

———. 1985. "Problems of Coalition-building: Women and Trade Unions in the 1920s." In *Women, Work, and Protest,* edited by Ruth Milkman. Boston: Routledge & Kegan Paul.

Kochan, Thomas. 1979. "How American Workers View Labor Unions," *Monthly Labor Review* 102:25.

Kochan, Thomas, Harry Katz, and Robert McKersie. 1986. *The Transformation of American Industrial Relations.* New York: Basic Books.

Komarovsky, Mirra. 1962. *Blue-Collar Marriage.* New York: Random House.

Koziara, Karen, Michael Moskow, and Lucretia Dewey Tanner, eds. 1987. *Working Women: Past, Present, and Future.* Washington, D.C.: Bureau of National Affairs.

Kruse, Douglas L., and Lisa A. Schur. 1992. 41. "Gender Differences in Attitudes toward unions." *Industrial and Labor Relations Review* 46 (October): 89–102.

Leinberger, Paul, and Bruce Tucker. 1991. *The New Individualists: The Generation after the Organization Man.* New York: HarperCollins.

Lerner, Stephen. 1991. "Let's Get Moving: Labor's Survival Depends on Organizing

Industry-wide for Justice and Power." *Labor Research Review* 18 (Fall/Winter) no. 2:1–16.

Lipset, Seymour Martin, ed. 1986. *Unions in Transition: Entering the Second Century.* San Francisco: ICS Press.

McMahon, June, Amy Finkel-Shimshon, and Miki Fujimoto. 1991. *Organizing Latino Workers in Southern California.* Los Angeles: UCLA Center for Labor Research and Education. June 28.

Milkman, Ruth. 1980. "Organizing the Sexual Division of Labor: Historical Perspectives on 'Women's Work' and the American Labor Movement." *Socialist Review* 10 (January–February):95–151.

———. 1991. "Labor and Management in Uncertain Times: Renegotiating the Social Contract." In *America at Century's End,* edited by Alan Wolfe. Berkeley: University of California Press.

———. 1993. "Union Responses to Work Force Feminization in the U.S." In *The Challenge of Restructuring: North American Labor Movements Respond,* edited by Jane Jenson and Rianne Mahon. Philadelphia: Temple University Press.

Milkman, Ruth, ed. 1985. *Women, Work, and Protest: A Century of U.S. Women's Labor History.* Boston: Routledge & Kegan Paul.

Needleman, Ruth. 1986. "Turning the Tide: Women, Unions, and Labor Education." *Labor Studies Journal* 10 (Winter): 203–35.

Nussbaum, Karen, and John Sweeney. 1989. *Solutions for the New Work Force.* Cabin John, Md.: Seven Locks Press.

Plewes, Thomas. 1988. "Understanding the Data on Part-Time and Temporary Employment." In *Flexible Workstyles: A Look at Contingent Labor.* Conference Summary, Washington, D.C.: U.S. Department of Labor, Women's Bureau.

Plotke, David. 1980. "Interview with Karen Nussbaum." In *Socialist Review* 10 (January–February):151–59.

Ratner, Ronnie, ed. 1979. *Equal Employment Policy for Women.* Philadelphia: Temple University Press.

Rix, Sara, ed. 1990. *The American Woman, 1990–91: A Status Report.* New York: W. W. Norton.

Rubin, Lillian. 1976. *Worlds of Pain: Life in the Working-Class Family.* New York: Basic Books.

Schor, Juliet. 1991. *The Overworked American: The Unexpected Decline of Leisure.* New York: Basic Books.

Silvestri, George, and John Lukasiewicz. 1985. "Occupational Employment Projections: The 1984–95 Outlook." *Monthly Labor Review* 108 (November):42–57.

Sirianni, Carmen. 1988. "Self-Management of Time: A Democratic Alternative." *Socialist Review* (October–December):5–56.

Sockell, Donna. 1990. "Research on Labor Law in the 1990s: The Challenge of Defining a Representational Form." Paper presented to the Second Bargaining Group Conference, Cornell University, May 6.

Strauss, George, Daniel Gallagher, and Jack Fiorito, eds. 1991. *The State of the Unions.* Madison, Wis.: Industrial Relations Research Association Series.

Strom, Sharon. 1985. " 'We're No Kitty Foyles': Organizing Office Workers for the Congress of Industrial Organizations, 1937–50." In *Women, Work, and Protest,* edited by Ruth Milkman. Boston: Routledge & Kegan Paul.

Tentler, Leslie. 1979. *Wage-earning Women: Industrial Work and Family Life in the United States, 1900–1930*. New York: Oxford University Press.

Time Magazine. 1990. *Special Issue on Women,* vol. 136 (19).

U. S. Department of Labor, BLS. 1991. *Employment and Earnings* 38. Washington, D.C.: GPO. January.

———. "Employment in Perspective: Women in the Labor Force." Report 823. Washington, D.C.: GPO. First Quarter.

———. Women's Bureau. 1989. "Facts on Working Women: Women in Labor Organizations." No. 89–2:1–4. Washington, D.C. August.

Wertheimer, Barbara. 1975. *We Were There: The Story of Working Women in America*. New York: Praeger.

Williams, Christine L. 1989. *Gender Differences at Work: Women and Men in Non-Traditional Occupations*. Berkeley: University of California Press.

Woods, Susan. 1979. "Waitressing: Taking Control of Our Work." *Quest* 5 (Summer):82–94.

Part I
Closing the Wage Gap

The problems of income inequality, poverty, and occupational segregation did not diminish for women in the 1980s, despite the dramatic decline of the gender wage gap. The position of some women (primarily white, professional, single, and without children) has improved relative to men, but as Hartmann and others in this section suggest, the shrinking wage gap has as much to do with the decline in male income as with an improvement in the economic situation of women.

One fundamental continuity exists for the U.S. labor movement as it moves into the twenty-first century: income and workplace opportunity issues will remain central for women as well as for men. But the means to achieve these ends for women may need reformulating. In an argument paralleling William Julius Wilson's proposals for African-Americans in *The Truly Disadvantaged* (1987), Margaret Hallock urges a fundamental strategic shift away from gender-based campaigns toward universal programs that address overall economic inequality. In those cases where pay equity *does* remain a focus, Hallock agrees with Jean Ross, Ronnie Steinberg, and others, that relying on job evaluations will likely yield disappointing results. Job evaluation procedures are riddled with gender bias and ultimately foster management control of wage-setting.

In her commentary, Marlene Kim agrees in part with this critique of job evaluation but she argues that job evaluation systems are key to wage-setting in the United States and that proponents of gender equity must not abandon reform efforts in that arena. Kim's point is reinforced in Gloria Johnson's account of the strategies pursued by the IUE: closing the wage gap, of necessity, must involve a struggle over value and the technical rationales used in wage compensation.

The blue-collar union women in Brigid O'Farrell and Suzanne Moore's case study illustrate the wisdom of adopting a broad, inclusive strategy to remedy gender inequity. These workers achieved their goals of integrating women into skilled, male-dominated jobs by refusing to give up their specific (gender-based) demands for legal redress for sex discrimination under Title VII, and they negotiated affirmative action and other "special programs" for women. They also fought for other workplace issues, such as improved health and safety standards and job posting, that benefited everyone and won them enduring supporters.

Affirmative action, as Barbara Bergmann, Anna Padia, and Carrie Donald argue, remains a viable remedy: It has the potential to raise wages as well as enhance career opportunities. Yet just as with pay equity, affirmative action cannot be successful without the support of the male work force. Educating and organizing men has to be taken seriously. A case must be made for the fundamental injustice of the workplace in the absence of affirmative action— what Bergmann refers to as the "white male quota system." But, as O'Farrell and Moore demonstrate, the real fears of men about job loss and loss of status cannot be ignored.

1
Unions and the Gender Wage Gap

Margaret Hallock

The wage gap between men and women workers in the United States has been remarkably intractable. Estimates by the U.S. Department of Labor showed that, in 1960, women who worked full-time, year-round, earned on average only 60.8 percent of the median annual earnings of men (1983:82). This gap remained roughly stable for two decades, but during the 1980s, when women's annual earnings rose to 68 percent of men's, progress was swift (U.S. Bureau of the Census 1990).

Although there have been some improvements, a sizable wage gap remains, which means that women are disproportionately low wage earners. The wage gap is of concern because it reflects a basic unfairness in the distribution of economic rewards and because, increasingly, women are poor. Women and their children now make up the majority of the poverty population, and this will be the case as long as women earn low wages (Kamerman 1986:42–43).

The wage gap has become an issue for unions because women account for a larger proportion of the work force and the labor movement than in the past. Unions have adopted pay equity as the major strategy to eliminate the wage gap. They have also adopted policies to combat sex segregation of occupations, a closely related issue.

I review what we know about the wage gap and analyze policies to diminish the gap, with particular emphasis on the achievements and disappointments of pay equity. The main conclusion is that pay equity has been of limited effectiveness because of technical and political factors. I argue that pay equity is still a useful and necessary policy but that it needs to be reformulated to diminish the emphasis on job evaluation.

In addition, unions could help close the wage gap by concentrating on policies and demands that promote overall wage equality, that will raise wages for low-wage jobs, and restructure work to help workers cope with work and family responsibilities, and by representing workers in a less secure economy by promoting apprentice, skill-training, and employment programs. In short, unions can reduce the gender wage gap by recommitting to an ideology of equality. Adequate and equitable wages for all workers has not been a prominent union theme in the United States, in contrast to the union platforms in Europe and Canada. Wage solidarity and equality programs are desperately needed to combat the growing inequality of incomes in the United States.

The Wage Gap: What We Know

Unions and policymakers must understand the wage gap in order to fashion policies and strategies that will address it successfully. In general, explanations for the wage gap can be sorted into the following: discrimination against women, sex segregation of jobs and the corresponding undervaluation of women's work, the characteristics of women workers, the interaction of work and family, and differences among firms and industries. Each explanation has policy implications. This section summarizes the literature on the nature of the wage gap and the next section describes policies that have been used to attack it.

Economists and other researchers often explain portions of the wage gap mathematically and claim that the unexplained portion is due to discrimination against women. For example, they have analyzed the impact of age and education on wages and estimated the portion of the wage gap that is related to differences in these characteristics among men and women workers. This approach is not wholly satisfactory if discrimination is built into the factors that explain the gap. Many feminists would say that education levels and sex segregation of jobs reflect historical discrimination against women and that economists therefore underestimate discrimination if these factors are used as explanatory variables.

The following generalizations emerge from the literature on the wage gap.

First, discrimination exists. After controlling for the characteristics of women workers and their jobs, a residual gap remains (Gunderson 1989). Part of the wage gap simply cannot be explained by the numerous quantifiable factors that economists use to explain wages. In other words, women earn lower wages because they are women.

Second, sex segregation of jobs and undervaluation of women's jobs account for a substantial portion of the wage gap. Especially when detailed occupations such as X-ray technician or executive secretary are analyzed, we find that men work with men, women work with women, and women earn less than men. Earning less for working at the same job is not the problem; segregation by occupation, combined with the lower value of women's work, is the problem.

Sorensen (1990) finds that crowding women into female-dominated jobs accounts for up to one-third of the wage gap. Further, these jobs are under-valued compared to male jobs. In five public jurisdictions where pay equity job evaluations were performed, nearly one-half of the overall earnings gap between men and women was due to the combined effect of occupational segregation and a lower pay structure for female jobs relative to male jobs (Sorensen 1987).

The origin of lower wages for women's work is not mysterious to feminists, who cite historical examples of sex segregation of men and women workers with separate salary schedules and explicit systems such as the family wage system under which women were assumed to be secondary earners (Hartmann 1976; Lewis 1988; Barrett and McIntosh 1980; Bergmann 1986).

Third, women's education, experience, and other measures of productiv-ity explain part of the wage gap. Women come to the labor market with different types of education than men, they make different choices, and they have less experience and job tenure (Gunderson 1989; O'Neill 1985; Blau and Beller 1988). In a market that values full-time work and careers and prescribes relatively rigid sex roles, women's nonmarket responsibilities have had an impact on their earnings. These factors are closely related to discrimination, sex segregation of jobs, and the household division of labor. Women's place in society has, to a large degree, determined women's place in the work force.

Fourth, the household division of labor and other factors outside the labor market reduce women's earnings (Gunderson 1989; Shelton and Firestone 1989; McAllister 1990). Women are still the primary workers in the non-market economy. The largest pay gap exists between married men and women, and the smallest gap exists for nonmarried women and men without children. Time spent on household tasks has a negative effect on both men's and women's wages, but the effect is much larger for women. Women are also more likely to work part-time due to the household division of labor, and this has an additional effect on earnings that is not measured by the wage gap for full-time workers.

Fifth, differences across firms and industries account for part of the wage gap (Gunderson 1989; Blau 1977; Hodson and England 1986). Industrial relations scholars and labor economists have long known that individual firms create internal labor markets in which wages and other factors such as seniority and promotion policies differ substantially from other firms and the prevailing market. The nature of the industry and the extent of union-ization within it also matter. Gill and Fletcher (1990) find that the pro-portion of the work force represented by unions is correlated with the amount of improvement in the wage gap in selected industrial countries between 1960 and 1980. The male-female wage gap is smaller for union members, and women earn higher wages if they are members of a union (Anderson, Doyle, and Schwenk 1990).

Sixth, improvements in the wage gap during the 1980s are related to stagnation in men's wages, women moving into higher paying jobs, and improvements in women's "productivity" characteristics such as education and job tenure (Gunderson 1989; O'Neill 1985; Hartmann this volume; Bernstein 1988). There have been some improvements in the degree of sex segregation as women move into mixed and male-dominated jobs. Men, however, are not entering traditionally female jobs. And the movement of women into men's jobs appears to have mixed effects. Blau and Beller (1988) demonstrate that women's relative earnings fall as they move into a male job, confirming earlier evidence that wages fall when a job becomes dominated by women. Perhaps more disturbing is that part of the improve-ment in the earnings gap is a result of the stagnation of male earnings and the sharp decline in the real wage of male high school graduates. The only good news in the recent improvement seems to be that the wage gap is smaller for young women, ages 16–24, now entering the labor force; the question now is if young women can maintain their relative earnings as they grow older.

Seventh, improvements in the wage gap hide the fact that earnings are becoming more unequal among women. Inequality in wages and income is increasing in the United States for all earners and among women (Thurow 1987; Wagman and Folbre 1988). A higher percentage of women workers were in high-wage jobs (earning more than $30,000 per year) in 1986 compared with 1979. But the proportion of women in low-wage (under $10,000 per year) or part-time jobs increased during the recession of the 1980s and has not yet declined to the level of the 1970s (Wagman and Folbre 1988).

These trends reflect women's higher level of education, the movement of women into managerial and professional technical jobs, and the stagnation of wages in the low-wage sectors. Wages grew fastest for professional and man-agerial jobs, and women increased their share of these jobs between 1975 and 1986. Further, professional and managerial women are often part of a dual-income white family, and this exacerbates the growing inequality of income among families.

The Wage Gap: What We Have Tried

For thirty years, women, policymakers, and unions have pursued policies and programs to reduce the wage gap. These policies can be discussed in two groupings: equal employment policies, including affirmative action, and equal pay policies, including comparable worth or pay equity. More recent policies include work and family initiatives that would facilitate fuller participation by women in the labor market and help with the problems of combining work and family duties (Cook 1987; York, Cowell this volume).

Equal employment opportunity (EEO) programs seek to prevent discrimination against women in the various phases of employment decisions such as recruiting, hiring, and transfers and promotions. Affirmative action attempts to overcome the cumulative effects of inequality and systemic discrimination by requiring aggressive action to recruit and hire women and members of minority groups (Gunderson 1989).

Although equal employment opportunity legislation and programs can work with strict enforcement, there is no clear evidence that U.S. laws have had a substantial positive effect on women's employment and earnings. The overall assessment of affirmative action is somewhat brighter: such programs result in employment gains for women and minorities in firms where the plans are required, but the number of such firms is small relative to the entire economy (Gunderson 1989).

Unions have attempted to help women in traditional women's jobs by bargaining affirmative action programs with employers and by establishing career development programs (see Padia this volume). Union career development programs bolster the promotion and transfer mechanisms that exist in contracts and assist workers in understanding and qualifying for new opportunities. More advanced programs seek to develop new opportunities for women workers by restructuring jobs and enhancing training opportunities.

Despite the significant amount of activity in affirmative action and equal employment programs, they primarily affect women in professional or managerial jobs and those who can and are willing to change jobs and enhance their skills. Such programs have little effect on the wages and employment of the millions of women who continue to work in the predominantly female jobs in the clerical and service occupations. Yet this is where the majority of women work, and the largest number of new jobs in the economy are being created in these areas. Relying on promotions to higher level jobs is a cruel hoax that will only disappoint the women who remain in these female-dominated jobs. Further, relying on these programs sends a message to those who remain in traditionally female jobs that reinforces the message of the capitalist market—that these jobs are less important and valuable than other jobs and that women who work in these jobs are inferior to those who can move into "nontraditional" and male-dominated jobs.

Recognition of the limitations of affirmative action and antidiscrimination programs led many to advocate comparable worth or pay equity (Blum 1987). Pay equity held the promise of *upgrading wages in the jobs where women work now* rather than requiring women to change jobs in order to earn a decent wage. Equal pay legislation did not have an impact on the wage gap because men and women do not work in the same jobs, and affirmative action required impossible shifts of women to different jobs. Clearly, a policy was needed that would attack the heart of the problem: the wage gap between male- and female-dominated jobs.

The Achievements of Pay Equity

Pay equity addresses the discrimination against women that is reflected in the low wages paid for work traditionally performed by women. It attempts to eliminate wage discrimination and the effects of gender by paying according to productivity or value.

The initial concept of comparable worth, developed in the early 1980s, called for "equal pay for work of equal value." In defining value, early advocates relied on the long-standing management practice of job evaluation in which jobs with different content and duties could be analyzed and compared for their levels of skill, effort, and responsibility and the nature of working conditions. Value to the employer was thus defined as job complexity, which could be measured by knowledge, skill, responsibility, and working conditions.

The dominant practice of pay equity that emerged from the 1980s involved comparing male- and female-dominated jobs with a job evaluation system that gives points for varying levels of skill or knowledge, effort or problem solving, responsibility or accountability, and working conditions.[1] Supporters of comparable worth asked that all jobs be treated consistently so that all wages would reflect skill, effort, and responsibility in the same fashion. After jobs are analyzed and compared, jobs with equal job evaluation scores should be paid similarly—regardless of the sex of the worker.

---

[1]These factors are known in the job evaluation field as "compensable factors" because they have historically been associated with wages and therefore presumably measure value to the employer. Traditional or standard job evaluation systems were developed by quantifying the relation between wages and compensable factors. These systems thus reflect market-wage relationships for the jobs for which they were developed, primarily management and white-collar jobs.

Pay equity became well-known and widespread for a relatively new program, but it did not meet the expectations of its proponents. Nevertheless, the achievements were significant.

First, where it was implemented, pay equity did raise the wages of women and minorities in low-wage clerical and service jobs. Job evaluation identified consistent gaps between male- and female-dominated jobs, and wages for selected jobs increased by 10 to 20 percent in most applications (Gunderson 1989; Sorensen 1987; O'Neill 1985). Minorities were helped because they were (and are) concentrated in the low-wage service and clerical jobs (Malveaux 1985).

Second, pay equity challenged historical wage patterns and empowered women to improve their status. Unlike affirmative action, which was targeted at individuals, pay equity was a collective reform, required collective action, and affected many more women (Blum 1987). This reform targeted jobs rather than people and looked at women as a class. For the first time many women collectively and publicly questioned wage determination practices and the ideology of the market that led to their lower wages. They discovered numerous contradictions in the relationship between skill and wages and the effect of market wages on firm-level decisions. They found that education, skill, and labor market shortages often led to higher wages for men's, but not women's, jobs.

Pay equity campaigns are empowering because they reinforce the importance of the work that women do. In Oregon, women held public testimonies before state legislators and displayed their pay stubs after describing their job duties and responsibilities. They asked why a child care worker in a university child development center should be paid less than the worker monitoring the animals in the science laboratory. They asked why workers who take care of *people* consistently earn less than workers who take care of *things*. They asked why the secretaries who coordinate the business of large departments earn less than shuttle drivers.

Words such as *dignity* and *respect* were common in such campaigns. Women who were formerly ashamed to admit they were clerical workers proudly asserted the value and importance of their work. Women who had felt belittled by the emphasis in affirmative action and the women's movement on moving into "higher level" jobs proclaimed the value of their jobs. Women in technical, professional, or other elite jobs became more aware of, and sympathetic to, the concerns and realities of working-class women.

Women's numbers and status in unions grew as they organized for pay equity, and they formed important and lasting coalitions with women's groups. Organizing for pay equity was the first political and collective bargaining activity for many women and an important point of solidarity between feminists and union women.

Third, pay equity proponents and practitioners made an important contribution to the technical field of job evaluation and compensation. Pay equity programs explicitly confronted the issue of the value of work as analysts examined traditional job evaluation systems for gender bias (see Acker 1987; Steinberg and Haignere 1987; Treiman and Hartmann 1981; Ontario Pay Equity Commission 1989; Remick 1984). Steinberg and others found that skills and duties traditionally associated with women's work are routinely accorded less value in job evaluation systems and in compensation plans. Practitioners made numerous proposals to reform traditional job evaluation systems or to create new systems that more adequately recognized the range of duties and skill often found in women's jobs.

Fourth, pay equity led to better data on women's jobs and more consistency in job classification and compensation. Because of the enormous effort put into recording and analyzing job duties, new information on the wages, duties, working conditions, and minimum qualifications of male- and female-dominated jobs emerged. These data will be a rich source of information on discrimination at the firm level, firm-specific practices of job identification and structure, and the role of gender. Further, the extensive data on job duties and skills in various jobs and job families can help unions and workers restructure career ladders, training programs, and promotion and transfer policies.

The Disappointments of Pay Equity

Although working women are better off because of the movement for pay equity, the proponents' early dreams have not been realized. The reform has been limited and constrained in many of its achievements and expected effects.[2]

The actual impact of pay equity on the wage gap has been small. Even where pay equity wage adjustments have occurred, the wage gap between male and female jobs of comparable value has not been fully eliminated. The potential of pay equity is to raise wages by 20 percent (Sorensen 1987 and 1990), but actual adjustments are more often in the neighborhood of 10 percent for *selected jobs only* (Gunderson 1989; Orazem and Matilla 1989).

[2]This section relies on Steinberg (1987), Brenner (1987), Blum (1987), Malveaux (1985), Acker (1989), various articles in Steinberg (forthcoming), Evans and Nelson (1989a and 1989b), and conversations and interviews with practitioners and proponents in unions and other organizations.

Wage adjustments for women have been reduced by a number of factors. Public sector budgets were constrained in the 1980s, and wage adjustments were lowered or phased in over a number of years. Often a set amount of money was reserved for pay equity before the job evaluation was complete, resulting in less than full adjustments.

Technical issues limited wage adjustments as well. Proponents often settled for an analysis of the wage gap that compared female-dominated jobs to all jobs rather than to male-dominated jobs. This approach had the effect of comparing jobs that have discriminatory wages with themselves, thereby underestimating the wage gap. Additionally, consultants and management often proposed that wages should be adjusted to be within a certain range of male jobs, creating a zone or band for equity and leaving a wage gap (see Steinberg this volume).

Political considerations also limited adjustments at a given establishment. Management frequently proposed to limit men's wage increases in some fashion to pay for pay equity, thus encouraging male workers to struggle to maintain their relative position. The result was lower wage adjustments for women (Orazem and Matilla 1989 and 1990). Implementing pay equity has been a highly political process, and political interests have affected the outcomes (Hallock 1990).

The limited wage impact is also a result of pay equity being confined to the public sector. Nearly all of the successful pay equity initiatives have been in the public sector and it is unclear if wage adjustments in the public sector have had a spillover effect on private sector wages.

Indeed, in some instances, pay equity became a technical reform that enhanced management control over personnel systems. Management succeeded in wresting control of the reform in several ways. First, management sought to achieve its own agenda in the name of pay equity. In Oregon and Minnesota, for example, managers learned that job evaluation and pay equity studies could be used to reshape the classification system and dilute the results of pay equity demands.

Second, management sought to control the technical aspects of studies. They were aided by the sheer magnitude and complexity of some studies. Feminists who lobbied for a legislative bill were frequently excluded by the time commitment necessary for involvement. Similarly, union representatives with competing demands in representing workers often could not diligently pursue the technical aspects of a study. Often only full-time employees, mostly managers, had the time to meet the technical demands of pay equity. Management control is not always detrimental. Evans and Nelson (1989a) show that pay equity implementation in Minnesota was successful because of numerous players in the technical issues. Thus the lesson appears to be that sympathetic management can resolve technical issues smoothly while a hostile management can use these same issues to obfuscate and block the pay equity process.

Moreover, pay equity proponents have not succeeded in significantly reforming traditional job evaluation systems or redefining the value of women's work. The basic problem with pay equity has been the lack of *operational definitions of value and equity*. Pay equity programs thus became a power struggle between women and men, labor and management, and feminists and nonfeminists. The process at times was divisive. No consensus existed on how to proceed with a pay equity study, the appropriate job evaluation system to be used, how to analyze pay relationships, and how to adjust wages. Despite the proponents' effort and diligence, no clear alternative to traditional job evaluation systems emerged. Pay equity reform ventured onto solid corporate/management turf and failed to achieve significant change (Acker 1989).

Traditional job evaluation systems have been criticized for ignoring many aspects of women's jobs, including care-giving, information management, administrative tasks, and dealing with dirt. Also, many of the duties that women perform are difficult to specify and evaluate. I have seen male job evaluators struggle with concepts such as coordinating workflow and schedules and the problem of frequent interruptions of complicated clerical work.

In most pay equity cases, there was no significant challenge to the *value* placed on duties found in female-dominated jobs. Social work or child care may be recognized to have a higher skill than before the job evaluation study, but fundamental changes in the value of taking care of people or children was often outside the scope of the technical study. Job evaluation factors and their weights were seldom altered, they were just applied more consistently.

Job evaluation reinforces the notion that wages are based on skill and that the solution to the wage gap is to eliminate gender bias in *measuring* skill or value (Lewis 1988). But wages themselves are a social construct with deep historical underpinnings relating to class and gender. Technical adjustments to management job evaluation systems are unlikely to alter fundamental social and cultural relationships that are reflected in the wage system.

Job evaluation is frustrating to workers and proponents because it is presented as a technical tool that has an air of objectivity but is, in reality, a political tool used to define value. Women who successfully campaigned for revaluing women's work in the political or bargaining process leading up to a study are often sorely disappointed by the ensuing technical discussions of value. The actual process of technical job evaluation is a far cry from the ideological and political arguments that were prominent before the actual study.

The focus of job evaluation often reinforced the concept of hierarchy and heightened conflicts between men and women, and between labor and management (Acker 1989; Hallock 1989 and 1990; Evans and Nelson 1989a; and Blum 1987). Pay equity can be divisive. Despite the progressive aim of revaluing women's work, job evaluation assigns each job a value and establishes a job hierarchy. Job evaluation can reinforce traditional hierarchies or challenge them by altering relative positions; but either course can cause legitimate anxiety and heighten divisions among workers. This aspect of pay equity is at once its radical potential and the source of many compromises that have limited its potential for reform.

Some of the most painful divisions occurred within unions, between men and women. Pay equity does more than ask for higher wages for women—it asks that women receive the same wages as men and requires comparisons with men's jobs. For instance, women clerical workers often say they deserve as much as warehouse workers whose jobs require less skill. This claim is obviously threatening to warehouse workers.

Unions have adopted various strategies to lessen pay equity's divisive tendencies. Many point out that dual-income families are forced to live on one and one-half incomes because of discrimination against women. The main strategy has been to concentrate on upgrading women's wages and holding men harmless in all respects, an approach difficult to achieve when management insists on paying for equity wage adjustments from existing wage sources. Management has created numerous strategic tactics to divide labor, from attempting to cut or freeze men's wages to rearranging bargaining units (Hallock 1990). Joan Acker (1989) artfully describes how pay equity can become a dilemma for unions facing competing demands from men and women members in her account of the Oregon project. Bargaining for pay equity can be a frustrating exercise if management seeks to impose job evaluation as a rigid determinant of wages or otherwise alter historical bargaining relationships.

In sum, pay equity has been limited because of internal contradictions and some very real political problems. In their understandable zeal to raise women's wages, practitioners adopted a technical approach in a management-controlled environment. Pay equity reformers sought legitimacy by compromising on technical issues, from job evaluation systems to compensation analysis. These technical compromises combined with political issues of budgets, collective bargaining, and gender divisions to limit the extent and impact of pay equity.

Yet despite the disappointments, pay equity is still a viable way to attack the wage gap. Pay equity is not dead, but it does need reformulating. In particular, as many union practitioners now recognize, the emphasis on job evaluation must be reduced and justifications for raising women's wages other than the value of work must be found (see Ross, this volume).

Recommitting to an Ideology of Equality

Unions are developing new strategies and policies to reduce the gender wage gap without requiring a technical comparison of male and female jobs. European and Canadian unionists in particular have demonstrated that an explicit campaign for equality among workers can have beneficial impacts on the gender wage gap and overall income inequality.[3]

The Swedish Wage Solidarity Policy

Many collective bargaining strategies focus on upgrading wages in the lowest wage areas and reducing the difference between high- and low-wage jobs in a bargaining unit. The most elaborate example of this strategy has been implemented in Sweden (Meidner 1987). The solidarity wage policy in Sweden, supported by the Social Democratic party and the government, called for coordinated bargaining among all member unions with the goal of equalizing wages for similar types of work and decreasing wage differentials throughout the country. State economic policies were consistent with this policy and allowed it to flourish by keeping unemployment low and by providing a strong welfare system to cushion the effects of the economic restructuring that was caused partially by the solidarity policy. That is, wage levels were based on concepts of equality and a living wage, not on the profitability of individual firms or even industries. Unprofitable firms rationalized their use of labor or left the market. Although the solidarity wage policy was not directed at women, it reduced the gender wage gap because women are disproportionately low-wage workers (Meidner 1988; Acker 1990). In 1983, Sweden's wage gap was smaller than in any other industrialized country: full-time, year-round women workers earned 81.5 percent of the earnings of men.

Unfortunately, the wage gap in Sweden is now increasing and the solidarity wage policy is less prominent.[4] In response, women in Sweden are now turning

[3]Similarly, the Australian case in which national institutions set wages based on policy norms demonstrates that explicit public policy regarding the wage gap can be effective (Gregory et al. 1987).

[4]The demise of the solidarity policy is the result of a number of economic and political factors. The Swedish economy is a highly international economy, and global economic changes

to pay equity programs to reverse the widening gender wage gap and to address the issue of the value of women's work (Acker 1990). One primary architect of wage and economic policy in Sweden has called for a national job evaluation system to establish norms for wage differentials and to halt the trend toward basing wages on profits (Meidner 1988).

Canadian Bargaining and Equity Platforms

Canadian unions best illustrate the gains possible through legislative initiative and the importance of taking pay equity into the private sector.

The province of Ontario passed major legislation, effective in 1988, that required public sector employers and private sector employers with ten or more employees to negotiate and post pay equity plans. All female-dominated job classes in an establishment must be evaluated according to an evaluation system free of gender bias and wages raised to match those of a comparative male job. A pay equity commission and hearings tribunal is responsible for resolving differences and arbitrating complaints.[5] In implementing the legislation first in the public sector and among large employers, unions encountered technical issues similar to those experienced in the United States, including the definition of establishments, exclusions for casual workers, finding a job evaluation system that is free of gender bias, and bargaining wage adjustments. Nevertheless, the Ontario Public Service Employees Union (OPSEU) bargained a settlement for public employees in which nearly 28,500 employees in female job classes received wage adjustments averaging $1.45 per hour and totaling $83.8 million over two years (OPSEU 1990). The true test of the legislation will be its effectiveness in the private sector.

The problems associated with the Ontario legislation have produced debate in Canada on alternative programs to attack the wage gap, particularly for women who work in the private sector, in small firms, at part-time jobs, and in low-wage manufacturing and service industries—in short, in the most marginal economic industries and jobs that are difficult to cover legislatively.

---

and internal economic restructuring have altered the political and institutional arrangements that allowed for coordinated bargaining and integrating bargaining with national economic policy. Real wages have been stagnant, and redistribution from high-wage to low-wage workers is thus more difficult. Wages are increasingly related to firm and industry profit levels rather than national norms.

[5] While this legislation is much more aggressive than anything in the United States, still a number of problems remain (OPSEU 1987a). Separate pay equity plans can be developed for separate bargaining units, and comparisons across bargaining units and establishments are not permitted, thus limiting the number of male comparators for female jobs, especially in female-dominated units such as health care. Employers are also protected from having to allocate more than 1 percent of payroll for pay equity adjustments.

Unions in British Columbia, for example, advocate deemphasizing the concept of equal pay for work of equal value. Instead, they favor relying on collective bargaining for organized workers, higher base wage rates, increasing unionization, raising the minimum wage, regulating wages for jobs that have been privatized, and establishing mechanisms for raising wages in problem sectors such as light manufacturing and retail trade (Lewis 1988; British Columbia Federation of Labour 1988). The British Columbia Federation of Labour currently is proposing legislation that would require actions to narrow the gender wage gap but not require job evaluation. The wage gap would be calculated for sectors; employers and unions would be permitted to use various methods to produce the proscribed result, from higher minimum and entry-level wages to wage adjustments based on the amount of gender-domination of a job. The proscribed outcome would be a decline in the *overall* wage gap.

Canadian unions have also followed a type of wage solidarity approach (Lewis 1988). Unions have employed flat dollar wage increases rather than percentage raises. The Canadian Union of Public Employees (CUPE) in 1979 instituted a demand for "equal base rates." The base rate was defined as the wage for full-time, entry-level employment in the public sector, and in practice was the living wage paid to full-time working men. In 1981 CUPE called for the entry-level wage for women's clerical work to equal the wage for laborers; this demand was an explicit attempt to avoid job evaluation and instigated a movement to equalize entry-level wages for men and women.

The Challenge for U.S. Labor

The U.S. labor movement has practiced a form of wage solidarity as well. It has always supported higher minimum wages, and many unions have successfully bargained flat dollar wage increases or a combination of flat dollar and percentage raises. Also, national collective bargaining agreements have tended to reduce regional wage dispersion. Nevertheless, U.S. unions have not promulgated wage equality as a major goal. A new emphasis on wage equality is needed, especially considering the increasing inequality of incomes in the United States. Reversing this alarming trend toward income polarization should be a key union platform, as it would benefit nearly all working people.

One approach could be a reformulation of the family wage. The notion that men should be paid more because they have families to support was, historically, an important rationale for paying lower wages to women (Carlson 1986). Recently, the concept of a family wage has not been prominent in bargaining or union ideology, in part because only a small fraction of families now depend on a single male income and women are more likely to be primary earners. But unions could take back the issue of a family wage by reformulating it as a demand for a living wage or a family wage for *all* workers. The demand would not be for a wage that allows a man to support a family but for a wage that permits any worker to contribute significantly to or support a household. Such a demand would force unions and firms to examine wage scales in light of statistics and figures on poverty income levels and partially return unions to demands based on need rather than demands based on ability to pay. Clearly, this could not be a technical demand, based on the number of people in each household or on each worker's level of contribution to a household, but an ideological demand to replace the outdated concept of a family wage for men. This is contrary to the increasingly technical nature of collective bargaining and would require ideological commitment combined with adequate bargaining power and community support.

Public sector unions in Oregon adopted this approach in their 1987 campaign for pay equity. After encountering problems with the technical approach to pay equity, the Oregon Public Employees Union (OPEU) embarked on a campaign to expose the low wage levels for state employees, primarily women, and to link these wages to the feminization of poverty (Acker 1989; Hallock 1987). State legislators were shocked and embarrassed by the revelations, and the governor promised to end the practice of paying wages so low that state employees qualified for welfare benefits.

U.S. unions also need to develop policies that simultaneously represent the new work force and combat the gender wage gap. The wage gap will widen if there is unequal access to the few "good jobs" that are emerging from economic restructuring and technological change. Workers need information on technological change and job opportunities, and they need access to training. Unions should aggressively negotiate new apprenticeship models that expand the concept of apprentice training beyond the traditional male trades to semiprofessional and technical jobs in industries such as health care and retail trade. More elaborate school-to-work structures are needed for young workers. Adult workers need negotiated benefits covering promotion, skill upgrading, and training. Unions should reassert themselves as champions of affirmative action and equal opportunity programs and apply these programs, along with education and training programs, to the changing nature of jobs.

Some workers may be better represented by a craft or occupational model than an industrial approach (see Cobble 1991). The trend toward smaller firms and less permanent employment also argues for a craft or apprentice model. Workers need skill certification and training that is portable, along with portable health and pension benefits.

Lastly, as detailed in other sections of this volume, a plan to represent the contingent work force that is disproportionately female and the adoption of policies addressing the work and family dilemma are crucial to closing the wage gap. These policies would mesh well with solidarity wage policies, a renewed emphasis on income equality, and a living wage for all workers. These program suggestions should be viewed as one part of a complete strategic initiative by unions to respond to the rapidly changing economy and world. Labor needs to develop a clear vision of the kind of economy it wants and how economic restructuring could be directed toward constructive and progressive ends. Unions must continue to represent individual workers and support individual advancement and opportunity, but these programs should be couched in a broader program directed toward greater equality and fairness in the distribution of economic resources.

New, more inclusive, less gender-specific approaches are necessary. Yet unions must not lose sight of gender-based discrimination and the undervaluation of women's work. A broader strategy focusing on the issues of the entire working class and combating overall income inequality is necessary, but inequality based on gender and the legitimate struggle of women for equal rights and economic equality must not be lost.

2
Roundtable on Pay Equity and Affirmative Action

Heidi Hartmann

I'd like to begin by commenting on the progress of women in the 1980s with respect to the wage gap. In August 1987, the Census Bureau released a major study on women's earnings (U.S. Bureau of the Census 1987) with a congratulatory tone that could be paraphrased, "Hey, women's wages are up to 70 percent—isn't that terrific!" Everybody I knew asked, "What's going on here? What happened to 59 percent? Has there been a sudden large change?" The confusion stemmed from the "big news" manner in which the Census Bureau released the study and from the existence of two different wage series, the annual and the weekly, both based on the median earnings of full-time workers. (The Census Bureau report was based on hourly wages, which are more or less consistent with the weekly wage series.) Looking at weekly wages, and comparing full-time workers, male and female, one does see that by 1987 women earned 70 percent of what men earned. The starting point of that series, however, isn't the 59 percent with which we all became familiar in the late 1970s. Because of inaccurate reporting in the media, everyone was led to believe that the wage ratio increased from 59 percent to 70 percent. That would be a large increase in just over ten years. The *real* starting point of that series, which began in 1970, was 62 percent. So over fifteen-plus years that series shows that the female-male wage ratio increased from 62 to 70 percent—that's fairly good, but not as dramatic as everyone thought. What about the wage series with that old familiar 59 percent? The wage ratio in that

These comments were originally presented at a colloquia series on women and labor sponsored by the Labor Education Department, Rutgers University, in the spring of 1988. They have been revised and updated for this volume.

wage series has also increased; in 1985, the ratio was 65 percent, it fell to 64 percent in 1986, and increased to 65 percent in 1987 and 66 percent in 1988 (National Committee on Pay Equity and Institute for Women's Policy Research 1989). Most recently, the ratio reached 68 percent for median annual earnings in 1989, showing continued increases since the report was released and a fairly large increase for the decade of the 1980s (U.S. Bureau of the Census 1991).

The Census Bureau report also stressed that, relative to men of their age grouping, young women do much better than older women. Young women have always done better than older women. Ten years ago, younger women did better than older women, and, twenty years ago, younger women did better than older women. The only problem is that younger women become older women. The real question is whether these younger women are going to be able to maintain the advantages that younger women have typically had. Or are they going to be penalized for the childbearing years, the family care-giving years, as older women have been? The evidence isn't in on that yet; we'll have to wait and see.

The Institute for Women's Policy Research looked at how much of the narrowing of the wage gap between women's and men's earnings had to do with the fall in men's wages. Because the economy is not doing so well, especially in the Midwest, with its heavy concentration of industrial jobs, and in New England, with its concentration of computer systems engineers, it seems likely that part of the improvement could be due to declines in men's real wages. The calculation of this proportion varies according to the years chosen for the starting and ending points of the comparison. We found that from 1978 to 1987, only 33 percent of the decrease in the gap was due to a decline in men's real wages. In other words, 67 percent of the improvement from 59 percent to 65 percent is indeed due to women earning better wages (National Committee et al. 1989). The Census Bureau notes that between 1987 and 1989 men's real wages fell, while women's real earnings grew only slightly. Thus, much of the improvement in the ratio of the last two years was due to the decline in men's real wages (U.S. Bureau of the Census 1991).

We weren't able to investigate how much of the real improvement in women's wages is due to the rise of women's wages in women's jobs, which is what comparable worth is about, or to women moving into nontraditional jobs, or at least integrated jobs. The common wisdom is that much of the improvement is due to women moving into men's jobs (or integrated jobs). Certainly, the data support the fact that occupational segregation by sex declined in the 1970s more than it ever has before, at least since occupational segregation has been measured, in the early 1900s. Between 1970 and 1980 the index of sex segregation fell about 10 percent; the index lost 6 percentage points from 66 to 60 (that is, about a 10 percent decline). And given how stable that index has been for decades, a 10 percent decline for one decade is a significant change (Reskin and Hartmann 1986).

The overall stability of the measures of sex segregation is amazing; it seems to stay more or less constant no matter how jobs change. Seamstresses and stitchers are not such an important part of our economy as they once were, and we have many new jobs, such as computer programming, that have emerged, especially since 1950. Yet, no matter how many old jobs disappear and how many new ones are created, this index of sex segregation stays at about two-thirds. There has got to be some magic out there that we just don't understand. Jobs are constantly changing and, new research shows, women and men are constantly moving between them, yet we still have a high degree of sex segregation.

Nevertheless, it is a hopeful sign that sex segregation has declined and that the wage gap has decreased. Political action has been crucial in bringing about these improvements: the women's movement, the union movement (that is paying more attention to women workers), and efforts for comparable worth that have involved both unions and associations of workers that perhaps wouldn't quite consider themselves unions. Comparable worth provides a legitimate way for workers to become collectively involved in the struggle over wages, whether or not they are members of a union (although most if not all successful campaigns have been led by unions). Collective action has been key in bringing about changes for women. Clearly, the more we struggle together, the stronger we are politically, the more we get.

I am often reminded of Shulamith Firestone's book, *The Dialectic of Sex,* which came to my attention in the late 1960s. In the beginning of the book, she is telling her friends or family that she is working on a book about "sexual inequality." At first, her friends and family didn't understand what she meant. After a while they said, "Oh that, you mean *that,* you can't change *that.*" That was the way people thought about gender inequality and many people still do: "You can't change human nature," they say. But we are.

We are changing the way men are taught to have a right to expect advantages and women are taught to endure. To bring about this change is an incredible political struggle. I really believe that it is a revolutionary change: that women will no longer make coffee, that, to get more intimate, women will no longer fake orgasms, that all these things women will no longer do. Some men still expect their male power and privileges and some women are still unable to resist. But overall, women's empowerment is really a very revolutionary change.

Public opinion about appropriate activities for women and men has changed, opinion polls show. Most men now believe that men should have an equal role with women in taking care of children. Does that mean that they are going to change as many diapers as women? I don't know. And that *is* the bottom line. Dealing with dirt does lower one's value and women have always cleaned up the messes in our society. Women rush to get the papers out on deadline. They get them typed and copied. If the time they are needed is 10 A.M., they are there in neat stacks, all stapled. How does that happen? Women clerical workers make that happen. They take stuff that looks like a mess and they make it look good.

Job evaluation studies, a fairly standard component of comparable worth struggles, have great political value. They can be important vehicles in changing women's minds about what they do. It's important to help women understand that these studies say what they already know. These studies say what we've been saying: "I am worth just as much as this guy over here. Can you believe it? He's making $5,000 more a year than me for over twenty years, but actually my work is worth as much as his." Sometimes women need that scientific backing to bolster their position within their labor organizations. Technical studies do not have to be done by an outside consultant, but often are. These consultants often seem to obfuscate their work to make it appear more complicated than it really is. In that case, a workers' committee could hire its own consultant to explain the technical aspects and how the study's findings can be used.

Let me now turn to the subject of the labor market and taking comparable worth into the private sector. Private enterprise is pretty well established in the United States, despite what the judge said in the Lemons case in Denver: Comparable worth "is pregnant with the possibility of disrupting the entire economic system of the United States of America" (Lemons 1978). In fact, comparable worth is not destroying capitalism, it isn't destroying the so-called free enterprise system as we know it. It is correcting—but not abolishing—the market, and that's okay. In some sense, pay equity is not a fundamental challenge to a class society. Workers are paid wages and what workers try to do when they rely on wages for nearly all their income is get a little bit more wages. In general, some workers are paid more than other workers; there is a wage hierarchy. If it comes as a shock, socialist societies have wages, too; workers in socialist societies often try to get more wages, but they also try to get more public programs that can substitute for wages or fringe benefits.

In this country, we need more public programs, more publicly provided child care, more publicly provided health care. Historically, the labor movement in the United States has been less interested in directly affecting public policy than unions in other countries have been. They have been more interested in wresting these gains from employers on behalf of the unionized workers and less interested in creating government programs that would benefit all people. I certainly don't want to blame the unions in the United States for the fact that the United States does not have state-run welfare systems like those in Western Europe, but the unions *are* one player. At least part of the reason unions have taken the strategy they have is that the United States seems to have a very virulent form of capitalism—a form of capitalism that could be called "cowboy capitalism." It is a very laissez-faire capitalism, with strong animosity to government regulation and government economic activity.

Comparable worth doesn't attack the market but it does seek a market that is consistent and bias free, a market that treats women and people of color the same way it treats white men. Sometimes that treatment even for white men is not so great, but it is nevertheless better than the way women and people of color are treated now.

How can we take comparable worth into the private sector? Barbara Bergmann, in her book *The Economic Emergence of Women,* makes an excellent proposal. She argues that the first target for pay equity should be federal contractors. The U.S. equal employment opportunity system has two parts. One is Title VII under the Civil Rights Act, which basically requires all employers not to discriminate. If you think your employer is discriminating against you, you can file a complaint and eventually pursue your case in court, either because an equal employment opportunity agency takes your case, or because you take your own case into court. These laws, Title VII and its amendments, apply to all employers with more than fifteen workers. The other equal employment opportunity system deals with employers who have a contract with the federal government. (Many state and city governments also have contract compliance regulations that generally require businesses with contracts with the government not to discriminate.) Regardless of whether a worker complains, government inspectors actually go around to businesses and make sure they are not discriminating. Although thorough use of this remedy depends on politics, and on the budget, contract compliance provides good possibilities for enforcement. A worker is not required to complain in order to initiate the enforcement mechanism; inspectors can initiate action.

Bergmann argues that these contract regulations should require pay equity. One problem employers have with adopting comparable worth is their fear that employers without comparable worth will drive them out of business. Employers argue that if they are going to have to implement changes like pay equity, parental leave, and child care, they will be at a competitive disadvantage. Therefore, a system that makes everybody comply all at once is actually better. (For example, the minimum wage "zaps" employers all at the same time; no competitive advantage or disadvantage to worry about.) Under Bergmann's proposal, the government would issue regulations requiring, for example, that several prominent occupations be treated comparably. In effect, the regulations would say to employers, "We don't care what you pay them, but these are the relationships that they must have to each other. Yes, you might be a low-wage industry; yes, you may be a high-wage industry; we don't care. You can place your firm wherever you want in the market. If you want to be a high-wage employer [which many firms want to be because they think they can get a better quality worker and they can afford it], fine. If you want to be a low-wage employer, fine. We don't care as long as the wage is not below the minimum wage. Just make sure whenever you have secretaries or truck drivers or salespeople, you follow these relative wage guidelines."

In contrast, enforcement under Title VII may not be an effective way to change wages. The Title VII model of equal employment opportunity, with its individual case-by-case approach, or even with its class-action lawsuits, is a frightening method—to employers—for changing something like wages. In many of the civil rights cases brought through Title VII in the South, wage rates were altered by the courts. Lawyers would say, "You know, the top wage of skilled black jobs pays less than the least skilled white job. We can't have this," and the judge would order new wages. Of course, courts can set wages in case-by-case review, but federal legislation, or executive orders such as those governing the contract compliance program, would be more effective.

If contractors to the federal government implemented pay equity, a spillover effect would most likely occur with other public and private sector employers. State and local governments might also require pay equity of their contractors. Sooner or later all employers would have to catch up, in order to be able to hire and retain workers. If the entire public sector implemented pay equity, 20 percent of U.S. workers would be covered.

Comparable worth, as a strategy for raising women's wages and changing women's lives, continues to have great potential. The pay equity movement has already achieved a lot. If anyone had asked me ten or twelve years ago if pay equity would have gotten this far by this point in time, I would certainly have said, "No." Yet the pay equity concept is now understood by the women's movement and the labor movement and the general public. Periodically, the pay equity movement receives substantial publicity. The movement has helped women say, "I am really worth something; my job is really worth something." This raised consciousness on the part of women workers is an important force.

If women earned as much as men in the labor market, our lives would really look different. Men would do more housework, or, perhaps, housework would not get done!

Jean Ross

During the 1980s, local affiliates of the Service Employees' International Union (SEIU) developed a number of strategies to narrow the wage gap between jobs held predominantly by women and those held by men and, in several instances, the gap between jobs held disproportionately by minorities and those held by white workers. The experiences I discuss draw primarily on my work with SEIU over the past several years.

First, it is useful to distinguish between pay equity as it has been defined by the women's movement and feminist academics and pay equity as it is often defined by the labor movement. Feminist advocates tend to use a narrow definition of pay equity to describe adjustments made as the result of a formal job evaluation study.[1] Labor advocates often use pay equity to refer to a broader range of strategies that raise wages paid to traditionally female jobs and/or reduce sex segregation in employment.

The most common image of how pay equity is achieved involves a job evaluation study, typically done by a consultant hired in conjunction with a labor-management committee (SEIU 1985; National Committee on Pay Equity 1987). The results of the study are then used to determine the wage adjustment needed to implement pay equity. I refer to this as the traditional approach. Nontraditional approaches used by SEIU locals include:

- Using a "piggyback" or matching study to determine the wage gap between predominantly male and female classifications.
- Reclassifying positions traditionally held by women to more fully reflect the skills and responsibilities of the job.
- Negotiating increases for all job classifications where 70 percent or more of the incumbents are women.
- Negotiating larger increases for predominantly female occupational groups, such as clerical workers, librarians, or nurses.

[1] Similar approaches can be used to raise wages for jobs disproportionately held by minority workers. However, in many instances, racial and ethnic wage discrimination occurs predominantly in hiring and promotions, and minorities fill jobs that are low-skilled as well as low-waged. If this is the case, pay equity should be combined with a broader strategy to reduce occupational segregation and wage discrimination.

- Negotiating additional longevity increases to raise the top salary for predominantly female jobs.

Much of the progress toward reducing the wage gap relied on these nontraditional bargaining strategies. In other instances, union negotiators won changes that reduce the wage gap in classification systems, promotional procedures, and career development programs. These victories are often inspired by the pay equity movement and have a similar impact, but receive little publicity and are often never termed "pay equity," due, in part, to employers' unwillingness to admit that they historically paid less for women's jobs than those jobs were worth.

The beginning of the pay equity movement is often attributed to the 1981 Supreme Court decision in *County of Washington v. Gunther,* which declared that wage inequities between similar, but not equal, jobs was illegal (Stone 1987). While most of the progress toward pay equity has taken place through collective bargaining, litigation has received the bulk of the publicity. The media, unfortunately and all too often, has judged the status of the movement by its progress in the courts, where advocates have suffered major setbacks over the last several years.

While I want to focus primarily on the role of collective bargaining in winning pay equity, it is useful to trace the history of pay equity in the courts, which shapes the public perception of the success of the movement and influences the balance of power at the bargaining table. SEIU began negotiating for equity adjustments for predominantly female jobs in the early 1970s. In at least one instance, the union used a dual-focused strategy of bargaining and filing discrimination charges with the Equal Employment Opportunity Commission (EEOC). Little progress was made at the bargaining table, however, prior to the 1981 *Gunther* decision. After *Gunther* and the initial Ninth Circuit Court ruling in *American Federation of State, County and Municipal Employees v. State of Washington,* advocates gained the upper hand at the bargaining table, where they were armed with the threat of legal action against employers who failed to act. By the mid–1980s, pay equity became a common demand in collective bargaining throughout the public sector.

The reversal of the initial ruling in *AFSCME v. State of Washington* in September 1985 marked the switch from a supportive court to one concerned with upholding employer rights and the role of the free-market economy. The standards set by *AFSCME v. State of Washington* made it virtually impossible to prove sex-based wage discrimination between dissimilar jobs without a "smoking gun" showing that the employer knew that salary policies had an adverse impact and that they were *intended* to discriminate.

The next setback occurred in 1987, with the U.S. District Court ruling in

UAW v. State of Michigan.[2] The *Michigan* decision affirmed the legality of market factors in salary setting and allowed evidence of market comparisons to supersede the results of job evaluation.

What is often forgotten is that in both of these cases the unions involved won significant gains through negotiations. AFSCME negotiated a substantial out-of-court settlement in Washington State. Although settling the case left a bad decision standing, the union did what it needed to do in order to protect the interests of its members when faced with the prospect of continuing through an increasingly hostile court system. In Michigan, while the case was pending, the state agreed to wage differentials for all predominantly female jobs.[3]

During this series of setbacks in the courts, pay equity activity continued and, in fact, increased. Why? First and foremost, employers realized that if they didn't increase the pay for predominantly female jobs they could no longer attract and retain a skilled work force. A majority of the fastest growing jobs in the economy are predominantly female jobs. This, and the entry of women into nontraditional jobs, heightens demand for workers in many occupations. Second, losses in the courts have had the perverse result of lessening employers' fears of legal action by removing the threat of massive back pay judgments. Employers are less fearful of accusations of discrimination for failing to fully remedy wage disparities and are more willing to negotiate partial or phased-in agreements. This combination of factors encouraged action at the bargaining table and, to a much lesser extent, legislative activity advocated by unions and their feminist allies.

The focus on collective bargaining maintained the vitality of the pay equity movement. In the long run, a membership-based strategy offers the best potential for concrete victories, while building the strength of the union. Many women who are now local and national leaders within their unions first became active through battles for pay equity. Although a legal strategy does not necessarily preclude strong membership participation, it is difficult for unions to sustain interest and involvement through years of court proceedings. In contrast, a campaign focused on bargaining or local political action must involve union members in order to succeed. Even if the legal climate were more promising, I would counsel against a singular focus on litigation due to the lessened opportunity for membership involvement.

The commitment to a bargaining strategy requires background work and

---

[2]The dismissal was upheld in 1989 by the Sixth Circuit Court of Appeals.

[3]Defined as classifications where 70 percent or more of the incumbents were female, these adjustments applied to predominantly female UAW-represented positions, as well as to jobs represented by other unions.

a number of strategy decisions. Prior to bargaining, unions need to analyze employment patterns, identify predominantly female jobs, and engage in membership education (National Committee on Pay Equity 1987; SEIU 1985). The first and most significant decision is whether or not to pursue a formal job evaluation study. The majority of SEIU locals that bargained pay equity during the late 1980s did so without a formal study. This strategy avoids the lengthy process and expense of hiring a consultant to conduct a study.

But without job evaluation, how can you calculate the wage increase necessary to bring predominantly male and female jobs into alignment? Often times, the gap can be approximated by matching job descriptions for the employer in question with those from another jurisdiction where a study has been done and calculating the results. This "piggyback" approach is faster, less costly, and can easily be completed by a labor-management committee working without professional consultants. Many of the most commonly used job evaluation methodologies produce quite similar and predictable results. In unpublished research, SEIU compared the results of five major job evaluation studies of state employees and one of city workers. This comparison showed the relative ranking of jobs between studies to be remarkably consistent despite the use of different consultants and different methodologies. Librarians usually ranked comparably to engineers. Secretaries ranked comparably to the skilled trades. A carefully done piggyback study, for most purposes, works just about as well as a study that may cost hundreds of thousands of dollars for a mid-size to large employer. The state of Minnesota publishes guidebooks for local government employers wishing to use matching studies to fulfill the requirements of that state's law mandating implementation of pay equity in the public sector (Minnesota Department of Employee Relations 1984). Where money is an issue, as it nearly always is, it is far better to put scarce resources into pay adjustments than outside consultants.

Another advantage to negotiating without a study is the problem of "undervalued" jobs. The process of using job evaluation to rank or score jobs and then calculating a pay line identifies some jobs as overpaid relative to their evaluated ranking.[4] This is always one of the most difficult issues confronted during pay equity negotiations. Unions argue that wages for women's jobs should be raised to the level of historically male-dominated positions, rather than an average of salaries of all positions somewhere in the middle. Unfor-

---

[4]Job evaluation techniques and the translation of the results of job evaluation studies into pay scales are discussed in the SEIU's *Pay Equity Bargaining Guide* (January 1985) and the National Committee on Pay Equity's *Job Evaluation: A Tool for Pay Equity* (November 1987).

tunately, a number of employers have proposed lowering or freezing the salaries of male positions until those held by women catch up. For unions, such an approach leads to divisiveness and endangers majority support for pay equity.

Speed is also a reason to consider a nontraditional approach to job evaluation. The state of Connecticut's job evaluation study took ten years to complete. By the time it was finished, many of the jobs studied at the beginning had changed so much that the evaluations were already outdated, but the study was well done. There were strong provisions for union participation and good appeal rights for workers who felt their jobs were misevaluated, but it was nearly a decade before workers received wage adjustments.

Another lesson that can be learned from Connecticut is that most classification systems, at least in the public sector, are seriously outdated and inadequate. In Los Angeles County, for example, many clerical job specifications have not been updated in over twenty years. Many of the county's jobs were totally transformed by computer technology during that period. There is the potential for tremendous problems when it becomes necessary to revise classification systems in order to accurately evaluate jobs. In many states, public employee bargaining laws permit bargaining over wages, but not over classification issues. Management can use its ability to reshape the classification system to undo whatever gains might be won through pay equity.

The history of pay equity for Oregon state workers is an example of the perils involved when pay equity becomes mixed up with a classification study. The process got off to a good start in 1983. A task force was appointed and chaired by the research director of the largest state employee union, SEIU Local 503/Oregon Public Employees Union. Midway into the study, management decided that the classification system needed an overhaul. The results of the classification study were disliked by all concerned, state personnel officers as well as the union, and the study was temporarily shelved. In the interim, the state signed a contract in 1987 providing $23 million in pay equity adjustments. But in the next round of contract negotiations in 1989, management came back with a reclassification proposal that resulted in downgrades for 15 percent of state workers. The union ultimately reduced the number of downgrades by more than 50 percent as well as won protections for incumbents. But had the issue of classification been avoided, there would have been no rationale for downgrading (Johnsen 1990).

Unions should secure agreement prior to any job evaluation study that there will be no downgrading. This is essential for building support among male union members. Never agree to implement the results of a job evaluation study before the study is complete. Reserving the right to negotiate over the results of a study offers a way to work out any problems that might come up.

Despite the pitfalls of job evaluation studies, there are times when job evaluation is strategically appropriate. Many employers want the more scientific approach job evaluation offers. They want a greater degree of accuracy than a piggyback study offers. Studies can also be used as a foot in the door during negotiations, allowing management to say, "We'll give you a study this year and come back in a year to talk about wage adjustments." Having well-documented evidence of wage disparities can help persuade reluctant managers, elected officials, and taxpayers that wage discrimination does exist.

But *if* a study is done, *how* it is done is very important. Factor definitions and weighting can have a significant impact on the results of a study. Recently, many consultants have fine-tuned their job evaluation methodologies, particularly in response to the Province of Ontario's mandate that gender-neutral job evaluation methodologies must be used to meet the stipulations of the provincial pay equity law. Most point-factor systems can be modified to increase the weight given to characteristics commonly associated with predominantly female jobs and to decrease the emphasis put on stereotypical male characteristics.

Two methodologies, however, consistently undervalue predominantly female jobs. Policy-capturing studies build from an employer's existing salary structure by measuring the value the employer places on various job-related characteristics. Historically, employers have valued characteristics associated with men's work more than those associated with women's work. Policy capturing eliminates the explicit negative impact on salary of the share of women in a job, but it does so within the confines of a male value structure.[5] The results can be startling. In New York State, for example, a policy capturing study done in 1987 declared that registered nurses were *over*paid by 10 percent. Another problematic methodology is the decision band method (DBM), which places a substantial weight on the types of decisions made by a position. Since women are generally underrepresented in decision-making positions, their jobs suffer.

A cross section of the union's membership needs to be involved in all facets of a study if its results are to be understood and accepted. Unions need to educate their members about how job evaluation works in order to help members provide thoughtful input. Job evaluation studies frequently survey workers on the content of their jobs. Many workers in nonprofessional positions have a difficult time describing the full range and responsibilities of their

---

[5] In most policy capturing studies, factor weights are determined from the study using a regression formula based on study results and the percentage of women in a job (usually a negative coefficient). The "equitable" pay for the job wages is then determined using the factor weights in the formula, but leaving out the negative coefficient on percent female.

work. They tend not to think in terms of budget impact and the responsibilities their jobs entail—the factors most job evaluation systems value highest.

Studies that provide input in the formulation of job descriptions that serve as the basis of evaluation give unions the opportunity to highlight the often complex and skilled nature of even the lowest paid jobs. Maintenance workers, for example, rarely think of their jobs in terms of the value of the equipment they maintain. Eligibility workers don't add up the dollar value of the benefits their clients receive. Helping workers analyze their jobs is one of the most important roles a union can play in the job evaluation process. Moreover, a job evaluation can serve as a tool to help workers appreciate the true importance of their work to the overall mission of the organization. For women, who are often socialized to underestimate and undervalue their own abilities, this process can be very powerful.

Strong membership participation can also prevent pay equity from becoming a divisive issue. In most instances, budgetary constraints limit the pot of money available for equity adjustments and cost-of-living increases. Allocating available resources between the two poses a tough choice for unions that represent both predominantly female and male jobs. In most instances, maintaining the support of a diverse membership requires a strategy that balances pay equity adjustments and other economic issues.

Some feminists have faulted unions for not prioritizing adjustments for historically discriminated jobs to the exclusion of other economic demands. But unions have a moral and legal obligation to best represent the concerns of their entire membership. Preserving unity may sometimes mean that pay equity must be phased in over a number of years.

In nearly all pay equity agreements, the negotiated wage adjustment is less than the wage gap identified. Women's jobs are typically paid 15 to 20 percent less than comparable male positions. Due to the cost of bringing up wages for predominantly female jobs, adjustments are often less than the full amount needed to establish equity. In other instances, a lengthy phase-in is utilized to lower initial costs. In Washington State and the city and county of San Francisco, for example, initially negotiated adjustments were in the range of 10 to 12 percent. Both of these are among the "big-ticket" settlements.[6] Most workers are quite pleased to receive a 10 percent equity adjustment.

Finally, most efforts at achieving pay equity have a significant political component. In the public sector, where most pay equity activity has occurred, elected officials strongly influence the context of bargaining and have the

---

[6]SEIU Local 790 negotiated additional increases of 3 percent in each of two years in a contracted signed in 1989.

ability to allocate funds for implementation. In Canada, where the pay equity movement is most advanced, provincial legislation mandates implementation of pay equity in Ontario and Manitoba. Ontario's law goes so far as to cover all but the smallest private employers. Minnesota state law mandates pay equity for state and local government workers.

Pay equity is politically popular. Polling data show that 60 to 80 percent of the public support pay equity. Getting there may not be easy, but it is a battle that generally draws strong public support. After nearly a decade of organizing, strategizing, and negotiating, San Francisco's city and county workers won pay equity at the ballot box. SEIU negotiated a $35 million pay equity fund, which then-mayor Dianne Feinstein vetoed three times. Each time the board of supervisors overrode the mayor's veto. Finally, to resolve problems created by the city charter's prohibition of collective bargaining for wages, the union put pay equity before the voters. By a margin of over 60 percent, city residents approved spending $35 million in tax monies for pay equity adjustments for city workers. The depth of public support for this issue is underscored by the voters' willingness to take money out of their own pockets for pay equity adjustments for city workers.

To conclude, my most important message is the need for creativity. Pay equity is most successful where unions have looked at the issues creatively, where they have mobilized and educated their membership, and organized internally to support the issue. Achieving pay equity often takes five, six, seven, or more years. Activists need to be prepared to hang in for the long haul. Often it is necessary to try several approaches until one works. The record is clear: with patience and planning, it is possible to make significant gains toward wage equity in the workplace.

Ronnie Steinberg

Too often pay equity initiatives have substituted technical solutions for what are really political issues. Technical expertise is critical for the success of a reform, but it must be protected from misuse in a political context.

The 1985 New York State comparable pay study provides an example of a situation where technical experts floundered in a political vacuum. The study involved the use of a policy-capturing approach to job evaluation that defined pay equity conservatively (see Ross, this volume). The political groups that could have pressed for a more progressive pay equity model failed to do that pushing. The feminist proponents who conducted the pay equity study were constrained from playing a political role because they had assumed the role of technical experts. As a result, the final pay equity adjustments were among the lowest yet announced.

In contrast, technical expertise can be a political resource for groups such as commissions on the status of women, unions, women's advocacy groups, and state legislators—groups that have the resources and political muscle to protect the use of that expertise. For example, at Yale University, Local 34 of the Hotel Employees and Restaurant Employees used an expert to help them figure out how to do a study themselves. They succeeded because the union bargaining committee achieved consensus among committee members over a new wage structure for the jobs they represent. They based their bargaining demands on this proposal, exerted political and economic pressure on Yale, and won average pay equity adjustments of over 20 percent from the university without a strike.

It is important not to talk about pay equity simply as a technical reform, but to see the interdependence between technique and politics. Because of the lack of political organizing, many so-called pay equity "victories" actually have produced highly constrained outcomes in which biased compensation systems perpetuate the two-tiered wage structures. The very structures that comparable worth was supposed to eliminate ended up even more firmly implanted.

Part of the problem has to do with union strategies and with unions' understandable view of pay equity as merely an extension of their normal responsibilities for bargaining over a wage package. Pay equity becomes one agenda among many, especially where there is a diverse membership. Feminist proponents of pay equity must fight to make sure that male union leaders are held accountable for what they do for their women workers at the bargaining table. Nonunion feminists need to build coalitions with women within unions to ensure that their needs are met.

Moreover, better methodologies for measuring wage discrimination as the basis for achieving pay equity must be invented. Some technical approaches to implementing comparable worth have far-reaching consequences for the extent to which sex and race bias is eliminated from compensation systems. Two standards of gender neutrality need to be used to assess compensation systems. First is what I call a consistency standard, which holds that if an employer *already* values a job characteristic for the purpose of paying wages in male work, then the same employer must value that work at the same wage for female- and minority-dominated work as for work done by a white male. For example, one extra year of education or one extra degree should be worth the same return in wages regardless of whether the educational requirement is for a female job or a male job, for a nonminority or minority job, and similarly for experience, for supervision, or for undesirable working conditions. The second standard, one that is more difficult to attain in the United States, is what I call a gender balance standard, which says that employers may not negatively value certain job characteristics differentially found in historically female jobs, thereby in effect lowering the wage rate when those job features are found and the value of job characteristics are taken into account. If an employer negatively values characteristics associated with female-dominated or significantly minority-held jobs, then the compensation system should be modified to compensate positively these regularly performed skills and responsibilities.

Researchers have found that there are all kinds of job content characteristics—many of which are associated with female-dominated jobs—that lower one's salary. Receiving work from multiple supervisors is valued negatively, for example. Working with dying patients or cleaning up other people's dirt has been found in many states to be valued negatively. This seems quite perverse. Local 34 at Yale University found that "support" staff who worked closely with students had lower salaries than other employees who did not work with students. Imagine how that information could be used politically at a press conference during a strike.

Comparable worth is not just about cleansing bias from compensation systems; it is also concerned with building a new political consensus to determine what is valuable and compensable and to revalue the work that women do. If we look at it this way, we can begin to see why pay equity adjustments are not being fully realized. A colleague of mine, Lois Haignere, developed an exercise that she and I have carried out with many union and feminist groups. We break a large group into small groups and give people positions: some are managers, some personnel workers, some blue-collar workers, some white-collar workers, etc. We give them a set of possible factors and weights and put them on committees to devise an equitable compensation system. We ask them which of these factors they think should be valuable and what the relative weights of selected factors should be. What we find is that almost all groups value education, claiming that the more education an employee has, the more she or he should be paid. Similarly, there is a moderate amount of consensus about such job content characteristics as supervision and experience. However, after that, the consensus almost always breaks down. The health groups want to place more value on working with clients. The operational units want to place value on working outdoors and lifting heavy objects.

Although not entirely arbitrary, decisions made about what is valuable are neither as objective nor as technical and inaccessible as management and the consulting firms that make huge profits off of pay equity studies claim they are. Compensation decisions are highly political decisions, where those with more power, that is to say, with more access to and control over decision making, end up having jobs with more valuable characteristics. I remember one example drawn from my experience as a technical monitor in a pay equity study of a small midwestern city. A draft of the final report proposed that, to implement pay equity, only job classes that were under-valued *more than* 20 percent below an average pay line should be brought up to 20 percent below the line. This recommendation *lowered* the cost of implementing pay equity to one-seventh of what it would be if all under-valued jobs were brought up to the average line. The consultants who pre-pared the report were not asked to delete this recommendation from the final report. But they were asked by management to modify their results for top managerial jobs, ensuring that the report would recommend that 16 out of 19 male department-head job classes received between 35 and 450 additional job evaluation points. The final report included no docu-mentation to justify assigning additional points to these jobs.

Feminist advocates lose control of the reform most frequently at the point when the government decides to do something about pay equity. I am not just talking about the negotiation and compromise that political scientists correctly claim is an inevitable part of the policy process in pluralistic democra-cies. Rather, the ways in which pay equity initiatives marginalize proponents from meaningful decision making follow distinctive patterns that serve to minimize the costs of pay equity adjustments, maximize managerial control over compensation decisions, and legitimize the compensation plan (Steinberg 1990a). Instead of cleansing compensation systems of sex and racial bias, governments are cleansing pay equity initiatives of their feminist critiques. Women are not receiving the substantial wage adjustments they would if the implementation process were carried out consistently and to equalize the gender balance in the value placed on male and female job characteristics. Pay equity adjustments routinely bring undervalued job classes up only to an arbitrary percentage below the line—in Washington State, to 5 percent below an average pay line,[1] and in San Jose, California, to 10 percent below the male

---

[1]The average pay line includes the existing salaries paid to female job classes. To the extent that the existing salaries are discriminatory, that discrimination will be embedded in the wage line to which *all* salaries are adjusted. Procedures have been developed to remove the impact of direct discrimination from the average pay line (Treiman, Hartmann, and Roos 1984).

pay line. Job evaluation systems are not being modified to make visible and value the characteristics differentially found in historically female and minority job classes.

One effective way management marginalizes pay equity proponents is to turn political decisions into technical decisions, making them technically inaccessible to workers. Another way is to divide union and feminist proponents. A third way involves piggybacking other political agendas with negative economic consequences for employees onto the pay equity initiative and then to blame pay equity for the negative economic consequences. This includes red circling,[2] contracting out, and the introduction of new, supposedly labor-saving technology. A final form of marginalization involves withholding information as confidential until the evaluation results are available, after which it is too late and too costly for proponents to develop a counterproposal.

In order to minimize the impact of managerial containment tactics, women's organizations, feminist advocates, and trade unions need to participate fully in the decision-making process at every stage of a pay equity initiative, and they must monitor the implementation process very carefully. Proponents cannot pass a law, appropriate money, and then let personnel or others who are paid to protect management's interests hire consultants who use lots of technical tricks to cut the costs of pay equity adjustments.

Despite these difficulties, however, proponents have accomplished a great deal through pay equity campaigns. There are over one million workers who have benefited from some pay equity adjustment. Some of these adjustments have been trivial but others have involved as much as six-thousand-dollar pay increases. Nonetheless, I believe that we can do better. Pay equity proponents—feminists, trade unionists, policymakers, and legislators—need to recognize the sophistication and resources of those who have worked hard to contain this reform.

Proponents must build a new political sophistication into their strategies for achieving pay equity. Almost every situation I have observed suggests that the struggle for pay equity is not merely an issue of the neutral application of technical expertise, but rather a struggle for power and control. At the broadest level, the struggle involves the power to define how we are going to debate pay equity, which means, for example, confronting that image of objectivity and fairness, the "invisible hand" of the market, and

[2]Red circling is the term used for a procedure that maintains the wage level for incumbents of a title but lowers the wage level of that same job for future incumbents. Based on job evaluation results, red circling identifies jobs that are found to be "overvalued"—overpaid—relative to measurable job content.

making visible the hand that has served white male management so well. But our arguments are no substitute for political muscle. True pay equity will emerge not when policymakers see the intrinsic validity of the arguments proponents are making, but when it is politically impossible for them *not* to agree with proponents.

Barbara Bergmann

I would put affirmative action as our number-one priority for advancing the position of women. Until we make more progress in getting women into nontraditional jobs, in getting rid of the idea that there are men's jobs and women's jobs, white jobs and black jobs, we will not be anywhere near our goal of equality for women. I am in favor of efforts to change the pay in women's jobs through comparable worth, but integration through affirmative action also will have positive wage effects. Additionally, affirmative action breaks up the pattern that arbitrarily assigns certain jobs low pay, and certain other jobs high pay. When women go into traditionally male jobs, the number of women entering traditionally female jobs decreases, which is already happening to some degree in occupations such as nursing and teaching. The movement of women out of female-dominated jobs will produce pressures to raise the pay in those jobs. So, affirmative action not only improves access to jobs, it also affects pay.

Many people perceive affirmative action as an injustice, that it is unfair. My students, for example, even after they have had a whole term of my lectures about discrimination, are still very much against affirmative action. As an experiment, I give them a questionnaire. I describe a factual situation, using the U.S. Supreme Court case in which a California woman wanted a job as a dispatcher (*Johnson v. Transportation Agency* 480 U.S. 616 (1987)). There were three hundred of these jobs and not a single one had been given to a woman. I ask my students what should happen in that workplace: (1) should the employer merely review the fairness of the selection process?; (2) should women candidates be selected and given special attention for future vacancies?; (3) should a more rigorous quota be set up? Most of my students choose the first option. The reason is that there are no arguments in favor of affirmative action published in the media. I never saw anything explaining and favoring affirmative action in *Ms. Magazine;* I have never seen anything in *New Directions for Women.* I have certainly never seen anything in *Signs* or in *Feminist*

Studies about affirmative action. We have to put out the word that when there has been discrimination, it is not affirmative action that is an injustice, it is the absence of affirmative action that is an injustice.

When writing my book, *The Economic Emergence of Women* (1986), and talking with my students, I concluded that affirmative action does cause some injustices. For example, one of my students, an older woman, said, "I was working in this library for ten years and I had my eye on a certain promotion and I asked my boss whether I could be considered for that job. He said 'Well, I am terribly sorry, but we are holding that for a black person.' " That certainly appears unjust to the person asked to step aside. Sometimes these excuses not to hire or promote someone are used falsely. But even so, some people do lose chances they would otherwise have. Nevertheless, what's important is that we emphasize that the absence of affirmative action does not result in a perfectly just situation. Quite the contrary, there are many jobs for which there is a quota of 100 percent white males. Affirmative action changes such quotas to make them more fair.

We need a lot more research and thinking about various aspects of the process that sorts men and women into different jobs. Heidi Hartmann, now the director of the Institute for Women's Policy Research but formerly with the National Academy of Sciences, told me something very striking. She said, "At the academy, we had some men in clerical jobs and the males in management couldn't stand it. They were always looking out for ways to promote those men and get them out of there. There was no comparable action on behalf of the women clericals." So, we need to understand the psychology of gender that leads to this kind of behavior and perpetuates sex segregation in jobs. We ought to be recruiting psychologists, anthropologists, and sociologists to do this work.

We need research on the specifics of how people get sorted when they are hired. Many organizations hire people with no skill prerequisites and all training is given on the job. Nevertheless, in such cases, the new employees are still sorted into all-male and all-female job categories. We need to study the actual procedures used to get that result. We need to understand how, in a department store, the women end up selling the nuts and panties and the men sell the vacuum cleaners for good wages, when neither the men nor the women come to the job knowing more about vacuum cleaners.

We need research on the arrangements and arguments and stratagems that are used to keep women out of certain jobs. In one of the examples in my book, a woman asked for a certain job and was told, "Sure you can have that, but to do the job you have to be able to lift this heavy machine all by yourself." It turned out that the men lifted it with a hoist. We need anecdotal material like that as well as statistical data.

We also need both research and action on why women clerical workers and others in female-typed occupations are seldom promoted. Why does a woman clerical worker who knows her boss's job not succeed her boss if he leaves? We need more research on sexual harassment of women in non-traditional jobs. We need to find out about other kinds of harassment as well. In my book, I give the example of a foreman who would always put a woman carpenter on the most repetitive, boring jobs as a way of harassing her, while males were given varied work.

Why and how have vocational schools remained so segregated? If a woman inquires into a vocational school, she is given a story that convinces her that she can't go there. In general, people accept such stories. The more light we can shed on that problem, the more scorn we can pour on it, and the more publicity we can give it, the sooner we can get rid of it. Vocational schools are an area where virtually no progress has been made.

Vocational training is very important for reducing the numbers of women living in poverty. Skilled blue-collar men make decent salaries. The women who haven't been to college have very few opportunities for any kind of salary that will keep them in comfort, keep their kids out of poverty, and keep them off welfare. If we want to solve the problem of poverty in this country, we have to do something about getting women into these blue-collar, skilled jobs that are available to noncollege-educated males.

Anna Padia

The experience of The Newspaper Guild (TNG) demonstrates that affirmative action programs have made a significant difference in the number of women and minorities in the news industry. Today, women make up 39 percent and minorities 18 percent of the U.S. daily newspaper work force at a time when women are 48 percent and minorities are 22 percent of the civilian labor force (Belden Associates 1990). Current population surveys offer a specific job comparison. Of all editors and reporters, 51.1 percent were women in 1991, up from 41.1 percent in 1972. Blacks and Hispanics held 13.3 percent of these jobs in 1991 compared to 1972, when 4.3 percent of these jobs were held by "Blacks, and Other Races" (BLS 1992).

While much remains to be done, I am convinced that the news industry would not have progressed this far without the pressures for affirmative action initiated by TNG. Nineteen years ago, TNG, which represents advertising, business, circulation, data processing, and editorial employees of newspapers and wire services in the United States, Canada, and Puerto Rico, began requiring its union locals to include affirmative action programs in their contract proposals to news industry employers. TNG believes that affirmative action is, and has been, extremely important in the hiring, training, and promotion of our female and minority members and that the number of women and minority reporters, editors, and publishers makes a difference in what we read and in how news is treated and prioritized.

Like most unions, TNG has used an array of mechanisms for correcting employment inequities, including collective bargaining, legislative, political, and legal actions, and demonstrations and other concerted pressure in coalition with various community groups. Collective bargaining, however, has been our principal approach. We define bargaining as the power to persuade and compel—persuading through intellectual arguments and compelling with the muscle of people and, in some cases, the law. It is an approach that has resulted in the inclusion of affirmative action provisions in Guild contracts and in conciliation agreements or consent decrees at a number of newspapers and wire services such as the Associated Press (AP), the *Washington Post,* the *Sacramento Bee,* and the *New York Times.*

Since 1976, all of the collective bargaining agreements negotiated between Time, Inc., and the New York Guild have included goals to hire, transfer, or promote women and minority employees in specific jobs during the life of each agreement. The contracts, covering all employees in the editorial departments of Time-Life Books and Time, Inc., magazines and editorial services, also established a joint committee to review progress to identify and solve problems in achieving affirmative action goals.

The current labor agreement between the *Cleveland Plain Dealer* and the Cleveland Guild Local includes a commitment that the employer will "continue its present policy of affirmative action" and "will actively recruit and promote women and/or members of minority groups." It continues a committee to study and issue recommendations regarding career opportunities and training programs for women and minority groups.

The accumulated experience of TNG bargaining has taught us more than a few lessons. Today, when TNG is asked what is the ideal plan of action to achieve affirmative action through bargaining, our response is: develop a multistep action plan that begins a year or more in advance of bargaining and which includes the following:

- Form a women's or minority caucus, or human rights or affirmative action committee or task force, that can energize support for and focus attention on affirmative actions. Caucuses could be especially effective in communicating and explaining how and why certain actions must be taken.
- Adopt resolutions that set or reaffirm policy at the local, regional, and/or international union level. This action will encourage discussion of the issue and give proponents an idea of where objections lie and how to neutralize them.
- Support related legislation and publicize this support in union newsletters to inform employers and the membership of the legislation's importance. (The AFL-CIO and some larger unions assign lobbyists to target key federal legislation, such as the Civil Rights Act of 1991.)
- Educate members by conducting special local discussion series, workshops, or seminars on the issue of affirmative action.
- Select a bargaining team that is not opposed to affirmative action. The people at the bargaining table will be required to carry the banner when it comes down to the final hours of crunch bargaining.
- Collect copies of employers' general employment policies and statements and any articles or memos on equal employment, affirmative action, or multicultural diversity efforts and review them for their impact on union proposals.
- Look at the history of bargaining with an employer. Is there a history of discrimination? What complaints have been filed against the employer? Have affirmative action remedies been proposed in the past? What was said and what was the outcome? Tracing an employer's employment patterns and practices over time will help build the legal basis to prove discrimination.
- Develop sound intellectual arguments for your collective bargaining proposals and support these arguments with documentation.

There are two primary sources for documentation. First, gather and analyze the employer's payroll data. Private sector unions have the right, granted by decisions of the National Labor Relations Board (NLRB) and the courts, to request and obtain any information that is presumed relevant to collective bargaining or to investigate potential violations of a contractual fair employment practice clause. Relevant data include the name, sex, and race of an employee; date of hire; date of birth; salary, merit increases, commissions, bonuses, and other compensation; work force analyses; and EEO reports and information on all charges or complaints filed by or on behalf of bargaining unit employees. Often employers balk at requests for data and the union has to file an unfair labor practice charge with the NLRB against the employer to obtain this information. But armed with this information, a union has the qualitative documentation to determine where discrimination may or may not be present. The data can help the union define the problem, design the remedy, and develop the legal basis for a proposal. Second, gathering anecdotal information will give life to the statistical patterns or practices found in the payroll data analysis and provide sharper definition of the problem and the proposed remedies.

But, how does a union develop the more difficult "power to compel"? First, in the early stages of bargaining, TNG organizes the people in the job classifications that are most immediately affected either in one-on-one or in small group forums. We discuss the facts, goals, and tasks required and prepare members of this group to become the core of any caucus, committee, or task force.

Another critical early step is to organize support from other job classifications not immediately affected, starting first with the identified leaders in these jobs. While such an undertaking is not without its problems and may require some quid pro quo politics, the potential opponents to affirmative action within the union membership will know the union is serious if it has been publishing articles, sponsoring forums, and doing legislative work, and has adopted and publicized resolutions on affirmative action. Members will recognize that affirmative action is an important policy of the union and will be more inclined to support it. It also helps if the membership is informed of other examples of affirmative action either from the industry or, to a lesser extent, from other unions.

A third way to build support is to work with outside organizations such as the National Organization for Women or the National Association for the Advancement of Colored People. An ongoing mutual relationship with these organizations can produce influential pressure at critical junctures in bargaining.

Finally, the most compelling and expensive action that a union can take is to file discrimination charges or to support charges brought by employees. This action can be done before, during, or after bargaining. The Newspaper Guild recommends that local unions seek to grieve, arbitrate, negotiate, and only then litigate discrimination disputes, but this approach is not inflexible and has been altered when circumstances warranted. In a few cases, the union has filed a charge and the charge itself has become the compelling factor that initiated bargaining. In other cases, the union threatened litigation in the middle of bargaining, informing the employer that, without an affirmative action provision, the Guild would file charges and pursue a case through the courts, a threat that has caused more than one employer to work out an agreement.

In some cases, Guild locals, in consultation with the international union office, have filed discrimination charges that resulted in either a conciliation agreement or a consent decree. Many of these have yielded the most dramatic and most expensive precedents and definitive changes. For example, a conciliation agreement reached in 1980 among the Washington-Baltimore Guild, the Equal Employment Opportunity Commission (EEOC), and the *Washington Post* established goals and timetables to hire, upgrade, and promote women over five years in the news, editorial, and commercial departments. The agreement resolved charges filed eight years earlier in 1972.

In another case, a 1976 conciliation agreement among the Sacramento Newspaper Guild, the EEOC, and the McClatchy Newspaper Company settled Guild charges of sex and race discrimination at the *Sacramento Bee.* The agreement included remedial provisions in recruitment, hiring, transfers, promotion, pregnancy leave, and newspaper "help-wanted" advertising practices. All of the Guild contracts negotiated since that agreement have included an affirmative action provision.

Likewise, the 1983 consent decree between the Wire Service Guild, the EEOC, and the AP included an extensive five-year affirmative action plan including goals and timetables for hiring and promotions, training, and other programs that settled sex and race discrimination charges filed with the EEOC in 1973. The employer extended and expanded the affirmative action plan in 1988 and agreed to a Guild contract that includes an affirmative action provision.

The results of Guild bargaining have ranged from precedent-setting, complex, and sophisticated plans to minimum contract provisions committing an employer to recruit women and minorities in all job classifications. And, where bargaining does not initially achieve contract language, the discussions often cause an employer to quietly review employment practices. At the very least, bargaining keeps the pressure on and the issue alive.

Today, three out of ten daily newspapers have affirmative action programs, many of which were established within the last ten years due to Guild prompting, legal precedents, and a growing industry awareness that affirmative action and employee diversity are simply good business. Most affirmative action programs are in place at large-circulation newspapers and 68 percent of all newspapers with programs rate the effectiveness of their program positively (Belden Associates 1990).

But there is much to be done. And we have to do it in the wake of 1989 Supreme Court decisions making it harder to prove discrimination and easier to challenge consent decrees. These decisions weakened the power to compel at the bargaining table and require legislative and political changes to repair the damage. Absent these changes, other affirmative actions such as career

development and alternative work schedules may have more chance of suc-
ceeding since they are driven less by legislative, judicial, or regulatory pressures
and more by an employer's need to accommodate the changing demographics
of the work force and to compete effectively. Most important, to keep, expand,
and go beyond affirmative actions to affirming diversity, we must continue to
make demands. For, as Frederick Douglass said, "Power never concedes without a demand. It never has and never will" (Douglass 1950).

3
Unions, Hard Hats, and Women Workers

Brigid O'Farrell and Suzanne Moore

After twenty-five years of affirmative action, gender segregation in the workplace persists and women continue to earn less money than men. Nowhere is this more evident than in the blue-collar world of carpenters, machinists, and truck drivers. In such trades, male coworkers and their unions are often singled out as two of the main reasons for women's slow progress toward equality in the workplace. In this chapter we examine the role of unions in integrating women into these jobs.

We contend that there is a potentially powerful symbiosis between blue-collar unions and the women who seek to integrate jobs. Women are a source of new membership, talent, and energy. Unions have the resources, mechanisms, and legitimacy to represent women's issues through existing industrial relations procedures. Why, then, hasn't more progress been made?

Our union case study provides an in-depth understanding of what forces promote successful partnerships between women and unions and suggests two important findings. First, the actions of women on their own behalf and their use of existing union structures, including grievance procedures, collective bargaining, committees, and legal actions, is critical. Second, men's responses to affirmative action are complex, fluid, and contingent on the specific work situation and the way affirmative action is implemented and perceived.

Our findings point to the pivotal role of union leaders, both national and local, not only in terms of responding to the demands of women, but in being aware of the diverse attitudes of men toward job integration and in helping design programs that will win the support of the uncommitted majority. Solidarity of women and men and support of rank-and-file union members on a wide range of issues is critical in the current period of union retrenchment.

Increasing evidence suggests that while job integration strategies can be divisive, they also provide some opportunity for new alliances between women and men that will strengthen unions, expand job choices for women, and improve the workplace for all.

Slow Progress

Data collected from 1979 to 1989 provide concrete evidence that women can enter and remain in blue-collar jobs historically done by men, even under very difficult circumstances (Padavic and Reskin 1990; Swerdlow 1989; Schroedel 1985; Waite and Berryman 1985; Deaux and Ullman 1983; Harlan and O'Farrell 1982; Walshok 1981). Occupational segregation among blue-collar jobs, however, remains virtually intact (table 3.1). Similarly, economic equity is still elusive and patterns of segregation are emerging in new occupations and industries (Reskin and Roos 1990).

There are only token levels of female participation within the best craft jobs, even in categories where there has been some growth in the total number of jobs. For example, the number of painters increased 12 percent, from 483,000 to 543,000, while the number of women who are painters increased 35 percent, from 24,150 to 32,580. Yet women are only 6 percent of all painters. The *percentage* of women carpenters actually *declined* from 1.3 to 1.2 percent, despite an increase in the total number of carpenters. The percentage of women increased in several machine and production jobs, such as telephone installer, but the number of women declined due to the overall loss of jobs in the industries.

There are some differences within occupations and industries, however. Women have made more progress among light truck driving than heavy truck driving jobs, and bus driver is now an occupation that is more than 50 percent women, one of the resegregation patterns discussed by Reskin and Roos (1990). Women have made the most progress in the entry-level laborer categories where the heaviest, dirtiest work is found. Some of these jobs are important, however, as possible routes to the more skilled jobs in both the production and construction trades. Still, 20 percent of the laborers in production are women, compared with just 3 percent in construction.

Why continue to make the case for integrating these blue-collar jobs when progress is slow, resistance strong, and jobs increasingly susceptible to attrition from technological change and structural shifts in the economy? Women need to focus on blue-collar jobs, in part because of their significantly higher wages and modest job growth. The U.S. Department of Labor, for example, has recently initiated a wide-ranging policy program to support women in skilled

Table 3.1. Women in Selected Nontraditional Occupations, 1979–1989

Occupation	1979		1989	
	Total number employed (in 1,000s)	Women as a percentage of all workers	Total number employed (in 1,000s)	Women as a percentage of all workers
Construction				
Carpenters	1,276	1.3	1,369	1.2
Electricians	640	1.3	702	1.8
Painters	483	5.0	543	6.0
Plumbers, pipefitters	450	0.4	456	0.8
Helpers[1]	930	2.7	123	4.1
Laborers	–	–	755	3.0
Precision Production, Repair				
Machinists	552	2.9	479	4.2
Tool and die makers	184	2.2	148	2.6
Telephone installers and repairers	302	9.9	193	10.8
Telephone line installers, repairers	82	2.4	54	4.2
Operators, Laborers, Helpers				
Lathe and milling	123	8.9	55	9.0
Welders	713	4.5	612	6.6
Production helpers	–	–	82	26.8
Laborers, except construction[2]	718	9.6	1,288	20.4
Transportation				
Truck drivers, heavy[3]	1,965	2.1	1,850	1.9
Truck drivers, light	–	–	766	8.9
Bus drivers	358	45.5	440	54.8

Source: Adapted from U.S. Department of Labor, *Employment and Earnings,* Table 23 (January 1980); Table 22 (January 1990).

[1] In 1979 there was one category: construction laborers, including carpenters helpers.

[2] In 1979 the category was all other nonfarm laborers excluding animal caretakers, construction laborers (including carpenters helpers), freight and material handlers, garbage collectors, gardeners, timber cutting, vehicle washers, equipment cleaners, warehouse laborers.

[3] In 1979 there was only one category: truck drivers.

trades as a way to improve their economic status. In 1991, President Bush signed into law the Nontraditional Employment for Women Act, to increase training and employment in skilled trades for low-income women served by the Job Training Partnership Act.

A shortage of workers is projected in some skilled jobs, as well as in newly developing semiskilled and skilled occupations. While actual and projected

Table 3.2. Projected Employment in Selected Occupations with 25,000 Workers or More

Occupation	1988–2000 Employment change[1] (%)
Construction trades	16
Mechanics, installers, repairers	13
Machinery and related mechanics, installers, repairers	18
Precision production	1
Operators, fabricators, laborers	1
Transportation and material moving	12
Helpers, laborers, and material movers, hand machine operators	2

Source: Adapted from Silvestri and Lukasiewicz (1989): Table 4: Civilian employment in occupations with 25,000 workers or more, actual 1988 and projected to 2000, under low, medium, and high scenarios for economic growth, pp. 56–59.
[1] Medium scenario for economic growth.

job growth is significantly higher in the service occupations, blue-collar trades such as construction and machining will continue to provide opportunities for women and men (table 3.2). Furthermore, while hostile male coworkers create barriers, they may not be as significant as originally suggested (Padavic and Reskin 1990; Swerdlow 1989; McIlwee 1982; O'Farrell and Harlan 1982; Walshok 1981). At the same time, the role of unions in creating opportunities for women has become more important as government enforcement of equal employment laws relaxed in the 1980s (Simon 1986).

The Union Role

Despite declining national memberships, workers in blue-collar jobs are more likely to be union members or represented by unions than those in other occupations (table 3.3). Although 16 percent of all wage and salary workers are union members, over 25 percent of blue-collar workers belong to unions. Blue-collar jobs are also found in the public sector, where 44 percent of employed wage and salary workers are represented by unions (U.S. Department of Labor 1990).

Government officials (Newman and Wilson 1981), corporate leaders (Shaeffer and Lynton 1979), and researchers (Hartmann 1976) have perceived unions as a major obstacle to job integration. The government has either sued unions along with employers for discrimination or they have excluded unions from agreements altogether.

In the building trades, for example, several unions have been charged with

Table 3.3. Employed Wage and Salary Workers by Occupation and Union Affiliation, 1989

Occupation	Total employed[1]	Members of unions (% of employed)[2]	Represented by unions (% of employed)[3]
Managerial and professional specialty	25,357	15	18
Technical, sales, and administrative support	32,633	10	12
Service occupations	14,410	14	15
Precision production, craft, and repair	11,906	26	28
Operators, fabricators, and laborers	17,399	27	29
Farming, forestry, and fishing	1,774	4	5
Total	103,480	16	19

Source: Adapted from U.S. Department of Labor, *Employment and Earnings,* Table 58; Employed wage and salary workers by occupation, industry, and union affiliation, p. 232 (January 1990).
[1] Data refer to the sole or principal job of full- and part-time workers over sixteen years of age. Excluded are self-employed workers whose businesses are incorporated, although they technically qualify as wage and salary workers.
[2] Data refer to members of a labor union or an employee association similar to a union.
[3] Data refer to members of a labor union or an employee association similar to a union as well as workers who report no union affiliation but whose jobs are covered by a union or an employee association contract.

implementing discriminatory hiring and placement procedures, and some industrial unions have been charged with negotiating discriminatory seniority systems (Wallace and Driscoll 1981). Even when charges against a union have been dropped, they are rarely part of affirmative action discussions; the steel industry is a notable exception. In general, government agencies have been hostile to union involvement in affirmative action programs (Newman and Wilson 1981).

Part of this hostility is based on documented discriminatory behavior. Some unions have excluded women members and some have strongly resisted attempts to integrate either jobs or membership (Wallace and Driscoll 1981; Milkman 1987). Seniority systems have been found to perpetuate the effects of previous discrimination (Kelley 1982). Women have filed complaints of discrimination against unions, and the harassment of women entering sex-atypical trades, by both union and nonunion workers, is well documented (Padavic and Reskin 1990; Swerdlow 1989; Schroedel 1985; Deaux and Ullman 1983; O'Farrell and Harlan 1982, 1984; Gruber and Bjorn 1982).

But some unions have been effective in influencing social legislation, such as the equal employment laws (Freeman and Medoff 1984). Richard B. Freeman and Jonathan S. Leonard (1987) found that, in the private sector, unions have a slight positive impact on reducing sex-based wage discrimination and they do not appear to deter the operation of affirmative action programs to increase female employment. Ruth Milkman (1987) provides historical data on men and unions fighting against gender inequality.

Several union procedures have also been strengthened through litigation under Title VII of the Civil Rights Act of 1964. For example, Supreme Court decisions have affirmed the legitimacy of seniority systems and the duty of fair representation, both important union benefits.

Although there has been little research on the union role in general, two factors appear important for encouraging unions to play a constructive leadership role. First, women members have learned to use the existing union structures to pursue their goals, including the legal framework and the committee structure. Second, while there is resistance and hostility on the part of male coworkers and union leaders which has to be overcome, there are also supportive men who can be encouraged, as well as men with neutral attitudes who need to become involved. Our case study, based on fifty intensive interviews with thirty-three women and seventeen men in a large industrial factory setting, illustrates how these factors interact. (For further description and analyses of the Harbor Company and United Workers Union, pseudonyms for the company and union involved, see O'Farrell 1980; Douglas 1981; Harlan and O'Farrell 1982; and Harlan 1989).

The Harbor Company

The Harbor Company is a large multinational industrial manufacturer of products such as engines and gears. At the time of our case study, over nine thousand Harbor workers (90 percent of the work force in two plants) were represented by Local 1 of the United Workers Union. The blue-collar work force was 15 percent female, with women concentrated in the lowest paid, least skilled factory jobs such as punch press operator. Clerical jobs were also unionized, but women were at the bottom of the job ladder; men occupied virtually all of the upper-level production, purchasing, and cost-accounting jobs. Affirmative action efforts spanned several years of rapid employment growth followed by a period of decline. The company, like the industry in general, was exporting jobs, shutting down plants, and laying off workers in selected parts of its U.S. operations.

The United Workers Union had over 200,000 members nationwide, but the majority of workers in the industry and in the Harbor Company as a whole were unorganized. Women received some support from the national union, which had a long history of worker equity, and where the total membership was one-third women. The union's constitution and national collective bargaining agreement prohibited discrimination. A women's council represented the locals' committees, and a staff director for women's activities provided a link to the national's male leadership.

Union Women Take Action

Collective bargaining and grievance procedures are the primary tools that unions use to establish and protect worker rights on the job. Legislation has been used by unions as an extension of the collective bargaining process (Newman and Wilson 1981). When union leaders or rank-and-file members failed to secure certain rights at the bargaining table or to resolve problems through the grievance and arbitration process, they have gone to government agencies and the courts. This has been most successful when addressing women's issues such as pregnancy disability, equal pay for equal work, and equal pay for comparable worth (Freeman and Leonard 1987; Hams 1984; Wertheimer 1984; Steinberg and Cook 1981).

All of these procedures were used by the women in Local 1 where comparable worth and job integration were at issue. The women seeking men's skilled jobs were very active in the process. They began their complex quest for better pay and jobs in the mid-1960s.

The two primary concerns of women in Local 1 were to improve the pay of factory and clerical workers, who were mostly women, and to gain access to the sex-atypical or higher-paying skilled jobs done predominantly by men. They went first to the union, which was unresponsive, and then to the government. One of the first female welders recalled:

> Another woman and myself, we got on our high horse. A lot of girls had tried, but it never worked, but we had never had an equal rights law behind us before. We decided we wanted to push women's rights on the men's jobs and we just told the union, "We're going into town to the State Equal Rights Commission and push it ourselves." So the union decided to go with us.

The local union leaders belatedly responded to a small but active group of women members. Relying on the grievance process, the shop stewards and officers tried to upgrade women's welding jobs and to introduce women to the higher-paying welding department. The grievances resulted in limited expansion of women's bidding rights on the men's jobs, but women's jobs were not upgraded. The union then filed complaints with the federal Equal

Employment Opportunity Commission (EEOC) and the Department of Labor, but the resulting affirmative action plan was not implemented.

In 1973, after a second set of sex discrimination charges were filed with the EEOC against several different Harbor facilities, the EEOC brought its own charges against Harbor and the United Workers Union (UWU) at the national level. The pattern was similar to that of other national initiatives where the EEOC charged both employer and union with employment discrimination. The EEOC later dropped the complaints against the UWU, but the commission denied the union any participation in the national settlement with Harbor.

In 1974, through collective bargaining, the local union negotiated a formal job-posting and bidding system, which benefited all workers. Promotion opportunities for all employees were better communicated. The union had tried for years to establish such a system, but without success. Such systems are often a required part of affirmative action programs, however, and not surprisingly, workers perceived the system as a product of the women's complaints and the pending government negotiations. One woman explained how the women's job action benefited everyone:

> There's special discrimination against women. . . . There's also discrimination
> that affects everyone. . . . For example, the upgrading system, a lot of guys
> got screwed over . . . but by dealing with it in the context of women and
> minorities they help everybody.

In 1978, the company signed a national settlement with the EEOC, but the women in Local 1 were not satisfied with the agreement. They again pushed the local union to sue the company to upgrade women's factory jobs and to develop a more aggressive affirmative action program to recruit and train women for skilled jobs. In addition, the union sought information on the work force by race and gender through the National Labor Relations Board (NLRB). After three years of legal activities, Harbor and Local 1 signed a new affirmative action agreement that was a marked improvement over the national plan. The agreement eliminated the two lowest job ratings, improved job posting and layoff procedures, and created over 80 new training positions for segregated jobs; some trainees could transfer with their pay and company seniority intact. Other changes included improved maternity benefits, equalized entry-level rates, and the award of back pay. The local also succeeded in receiving information from the company to help monitor the agreement. The number of women in the more skilled jobs gradually increased. By 1980 for example, 54 of the 289 apprentices (or 19 percent) in the all-around machinists training program were women.

Importantly, the women began to organize. Through a women's committee they developed support not only among male coworkers, but also among women in the predominantly female factory and clerical jobs. Individual women and the women's committee became active in both the internal union negotiations and the external legal activities.

The women's committee was started in the early 1970s by a small group of women, most of whom were recently hired into the machinist apprenticeship program. They met after the regular union meetings. In 1976, the women petitioned the union to have their committee recognized as a standing union committee, with all the legitimacy and union resources that this status would confer. Four years later, after hard opposition from some quarters, the status was approved.

Whether to create a separate, highly visible caucus within an organization has been a strategy question in most political movements. The interviews conducted for this case study revealed ambivalence even among activist women because a separate caucus meant risking the alienation of the union mainstream majority. A woman machinist expressed her ambivalence about forming a committee:

> The best thing the women's committee could hope to accomplish is to be able to organize women in the shop floor to fight discriminatory practices of the company through encouraging [women] to file grievances, . . . and participate more in the union. . . . I'm afraid it will gear itself too much to women's issues. It's important to make a distinction between the guys on the floor and managers . . . then they won't alienate the guys in the shop.

The women's committee resolved the dilemma by forming coalitions with sympathetic coworkers, male and female, and a strong alliance formed between the women's committee and the occupational health and safety committee. The two committees worked together on issues particularly important to the blue-collar women integrating skilled jobs and they took up issues relevant to women in clerical jobs, such as the health effects of VDT terminals. They also pushed issues of concern to men. One woman explained the importance of health and safety in the jobs they were integrating:

> Health and safety is going to be a big issue at Harbor Company. A lot of people take a sort of 'oh well, it won't hurt me' attitude, but I think that's changing 'cause a lot of people are getting hurt and people are starting to realize some long-term effects. . . . They still use asbestos . . . cut asbestos fibers and stuff like that. They do that right on my floor.

The Local 1 women's committee remains active today. According to a recent article in the union's national newspaper, the committee is seen as a positive force fighting for all workers. The committee has taken up family care and is credited by the union leadership for negotiating in the collective bargaining agreement a flexible spending account that provides a tax break for men and women who are paying for child or elder care. It continues to focus on health and safety issues.

Union Men

Although the women in Local 1 worked with supportive men, they also faced male hostility, as have women in other studies (most recently, Padavic and Reskin 1990). Most union officers were aware of their legal responsibilities, but some resisted the establishment of the women's committee; they appointed conservative women to serve on it. Some women perceived little real change in male union attitudes; they thought that the men were forced to go along with equal employment ideas because of pressure from the women as well as the government. They did, however, see changes in male behavior over time. As one woman explained, "With some of the people that are in there now, I'm very satisfied. If you had asked me ten years ago I would have said, 'Throw it all out.' But not now."

Union leaders and the men they represent are at the core of the job integration struggle. No discussion of strategies to integrate blue-collar jobs can be relevant without some understanding of the roughly twenty-five million men who are blue-collar workers. As union power brokers, incumbent gatekeepers to disputed job territory, and women's coworkers, they exert a tremendous influence on how unions and employers distribute jobs and benefits, how workers are trained, and thus their subsequent job satisfaction.

Blue-collar men share several common experiences (see Halle 1984; Shaiken 1984; Gray 1984; Shostak 1980; Riemer 1979). Much of their work is physically demanding, noisy, dirty, and high-pressure. In an industrial setting that is increasingly buffeted by technological change, foreign competition, and a weakening economy, job deskilling and unemployment are constant threats, underlying a sense that manual work is not highly valued by society. At the same time, the men we interviewed, like those in other studies, share a traditional pride in doing manual labor. They enjoy stories of the legendary feats and skills of other workers, and there is ritual and special language surrounding the tools and work that are institutionalized through programs such as apprenticeships.

The social upheavals of the past quarter century have profoundly challenged and threatened these men, not only their economic security, but their values, beliefs, and self-image. The superimposition of the demands of minorities, environmentalists, and women onto their workplace has brought stress, conflict, and greater job insecurity. None of the changes has had greater impact than the women's movement, because it has affected the women in their lives at home as well as at work.

Yet blue-collar male attitudes are diverse, complex, and sometimes surprising. Women who were interviewed in the case study described male harassment as most severe for the first women who integrated the male-dominated jobs; it then lessened over time. Men seemed to fit into three categories: a small group of actively supportive men, a minority of very hostile men, and the majority, who were neutral or ambivalent. Similar categories have been found in other studies. (See, for example, Martin's 1980 study of police work, Gray's 1984 study of a production plant, and Swerdlow's 1989 account of transit workers.)

Progressives

In Local 1, less than 20 percent of the men interviewed could be termed actively supportive of women's changing job roles. Generally, they were young (under forty) and active in the union as officers, committee members, and shop stewards concerned with a range of issues such as health and safety as well as affirmative action. For these men, women's abilities were not an issue. They believed that women's exclusion from company jobs was the direct result of discriminatory company practices. If a woman could not perform a plant job, it was because the machinery was designed especially for men, or male coworkers or managers were not teaching the women. One machinist explained:

> Now if you're not taught to do that work, you could break your back. But if someone took the time and said, "Now look, take it easy. Let the crane pick it up. Now just take it with two fingers and balance" . . . you could show someone how to do it without working up a sweat. If you say, "just pick it up and stack it," they'd kill themselves.

The progressives wanted their union to take an active lead rather than a reactive role on questions of race and sex. They believed that the union leadership had not addressed the prejudice of its male members and the role its overt expression had in retarding women's advancement. Some also thought that the women were too passive. They considered the union's lawsuits a way of letting the legal system deal with a people problem that the union should be handling internally. "People have to participate in [solving] their problems," one man said. "You have to educate people so you can't be used against each other."

Hostile Hard Hats

Hostile men also made up less than 20 percent of the men interviewed, but they caused a disproportionate amount of trouble for women. Regardless of age, they thought women should be home or at least not in a "man's job." As a new woman recruit on the all-male assembly line commented: "It's only a small group, but when they all stand by the water fountain right outside the ladies' room, it can seem like a whole lot."

These men felt threatened, angry, and betrayed. One older worker described his bitterness about affirmative action efforts at Harbor:

> There's gonna be an explosion. A person like me, I don't care if a black or woman gets a job as long as they're qualified. . . . But I'm a product of the depression days. If anyone was discriminated against and stepped on, it's people from that era. . . . Then thirty years later you have children of your own and they're being discriminated against the way you were. . . . This is wrong. Where is a twenty-one-year-old white male to go? There is no place for him.

Unlike the progressives, the men in this hostile minority were all different ages. They were not active union members, but they were critical of union activities, although they were not well-informed. They had very conservative attitudes about women's place and thought women, especially those with young children, should be at home. One man said, "I'm a firm believer, if you're a woman, work in the office or stay home and make babies."

They believed that women did not have the qualifications to do all aspects of a job, including the heavy, dirty, and "bad" work. These men thought that women didn't have the knack to learn the jobs or that supervisors might give the women the easier work and the men would have to take up the slack.

These men also reflected the larger male work culture itself. As Norma Briggs (1979) noted, often the barrier is not the difficult or dirty nature of some jobs, but breaking a taboo and heading into territory that has been the preserve of men. Blue-collar men see themselves doing men's work in a man's world, an image important to their self-esteem. The work group cohesiveness enables the men to work together, often in close quarters and in high-risk situations. The buddy bonding continues after hours in "masculine" interests: gambling, drinking, and sports.

Overt sexist treatment of women is a stereotypical aspect of the hard-hat culture: girl watching, looking at pornography, telling sexual jokes, and teasing women seem to reinforce and reassure them of their masculine identity. Research suggests that these constant sexist overtones are ways that men working in close interdependency and physical contact redirect "unacceptable feelings" they have for each other into socially acceptable fraternal bonds and loyalty to the all-male group (Halle 1984; Gray 1984; Martin 1980).

The culture also demands a clear dichotomy of what constitutes acceptable behavior at work and at home among women. The more conservative the man, the more he will object to exposing women to an all-male work environment. Some men also view women's intrusion into the work ranks as inherently deflating the intrinsic worth of their jobs. Women's work is not considered to be valuable (Williams 1989). Many blue-collar men are "status anxious"; that is, their own jobs are of such low status that there is no margin for further devaluation (Shostak 1980).

The Harbor case study interviews identified a broad range of concerns and issues shared to a lesser or greater degree by a much larger population that includes, but is not limited to, the overtly hostile male coworkers. What sets this small group apart is their active expression of attitudes that seemed to be based more on stereotypes about women and less on the reality of how women perform their jobs or the real threat to the men's job security.

Ambivalent Moderates

The majority of the men interviewed expressed an ambivalence that is a cause for concern, but also for optimism about future outcomes. As Stan Gray (1984) argues in his study of an electronics plant in Canada, these are the men who may remain quiet in the face of a small, very aggressive group of hostile men, or they may become extremely helpful or at least remain neutral with progressive leadership.

These are the men who train women on the job and who, in the Harbor case, ultimately voted for the women's committee. Among this group one cannot generalize about age or level of union participation. What characterizes them is a passive ambivalence about workplace issues that extends to their attitudes about the company and their union in general. Most espouse traditional values about women's roles, but are tolerant of the evolution taking place around them. One man explained his understanding of why women work:

> The forklift driver, she just wanted to get out and work. That was it. She likes being home and taking care of her little girls, but she needs to get out and be with people, have a way of independence in the same way that her husband would. . . . I think the [wage] scales should be brought up because there are more and more women who are becoming independent as far as even having a family. They'll get along without a husband and still have to raise a family.

And they have to work, pay rent, so they should have the same opportunity to make enough money to be able to raise the family.

These men characterized as tradition what feminists call discrimination. They denied that women are harassed on the job, although they acknowledged that some "joking" and "teasing" went on when women first integrated the jobs. They did not express deep anger about affirmative action at the plants or characterize the company's integration efforts as "special treatment" of women and minorities: "The workers would stop that." Nor did they object to working with qualified women as long as their own jobs were not threatened. Those who had positive experiences with women coworkers described them as intelligent and aggressive, good trade unionists who worked out of financial need and a desire for independence.

Although moderates may be inclined to hold negative, stereotypical views about women, they, unlike the more rigid hostile men, can be influenced to be more accepting by their personal experiences and by the opinions of their coworkers, union leaders, and managers. Circumstances these men consider unfair, however, can trigger resentment and hostility. In one case, management transferred women from other departments with their seniority and pay intact, as well as with significant incentive bonuses. Male coworkers were then expected to train the women from scratch, even though the women were making more money. The men refused:

> Well, two of them came up with five more years service than I did and they came right in on the job. Now the foreman says, "Break them in." I says, "No way am I breaking them in because they got more service than I got. You're the foreman. You break them in. You did the hiring." . . . The other fellow felt the same way.

Women who failed on the job also reinforced the men's negative stereotypes and attitudes:

> Maybe I'm prejudiced, but like I say, women are getting jobs when they aren't qualified. . . . If they are qualified, all right, but to give them a job because they are a woman, I can't see it. . . . She knew absolutely nothing about it. That's what I guess upset most people. Everything she wanted done she had to go see someone else. . . . Whereas if somebody had come in there who was qualified, that knew the job, you know there is lot of stuff they'd know or have some knowledge of, or be able to at least pick it up. . . . Nothing, that was the gall of it.

Affirmative action programs often necessitate tampering with and modifying the old personnel practices in order to remedy the effects of a discriminatory past. Integration of the white male jobs can require breaking faith with male workers on established job practices and entitlement in order to provide greater opportunities for women. As we saw earlier, however, job-posting and upgrading systems can be introduced that also help white men. Men and women on the plant floor must be involved in developing programs that will best meet their needs.

Hostility and resentment can also be influenced by the deskilling of jobs or the threat of losing jobs altogether. The historical relationship between the entrance of women into specific job categories and the "deskilling" of those jobs has been established (Hacker 1979). In the modern industrial economy, many skilled blue-collar jobs are being eliminated totally. Computerization is having the greatest impact on the highest-skilled machinists (Shaiken 1984). At Harbor Company, the men interviewed were able to give specific examples where the least-skilled part of men's jobs were separated and filled by women at reduced pay. Layoffs and plant closings were a constant threat.

Conclusions

The Harbor case study supports the idea that by working through existing legitimate organizations such as unions women can achieve progress, although the path is not easy. The women at Harbor chose to work through a union that, at first, did not respond to their needs. They filed grievances, altered the committee structure, used the union to monitor and expand legal actions, and in the process formed coalitions with other workers that helped to make affirmative action possible. The affirmative action plan adopted by the local company and union was a much stronger agreement than an earlier national plan negotiated between the company and the federal government without the union's involvement.

The study also corroborates other research on blue-collar men that reveals much more complex attitudinal profiles than the "Archie Bunker" stereotypes. Sexual bullies are a troublesome but distinctly small minority of male co-workers. Some men are very helpful, while the negative attitudes of others can be alleviated by addressing issues of fairness and job security. Overt hostility directed toward women can be reduced or avoided when the men's jobs are not threatened and men are educated about the process and the impact of job integrations (Swerdlow 1989; Harlan and O'Farrell 1982).

An enlightened leadership would do well to widely disseminate success stories of female performance in "men's jobs." They should also minimize disruption to the existing job structures and emphasize the benefits that may result for men and women. The strains and sources of potential conflict inherent in any new integration setting, while unlikely to be eliminated, can be managed and minimized with proper planning, progressive leadership, and the active involvement of union women.

Unions are in a unique position to help women in a number of ways consistent with their industrial relations roles (Newman and Wilson 1981). Through collective bargaining women and men can negotiate color-blind and gender-blind wages and working conditions for all of their members; through the grievance process they can identify discriminatory acts and represent victims; they can inform workers about their rights and provide both financial and legal assistance to victims and activities for redress and change; they can reduce coworkers' hostility by instituting education and training programs and serving as role models for attitudinal change within the union; they can monitor affirmative action agreements to mitigate the stress and conflict that come with change.

But they must work within the economic constraints of the industry and region and be realistic about the attitudes and experiences of the workforce. A concrete plan should begin with an identification of hostile elements within the workforce and a realistic assessment of women's job qualifications and training needs with remedial support where necessary. The union must be sensitive to real or imaginary fears about change, especially related to job security.

There is no one model plan or paradigm for unions that will fit every situation or set of problems, because integration is a "people problem" as well as a legal or economic issue. Union solutions require positive leadership, flexibility, communication, and common sense on the part of both women and men. For some, government force or the threat of force will continue to be necessary. In an imperfect world, however, unions are still one of the best vehicles for bringing equality to the workplace.

Comments

Marlene Kim

A historical examination of the wage gap confirms the dramatic improvements in the 1980s noted by Hartmann and Hallock. According to the Bureau of the Census, in 1939 women earned 58 percent of male earnings (O'Neill 1985). This ratio rose to 64 percent in 1955 but fell quickly to 59 percent by 1961, where it stubbornly held to this level throughout the 1970s (the 59 cents to which Hartmann refers).[1] In the 1980s it gained steadily, so that by 1991 women received 71 percent of male earnings (see figure 1). The Bureau of Labor Statistics (BLS) supports this pattern. In the 1960s, when this data series began, women earned 60–65 percent of male earnings. This ratio held throughout the 1970s, but during the 1980s, it gradually improved. In 1991, women earned 72 percent of what men earned.[2]

Researchers cannot fully explain why women's earnings improved relative to men's during the 1980s. Gains in women's education, work experience, and other human capital explain only 6 percent of the improvement. (Sorensen 1991). In fact, as Hallock and Hartmann suggest, most of the change in the wage gap, of the portion that can be measured statistically, is due to the fact that men's earnings fell. Figure 2 illustrates these losses for men: from 1967 to 1991, real earnings (earnings adjusted for inflation) declined for both

---

[1] The Census Bureau collected earnings data by gender in 1939; however, the series was not collected annually until 1955.

[2] The Census Bureau and BLS wage ratios differ because the BLS measures weekly earnings and excludes self-employed workers. In contrast, the census measures annual earnings, includes self-employed workers, and counts only year-round workers. Historically the census portrayed poorer earnings ratios; however, recently the BLS and census indicate similar—71 percent versus 72 percent—earnings ratios.

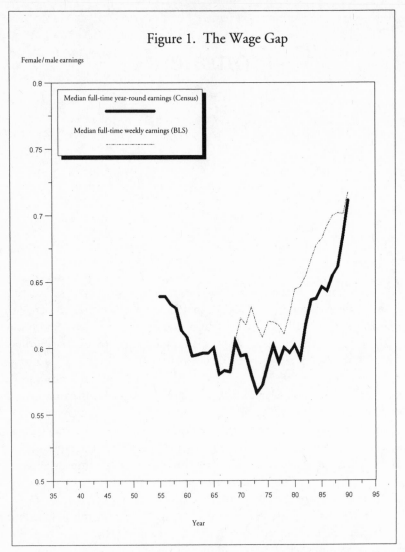

Figure 1. The Wage Gap

Female/male earnings

Median full-time year-round earnings (Census)

Median full-time weekly earnings (BLS)

Year

Source: O'Neill 1985; Goldin 1990; U.S. Census (various); U.S. Department of Labor (1991a, 1991b, 1979).

African-American and white men, while rising slightly for African-American and white women.

African-American men were hit especially hard, suffering disproportionate losses in highly paid unionized manufacturing jobs (Sorensen 1991). Consequently, the race wage gap widened during the 1980s: whereas the wage

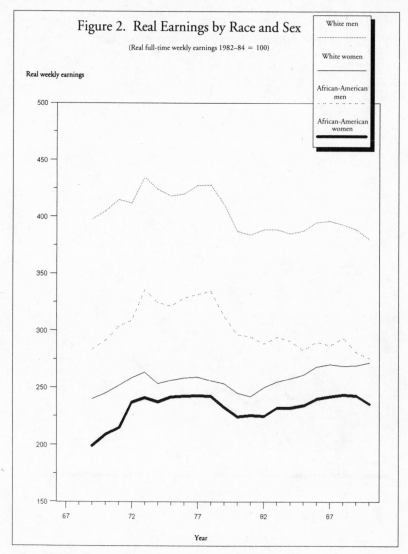

Figure 2. Real Earnings by Race and Sex

(Real full-time weekly earnings 1982–84 = 100)

Real weekly earnings

White men

White women

African-American men

African-American women

Year

Source: U.S. Department of Labor (1979, 1991a, 1991b).

difference between African-American and white men's earnings declined through the late 1970s, the trend then reversed and the difference has been increasing (see figure 3). Earnings differences between African-American and white women follow a similar pattern, although the reasons for this retrench-ment are unclear (Sorensen 1991). Thus, although the 1980s brought im-

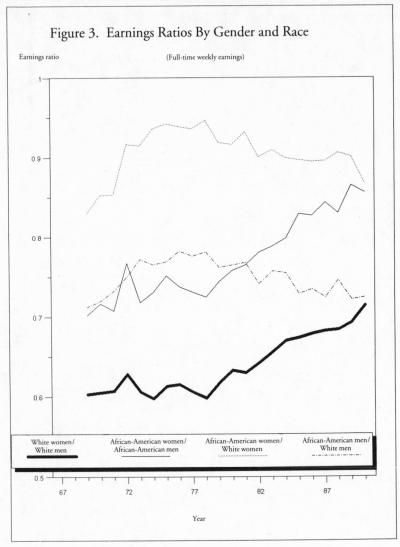

Figure 3. Earnings Ratios By Gender and Race

Earnings ratio   (Full-time weekly earnings)

| White women/ White men | African-American women/ African-American men | African-American women/ White women | African-American men/ White men |

Source: U.S. Department of Labor (1979, 1991a, 1991b).

provement in the *gender* wage gap, the *race* wage gap suffered miserably. This reverses the trend during the 1970s, when the race wage gap improved but the gender wage gap remained constant.

The decline of the wage gap, therefore, is not an entirely happy story. Gains in education and work histories—events in which women have relatively more control—have only a small effect on the wage gap. Much of the change in the wage gap is due to men—especially African-American men—receiving lower pay and fewer job protections. In short, although women made progress relative to men in the 1980s, the declining gender gap did not reflect a decline in gender or race discrimination. African-American women lost ground relative to white women, and African-American men lost even more.

The Need for Dual Strategies

Thus employment discrimination and economic inequality between men and women were not eliminated in the 1980s. To begin to remedy these inequities, I argue that we still need *both* affirmative action and comparable worth policies. We need affirmative action so that women have *access* to high-paid jobs and comparable worth so that the jobs women hold (or will hold) are not *undervalued* because women are employed.

Clearly one reason why women continue to earn less than men is occupational segregation. Affirmative action is a common solution to occupational segregation because it ensures that employers adequately advertise job and promotional openings and train workers, so that hiring, training, promotions, and layoffs are gender- and race-neutral.

But women also earn less than men because of what I call "direct wage discrimination": jobs that women hold may be underpaid simply because women perform the work. In other words, if men held the same jobs, the jobs would pay more simply because a man is doing the work. As Hallock argues, historical studies indicate that as women entered certain occupations, such as bank telling and clerical work, the pay and status in these jobs declined. In addition, statistical analyses of pay by occupation show that as the proportion of women in an occupation increases, the pay declines, even after accounting for education and years in the labor force. Finally, case studies indicate that historically employers had separate and lower wage scales for the same job if women performed the work (Newman 1976), or they simply paid lower salaries for occupations held predominantly by women (Kim 1989). Once these discriminating pay scales were established, they were maintained into the 1970s and 1980s.

The comparable worth strategy recognizes the existence of direct wage discrimination and that affirmative action and job integration do not necessarily correct it. Even if affirmative action were successful and women entered male-dominated jobs in large numbers, the pay and status in these jobs would decline because *pay is determined by who performs the work.* Thus the comparable worth strategy mandates that pay structures be re-evaluated so that jobs are not undervalued simply because women perform the work.

Therefore, we need to continue to pursue *both* comparable worth and affirmative action strategies to ensure access to jobs as well as fair pay. Affirmative action may not raise women's salaries in their current positions, but it is still an important remedy for the problem of women being stuck in dead-end jobs. Recent research indicating that women have not reaped benefits from affirmative action (Hartmann 1991) underscores the need to redouble our efforts to enforce the existing laws. These efforts, however, cannot be to the exclusion of comparable worth.

A Defense of Comparable Worth and Job Evaluation

As the authors in the previous chapters noted, we should not abandon comparable worth due to disappointments during implementation. When comparable worth failed, the failure was not due to the technical limitations of comparable worth but to the inherently political nature of the pay arena. Indeed, during the past decade of implementing comparable worth, the real crux of wage setting surfaced: pay is a political decision, and wages reflect power.

By definition, job evaluations determine the value of jobs. Every decision during this process is thus a value judgment and is political—from choosing what aspects of a job to reward, measuring these aspects, and deciding how much each should be rewarded. Feminists wrongly turned their backs on job evaluation because they thought it dry and lacking politics and ideology; in fact, it is full of ideology and value.

Although political, job evaluation does not automatically enhance management's control. Job evaluation is a tool: it has no allegiance to management and can be used effectively by workers to achieve workers' goals. Job evaluations have been controlled by management and used for management's own purposes because management had more power, not because of the inherent limitations of job evaluations. If workers exercised control over the job evaluation process, many of the disappointments of job evaluations discussed by Hallock and Steinberg would not have happened.

Job evaluation is too important a tool for labor to ignore: 90 percent of all employers use job evaluations to set wages. By changing job evaluations, pay can be changed. Current wages reflect gender, class, and racial biases, but these biases become institutionalized through formal procedures, including job evaluations. Job evaluations can alter these fundamental underpinnings of social and cultural evaluations, and subsequently allow for fairer wages.

Job evaluations can be redesigned to value any aspect of work and therefore potentially redefine the value of women's work. If traditional job evaluations ignore traditional female tasks, such as care-giving, they can be changed to include these values by giving more points to skills in women's jobs, *and* by changing the weights for these skills. Employers can create additional categories of value, such as direct patient care, thus valuing women's work more. In the case of clerical work, employers can increase the points for difficult working conditions because of frequent interruptions of work, as well as increase the weight (value) given to repeated types of stress. In Ontario, comparable work regulations mandate that job evaluations be gender-neutral and include the skills and job conditions in women's work (Steinberg 1990). The same can be done in the United States.

As Steinberg indicates, unions and feminists have the capacity to understand and use this tool for their gain. The real barrier is not technical but political: job evaluation involves building a consensus about which aspects of jobs should be rewarded with higher pay. It may pit workers against each other, and those who believe one person's pay increase comes from another's pocket will resist pay equity. Even if pay increases are not taken out of others' wages, members not covered by pay equity may feel their issues are being ignored while resources are put into the pay equity strategy.

Thus, as Steinberg admonishes, organizing and coalition-building is imperative. In addition, feminists and unions must be involved with all aspects of pay equity, including the development, implementation, and technical aspects—since this is the process that revaluates pay. Such involvement will minimize the shortfalls and divisiveness that can occur. As Padia and O'Farrell and Moore suggest, this is also important in implementing affirmative action, since allocating jobs is also inherently political.

Education is critical as well. Education not only informs members about job and pay policies and how these will affect them, it also builds a consensus about what is fair and just. In many cases, the success of comparable worth was a direct result of years spent educating members about why there was a need for such a policy. In contrast, as O'Farrell and Moore suggest, the failure of affirmative action is due in part to the lack of education and debate over how jobs should be allocated and how the current methods of hiring and promotion may be discriminatory.

Wage increases for men did not happen overnight, and certainly not over a decade. They resulted from centuries of organizing and battle—and much bloodshed. That comparable worth has increased women's wages—about 7 percent over a decade—is still, as Hallock states, quite an accomplishment.

Strategies for the Future

Clearly our work has not been completed. We need to continue to reduce the wage gap as many of the previous authors have suggested: extending comparable worth by requiring it of federal contractors or mandating it in the public sector; implementing family policies, such as family leave and child care; focusing on reducing wage inequality in general. In addition, however, we need to address wage, job, and family policies *across* national boundaries, because now labor knows no borders. With the many free trade negotiations underway, it is imperative to formulate minimum international labor standards. Without these standards, the wages and benefits that prevail will be those of the lowest-paid country. Without international standards, we may win higher wages for women and minorities in this country, but then the work will simply go offshore.

Unions need to work together internationally to counter these trade agreements and the global search for cheaper labor. A handful of unions, including ACTWU, CWA, and ILGWU, are beginning to work with their international counterparts. Although unions have spoken for many years about the need for international solidarity, the time to execute is now.

Comments

Gloria Johnson

In most cases it is the woman who is responsible for the home, for taking care of her family and its needs. She is the caretaker and the caregiver. Historically, these roles have been viewed as her primary ones. Unfortunately, when this view has extended into the workplace, it often has translated into jobs for women that are an extension of this role. These "female" jobs and "female" skills have been undervalued and underpaid.

Ronnie Steinberg addresses this reality in her discussion of comparable worth as a strategy to close the wage gap. She states: "Comparable worth is not just about cleansing bias from compensation systems; it is also concerned with building a new political consensus to determine what is valuable and compensable and to revalue the work that women do" (p. 58). This is not an easy task: stereotypes and tradition are difficult to overcome. We have made some progress in this direction, but even that has not been easy.

Our experience at the International Union of Electronic, Electrical, Salaried, Machine and Furniture Workers (IUE) has been that efforts to change the way women's work is valued must include changing the way many women view the value of their work. A situation which arose in an IUE plant in Indiana in the late 1970s illustrates this point. The local union president urged women to advise IUE of their discrimination complaints, and a great deal of newspaper and TV attention was given to IUE's intention to file an employment discrimination lawsuit. But only eighty of the two thousand women in the plant authorized IUE to file a suit on their behalf. The settlement resulted initially in an average increase of about 35 cents per hour for 350 women, and about $350,000 in back pay. Nevertheless, after the settlement was made and publicized among the employees, the union found itself in extreme disfavor with many women members. Women filed charges of discrimination against the union. These women were not charging that there was any sex discrimination in the plant. Rather, they were charging that, by giving certain women a wage increase, a wage inequity had been created among other women! They compared themselves with other women, not with the men whose work was of the same value as theirs!

IUE experience also suggests that there is no single strategy for reducing the wage gap. Our first approach has been through the collective bargaining process, but we define the collective bargaining process as reaching beyond negotiations and beyond handling grievances to include the right to file charges with appropriate agencies and, where necessary, the right to file lawsuits. As Winn Newman, former IUE general counsel, said in his 1981 speech to the National Council for Civil Liberties, Positive Action for Women at Work Conference, "The IUE has recognized that discrimination will generally not be corrected at the bargaining table, at least not without using the law for support." Anna Padia's discussion of affirmative action within the newspaper industry also makes this point.

Since its inception in 1949, the IUE has used a multipronged approach to closing the wage gap and ending sex- and race-based discrimination. Our constitution was among the first to include "sex" discrimination in its anti-discrimination provision (1949). The IUE, according to a 1961 Bureau of Labor Statistics study of 1,717 contracts covering one thousand employers from every job sector except the railroads and airlines, was the leader in contracts with antidiscrimination clauses (67.4 percent) and number two in the number of workers covered by antidiscrimination clauses (72.8 percent). In 1957, IUE held one of the first union women's conferences, which 257 women attended. They met, they talked, they debated, and the union learned about the problems, aspirations, and issues facing women. The number one priority adopted by this body was "Equal pay for equal work." I quote their position: "We call upon these corporations [GE and Westinghouse] to negotiate with our union and make effective clauses providing for equal pay for equal work. By this we mean not only equal pay for identical work but equal pay for work of equal value, no matter where it is done."

IUE had some success in carrying out this mandate in the late 1950s and early 1960s, but some of IUE's larger employers resisted. We did discover however, that many IUE women were doing work that was equal, similar, or comparable to men's work in the plants but were being paid less than the men. Through a very simple questionnaire we learned that in many plants the highest-paid woman worker, whose job required education, some training, and some degree of skill, received less than the lowest-paid male in the shop, often the janitor or the cleaner—a job with few, if any, skills and education requirements. For example, women quality checkers employed at the highest women's wages received the same base pay that sweepers received (the lowest-paid male job). The quality checkers were also required to have more education and experience and were regarded as skilled workers.

The Equal Pay Act (EPA) was finally passed in 1963—as some would say, "a foot in the door"—and it helped in our fight to close the wage gap. IUE filed many lawsuits under EPA but one case filed in 1965 stands out in my memory. The suit alleged that the company had paid female employees less than males doing comparable or nearly comparable work in twenty-one different job categories. The male classifications were paid higher, with hourly differentials up to 94.5 cents per hour. IUE won $300,000 in back pay, retroactive rate adjustments for nineteen of the twenty-one women's classifications, plus the institution of job-posting and upgrading procedures. The rate adjustments plus the job-posting and upgrading processes served to eliminate separation of male-female classifications.

IUE pursued with equal vigor the passage of Title VII of the Civil Rights Act (1964) and the Pregnancy Disability Act (1978). With passage of Title VII, IUE adopted a union-wide education program on the new law. A "team" from national headquarters went into every IUE district and into as many local unions as possible to explain workers' rights under the new law. As expected, in some locations there was resistance and resentment, similar to that reported by O'Farrell and Moore in their case study. And as was true in their case, it was a vocal minority of men who resented women doing their work. Nevertheless, the IUE education effort resulted in some wage inequity adjustments and promotions through changes of contract language as well as through grievance and arbitration. As Padia and Ross also observe, education is an important and necessary tool in addressing wage discrimination.

To implement the still relatively new equal employment laws, IUE recognized the need to spell out a specific course of action to correct discrimination. Delegates to the 1972 IUE Convention adopted such a program, the Title VII Compliance Program, which is remarkably similar to The Newspaper Guild's affirmative action program. The IUE's compliance program emphasized the elimination of systemic discrimination and consisted of the following elements:

- an education program for staff and membership;
- a systematic review of the number and status of minority members and females at each of the IUE plants;
- a systematic review of all collective bargaining contracts and plant practices to determine whether specific kinds of discrimination exist; and

- most important, requests to employers for detailed information broken down by race, sex, and national origin, relating to hiring and promotion policies, initial assignments, wage rates, and seniority, copies of the employer's affirmative action plan (AAP) and work force analysis, and copies and information concerning the status of all charges filed against them under the Equal Pay Act, Title VII, Executive Order 11246, and state EEO laws.

Local unions were requested to examine existing contracts and practices, using guidelines prepared by IUE, to determine if there was discrimination. If they found practices believed to be discriminatory, the international urged them to seek immediate voluntary changes from the employer. When the international failed to obtain precise data from its locals, it requested the information directly from employers.

After IUE analyzed the data and concluded that discrimination existed, it:

- requested bargaining with employers to eliminate the illegal practices or contract provisions;
- filed NLRB refusal-to-bargain charges against employers who refused to supply information or to agree to eliminate the illegal provisions;
- followed up these demands by filing Title VII charges and lawsuits under Title VII and Executive Order 11246.

The Title VII Compliance Program achieved significant results in modifying employers' future practices and in providing relief to employees for prior discrimination. For example, as a result of a 1972 IUE Title VII lawsuit involving height restrictions at a plant in Tyler, Texas, the company agreed to discontinue its requirement that all employees be at least 5 feet, 7 inches tall. It further agreed "to make whole" all females who were discriminated against by hiring them, paying back pay, and providing seniority, pension, and other benefits. IUE cases also ended discrimination in initial and other job assignments and promotions, produced job posting and bidding for promotions and transfers, and brought about the transformation of narrow seniority systems into true plant-wide seniority, resulting in promotions of low-paid minorities and women from within.

IUE wage discrimination lawsuits in particular have been pathbreaking. In early 1970, long before comparable worth became fashionable, IUE filed what was one of the first sex-based wage discrimination lawsuits, alleging, among other things, wage structure bias at an Ohio plant. The 1977 settlement provided for increasing the rates for nine job classifications that had been restricted to women and for $166,000 in back pay (*Rinehard v. Westinghouse Electric Corp.*, No. 70-537 (N.D. Ohio 1979)).

Another key case was *IUE v. Westinghouse.* In the late 1970s IUE contended that the company's policy was to pay women at its Trenton, New Jersey, plant significantly less than men although the company's own job evaluation indicated that the women's jobs required equal or more knowledge, training, skill, and responsibility. A settlement was negotiated that included increased wages and back pay before the case was resolved by the courts.

The support of union officers, the executive board, and legal staff in countering sex and race discrimination made a big difference for the IUE. It meant financial support, it meant strong resolutions, strong affirmative action programs, it meant implementation of strong antidiscrimination policy. Support and commitment at the top would prevent what Ronnie Steinberg sees as one of the problems in addressing the pay equity issue: the unions' "understandable view of pay equity as merely an extension of their normal responsibilities for bargaining over a wage package. Pay equity becomes one agenda among many, especially where there is a diverse membership" (p. 57). Having the commitment and support at the top provides some of the power and control she deems necessary if pay equity initiatives are to work.

The Politics of Pay Equity

Ronnie Steinberg and Anna Padia agree that pay equity is primarily a struggle for power and control, and there must be "political muscle" for it to succeed. In Hartmann's words: "the more we struggle together, the stronger we are politically, the more we get" (p. 45). Similarly, O'Farrell and Moore report that the women in their case study felt the necessity of working collectively in order to be a "political" force in their union. I don't think there is any doubt that politics—power, control, strength—is an important part of our struggle to eliminate the wage gap.

Let me offer two examples that illustrate the politics of the problem. During World War II, the War Labor Board (WLB) regularly examined the content of "women's jobs" to determine whether those jobs were being paid according to the requirements of the jobs and not according to the sex of the person performing the job. The WLB used job evaluation and other techniques to resolve "intraplant inequality" cases—disputes over the correctness of rates paid for jobs in relation to rates for other jobs in the same plant, whether occupied by men or women.

One of the WLB's last and most famous cases involved General Electric and Westinghouse in 1945. There was clear evidence that, despite a job evaluation system, these companies were deliberately paying women less than men for jobs that, although different, involved substantially equal skill, effort, and responsibility. The WLB analyzed the job content of the "women's" and "men's" jobs to determine whether the "women's" jobs were being paid below what the content of the job performed would indicate.

Based on statements and also data provided by one company, the WLB found that General Electric had hired professionals to determine the degree of skill, effort, and responsibility the jobs required, and reduced the wage rate by one-third if women were performing the job. Westinghouse admitted to following a similar practice, reducing the rate by 18 to 20 percent if women held the job. The WLB concluded that sex alone explained the low wages paid to women and found that the companies had discriminated in setting lower rates for women. Unfortunately, the WLB was disbanded before it could implement a remedy (see also Milkman 1987:80–82).

Ronnie Steinberg provides a similar example. When she served as a technical monitor in a pay equity study, consultants were asked by management to modify their results for top managerial jobs, ensuring that the report would recommend that 16 out of 19 male department head job classifications would receive between 35 and 450 additional job evaluation points. What is clear is that in both cases, management's decisions altered the findings of job evaluation plans to their benefit—they had the power, the control referred to as "political muscle."

Where do we go from here? Many good ideas were raised in the preceding chapters. I would like to add some others. There must be a greater effort in the labor movement to get women on negotiating committees and to involve them in the collective bargaining process. Greater representation of women at all levels of the union must be achieved, but particularly on executive boards of unions where policy is made. We also need increased involvement of unions in coalition with other organizations in the legislative and political action arenas. We need to elect an administration in Washington that supports and is sensitive to the problems of the changing work force. Increasing numbers of women must be there to raise the issues and, as O'Farrell and Moore indicate, we must also seek the support of male coworkers. Equally important is that the real message of pay equity gets out. Unfortunately, many see pay equity as simply "job evaluation." I think this misconception limits its effectiveness and appeal.

We need to develop "strategy packages" on the wage gap and establish forums where they can be discussed. A strategy package would provide information about what has proven successful in closing the wage gap—from education to litigation, job evaluation to legislation. Several of the writers suggest we need to be creative, which is true, particularly in light of the changing work force, the unresponsiveness of the political arena, and the development of a nation of haves and have-nots.

I thought it was quite creative when, in 1963, one of IUE's districts developed a program called "No Bias in Hiring." The union set out to get no-bias-in-hiring pledges from every employer in the district whose workers were represented by the IUE. It was good publicity and it also got some results.

The most pressing need now is to bring pay equity into the private sector. From all appearances private sector employers will do very little to correct discriminating pay patterns until forced to do so. Some believe that, as unions achieve more success with public employers, private employers will be pressured to change. I'm not convinced this will happen. I believe the real pressure must come from women employed in the private sector in coalition with women's organizations and other support groups. Women working within their unions must develop strategies to address wage gap issues through collective bargaining and legislative activity. Progress in closing the wage gap is in our hands.

Comments

Carrie Donald

Pay equity continues to be a viable tool for addressing the wage gap, but its limitations should be recognized. I agree with Margaret Hallock that technical issues, budget limitations, and political concerns have diminished the effectiveness of pay equity assessments and implementation. As noted in the preceding chapters, job evaluation studies can be costly, time-consuming, and subject to employer domination. Pay equity studies are not conducted in antiseptic economic laboratories and are less than scientific. As Ronnie Steinberg argued, pay equity studies often become the site of struggles over power and control rather than the product of the neutral application of technical rules. Moreover, pay equity studies are at times divisive since the studies require comparing men's jobs with women's jobs. Lastly, although pay equity studies, when conducted properly, have brought wage gains for women, the adjustments do not reflect complete equity. For the most equitable results, unions must be involved in every phase of a study, from the selection of a technical consultant, through the study design, to the application and evaluation of the results. Otherwise, as Steinberg notes, management can employ tactics to lessen the impact of the study. Despite these formidable problems, however, the strategy of formal studies can and should be pursued.

Ultimately, the nontraditional approaches to pay equity advocated by Hallock and Ross in particular are the most viable strategies for improving the relative wage rates of many women workers. These strategies include "piggyback" or matching study, collective bargaining without job evaluation, flat dollar wage increases instead of percentage increases, higher minimum and entry-level wages, increases based on the percentage of incumbent women, larger increases for predominantly female occupational groups, position reclassification, and longevity. The piggyback or matching study approach, for example, is capable of yielding results similar to a full-scale job evaluation study, but with much less expense and controversy. Through the collective bargaining process, joint employer-union committees can be established to study job rates and correct the pay of historically undervalued female jobs (Newman 1982). And, as Hallock advocates, the demand for a living wage for all workers should again be a central rallying point for the union movement.

These nontraditional programs should not replace programs directed specifically at sex discrimination. Nevertheless, they have the potential for making possible some of the same wage gains for women.

Pay equity proponents also should continue lobbying for legislative initiatives at the local, state, and federal levels. The suggestion that pay equity be made a condition of receiving a federal contract is an excellent one and could be achieved through a presidential executive order, as is the case with affirmative action under Executive Order 11246, or realized through federal legislation, as are numerous other workplace requirements.

Affirmative Action and Unions

As O'Farrell and Moore carefully document, a number of barriers exist within unions to the integration of women into skilled blue-collar jobs. Nevertheless, the Harbor Company case study in chapter 3 also reveals that women can work successfully within the union structure for gender integration into nontraditional jobs. The avenues for change include the union committee system, the grievance procedure, and the election process. Internal support groups can be formed to ensure better job training for women and provide them with the necessary skills to perform well in their new jobs. Women and their supporters in the union must work with the employer to develop a gender integration program that ensures proper job training for women without giving them special treatment. This same coalition must also develop cultural diversity training programs to sensitize fellow workers and address worker biases that can hinder successful job integration. The training may not be successful for those workers that O'Farrell and Moore characterize as the "hostile hard hats." However, substantial gains could be made through training the "ambivalent moderates."

Even before effective affirmative action programs can be established and implemented, unions should work to eradicate intentional discriminatory policies, practices, and actions in the workplace. Unions should aggressively enforce their nondiscrimination clauses, which are contained in 80 percent of collective bargaining agreements (Patton 1988). A nondiscrimination clause should be an important part of the bargaining agenda in bargaining arrangements where such clauses have not yet been negotiated.

Unions are in a unique position to contribute significantly to the enforcement of equal employment laws through development of assistance programs (Newman and Wilson 1981). These programs should inform workers of their rights and provide legal and financial assistance to individual victims of discrimination. When a woman has been the subject of discriminatory actions at work, she should be able to enlist competent and effective assistance from the union. In fact, unions that do not press for an end to discrimination may be liable under the duty of fair representation as well as under Title VII of the Civil Rights Act of 1964 (Volz and Breitenbeck 1984; Cathcart and Ashe 1989).

Where well-designed and conscientiously implemented affirmative action programs have been undertaken, the results have been positive in integrating women into the work force. A cornerstone of affirmative action is training, and with it, lines of progression to better positions with more opportunities. The expansion of promotional opportunities through affirmative action must be part of any comprehensive equal opportunity program. The new apprenticeship model advocated by Hallock is needed to expand training from the trades to professional technical jobs. Unions must play a much larger role in bargaining for training and skill acquisition. These issues should be just as important as negotiating for seniority rights, job protection, and wage packages. The Newspaper Guild's successful bargaining model, described by Anna Padia, should be used as a plan of action to achieve affirmative action.

To date, affirmative action has had only marginal impact on the wage gap, in part because the movement of women into nontraditional jobs has not matched the growing number of women workers in traditionally low-paid female occupations. Nevertheless, as Bergmann notes, affirmative action has the potential to increase the rate of pay of female-dominated jobs as well. As more women go into nontraditional jobs, the supply of workers for jobs traditionally held by women will decrease and the pay will increase accordingly.

Division within the Union Movement

The crux of the problem is not *how* the labor movement can realize the measures of pay equity and affirmative action but *whether* labor unions will choose to place these issues high on their agendas. Although some union leaders have resolved to push equal employment efforts, others have blocked such measures (Horrigan and Harriman 1988). As O'Farrell and Moore note in chapter 3, certain unions supported protective state laws that severely restricted job opportunities for women, and, in passing the Civil Rights Act of 1964 and related measures, Congress found it necessary to prohibit employment discrimination not just by employers but also by unions (Schlei and Grossman 1983). Nevertheless, some unions continued engaging in employment discrimination (*Farmer* 1981; *Sheet Metal Workers Local 28* 1986). For example, "the first two contempt citations issued by federal courts under Title VII of the Civil Rights Act of 1964 were against construction labor unions: Local 189, the Plumbers Union in Columbus, Ohio and Local 46 of the Lathers Union in New York City" (Hill 1984). The record of a sector of the labor movement's opposition to women and minorities in the workplace has been documented in highly publicized litigation. Unions have carried the "reverse discrimination" banner in a number of the major employment discrimination cases decided by the U.S. Supreme Court (*Firefighters* 1984 and *W. R. Grace Co.* 1983).

Obviously, the few unions that opposed affirmative action have not acted alone. They have acted in concert with employers and in conformity to the invidious attitudes of a large segment of the general public. Nevertheless, such unions have failed to show positive leadership on this issue and have sought to preserve an economic spoils system for white males. Indeed, affirmative action has flourished more as a government requirement than as an issue championed by unions. In contrast, the gains made in the pay equity movement can, in large part, be credited to union leadership and involvement (Koziara, Moskow, and Tanner 1987; and Newman 1982).

What explains this divergence in union responses to affirmative action and pay equity? First, affirmative action followed shortly after the passage of Title VII in 1964; the concept that women and minorities had equal rights, let alone the idea of providing preferential treatment to secure those job rights, had not gained public acceptance. Pay equity, however, emerged as an issue in the late 1970s, when equal employment rights were more accepted and women and minorities represented a growing percentage of the work force. Second, affirmative action programs place women in direct competition with men for jobs. As O'Farrell and Moore observe, white males, especially in the blue-collar sector, are concerned about job deskilling and security. Affirmative action threatens job opportunities for men whereas pay equity potentially endangers *only* their level of pay increases and job status vis-à-vis other positions. Third, much misinformation related to affirmative action is circulated among the general public, employers, and labor organizations. Reliable and accessible information is often missing.

In short, two classes of unions have emerged, one group potentially receptive to issues related to women and minorities, and another, smaller group that actively opposes or renders only token interest in these issues. O'Farrell and Moore argue that women and their proponents can work within the union structure to make a union more receptive to equal opportunity and affirmative action issues. This process is decidedly easier and will garner more immediate results within some union hierarchies than others. The integration of women into certain unionized work settings will in many instances require extensive internal union coalition-building and training (Pecorella 1988). Therefore, when evaluating programs to end the wage gap, one must first assess the receptiveness of the union to a particular strategy.

In summary, within a unionized setting, proponents must use a combination of strategies in order to achieve equal employment opportunity and pay practices. The selection of strategies, as well as the way they are combined and weighed, will vary over time and according to situations. The resolve by unions to aggressively pursue equal employment and pay practices depends in the final analysis on the commitment of its members, staff, and leaders. The growth unions of the twenty-first century will be those that stay the course and steadfastly pursue the route leading to wage and employment programs free of discrimination.

References to Part I

Acker, Joan. 1987. "Sex Bias in Job Evaluation: A Comparable Worth Issue." In *Ingredients for Women's Employment Policy,* edited by Christine Bose and Glenna Spitze, 183–96. Albany: State University of New York Press.

———. 1989. *Doing Comparable Worth: Gender, Class and Pay Equity.* Philadelphia: Temple University Press.

———. 1990. "Pay Equity in the Nordic Countries." Paper presented at the Conference on Pay Equity: Theory and Practice, York University, York, Ontario, May 10–12.

American Federation of State, County and Municipal Employees v. Washington 770 F.2d 1401 (9th Cir. 1985).

Anderson, Kay E., Philip M. Doyle, and Albert E. Schwenk. 1990. "Measuring Union-Nonunion Earnings Differences." *Monthly Labor Review* 6(113):26–38.

Bailey, Thomas. 1990. "Jobs of the Future and the Skills They May Require." *American Educator* (Spring):10–15, 40–44.

Bakker, Isabella. 1990. "Pay Equity and Economic Restructuring: The Polarization of Policy?" Paper presented at the Conference on Pay Equity: Theory and Practice, York University, York, Ontario, May 10–12.

Barrett, Michele, and Mary McIntosh. 1980. "The Family Wage: Some Problems for Socialists and Feminists." *Capital and Class* 11:51–72.

Belden Associates. 1990. *Employment Survey of Minorities and Women in U.S. Daily Newspapers.* Conducted for the American Newspaper Publishers Association.

Belous, Richard S. 1989. *The Contingent Economy: The Growth of the Temporary, Part-Time and Subcontracted Workforce.* Washington, D.C.: National Planning Association.

Bergmann, Barbara. 1986. *The Economic Emergence of Women.* New York: Basic Books.

Bernstein, Aaron. 1988. "So You Think You've Come a Long Way, Baby?" *Business Week* (Industrial/Technology Edition, February 29):48–52.

Blau, Francine. 1977. *Equal Pay in the Office.* Lexington, Mass.: Lexington Books.

Blau, Francine D., and Andrea H. Beller. 1988. "Trends in Earning Differentials by Gender, 1971–1981." *Industrial and Labor Relations Review* 41(4):513–29.

Blum, Linda. 1987. "Possibilities and Limits of the Comparable Worth Movement." *Gender and Society* 1(4):380–99.

Brenner, Johanna. 1987. "Feminist Political Discourses: Radical versus Liberal Approaches to the Feminization of Poverty and Comparable Worth." *Gender and Society* 1(4):447–65.

Briggs, Norma. 1979. "Apprenticeship." In *Women in the U.S. Labor Force,* edited by Ann F. Cahn, 225–36. New York: Praeger.

British Columbia Federation of Labour. 1988. *A Legislative Model for Achieving Pay Equity.* Submitted to the Pay Equity Conference, Vancouver, British Columbia, March 11–12.

Carlson, Allen C. 1986. "What Happened to the 'Family Wage'?" *The Public Interest* 83:3–17.

Cathcart, David A., and R. Lawrence Ashe, Jr., eds. 1989. *Five-Year Cumulative Supplement to Schlei and Grossman's Employment Discrimination Law.* 2d ed. Washington, D.C.: BNA.

Cobble, Dorothy Sue. 1991. "Organizing the Postindustrial Work Force: Lessons from the History of Waitress Unionism." *Industrial and Labor Relations Review* 44(3):419–36.

Cook, Alice. 1980. "Collective Bargaining as a Strategy for Achieving Equal Opportunity and Equal Pay: Sweden and West Germany." In *Equal Employment Policy for Women,* edited by Ronnie Steinberg Ratner, 53–78. Philadelphia: Temple University Press.

———. 1985. *Comparable Worth: A Casebook of Experiences in States and Localities.* Manoa: Industrial Relations Center, University of Hawaii at Manoa.

———. 1987. "Family and Work: Challenges to Labor, Management and Government." *Industrial Relations* 42(3):520–26.

County of Washington, Oregon, v. Gunther 452 U.S. 161 (1981).

Deaux, Kay, and Joseph C. Ullman. 1983. *Women of Steel: Female Blue-Collar Workers in the Basic Steel Industry.* New York: Praeger.

Douglas, Priscilla H. 1981. "Black Working Women." Ph.D. diss., Harvard University.

Douglass, Frederick. 1950. "West India Emancipation." Speech delivered at Canandaigua, New York, August 4, 1857. In *The Life and Writings of Frederick Douglass,* ed. Philip S. Foner, vol. 2:437.

Ehrenberg, Ronald G. 1987. "Empirical Consequences of Comparable Worth." In *Comparable Worth: Analysis and Evidence,* edited by Ann M. Hill and Mark R. Killingsworth, 90–106. Ithaca, N.Y.: ILR Press.

Ehrenberg, Ronald, and Robert Smith. 1987. "Comparable Worth Wage Adjustments and Female Employment in the State and Local Sector." *Journal of Labor Economics* 5(1):43–62.

Evans, Sara M., and Barbara J. Nelson. 1987. "The Impact of Pay Equity on Public Employees: State of Minnesota Employees' Attitude toward Wage Policy Innovation." In *Pay Equity: Empirical Enquiries,* edited by Robert T. Michael, Heidi I. Hartmann, and Brigid O'Farrell, 200–221. Washington, D.C.: National Academy Press.

————. 1989a. "Comparable Worth: The Paradox of Technocratic Reform." *Feminist Studies* 15(1):171–90.

————. 1989b. *Wage Justice: Comparable Worth and the Paradox of Technocratic Reform.* Chicago: University of Chicago Press.

Farmer v. ARA Services, Inc. 660 F. 2d 1096, no. 79–1295 (U.S. 6th Cir. Ct. of Appeals, 1981).

Feldberg, Roslyn. 1984. "Comparable Worth: Toward Theory and Practice in the United States." *Signs* 10:311–28.

Figart, Deborah M. 1989. "Collective Bargaining and Career Development for Women in the Public Sector." *Journal of Collective Negotiations* 18(4):301–13.

Firefighters Local 1784 vs. Stotts. 467 U.S. 561, 34 FEP 1702 (U.S. Supreme Ct. 1984).

Freeman, Richard B., and Jonathan S. Leonard. 1987. "Union Maids: Unions and the Female Work Force." In *Gender in the Workplace,* edited by Clair Brown and Joseph Pechman, 189–212. Washington, D.C.: Brookings Institution.

Freeman, Richard B., and James L. Medoff. 1984. *What Do Unions Do?* New York: Basic Books.

Gill, Sandra, and Jean Fletcher. 1990. "The Wage Differential between Men and Women: Explaining Recent Changes in Industrialized Nations." Manuscript. From Gettysburg College. Prepared for presentation to 1990 World Congress of Sociology.

Goldin, Claudia. 1990. *Understanding the Gender Gap: An Economic History of American Women.* New York: Oxford University Press.

Gray, Stan. 1984. "Sharing the Shop Floor: Women and Men on the Assembly Line." *Radical America* 18:69–88.

Gregory, Robert G., and R. C. Duncan. 1981. "Segmented Labor Market Theories and the Australian Experience of Equal Pay for Women." *Journal of Post Keynesian Economics* 3(3):403–28.

Gregory, Robert G., et al. 1987. "Women's Pay in Australia, Great Britain, and the United States: The Role of Laws, Regulations, and Human Capital." In *Pay Equity: Empirical Enquiries,* edited by Robert T. Michael, Heidi I. Hartmann, and Brigid O'Farrell, 222–42. Washington, D.C.: National Academy Press.

Gruber, James E., and Lars Bjorn. 1982. "Blue-Collar Blues: The Sexual Harassment of Women Autoworkers." *Work and Occupations* 9:271–97.

Gunderson, Morley. 1989. "Male-Female Wage Differentials and Policy Responses." *The Journal of Economic Literature* 27(1):46–72.

Hacker, Sally L. 1979. "Sex Stratification, Technological and Organizational Change: A Longitudinal Case Study of AT&T." *Social Problems* 26:539–57.

Haignere, Lois. 1990. "Pay Equity Implementation: Experimentation, Negotiation, Litigation, Aggravation, and Compensation." Paper presented at the Conference on Pay Equity: Theory and Practice, York University, York, Ontario, May 10–12.

Halle, David. 1984. *America's Working Man: Work, Home, and Politics among Blue-Collar Property Owners.* Chicago: University of Chicago Press.

Hallock, Margaret. 1987. "Working Poor Push for Pay Equity." *Unison Magazine:* 14–16.

————. Forthcoming. "An Analytical Guide to Implementation Issues." In *The*

Politics and Practice of Pay Equity, edited by Ronnie Steinberg. Philadelphia: Temple University Press.

————. 1990. "Pay Equity Outcomes in the Public Sector: Resolving Competing Interests." *Policy Studies Journal* 18(2):421–32.

Hams, Marcia. 1984. "Women Taking Leadership in Male-Dominated Locals." *Women's Rights Law Reporter* 8:71–82.

Harlan, Sharon L. 1989. "Opportunity and Attitudes toward Job Advancement in a Manufacturing Firm." *Social Forces* 67(3):766–89.

Harlan, Sharon L., and Brigid O'Farrell. 1982. "After the Pioneers: Prospects for Women in Nontraditional Blue-Collar Occupations." *Work and Occupations* 9:363–86.

Hartmann, Heidi I. 1976. "Capitalism, Patriarchy, and Job Segregation by Sex." *Signs* 1:127–69.

————. 1991. "Beyond Affirmative Action: Promoting Diversity and Upward Mobility." Testimony for the Joint Center for Political and Economic Studies. December 10, Washington, D.C.

Hill, Herbert. 1984. "Race and Ethnicity in Organized Labor: The Historical Sources of Resistance to Affirmative Action." *The Journal of Intergroup Relations* 12:5–49.

Hodson, Randy, and Paula England. 1986. "Industrial Structure and Sex Differences in Earnings." *Industrial Relations* 25:16–32.

Horrigan, June, and Ann Harriman. 1988. "Comparable Worth: Public Sector Unions and Employees Provide a Model for Implementing Pay Equity." *Labor Law Journal* (October):704–11.

Johnsen, Jim. 1990. "The State of Oregon and the Service Employees International Union." In *Bargaining for Pay Equity* (National Committee on Pay Equity, May):50–52.

Johnson, George, and Gary Solon. 1986. "Estimates of the Direct Effects of Comparable Worth Policy." *American Economic Review* 76(5):1117–25.

Kelley, Maryellen. 1982. "Discrimination in Seniority Systems: A Case Study." *Industrial and Labor Relations Review* 36(1):40–55.

Kim, Marlene. 1989. "Gender Bias in Compensation Structures: A Case Study of Its Historical Basis and Persistence." *Journal of Social Issues* 45(4):39–50.

Koziara, Karen Shallcross, Michael H. Moskow, and Lucretia Dewey Tanner, eds. 1987. *Working Women: Past, Present, Future.* Washington, D.C.: BNA.

Lemons, Mary, et al., v. City and County of Denver. 1978. 17 FEP Cases 906, 907 (U.S. District Ct., D.C.): Civil Action No. 78–1499, U.S. Court of Appeals for the Tenth Circuit.

Levine, Marvin J. 1987. "Comparable Worth in the 1980s: Will Collective Bargaining Supplant Legislative Initiatives and Judicial Interpretations?" *Labor Law Journal* 38(June):323–34.

Lewis, Debra J. 1988. *Just Give Us the Money: A Discussion of Wage Discrimination and Pay Equity.* Vancouver, B.C.: Women's Research Centre.

Malveaux, Julianne. 1985. "Comparable Worth and Its Impact on Black Women." *The Review of Black Political Economy* 14 (2–3):47–62.

Martin, Susan E., 1980. *Breaking and Entering: Policewomen on Patrol.* Berkeley: University of California Press.

McAllister, Ian. 1990. "Gender and the Household Division of Labor." *Work and Occupations* 17(1):79–99.

McIlwee, Judith. 1982. "Work Satisfaction among Women in Nontraditional Occupations." *Work and Occupations* 9:299–335.

Meidner, Rudolph. 1987. "A Third Way—The Concept of the Swedish Labour Movement." Paper presented at the International Conference on Social Democratic Futures, University of Ottawa, November 18–21.

———. 1988. *The Wage Policy of Solidarity and Its Impact on the Swedish Model.* Stockholm: Arbetslivcentrum.

Milkman, Ruth. 1987. *Gender at Work: The Dynamics of Job Segregation by Sex during World War II.* Urbana, Ill.: University of Illinois Press.

Minnesota Department of Employee Relations. 1984. *A Guide to Implementing Pay Equity in Local Government.* August.

National Committee on Pay Equity. 1987. *Job Evaluation: A Tool for Pay Equity.* November.

———. 1990a. *Bargaining for Pay Equity.* May.

———. 1990b. *Collective Bargaining for Pay Equity: A Strategy Manual.* Washington, D.C.: National Committee on Pay Equity.

National Committee on Pay Equity and Institute for Women's Policy Research. 1989. "Briefing Paper No. 1: The Wage Gap." Washington, D.C.: Institute for Women's Policy Research.

Newman, Winn. 1976. "Presentation III." In *Women and the Workplace,* edited by Martha Blaxall and Barbara Reagan. Chicago: University of Chicago Press.

———. 1982. "Pay Equity Emerges as a Top Labor Issue in the 1980s." *Monthly Labor Review* (April):49–51.

Newman, Winn, and Carole W. Wilson. 1981. "The Union Role in Affirmative Action." *Labor Law Journal* 32(June):323–42.

Northrup, Herbert R. 1980. "Wage Setting and Collective Bargaining." In *Comparable Worth: Issues and Alternatives,* edited by Robert E. Livernash, 107–36. Washington, D.C.: Equal Employment Advisory Council.

O'Farrell, Brigid. 1980. "Women and Nontraditional Blue-Collar Jobs: A Case Study of Local 1." Washington, D.C.: U.S. Department of Labor, Employment and Training Administration.

O'Farrell, Brigid, and Sharon L. Harlan. 1982. "Craftworkers and Clerks: The Effect of Male Coworkers' Hostility on Women's Satisfaction with Nontraditional Jobs." *Social Problems* 29(3):252–65.

———. 1984. "Job Integration Strategies: Today's Programs and Tomorrow's Needs." In *Sex Segregation in the Workplace,* edited by Barbara F. Reskin, 267–91. Washington, D.C.: National Academy Press.

O'Neill, June. 1985. "The Trend in the Male-Female Wage Gap in the United States." *Journal of Labor Economics* 3(1, pt. 2):S91–S116.

Ontario Pay Equity Commission. 1989. *How to Do Pay Equity Job Comparisons.* Toronto: Pay Equity Commission.

OPSEU. 1987a. *Equity at Work: A Pay Equity Manual for Practitioners.* Toronto: OPSEU Collective Bargaining Department.

———. 1987b. *Pay Equity in Ontario: Time for Action!* Toronto: OPSEU Collective Bargaining Department.

————. 1990. *Ontario Public Service Pay Equity Plan.* Toronto: OPSEU Collective
Bargaining Department.

Orazem, Peter F., and Peter J. Mattila. 1989. "Comparable Worth and the Structure
of Earnings: The Iowa Case." In *Pay Equity: Empirical Inquiries,* edited by Robert
T. Michael, Heidi I. Hartmann, and Brigid O'Farrell, 179–99. Washington, D.C.:
National Academy Press.

————. 1990. "The Implementation Process of Comparable Worth: Winners and
Losers." *Journal of Political Economy* 98(1):134–52.

Padavic, Irene, and Barbara F. Reskin. 1990. "Men's Behavior and Women's Interest
in Blue-Collar Jobs." *Social Problems* 37(4):613–28.

Patton, Thomas H., Jr. 1988. *Fair Pay: The Managerial Challenge to Comparable Job
Worth and Job Evaluation.* San Francisco: Jossey–Bass.

Pecorella, Robert F. 1988. "Remediation and Equity: A Case Study of Gender Integration." *Public Personnel Management* 17(Spring):73–80.

Remick, Helen. 1980. "Strategies for Creating Sound Bias-free Job Evaluation Plans."
In *Job Evaluation and EEO: The Emerging Issues.* New York: Industrial Relations
Counselors, Inc.

————. 1984. "Major Issues in *a priori* Applications." In *Comparable Worth and Wage
Discrimination,* edited by Helen Remick. Philadelphia: Temple University Press.

Reskin, Barbara F., and Heidi I. Hartmann, eds. 1986. *Women's Work, Men's Work:
Sex Segregation on the Job.* Washington, D.C.: National Academy Press.

Reskin, Barbara F., and Patricia A. Roos. 1990. *Job Queues, Gender Queues: Explaining
Women's Inroads into Male Occupations.* Philadelphia: Temple University Press.

Riemer, Jeffrey W. 1979. *Hard Hats.* Beverly Hills, Calif.: Sage Publications.

Schlei, Barbara Lindemann, and Paul Grossman. 1983. *Employment Discrimination
Law.* Washington, D.C.: BNA.

Schroedel, Jean R. 1985. *Alone in a Crowd: Women in the Trades Tell Their Stories.*
Philadelphia: Temple University Press.

SEIU. 1985. *Pay Equity Bargaining Guide.* January.

Shaeffer, Ruth G., and Edith F. Lynton. 1979. "Corporate Experiences in Improving
Women's Job Opportunities." Conference Board Report 755. New York: The
Conference Board.

Shaiken, Harley. 1984. *Work Transformed: Automation and Labor in the Computer
Age.* New York: Holt, Rinehart and Winston.

Sheet Metal Workers Local 28 v. EEOC 478 US 421. No. 84–1656, 41FEP107 (U.S.
Supreme Ct. 1986).

Shelton, Beth A., and Juanita Firestone. 1989. "Household Labor Time and the
Gender Gap in Earnings." *Gender and Society* 3(1):105–12.

Shostak, Arthur B. 1980. *Blue-Collar Stress.* Reading, Mass.: Addison-Wesley.

Silvestri, George, and John Lukasiewicz. 1989. "Projections of Occupational Employment 1988–2000." *Monthly Labor Review* 112(11):42–65.

Simon, Sharon. 1986. "The Survival of Affirmative Action in the 1980s." *Labor
Studies Journal* 10(3):261–77.

Smith, James, and Michael P. Ward. 1984. "Women's Wages and Work in the
Twentieth Century." Santa Monica, Calif.: Rand Publication Series.

Sorensen, Elaine. 1987. "Effect of Comparable Worth Policies on Earnings." *Industrial Relations* 26(3):227–39.

————. 1990. "The Crowding Hypothesis and Comparable Worth Issue: A Survey and New Results." *The Journal of Human Resources* 25(1):55–89.

————. 1991. "Gender and Racial Pay Gaps in the 1980s: Accounting for Different Trends." Washington, D.C.: The Urban Institute.

Steinberg, Ronnie. 1987. "Radical Challenges in a Liberal World: The Mixed Success of Comparable Worth." *Gender and Society* 1 (4):466–75.

————. 1991. "Job Evaluation and Management Control." In *Just Wages: A Feminist Assessment of Pay Equity*, edited by Judy Fudge and Patricia McDermott, 193–218. Toronto: University of Toronto Press.

————. 1990b. "Social Construction of Skill: Gender, Power, and Comparable Worth." *Sociology of Work and Occupations* 17(4):449–82.

Steinberg, Ronnie, and Alice Cook. 1981. "Women, Unions, and Equal Employment Opportunity." Working paper no. 3. Albany Center for Women in Government, State University of New York.

Steinberg, Ronnie, and Lois Haignere. 1987. "Equitable Compensation: Methodological Criteria for Comparable Worth." In *Ingredients for Women's Employment Policy*, edited by Christine Bose and Glenna Spitze, 157–82. Albany: State University of New York Press.

Steinberg, Ronnie, ed. Forthcoming. *The Politics and Practice of Pay Equity*. Philadelphia: Temple University Press.

Stone, Diana. 1987. *Pay Equity Sourcebook*. San Francisco: Equal Rights Advocates and National Committee on Pay Equity. December.

————. 1990. "The Crowding Hypotheses and Comparable Worth Issue: A Survey and New Results." *The Journal of Human Resources* 25(1):55–89.

Swerdlow, Marian. 1989. "Men's Accommodations to Women Entering a Nontraditional Occupation: A Case of Rapid Transit Operatives." *Gender and Society* 3:373–87.

Thurow, Lester. 1987. "A Surge in Inequality." *Scientific American* 256(5).

Treiman, Donald J., and Heidi I. Hartmann, eds. 1981. *Women, Work, and Wages: Equal Pay for Jobs of Equal Value*. Washington, D.C.: National Academy Press.

Treiman, Donald, Heidi Hartmann, and Patricia Roos. 1984. "Assessing Pay Discrimination Using National Data." In *Comparable Worth and Wage Discrimination, Technical Possibilities and Political Realities*, edited by Helen Remick, 137–54. Philadelphia: Temple University Press.

U.S. BLS. 1992. Unpublished report.

U.S. Bureau of the Census. 1987. *Male-Female Differences in Work Experience, Occupation, and Earnings: 1984*. Current Population Reports, Household Economic Studies. Series P–70, No. 10. Washington, D.C.: U.S. GPO.

————. 1990. *Money, Income and Poverty Status in the United States, 1989*. Current Population Reports, Consumer Income Series P–60. Washington, D.C.: U.S. GPO.

————. 1991. "Money Income of Households, Families, and Persons in the United States: 1988 and 1989." Current Population Reports Series P–60, No. 172. July.

————. Various years. "Current Population Report P–60 Series." Washington, D.C.: U.S. GPO.

U.S. Congress. House. Committee on Education and Labor. 1991. *Civil Rights and Women's Equity in Employment Act of 1991*. 102d Congress, 1st sess.

U.S. Department of Labor. 1979. *Employment and Earnings.* January. Washington, D.C.: BLS.

————. 1980. *Employment and Earnings.* January. Washington, D.C.: BLS.

————. 1990. *Employment and Earnings.* January. Washington, D.C.: BLS.

————. 1991a. *Employment and Earnings.* January. Washington, D.C.: BLS.

————. 1991b. *Handbook of Labor Statistics.* January. Washington, D.C.: BLS.

U.S. Department of Labor, Women's Bureau. 1983. *Time of Change: 1983 Handbook on Women Workers.* Bulletin 298. Washington, D.C.: GPO.

Volz, William H., and Joseph T. Breitenbeck. 1984. "Comparable Worth and the Union's Duty of Fair Representation." *Employee Relations Law Journal* 10:30–47.

Wagman, Barnet, and Nancy Folbre. 1988. "The Feminization of Inequality: Some New Patterns." *Challenge* 31(6):56–59.

Waite, Linda J., and Sue E. Berryman. 1985. "Women in Nontraditional Occupations: Choice and Turnover." Santa Monica, Calif.: Rand Corporation.

Wallace, Phyllis A., and James W. Driscoll. 1981. "Social Issues in Collective Bargaining." In *U.S. Industrial Relations 1950–1980: A Critical Assessment,* 199–254. Madison, Wis.: Industrial Relations Research Association.

Walshok, Mary L. 1981. *Blue-Collar Women: Pioneers on the Male Frontier.* Garden City, N.Y.: Anchor Press.

Wertheimer, Barbara. 1984. "The United States of America." In *Women and Trade Unions in Eleven Industrialized Countries,* edited by Alice H. Cook, Val R. Lorwin, and Arlene Kaplan Daniels, 286–311. Philadelphia: Temple University Press.

Williams, Christine. 1989. *Gender Differences at Work: Women and Men in Nontraditional Occupations.* Berkeley: University of California Press.

Wilson, William Julius. 1987. *The Truly Disadvantaged: The Inner City, the Underclass, and Public Policy.* Chicago: University of Chicago Press.

W. R. Grace & Co. v. Rubber Workers Local 759 461 US 759 No. 81–1314 (U.S. Supreme Ct. 1983).

Part II
Meeting Family Needs

The tension between work and family, like the concern over adequate and equitable pay discussed in part one, will be of central importance to the work force of the future. The demands on wageworkers in the new competitive global marketplace are expanding relentlessly: workers are putting in longer hours, are undertaking more specialized and frequent job training, and are under pressure to accelerate productivity. Yet the requirements of family life—the time required to maintain an emotionally sustaining personal life and to care for children and aging parents—remain labor-intensive and resistant to further commercialization.

The challenge for unions is to unite men and women on this issue, and to devise policy that can appeal to young and old, to the childless couple and the single mother, to those who desire more time for the family and those who desire less. That possibility is not far-fetched. As Susan Cowell discusses, the proposed federal legislation granting parents job-protected leave for the care of family members united the needs of those with children and those caring for elderly parents. A broader policy approach that argued for paid time off for training, education, and other personal and professional necessities might have forged an even larger coalition, bringing in men and women of all ages and family situations. As Alice Cook so presciently suggests, paid leave, the shorter workday, and the restructuring of work time has the potential to forge a new coalition between feminist groups concerned with preserving and valuing family life and labor unions seeking to upgrade and retrain a work force stung by economic restructuring and job loss.

The essays by Susan Cowell and Carolyn York offer a rarely told tale: They chart the evolution and accomplishments of the union movement on work and family issues. They argue that not only did the labor movement show concern for work-family tensions earlier than corporate America but that the solutions proposed by labor have differed consistently from those put forward by management. As Cowell points out in her assessment of legislative policy regarding the family, management has touted private, voluntary reforms such as the new, flexible workplace (and to a lesser degree child care) as the solution to work-family conflicts; whereas the union "family bill of rights" emphasizes governmental intervention and argues that adequate family income, job security, health care coverage, and family supports, such as child care, are essential. York focuses on the bargaining arena. She compares the family-related benefits of unionized and nonunion workers and offers three case studies of how contract breakthroughs on family policy were achieved. In doing so, she documents not only the divergence of labor and management on family policy, but also the areas of agreement.

Joyce Miller provides further support for the Cowell and York viewpoints. The Coalition of Labor Union Women and union feminists generally were early, persistent proponents of child care and of contract language that would help parents fulfill their family obligations.

Alice Cook, however, offers a more critical view both of union evolution and of current union policy. Unions, she argues, always had a pro-family orientation but theirs was essentially a conservative philosophy—one that viewed women's primary role as domestic and gave priority to the income advances of male breadwinners. As the labor movement feminized, union leaders adjusted to the demands of their new female rank and file and evolved policies that addressed workplace equity for women and recognized the parental role of men. According to Cook, current union policies, although different from corporate policies, are still inadequate. The work-family dilemma will never be resolved until the needs of the family are given equal weight to those of the workplace and until policies are developed that encourage the equal participation of men in the daily labor of the home.

4

Family Policy

A Union Approach

Susan Cowell

"Work and family"—a code phrase for the dramatic rise in labor force participation by mothers, particularly mothers of young children, and the resulting tension between their work and family roles— became a hot topic in the 1980s. Politicians paid lip service to the needs of working mothers. Media commentators pronounced the death of the Ozzie and Harriet family—the mother at home, the father bringing home an adequate wage. Polls showed overwhelming public support for subsidized child care and family leave provisions. But at the end of the 1980s the United States remained the only industrialized country (except South Africa) without legislation providing for job-guaranteed and (usually) paid maternity leave, without a national system of child care, and without an explicit family policy.

During the 1980s, the labor movement was an active part of the coalitions supporting child care legislation and family and medical leave. These issues rose, if not to the top, at least near the top of labor's legislative agenda. Equally important, if not yet fully realized, was the emergence of a distinctive union approach to family policy, most clearly articulated in the Coalition of Labor Union Women's (CLUW) American Family Celebration in 1988 and CLUW's subsequent efforts to promote a family bill of rights.

The labor movement offers a distinct approach to family policy, one that is quite different from the flexible workplace touted by corporations as the solution to work-family conflicts. The labor movement advocates federal government policies to ensure adequate income, family and medical leave, and high-quality, affordable support services, including child care, elder care, and health care. Although rooted in labor traditions that predate the current women's movement, family policy has been advanced within the labor movement by union women seeking to integrate a women's rights agenda with a more traditional labor agenda.

Labor's approach is the closest American equivalent to European versions of family policy. Throughout Western Europe, family policies were generally initiated by socialist and labor governments but are now endorsed by all parties. These well-developed, long-standing plans include paid, job-guaranteed maternity or parental leave, national systems of child care, and family allowances to protect the incomes of families with children.

Despite the media and political attention paid to family issues in the 1980s, the debate in the United States has been dominated by a corporate agenda that stresses private sector and voluntary solutions to the conflicts of work and family. Unions have joined broad-based coalitions supporting the Act for Better Child Care (1988) and the Family and Medical Leave Act (1987). But labor's ability to advance its own agenda has been limited in a debate often framed by Reaganite assumptions about the role of government.

The 1990s may offer a more favorable environment for the labor movement and its traditional allies, as Americans reassess many of the assumptions about deregulation and the free market that were dominant in the 1980s.

Labor's Traditional Family Agenda

As the labor movement began to articulate an explicit family policy after 1985, a key premise was that labor's core agenda had always been pro-family. As the first resolution on family policy submitted to the AFL-CIO Convention in 1985 by the Communication Workers of America (CWA) noted: "Organized Labor throughout its history has been in the forefront of addressing the needs of workers and their families. Our achievement of minimum wage laws, free public education, protective child labor laws, the eight hour work day and social security have served to improve the quality of working and family life" (AFL-CIO, *Proceedings 1985*). The AFL-CIO restated that theme a year later: "To strengthen the family is at the heart of the labor movement's long struggle to raise wages and living standards, to democratize education, leisure and health care, to broaden individual opportunity and secure dignity in old age" (AFL-CIO Executive Council 1986).

These attempts to root family policy in labor's traditions were both defensive and strategic. Some in the labor movement were attempting to retake the issue of family from the new right and the moral majority. The 1986 executive council statement was subtitled, "Who Is Really 'Pro-Family'?" Others cited labor's traditional family agenda in order to broaden support within the largely male-dominated labor movement for the newer issues of particular importance

to working women. Yet, beyond the propaganda value, labor viewed its traditional agenda—including better wages, working conditions, health care,
pensions, leisure time, job security, and education—as providing the best
foundation for today's families.

Labor's long-held goals are truly pro-family because they demand that the
workplace and society accommodate workers as people—as members of families and communities, not merely as factors of production. Thus, while the
marketplace rewards productivity, unions insist on protecting workers during
nonproductive periods. Union contracts provide sick leave, disability, health
insurance, pensions, seniority, and job security, which are intended to protect
the incomes of individuals and their families throughout the life cycle, particularly in periods of vulnerability. This principle is just as important for women
who are trying to combine work and family obligations as it always has been
for the traditional male breadwinner.

The Family Wage and the Eight-Hour Day

Labor's traditional family policy is most clearly articulated in two important
issues from the early days of the American labor movement—the family wage
and the eight-hour day. The family wage meant that a worker (presumed to
be male) should earn enough to support a family. The term "family wage" is
not used today because of its built-in assumption that women ought to be at
home supported by a male worker. The principle, however, was an important
one—a worker is not just an individual rewarded for individual output but a
member of a family with responsibilities for others.

A nonsexist version of that principle should be at the core of labor's agenda
today—that every full-time worker, male or female, should be able to support
not merely him- or herself but a family. A modern version of the family wage
is particularly important at a time when more and more full-time workers
earn below the poverty line for families and when a growing number of
children—particularly in single-parent households—are living in poverty.

The eight-hour day was central to the early struggles of the American labor
movement. The fight for shorter work hours was explicitly intended to enable
workers to build a space between work and rest for personal, family, or social
enrichment. The nineteenth-century rallying cry was "eight hours for work,
eight hours for rest, eight hours for what we will" (Rosenzweig 1983).

The need for shorter work hours takes on special meaning today when most
adults work. Although the current obsession with international competitiveness is not conducive to a serious campaign to reduce working hours, this is
an essential part of a progressive family policy. The corporate response to the
need of women to work and care for children has been to track women into

poorly paid, insecure part-time work. A progressive family policy needs to shorten working hours for all workers—and ensure that part-time work is secure, decently paid, and covered by benefits.

The shorter workweek has long been part of labor's agenda—as a solution to unemployment and as a means to humanize the lives of workers. The AFL-CIO, for example, called for "a shorter workweek, reduced working hours per year and higher overtime penalties to increase opportunities for family life" (AFL-CIO Executive Council 1986). The International Ladies' Garment Workers' Union (ILGWU) attained a thirty-five-hour week decades ago for most garment workers, in part because so many of the union's women members wanted to be home early when their children returned from school. Many unions have negotiated limits on mandatory overtime, because it is particularly onerous for workers with family responsibilities. The United Food and Commercial Workers (UFCW), which represents many part-timers in retail work, has bargained innovative clauses to ensure that part-time workers get pay, security, and benefits equivalent to those of full-time workers (Nulty, this volume).

Labor's Evolving Position on Work and Family Issues

As more and more women, particularly mothers of young children, enter the work force, public discussion of work and family issues has focused more often on the need to find substitutes for the dependent care women have traditionally done without pay than on the broad range of concerns voiced by working parents. Child and dependent care and family leave—two ways to care for young children (or sick family members) if the parents are working—have become the top priorities.

Labor's interest in child care and leave issues predates the media's attention to these concerns. This may seem surprising since women have long been underrepresented among labor's ranks. The labor movement, however, has always represented the many working-class women who had to work while they raised children. The media didn't report the phenomenon until middle-class mothers faced the same problems during the inflationary 1970s and the struggling-to-stay-in-place 1980s.

The labor agenda for women workers as articulated by AFL-CIO convention reports has developed over the years, but its key elements have been stable since the 1950s. In 1959, the AFL-CIO laid out a program that was not dramatically different from today's: an end to job discrimination, equal pay for comparable work, maternity leave, expanded child care, and greater participation of women in their unions. Over the next three decades, the agenda broadened to include sexual harassment; discrimination in pensions, insurance, and Social Security; and pay equity. Maternity leave evolved into family leave and the push for leave legislation became a supplement to collective bargaining (AFL-CIO 1955–89).

A more subtle shift has been in the perception of why women work, their role in the family, and how "family" is defined. In 1955, labor still saw a woman's income as supplementary to her husband's and her role as family caregiver as primary:

> While we shall continue union efforts to increase the earning capacity of all workers so that wives and mothers are not driven into the labor market by substandard family incomes, we recognize that increasing numbers of women are seeking jobs in order to obtain more adequate family living levels and to contribute to community affairs. We support programs that make it easier for women to earn a living without endangering their own health or the welfare of their families (AFL-CIO 1955).

Later AFL-CIO convention reports, however, stressed women workers' significant economic contributions, their role as essential and often primary wage earners, and the discrimination and dual burdens they faced. According to a 1967 resolution adopted by the convention: "Nearly 60 percent of women workers are married, carrying home responsibilities as well as contributing to the economic support of their families through paid employment. Nearly 10 million working women have children under the age of 18, and 2½ million are heads of families" (AFL-CIO 1967).

In the 1970s, there was a growing concern about the rights of women workers as individuals, not just as contributors to the family.[1] In 1975 the AFL-CIO stressed the similarities between men and women workers: "The majority of women work for the same reason as men—economic necessity" (AFL-CIO 1975). Rather than emphasize the difficulties of accommodating the dual burden of work and family, the 1975 statement focused on gender discrimination: the concentration of women in low-wage, nonunion industries; lower pay for equal work; and less access to training and apprenticeships.

By the early 1980s, a new focus emerged: the desperate state of working families, especially minority and women-headed, in the face of high unemployment and social-service cuts. Child care and unpaid family leave might be sufficient supports for professional and business women but working-class mothers needed those supports and much more to survive the economic hardships of the 1980s. Acknowledging the depths of the crisis that working

---

[1]Beginning in 1971, a debate took place within the AFL-CIO over labor's position on the Equal Rights Amendment, a debate won by ERA supporters in 1975.

families faced prepared the way for the broader family policy agenda articulated in the late 1980s.

A Labor Program for Child Care

Child care is one example of the stability of labor's agenda on one of the key work and family issues.[2] Historically, labor has emphasized federal funding and standards to create a national child care system (AFL-CIO 1955–89).

In 1959, the AFL-CIO called upon affiliated unions to "seek the cooperation of communities and government agencies in the provision of child care facilities for the children of working mothers." In the 1960s, statements were more specific, calling for expanded federal funding and for liberalization of tax deductions for child care expenses.

In 1971, the AFL-CIO Executive Council supported draft legislation that would provide "for eventual universally available child development programs for all families who need and want them." Following President Nixon's veto of comprehensive child care legislation in 1971, the AFL-CIO conventions in 1973 and 1975 adopted programs that were the first to spell out labor's principles for child care legislation.

These principles have been fairly consistent over two decades. First, the AFL-CIO called for a massive financial commitment by the federal government. Second, it strongly endorsed *federal* standards to ensure quality. Third, it called for a universal system, not a two-tiered one. The convention reports preferred that child care be offered by the public schools where appropriate and strongly opposed subsidies to profit-making facilities (AFL-CIO 1973 and 1975). While the role of public schools has been controversial among child care advocates, labor's concern was not merely to ensure unionized jobs with decent pay, benefits, and security, but also to look to public schools as a model of universal, free service.

Although the AFL-CIO has consistently called on unions to negotiate child care facilities, it has long maintained that a comprehensive child care system can be created only by the federal government. In 1983, the AFL-CIO laid out a detailed program for bargaining over child care, specifically because labor leaders despaired of a national solution at the height of the Reagan revolution (AFL-CIO 1983).

The media and experts look to labor primarily as a potential private sector supplier of child care, but labor's principal role thus far has been as a political supporter for a high-quality, federally subsidized national system of child care

---

[2]For example, labor supported the creation of child care centers during World War II when many women entered the work force, and it opposed the dismantlement of most of those centers after the war.

for all children whose families need and want it. Labor played a key role in the coalition supporting the Act for Better Child Care, despite some differences over whether to accept a compromise on federal funds supporting church-sponsored facilities.[3] The American Federation of State, County and Municipal Employees (AFSCME), which represents significant numbers of child care workers, mainly in New York City, has been especially active in the coalition.[4]

New Initiatives in the 1980s: The American Family Celebration

The most ambitious effort to define a labor-based family policy was CLUW's American Family Celebration on May 14, 1988. CLUW attempted to reframe labor's historic concern with adequate income, family leave, child care, and equity for women into a broad family policy and to integrate a traditional labor agenda for decent jobs, health care, housing, and other basic needs with the issues of particular concern to working women—child care, family leave, and pay equity.

The effort to develop a family policy had many origins. Labor hoped to counter the right-wing ideology of the Reagan era by promoting child care and family leave as the real needs of working families and by framing labor's traditional agenda as pro-family. This policy reformulation was more than a defensive ploy: it reflected a deeply felt belief that the range of labor's program reflected the real needs of contemporary families. While the new right portrayed the increasing numbers of working women as a middle-class phenomenon, unionists knew that the struggle to balance work and family had long been a constant of working-class life.

In addition, many labor activists, particularly women, feared that issues such as child care and family leave were being stigmatized within the labor movement as "women's issues." Progressive trade unionists undertook to sell these issues as "family issues" to the largely male leadership and, in a sometimes

[3]The labor movement opposed federal funding of programs sponsored by religious groups, but there was disagreement over whether the issue was important enough to withdraw support from the bill. The AFT was the union most strongly opposed to accepting public funding of church-based programs, while most other unions were willing to accept a compromise that seemed politically essential.

[4]AFSCME's president, Gerald McEntee, was appointed chair of the AFL-CIO's Ad Hoc Committee on the Working Family. The committee developed the AFL-CIO's Children's Day on the Hill, a well-publicized and effective lobbying day on June 21, 1989, which brought union parents and children to Washington, D.C., from every state to lobby for passage of the Act for Better Child Care.

more difficult task, to male rank-and-file unionists. For example, to support the tiny but growing number of female miners, activists within the United Mine Workers (UMW) organized grassroots support for the Family and Medical Leave Act and for family leave in collective bargaining. The work and family committees created by Local 8–149 of the Oil, Chemical and Atomic Workers (OCAW) in New Jersey are another example of an innovative effort to involve male and female unionists in family issues. Formed in the early 1980s, these committees attempted to mobilize the locals' members to address family problems in the workplace and the community.

Underlying all these activities was a recognition of the plight of the American family. The drastic budget cuts and high unemployment rates of the early Reagan years focused attention on families in trouble. Poverty among women and children was reaching appalling levels. Unemployment was tearing apart many families. The family was no longer a private sphere, but a problem for public policy.

The American Family Celebration evolved from a resolution adopted at the 1986 CLUW convention that called for a national demonstration on family policy. Although not widely reported in the press, the cheerful May 14, 1988, rally—designed to include children in games and activities—drew about forty thousand trade unionists and family members to Washington, D.C., from throughout the Northeast.[5]

Although AFL-CIO and international union contributions provided funding for the full-time organizers in Washington, local CLUW chapters and women labor activists organized the effort to bring hundreds of union-sponsored buses to the nation's capitol. For most of these women, organizing the celebration provided a rare opportunity to play a leadership role within their local unions on an issue of particular concern to women. For some, the May 14 gathering was the first opportunity to involve children and other family members in a union activity.

As the organizing proceeded, the organizers felt the need to better define the goals of the rally and to prepare a labor agenda on family policy. The result, introduced as a Congressional resolution by senators Christopher Dodd and John Heinz, and representatives Augustus Hawkins and Marge Roukema,

[5]The UMW delegation to the CLUW Convention submitted a resolution proposing that CLUW unite with "pro-family and parental leave forces, especially our unions, to call for and to help coordinate a national demonstration in Washington, D.C. in 1987." The adopted resolution broadened the issues involved and suggested 1987 or 1988. Joyce Miller, national president of CLUW, and I served as cochairs of the National Coordinating Committee of the American Family Celebration. The observations in this section are based on my recollections and notes.

to publicize the rally, was later adopted as a statement of CLUW's family policy, the American Family Bill of Rights (see the appendix for the complete text).

The preamble described a vision of the new American family and stressed the growing diversity that was the result both of new freedoms and of economic and social pressures on the family. Families, particularly minority families, were acknowledged to be operating under great stress and in greater need than ever of government support programs. The bill of rights listed ten areas of support that should be viewed as rights to which all families are entitled:

1. The right to a job and economic security.
2. The right to health care.
3. The right to child and elder care.
4. The right to family leave.
5. The right to services for the elderly.
6. The right to quality education.
7. The right to equal opportunity.
8. The right to equal pay for work of equal value.
9. The right to shelter.
10. The right to live and work in a safe environment.[6]

Although CLUW was supporting specific pieces of legislation, rally organizers wanted to move beyond specific legislation and issue a call for a broad progressive agenda to meet the needs of changing families.

The CLUW discussions over family policy raised some underlying tensions within the group and among women trade unionists. Gays and lesbians, single mothers, and other single women were concerned that the term "family" implicitly excluded nontraditional families, despite the qualifying language about diversity. As a result, at its 1988 convention, CLUW revised the Family Bill of Rights to be more specific: "Single parent families as well as gay partnerships, extended families, unmarried couples and those with and without children are also families with the same needs" (CLUW 1988).

More generally, feminists worried that family issues would weaken labor's commitment to women's equity issues. Their fears were not unfounded. During the 1980s, the number of resolutions submitted to AFL-CIO conventions on equity issues (pay equity, the Equal Rights Amendment, sexual harassment) declined drastically as the number of resolutions on family issues

---

[6]The full text of the resolution as circulated by CLUW is in the appendix. The drafting of the statement, particularly on the issue of diversity, was hotly debated. Also, the right to shelter was changed to "the right to permanent housing" and the final item was amended to "the right to live and work in a safe *and accessible* environment," to include the rights of the handicapped.

(child care, family leave, work and family) increased in 1987 and 1989 (AFL-CIO 1981–89).[7]

Despite the risks, the increasing emphasis on family issues is not a retreat from women's issues for the labor movement, but is an effort to position our issues at the heart of labor's broad social agenda.

A Labor Program for Families

Labor has not advanced a comprehensive legislative package embodying its family policy, but rather has worked through coalitions backing legislation, including expanded child care funding and the Family and Medical Leave Act. Nonetheless, labor's positions embody broad principles that can form a distinctive union approach to family policy in the 1990s.

Labor's approach to the needs of families is comprehensive. Unions represent the complex and sometimes contradictory needs of real working families. Real families have to balance their needs for health care, retirement, child care, leisure time, adequate income, housing. Family needs are not limited to the care of young children or other dependents.

Labor's family policy is intergenerational. Families *are* intergenerational, and so is labor. Labor represents workers and retired workers of all ages, although in many ways labor's core constituency is the "sandwich generation" that is responsible for parents *and* children. Social Security is a key issue for older workers and retirees, but also for workers whose parents are aging. Family leave and child care may be of primary concern to younger workers, but retirees and older workers worry about their adult children and are often recruited as emergency child care providers.

Labor supports adequate federal funding for a national system that is affordable and accessible to all. Going against the grain of current American political thought, the labor movement has looked to the federal government to provide basic benefit systems that are universal, not means-tested. Unions know first-hand the limits of private sector solutions to social problems. Because unions in the United States have had to bargain at the employer level for such benefits as health care, they have learned that the private sector's approach leaves gaps in coverage and puts unionized companies at a competitive disadvantage with domestic nonunion companies that do not provide benefits and international competitors with socialized benefits. Moreover, labor knows from experience

[7]Resolutions on equity issues declined from ten in 1981, to seven in 1983, six in 1985, two in 1987, and one in 1989. In contrast, the number of resolutions submitted on family issues increased from two in 1981, one in 1983, six in 1985, ten in 1987, and nine in 1989.

that a state-by-state system would encourage businesses to move to states with lower taxes and labor costs.

Labor represents the providers of services as well as the consumers. Providing adequate social services is highly labor-intensive. Privatization and public underfunding lower labor standards and quality; unionization helps maintain high quality and prevents exploitation of the largely female work force that provides dependent care.

Labor knows that dependent care is no substitute for adequate income. In the long run, the well-being of working families is better served by jobs that offer good pay, full benefits, and job security than by low-wage jobs that tie women to a single employer that provides child care. Dependent care should be a right for all who need it, not a favor extended by one's employer.

Labor's approach to family policy would lead to a broad, progressive agenda that promotes good, secure jobs and adequate income for the nonworking population; national systems ensuring universal and affordable health care, child care, and elder care; adequate housing for all; guaranteed and paid leave for family or medical reasons; and an end to discrimination. Such a program would go far beyond any legislation likely to pass in the foreseeable future.

The Corporate Family Agenda

In the 1980s, work and family issues in the United States were dominated by a corporate agenda quite different from the labor approach. While spokespersons for the extreme right advocated a return by women to the home and rejected any public involvement in family life, significant segments of the corporate world, motivated by a need to recruit and retain women workers, have espoused work and family issues. The media and federal and state government have focused on educating business leaders about the advantages of voluntarily implementing parental leave or supporting child care for their employees. The federal and state government's role, beyond encouraging and educating, is limited to "partnership" with the private sector or serving as a model employer.

The flexible workplace, put forward as one solution to work and family problems, has been defined principally by corporations seeking flexibility for their own ends, not as a way to meet the needs of the new work force. "Flexible," from a corporate point of view, meant easy-to-replace workers, low benefit costs, and low overhead. Many women with young children were drawn into the new "flexible" jobs—part-time, temporary, or contingent work with no benefits, no security, no union—because they were single providers or because their husbands' hours or wages were being undermined by the corporate search for lower labor costs.

If there is one issue on which the corporate and labor family agendas differ most dramatically, it is adequate income. Labor has always argued that adequate income to provide for a family, preferably income derived from access to good, secure jobs, is the most basic need of all families. The corporate agenda excludes issues of income and job security from the area of family policy. Despite its pro-family rhetoric, the corporate agenda is primarily concerned with creating and sustaining a low-wage work force, not with creating good, secure jobs on which families depend.

Prospects for the Future

The debate on work and family will continue throughout the 1990s in a very different environment, one far more favorable to labor's perspective. Women are maintaining extremely high levels of labor-force participation. Unions are stronger and the most rapidly growing are those with large percentages of women.

Union leaders are very aware of the importance of women workers to labor's survival. The traditional belief that women are harder to organize than men is being replaced by an intuitive awareness, backed by recent poll data that show that women are more receptive to unionization than men. One statistic is revealing: in 1988, unions lost 200,000 male members and gained about 160,000 female members. Women are underrepresented in the labor movement not because they are less likely to want to join unions, but because their entry into the work force increased at a time when labor faced many obstacles to organizing. Family issues offer an important opportunity for labor to reach out to nonunion working women—as well as to labor's own women members.

The labor movement is well positioned to formulate a progressive family policy for America. Unions by their nature integrate the concerns of a broad range of ordinary Americans. No political force in America is as diverse in age, race, gender, geography, even income and occupation—from white, male airline pilots to Asian and Hispanic garment workers; from professional baseball players to nursing-home aides; from professors and teachers to unskilled laborers. As I have argued, labor's core principles suggest a broad and progressive program for America's families—one that could revive the labor movement's appeal and also offer the weakened liberal forces in this country a program around which to unite and rally public support.

Labor still suffers from a defensive posture, resistant to the assaults of corporate greed and government reaction but less willing to redefine the way we structure work and family. Unions rightly see flexibility as an employer strategy to weaken workers' strength and lower labor costs. But labor must act to develop a strong program, both legislatively and through bargaining, to create *good* part-time jobs with security, opportunity, benefits, and equal pay. Whatever its limitations, the labor movement is, in fact, the best vehicle for creating a society that accommodates the needs of work and family, a society that provides equality for women and security and opportunity for all.

Europe's family policy measures range from the conservative to the progressive, particularly for women. In Europe, differences over family policy have centered on whether to encourage women with young children to stay home or to make it possible for women to gain greater equality at work and at home.[8] In the United States, where female labor force participation is very high, even without social supports for working mothers, and where corporate demand for women workers is high, the issue will not be *whether* women work, but on what terms.

Will public policy help create good jobs for women *and* men, with family leave a right under law and union contract, or will it encourage jobs that are insecure and underpaid with leave and dependent care determined by employer whim? And will high-quality dependent care be accessible and affordable for all, or will dependent care, like health care, be an inefficient patchwork of private and public services with quality linked to a family's ability to pay? Labor's ability to articulate and implement its own family policy will determine the answers to these questions for all Americans.

[8]These generalizations are my own, based on discussions at the conference "New Developments in Parenting Policies for Young Children: An International Working Group," sponsored by Columbia University's School of Social Work, from April 26 to 28, 1990. Participants included experts from France, the Federal Republic of Germany, Austria, Sweden, Finland, and Hungary.

In broad terms, German and Austrian family policies encourage women to stay home to care for preschool children by providing long periods of paid leave and by underfunding child care. In Sweden, family policy encourages women to return to work part-time and encourages men to share family responsibilities. Sweden, Finland, and France have also invested heavily in child care for young children. Female labor-force participation rates in these countries are high, while those in Germany and Austria are relatively low.

France is somewhat of an anomaly. Its family policy—like Germany's—is heavily influenced by conservative forces. But its extensive network of subsidized child care (free for all three- to five-year-olds and many two-year-olds, subsidized for infants and toddlers) is rooted in the French belief that out-of-home care is good for children rather than in a concern for working women, as in Scandinavia.

Appendix

American Family Bill of Rights

Whereas, American families are fundamental building blocks of our society; and

Whereas, families provide a web of mutual support for their members; and

Whereas, this support system comes in many varieties, because families are diverse; and

Whereas, families have both greater choice in life-style and increased economic and social constraints, including the growing number of jobs which are low-paid and without adequate benefits; and

Whereas, families are facing unprecedented challenges in job security, homelessness, lack of affordable health care and child care, drug abuse, and other pressures; and

Whereas, these problems are compounded by the still prevalent problems of racism and discrimination for Black, Hispanic, Native American, and Asian American families; and

Whereas, the web of support provided by our families is only so strong as the strands within it, and the threat to one strand jeopardizes the whole; and

Whereas, it is our strong belief that the federal government has an essential role in strengthening basic rights for American families;

Therefore, be it resolved that Congress hereby recognizes that in order for families to thrive, all families must have affordable, quality support, including,

1. The right to a job and economic security.
2. The right to health care.
3. The right to child and elder care.
4. The right to family leave.
5. The right to services for the elderly.
6. The right to quality education.
7. The right to equal opportunity.
8. The right to equal pay for work of equal value.
9. The right to shelter.
10. The right to live and work in a safe environment.

5
Bargaining for Work and Family Benefits

Carolyn York

There is a myth that labor unions have jumped on the work and family bandwagon only as a way to attract more women members. In this scenario, unions latch onto child care, parental leave, and other work and family benefits in a desperate attempt to add to their diminishing ranks. They are not acting out of a belief in these benefits or as a result of member support, but rather out of a calculated strategy that these issues will bring them more members. It is an unfair myth and one that is insulting to the women who have struggled, in many cases for fifteen years or more, to establish child care programs for themselves and their fellow union members.

The real story of how and why unions have won work and family benefits is far different. Unions were early advocates of these benefits and remain pioneers in expanding work and family provisions. The roots of this struggle can be traced to the 1970s, when persistent, committed women labor leaders championed these issues within their unions and, undeniably, when truly cooperative managers emerged and helped make the most of labor-management child care committees.

Union-Won Family Benefits

Parental Leave

Unions have been remarkably successful in winning parental leave contract provisions. An overwhelming majority of large, unionized public sector employers provide parental leave with a guaranteed right to return to the job, and even most unionized workers in low-wage service industries have the right to job-protected leave. Predominantly nonunion, salaried employees of private sector companies, however, are much less likely to receive parental leave. A 1991 report by Hewitt Associates found that only 51 percent of surveyed employers offer parental leave to these employees. The survey included 1,006 private sector employers, typically employing one thousand or more employees (Hewitt Associates 1991).

The National Council of Jewish Women produced a report that examined the impact of unionization on parental leave; they too found that unionized workers were much more likely to have the right to parental leave than nonunion employees. The council reported that while 55 percent of the union members in the survey had the right to job-protected leaves of eight weeks or more, only 33 percent of nonunion workers had the same right (Bond 1987).

Although no comprehensive information is available on the number of union contracts that contain parental leave clauses, several union surveys provide useful estimates of the extent of negotiated leave provisions. A 1988 survey by the American Federation of State, County and Municipal Employees (AFSCME), which examined all of its contracts covering one thousand or more public sector workers, showed that seventy-two of the eighty-five surveyed contracts (85 percent) guaranteed maternity or parental leave with the right for employees to return to their jobs. Of the seventy-two contracts containing leave provisions, nearly 70 percent offered leaves lasting four or more months. The contract between the City of New York and AFSCME District Council 37, containing one of AFSCME's strongest parental leave provisions, provides up to forty-eight months of leave to natural or adoptive parents (AFSCME 1988).

A similar survey by the Service Employees' International Union (SEIU) found that among its public sector contracts, 84 percent provide six months or more of job-guaranteed leave, with nearly all of the contracts continuing health benefits during the leave of absence. In the private sector, where SEIU represents predominantly low-wage service workers, the union reported that they have encountered much stronger resistance from employers. Nevertheless, nearly two out of three of their surveyed private sector contracts provide job-guaranteed leave of three months or more, and 45 percent continue health benefits during the leave (SEIU 1987).

Since the surveys were conducted, both unions report that efforts to win or improve leave provisions are continuing. In particular, unions are expanding the concept of parental leave to "family" leave to care for sick or elderly family members, as well as newborn or adopted children. In the most recent contract between the city of Los Angeles and AFSCME Local 3090, city clerical workers won leave of up to four months for childbirth, adoption, or family illness, with the right to return to the same job following the leave. The leave provision also covers domestic partners (CLUW 1989).

The SEIU *Settlements Report,* a semiannual publication of the union's research department that highlights major settlements in the preceding six months, reported thirteen examples of contracts with new or improved parental leave language in 1989 and the first half of 1990. The most frequently cited gains were in the areas of extending health benefits while on leave and winning the right to leave to care for sick family members (SEIU Research Department 1989a, 1989b, 1990).

Child Care Programs

Child care benefits have generally been tougher to win than leave provisions, due to the high cost of establishing most child care programs. Likewise, the least expensive child care option—a dependent care assistance program (or dependent care reimbursement account)[1]—has been the most frequently won benefit, while on-site centers and child care subsidies (a direct cash benefit to employees to help pay for child care) have been the most difficult to negotiate. Other union-negotiated child care benefits include resource and referral programs, after-school programs, and sick child care programs. Many of these programs grew out of joint labor-management child care committees that were originally established when the union and the employer could not agree to a specific child care program during negotiations but could agree to set up a committee to work further on the issue (CLUW 1991).

The Hewitt survey on work and family benefits among large, private sector employers confirms the preference of employers for low-cost child care options. Although 66 percent (or 666) of surveyed employers reported offering one or more child care benefits to their salaried employees, low-cost items led the list, with 91 percent of those providing child care benefits offering a dependent care assistance program and 39 percent offering resource and referral services. Only 9 percent of the employers who provide child care benefits are involved with on-site/near-site or consortium child care centers, both subsidized and nonsubsidized (Hewitt Associates 1991).

As with parental leave, there are no statistics on the extent of child care benefits in union contracts. In 1988, however, SEIU surveyed other unions to collect information on union child care programs. The survey found more

---

[1] A dependent care assistance program offers employees the option of redirecting up to $5,000 per year of their pretax salary into an account from which they are reimbursed for their dependent care expenses. The money put into this account is not subject to federal income tax, social security tax, or, in most states, state income tax.

than fifty examples from sixteen unions in twenty-three states (SEIU Public Policy Department 1988).[2]

Since the SEIU survey, unions have added to the list of union-negotiated child care programs. In *A Labor of Love: AFSCME Child Care Examples,* a 1990 publication of the AFSCME Women's Rights Department, the union summarizes twelve AFSCME child care programs, including reimbursement programs, subsidies, and on-site centers. Three of the programs, all on-site centers, were established between July 1989 and April 1990 (AFSCME Women's Rights Department 1990). In addition, AFSCME's first contract for clerical and technical workers at Harvard University included provisions for a $50,000 annual fund to provide child care subsidies and a labor-management commitment to expand the number of child care centers for children of bargaining unit employees (Harvard University and HUCTW, AFSCME, AFL-CIO 1989). SEIU's *Settlements Report* for 1989 and the first half of 1990 also notes eleven new child care programs, including three joint committees, three reimbursement accounts, two subsidy programs, two funds to develop child care programs, and one pilot child care center (SEIU Research Department 1989a, 1989b, 1990). Also in 1989, the Communications Workers of America (CWA) and the International Brotherhood of Electrical Workers (IBEW) won their comprehensive work and family package in negotiations with AT&T, as well as achieving similar gains in contracts covering regional phone company employees.

Attitudes toward Flexible Work Arrangements

The extent to which unions have negotiated provisions for flexible work arrangements, including flextime, job sharing, and voluntary reduced work hours programs, all potential benefits to working parents, is difficult to determine because no surveys have focused on this issue. What is clear, however, is that many unions have mixed feelings about such programs. The primary concern is that flexible scheduling will "erode the long-fought for eight-hour day by allowing employees to work more than eight hours without premium overtime pay" (Women's Labor Project 1981). Unions have also feared that flextime programs could increase the use of part-time employees and hence erode the number of jobs that provide a living wage. Moreover, flextime programs could have a negative impact on employee safety and health when already tired employees work longer hours in a single day. Nevertheless, flexible arrangements tend to be popular with employees. Unions have proceeded

[2]The unions that reported child care programs were: ACTWU; AFGE; AFSCME; AFT; APWU; CWA; IBEW; ILGWU; IUE; NALC; NTEU; TNG; UAW; UFCW; and USWA (SEIU Public Policy Department).

cautiously when implementing flextime programs, often beginning with a trial period. AFSCME's position echoes that of many unions: "If used properly, alternative work schedules can have positive results; nevertheless, they contain pitfalls and the potential for abuse. A local union considering an alternative work pattern should carefully weigh the pros and cons" (AFSCME Research Department 1985).

Behind the Scenes of Work and Family Bargaining

In order to look more closely at how and why unions have won work and family benefits, I now turn to three case studies: AFSCME and New York State, where a joint labor-management committee oversees a network of nearly fifty child care centers; SEIU and Santa Clara County, California, which worked together with a local school district and the YWCA to set up an innovative before-and-after-school care program; and CWA and AT&T, which put together a comprehensive package of work and family benefits in their last contract. While my focus is on child care benefits, I will also discuss efforts to win parental leave, flexible work schedules, and other work and family benefits.

AFSCME and the State of New York

By March 1991, New York State had fifty on-site child care centers operating for state employees. This network did not grow overnight: It is the result of nearly two decades of work by the state and its employees' unions, who together administer the network through a joint labor-management child care committee.

New York State's largest union, the Civil Service Employees Association (CSEA), which represents approximately 110,000 state employees and has been affiliated with AFSCME since 1978, first addressed child care in the early 1970s when they won contract language stating that the union and the state would study the feasibility of a child care program for state employees. However, no money was committed to child care, and the project didn't get off the ground for nearly six years (AFSCME Women's Rights Department 1990).

During this time, Irene Carr, a New York State employee and union activist, rose to leadership in the CSEA and took on the challenge of developing a child care program. Carr says that in 1976, when she first became CSEA

Unless otherwise noted, my interviews with Irene Carr, CSEA Statewide Secretary, on June 27, 1990, and July 5, 1990, are the source of information for this section.

statewide secretary, she "just took notes." The following year, AFSCME sponsored Carr and several other women as observers at the First National Women's Conference in Houston. While in Houston, Carr met other union women attending as representatives of the Coalition of Labor Union Women (CLUW). The impact of the conference is clear—the CSEA women returned to Albany determined to form a women's committee within CSEA and took their request to the CSEA board of directors. The board approved, and in 1978, CSEA had a women's committee for the first time, with Carr as its chair.

Carr, as head of the women's committee, found herself in the middle of the child care issue. Women began calling her to find out why nothing was being done about child care, and she in turn asked the state the same question. Then, in 1979, in response to growing pressure from state employees, CSEA's president, William McGowan, and Sandy Frucher, a representative of the governor's office, approached Carr with a plan to use a federal grant to start a child care center for state employees. Less than six months later, the Children's Place in the Albany Capital Plaza Mall opened its doors.

In their next contracts, the state and the unions agreed to establish a separate sum of money to be used for child care programs, and with each subsequent contract, the commitment to child care grew. The 1988–1991 contracts allocated $16.6 million for child care over the three-year period, including $9.5 million in the CSEA contract alone. The child care network is run by a joint labor-management child care committee that includes a representative from each union, several management representatives, and twelve full-time staff.

Traditionally, grants from the child care fund have been used to help new centers pay for start-up costs, but the committee has also approved funds for a variety of other purposes including establishing pilot projects for evening child care, training child care workers, and helping child care workers buy health insurance or establish individual retirement accounts (IRAs). Recently the committee decided to approve funds to establish a dependent care reimbursement program and a program to train family day care providers and provide parenting seminars for state employees.

Requests for money from the child care fund generally make their way up to the statewide committee from workplace committees consisting of representatives from all of the unions in that workplace. The committee conducts a needs assessment survey to prove that there is a demand for the type of child care they hope to provide, reaches agreement with management to provide the space and make any necessary renovations, and completes the process of licensing and incorporating the center. Only at this point, after the unions and management have demonstrated their commitment to the project, do projects typically receive money from the child care fund for start-up costs. Carr estimates that it takes from two to three years to get a child care center up and running. "Someone," says Carr, "must be very dedicated."

Until recently, Carr reports little, if any, resistance among CSEA's membership to the union's commitment to child care. The situation began to change during the ratification process for the 1988–1991 contract. At membership meetings around the state, some members voiced opposition to the amount of money being put into child care—not because they don't support child care but because most of the children in the state centers are not children of CSEA members.

The state centers are self-sufficient, with full support coming from parents' fees, which are set on a sliding scale based on income. Despite this arrangement, many parents, particularly the lower-paid state workers CSEA represents, cannot afford to send their children to the state centers. In 1990, 2,900 children were enrolled in the state centers, but of those, only 450 were children of CSEA members. CSEA has bargained for subsidies to make the centers more affordable for its members, but, to date, the state has steadfastly refused to agree to subsidize the centers. Carr expects opposition within CSEA to increase until the union and state are able to resolve this problem.

In the next round of negotiations, which will take place in 1991, Carr believes that bringing down the cost of child care in order to increase members' access to the centers will be the major child care item on the table. She sees two possible resolutions: winning subsidies to help members pay for care or finding ways to help the centers bring down the cost of care. If the CSEA is not able to make progress on this issue, Carr says they will have to reevaluate their involvement in the child care network because they cannot continue to negotiate for funds that support centers their members cannot afford to use. She is hopeful, however, that the commitment to the child care network is strong enough that the state and the union will work out a solution. In the 1991 negotiations, Carr would also like to see the child care workers in state centers become state employees, thereby providing them with state wages and benefits and the opportunity for union membership.

The state's reluctance to subsidize child care programs, although unfortunate, is not unusual. Other employers, including AT&T, have drawn a sharp distinction between providing one-time funds for setting up child care programs and subsidizing the ongoing operating costs. Employers typically defend their position by saying that child care subsidies, which provide a set amount of cash to employees with child care expenses, could be viewed as unfair by employees without child care expenses. But the high cost of providing even a small subsidy to all employees with child care expenses is undoubtedly the major reason most employers have not agreed to provide them.

In addition to the child care fund, CSEA has bargained for parental leave to help members balance their work and family responsibilities. The CSEA contract provides for an unpaid, seven-month parental leave for natural or adoptive parents, in addition to leave for women disabled due to pregnancy or childbirth. The period of disability is defined in the contract as four weeks prior to delivery and six weeks following delivery, unless complications warrant a longer disability leave.

The CSEA contract, however, does not contain language on flexible work hours. Instead, both the union and the state prefer to address this issue through agency labor-management committees. Using this mechanism, several agencies, including Higher Education, Audit and Control, Motor Vehicles, and Tax and Finance, have customized voluntary flexible scheduling policies that meet their particular needs.

SEIU and Santa Clara County, California

In contrast to New York's large statewide network, the before- and after-school center set up by SEIU Local 715 and Santa Clara County, California, to respond to the child care needs of the county's 5,400 employees represented by the local, shows one way to provide child care on a smaller scale.

Local 715, like CSEA, has had a long-term commitment to child care. Kristy Sermersheim, executive secretary of Local 715, reports that since the mid–1970s, the union has put child care proposals on the bargaining table during each set of negotiations but, until the early 1980s, dropped the proposals before an agreement was reached.

Before each round of negotiations, the union conducted a survey to determine members' bargaining priorities. Although the unit was 70 percent women, child care did not rank as one of the highest priorities. The local later learned that the surveys had not uncovered the members' greatest child care need: before- and after-school care. Sermersheim, however, also believes that only the highest paid workers have the luxury to make child care a top priority. Others, like Santa Clara County employees, must place wages and benefits above their child care needs.

Nevertheless, many members were experiencing problems related to child care, and the union continued to push the county to address this issue. In

Unless otherwise noted, an interview with Kristy Sermersheim, SEIU Local 715 Executive Secretary, July 5, 1990, is the source of information for this section.

1982, the union finally won contract language setting up a labor-management child care committee, although the county insisted that the contract specify that the child care program would be "at no cost to the county."

The committee, because of the commitment of those assigned to it—a cooperative county manager and a dedicated union staff representative, who as a single mother knew first-hand about child care problems—proved to be an excellent vehicle for addressing workers' true needs. The committee conducted a needs assessment survey of all county workers and discovered that before- and after-school care was a much bigger problem for employees than the committee had realized.

At the same time, the superintendent of a nearby school district called to suggest that the county and the union work with him to solve each other's problems. The superintendent was looking for a way to boost the district's shrinking enrollment, a result of the area's increasing industrialization. He planned to set up a before- and after-school program that would attract the children of parents who worked nearby and wanted to take advantage of the program and its proximity: the school is within walking distance of two large county office buildings. The labor-management child care committee enthusiastically agreed with his proposal.

At this point, the county, the union, and the school district asked the YWCA to run the program, and the four groups signed an agreement to operate the before- and after-school program. The union's commitment included advertising the program to its members and helping employees with the administrative task of transferring their children into the Orchard Park School District.

The program opened in 1983 and is still operating; in 1990 it served 68 children during the school year and 35 in the summer. During this time, school enrollment has increased from about 200 to almost 350 (BNA 1989c). The center is self-supporting, but the cost to parents is "fairly inexpensive," according to Sermersheim. Parents are attracted to the center both for its modest fees and its convenience. The center stays open all day on school holidays, generally a difficult time for working parents to find child care.

Local 715 has also addressed work and family concerns through a long list of negotiated benefits including a six-month unpaid parental leave, the right to use sick leave for family illness, a dependent care reimbursement account, and a variety of voluntary flexible work arrangements. These flexible arrangements include flextime, a compressed workweek schedule under which employees may work four ten-hour days, and a reduced work hours program that allows employees to work fewer hours while retaining full-time status and benefits. "Employees love this program," reports Sermersheim, "especially new parents who need the flexibility to take care of their kids" (SEIU Clerical Division 1987).

When negotiating flexible work schedules, CSEA is careful to include adequate overtime provisions. For example, under their four ten-hour day schedules, Local 715 generally waives the right to overtime pay for the ninth and tenth hours but provides for overtime pay for any hours over ten per day and for any hours on the fifth, sixth, and seventh days.

In future negotiations, Local 715 hopes to improve their parental leave language to require the county to provide health insurance to fathers and adoptive parents on leave, a benefit currently available only to birth mothers.

CWA and AT&T

When the Communications Workers of America and the International Brotherhood of Electrical Workers settled their 1989–91 contract with American Telephone and Telegraph Company (AT&T), the press reported extensively on the ground-breaking work and family package contained in the agreement. But like the other examples in this chapter, the roots of the unions' attention to these issues extend to the 1970s. Dina Beaumont, executive assistant to the president of CWA, says that 1974, the year CWA established a national women's committee, was a turning point in the union's fight for work and family benefits. The women's committee pushed not only for child care but also for fairer pay for clerical jobs and opportunities for women in craft occupations. During this period, many union women, Beaumont notes, were energized by the women's movement and went on to seek leadership positions within their unions and to fight for contract language to meet their needs.

CWA's newly formed national women's committee first took up the task of educating its membership through national and regional conferences, which served two purposes: to provide information on women's issues and to teach women leadership skills. According to Beaumont, as a result of attending these workshops, many more women gained power within their local unions and had learned how to use it.

By the late 1970s, the union had won both paid and unpaid leave provisions for parents in the AT&T contract. A short-term disability insurance program provided full or partial pay, depending on seniority, for mothers following delivery, and parental leave provided an unpaid, job-guaranteed leave of up

Unless otherwise noted, an interview with Dina Beaumont, executive assistant to the president of CWA, June 22, 1990, is the source of information for this section.

to six months (extended to twelve months in 1989) to mothers and fathers, including adoptive parents.

In the early 1980s, work and family issues again received attention—this time from the union's Committee on the Future, created at the 1981 CWA convention to "analyze strategic options open to the Union for dealing in a positive way with important changes taking place in our environment" (CWA 1983). Among the extensive list of issues addressed in the committee's far-reaching and candid report is family care. The Committee on the Future recommended that "CWA bargain for family-care plans so Members can have time off to take care of sick children or other family members and not fear harassment from their employer or the loss of their jobs. We also recommend a closer look at flextime as a way of helping our Members meet the obligations of both their home and their work" (CWA 1983). The union subsequently submitted proposals on work and family issues in several rounds of negotiations with AT&T but settled each contract without winning improvements in this area.

The next major step toward addressing work and family issues came in 1988 when CWA held its first industry-wide bargaining conference to prepare for negotiations covering approximately 525,000 workers in the telecommunications industry. At the conference, chaired by CWA president Morton Bahr, delegates set seven major bargaining goals, reflecting the members' priorities, which they agreed would be proposed in every set of negotiations that year. One of these goals was to win contract language on work and family issues.

Beaumont remembers that "I was a little concerned because there wasn't much debate at the conference over choosing work and family issues as one of the bargaining goals. And I wondered, 'Are they taking these issues seriously?' But they did. The timing was right, and because of the groundwork the union had laid over the years, they saw the importance of these issues."

As 1989 negotiations began, the CWA launched a major campaign to mobilize its members behind the goals chosen at the 1988 conference. The union wrote issue papers on each of the goals and publicized the goals through posters and buttons. Work and family issues received attention equal to that given the other goals.

The union's groundwork, Beaumont feels, also sensitized AT&T to the importance of these issues. In addition, AT&T did its own research. A survey of managers showed that employees experienced a wide range of family-related problems, and AT&T decided that a high-quality employer, which they considered themselves to be, had a responsibility to support employees through work and family programs.

In negotiations, the union sought to win nineteen specific benefits in five broad areas: increasing the supply of family care providers; financial assistance; flexibility; information and education; and a joint union-management committee. Table 5.1 compares the union's initial proposals to the work and family package included in the final contract.

The union was successful in winning at least one improvement in each of the five areas designated. When presenting their proposals to management, CWA stressed the potential benefits to AT&T of agreeing to the union's proposals: reduced absenteeism and turnover; and improved recruitment, retention, productivity, morale, and loyalty. Beaumont reports that despite the other difficult issues on the table in this round of negotiations, most notably health insurance, AT&T did not fight strongly against many of the union's proposals. In part, she feels "the company got serious because the union was serious." Through its extensive grassroots campaign, the union had made it clear to AT&T that they would not drop these proposals in the heat of bargaining. Also, she believes the company finally realized that the time had come to implement these changes.

Where CWA will go with this issue in the next round of bargaining with AT&T is still to be determined. Another industry-wide bargaining conference is set to begin in 1991, and Beaumont expects that the union will analyze the lessons learned from the programs put into effect in this contract before setting their bargaining priorities for the next round of negotiations. One issue that may be a priority is an expansion of the "excused workday" concept (if the program works out well during this contract) to give employees more flexibility, although Beaumont stresses that any program involving flexible working arrangements must be voluntary.

Meanwhile, CWA has added to their success with AT&T by winning work and family benefits in all telecommunications contracts of any significant size negotiated since the AT&T contract. Generally, these contracts have followed the AT&T pattern, but, depending on the priorities of each bargaining unit, may include other components, such as well-baby care. According to Beaumont, the union's formula for success is simple: educate the membership and communicate to the employer that work and family is a bottom-line issue.

Lessons for the Future

The case studies presented in this chapter are more than examples of individual victories; they can serve as a guide for the future. The case studies show that victory primarily depends on the dynamics within the unions that

Table 5.1. Comparison of CWA Proposals to Final Contract

Proposal	Final Contract

Increase Supply of Providers

Proposal	Final Contract
• Seventy-five new child care locations (on-site, near-site, or consortium). • Ten million dollars to open or expand existing facilities. • Set aside space in AT&T buildings for child care and provide start-up money for the centers.	Five million dollars to fund projects to increase the supply or enhance the quality of community options for child and elder care. Fund will support projects including expansion grants, start-up of new programs, and quality improvement grants.

Increase Financial Assistance

Proposal	Final Contract
• Establish Dependent Care Reimbursement Account. • Sixty dollars per week per employee voucher for family care services.	Dependent Care Reimbursement Account. Adoption assistance of up to $2,000 per child.

Leave Flexibility

Proposal	Final Contract
• Six-month paid parental leave with phased-in return to work. • Six-month paid leave to care for seriously ill relative. • Part-time scheduling with full benefits for family care responsibilities. • Four paid sick days to care for sick relative. • Right to refuse overtime based on inability to make child care arrangements. • Flexible work schedules. • Allow vacations to be taken on a day-at-a-time basis.	Twelve-month unpaid parental leave (improved from six months). Twelve-month unpaid leave to care for seriously ill relative. "Excused work day" for personal reasons; may be taken in two-hour increments (one-year pilot program).

Information and Education

Proposal	Final Contract
• Resource and referral program for child care and elder care services. • Employee Assistance Program to handle work and family problems. • Parenting seminars for employees. • Seminars for management on work and family issues.	Resource and referral program for child care and elder care services.

Create a Joint Union-Management Committee

Proposal	Final Contract
• Joint committee to address child care issues including selection of locations to receive funds.	Joint Board to review proposals and direct $5 million fund to selected local community programs.

Source: Proposal information is from materials provided by CWA, which were used in their work and family presentation to AT&T during 1989 negotiations. Final contract provision information is from BNA Special Report Series on Work and Family 20 (August).

made work and family issues a priority. In particular, the following activities seem to be key to winning work and family benefits at the bargaining table:

- *Developing women union leaders and staff at the local and national level and electing union leaders, male or female, who are committed to work and family issues.* In all of the case studies, women union leaders led the way with the encouragement of union presidents who supported their goals. Many of these women developed their leadership skills through union-sponsored women's committees. The CLUW has also played an important role in developing women union leaders and providing them with training on working women's issues.
- *Emphasizing internal education of the union's membership.* In the cases studied, the union encountered little resistance from members to making work and family benefits a priority. The unions attribute this to years of workshops, union meetings, and publications stressing the importance of these benefits for all members.
- *Nurturing cooperative relationships with management.* In all of the cases studied, management was ready to seek a joint solution to work and family problems. Although a union cannot create a cooperative attitude where one does not exist, the union can make sure the employer recognizes that work and family issues are important to employees and the union and that addressing these problems may result in benefits to the employer.
- *Developing a long-term perspective.* Improvements resulted after years of hard work in every case studied. Clearly a long-term commitment is essential for success.

Anticipated Bargaining Trends

Given the long time period over which unions have built their work and family programs, we can look forward to many more victories that are currently germinating. The case studies and union surveys provide information on where we can expect bargaining for work and family benefits to go in the future, with the following items likely to top labor's work and family agenda in the coming years:

- *More of the same.* Unions have been most successful in winning unpaid parental leave, the right to use sick leave for family illness, and dependent care reimbursement accounts. Because these are low-cost items for employers to provide, we can expect a steady stream of new and improved benefits in these areas.
- *A broader definition of the family.* Due to both a growing awareness of employees' elder care needs and sensitivity to the variety of alternative families in society today, unions and employers are increasingly negotiating benefits that meet the work and family needs of all families. We can expect to see a greater emphasis on elder care services and on benefits that offer both elder and child care services, such as family care resource and referral programs. Leave provisions

will gradually more broadly define who can take a leave and the reasons for taking a leave.

- *Tackling the cost of parental leave and child care.* Paid parental leave provisions and programs that subsidize the cost of child care are almost nonexistent in this country. Hewitt Associates reported only 3 percent of surveyed employers provided paid parental leave in 1991, while at most 9 percent offered any type of subsidized child care (Hewitt Associates 1991). Likewise, although some unions have negotiated child care subsidies and small amounts of paid parental leave, such programs are not yet widespread. As the case studies show, even some of the most cooperative employers strongly oppose programs that require them to pay for parental leave or child care.

Although unions will continue to push for such benefits and can be expected to win more improvements, the course that unions and employers take will be strongly influenced by activity at the federal level. As unions and employers continue to address their employees' work and family needs, society as a whole must address the larger questions of how we will provide, regulate, and pay for the care of our children. Unions, realizing that these issues cannot be solved at the bargaining table alone, have lobbied extensively to enact federal laws on parental leave and child care. Only then will unions be able to win programs that complement and enhance a national program.

Comments

Joyce D. Miller

Both papers are extremely thorough and well documented. I agree with almost all of both authors' conclusions. My comments are mostly to augment their papers, not contradict either essay.

In response to York, I would like to point out that unions have been involved in child care for much longer than fifteen years. My own union, the Amalgamated Clothing and Textile Workers (ACTWU), established child care centers almost twenty-five years ago. In the early 1960s ACTWU established child care centers in Baltimore, Chicago, and other cities, caring for over 1,800 children of union members. ACTWU in fact was providing child care for more children than any other private institution in the United States at that time. In 1968, the AFL-CIO worked to amend the Taft-Hartley Act to make child care a permissible issue for labor-management negotiations. The labor movement also played a key role in promoting and developing the Comprehensive Child Care Act of 1971, and has promoted child care issues and legislation ever since.

For example, York mentions CSEA leader Irene Carr, who was part of the Coalition of Labor Union Women child care project that examined child care in Israel, Sweden, and France in 1977. The project resulted in the publication of the widely distributed study "A Commitment to Children" (CLUW 1977). Unfortunately, the problem Irene Carr describes—of CSEA members being unable to use the established child care centers because of cost—is a universal problem: the very people for whom the centers are established cannot afford to use them.

York's account of the story of the CWA-IBEW-AT&T contract is outstanding. This contract, and its innovative approach to work and family issues, is a beacon for the entire labor movement. Dina Beaumont's succinct analysis says it all: "The union's formula for success is simple: educate the membership and communicate to the employer that work and family is a bottom-line issue."

But I disagree with York's assertion that, in all cases, women union leaders led the way on work and family issues with the encouragement of union presidents. There are many unions—AFSCME, ACTWU, UMW—where men led the way with the support of women. Even within CWA, if President Morton Bahr had not been committed to these issues—regardless of the pushing of female leaders—they probably would not have been raised during bargaining nor would the breakthroughs have been achieved.

I also stress that while feminism has affected union women, CLUW and feminists based in the unions have sensitized the women's movement to the importance of working women's issues.

Let me also add that one reason unions have not encountered much resistance on work and family issues is because their members have *lived* these issues. They experience daily the conflicts between work and family. As an older ACTWU member in Joliet, Illinois, said at a meeting I addressed on the need for child care: "It may be too late for me, but I remember what it was like and I support it for our younger members."

I agree with York's overall conclusions and particularly would underscore the need for federal legislation and governmental support.

In commenting on the well done paper by Susan Cowell, I would add the issue of reproductive freedom to the excellent "Family Bill of Rights" she cites. CLUW maintains that decisions about contraception, abortion, sterilization, the timing of childbearing, and the number of children a family has should not be made by governments, courts, employers, or any person or institution other than the individual woman. CLUW advocates policies that support working women as mothers—affordable prenatal care, parental leave, and child care—at the same time that we defend the full range of safe, legal family planning services without restrictions based on income or economic status.

Cowell's point on the growing number of women joining unions is well made; in time, a higher percentage of women will make up the membership of the American labor movement. Let me add, however, that the determining factor in union growth is not sex but rather the decrease in jobs in manufacturing versus the increase in jobs in the public sector and service industries. For example, we see a decrease in membership in unions such as ACTWU and the ILGWU because of the loss of jobs, even though each union has a high percentage of women members.

Cowell's point that the complex and contradictory needs of working families are of key importance to developing an adequate, comprehensive family policy is well taken. She is also on target when she discusses the "sandwich generation." I do not agree, however, that attention to family issues has weakened labor's commitment to women's equity issues. For example, in the early 1980s, passage of the Equal Rights Amendment was prominent on labor's agenda and the AFL-CIO fought hard for it. The legislation failed, shy of the ratification votes of three additional states. But the AFL-CIO marshaled its considerable lobbying power and got an extension on the ratification deadline. Even now, in the early 1990s, the ERA remains a rallying cry, despite the pessimism many feminists feel and their sense that, until the composition of state legislatures changes, an all-out ERA effort is an exercise in futility. Labor's commitment to pay equity is another example of the importance of women's issues. CLUW still gives considerable attention to sexual harassment. Again, there has not been a trade-off. Labor has pursued both equity and family issues.

Some general comments on the transformation of the family are in order. Yesterday's extended families and involved neighbors have been replaced by television, impersonal shopping malls, and hostile streets. Institutions that might compensate for what overwhelmed parents are unable to do are themselves undermined by less than adequate public policies. The fragmentation of American families is not simply an issue of personal morality or individual fidelity but is powerfully linked to changes in the economy.

The United States is the only advanced Western nation where family life is regarded as a private matter, where workplaces operate oblivious to family pressures, and where a lingering frontier mentality creates ambivalence about support from corporations or government—even help that would enable a parent to stay home with a newborn. We must promote an environment that provides child care, elder care, family support, and a sense of belonging to old and young alike. I believe we must make it easier to combine work and family, and provide more time and support for parenting.

Our institutions must be more responsive to children and families. There is a consensus among people of widely divergent ideologies that the family is central to our well-being as individuals and as a society, and that if children are to grow into self-sufficient adults, the family must be supported by social institutions, both public and private.

Bargaining for Family Benefits: A Union Member's Guide (1991), published by the CLUW, is a guide for union members to negotiate family benefits.*

*Available for $5 from CLUW, 15 Union Square West, New York, NY 10003.

The labor movement's ongoing commitment to work and family issues is exemplified in the guide; in the AFL-CIO Executive Council's creation of a work and family committee; in the committee's sponsorship of Children's Lobby Day and the support that event received from the entire labor movement; and of course, in the CLUW-initiated American Family Celebration discussed in the Cowell paper.

Comments

Alice H. Cook

In response to the essays of Susan Cowell and Carolyn York, I shall comment on two points. First, unions' positive recognition of working women's predicament came long after the problem arose, for substantial numbers of women have been in the labor force from the beginning of waged work, and these numbers have been visibly growing since at least the mid-1950s. Union attention to the ensuing issues can be dated to within the last fifteen years.

Second, the approach of unions to the conflicting demands of family and work has been to treat these issues as particularly adhering to women rather than to their male partners. It is only within the last five years that unions have begun to discuss them as family problems.

Unions' Early Responses

Historically, union men feared women as cheap competitors to their hard-won standards of wages and working conditions. They shared their employers' judgment that women were worth less than men because they had inferior training; they were physically less able to undertake the heavy work that largely characterized men's jobs in the growing industrial and construction sectors; and, if women *were* to undertake such work, they endangered their reproductive systems and thus their essential reason for being. The unions' slowness to react to women's needs in the work force arose from the belief that women would not remain in the labor force after they married. Women were perceived as hard to organize because their long-term interests and "proper place" were not in wage work. At the same time, their presence in jobs outside the restricted areas of "women's work" represented low-wage and low-skill competition. Women in the United States and abroad tended to form their own separate organizations. The Women's Trade Union League existed from early in the twentieth century both in the United States and in England. Eleanor Marx led a union of match workers. German women under Clara Zetkin formed women's divisions within their unions.

The unions' first recognition of women's special needs as they went out to work was to support protective legislation, although most unions deeply distrusted any state intervention in their own affairs. Unions adopted the view that the problems of wage-earning women were the government's, rather than the unions', responsibility (Steinberg 1982:78–81; Brandeis 1953). The state was to draft and enforce legal requirements to be followed by the employers of all women. The state would, for example, limit the hours women could work and the amount of weight they could lift; restrict night work; and, in some instances, stipulate the provision of rest periods during the working day and chairs for women in retail sales so that they could sit when they were not engaged in service to customers. These laws would constitute a set of minimum standards, below which the exploitation of women could not fall, thus ensuring union men of a bottom line of competition from women. Historically and until very recently unions regarded women as a threatening, deviant group of workers to be dealt with differently than men (Kessler-Harris 1982).

Although legislation may have assisted women, it also limited the kinds of work to which they were assigned, and so contributed to an established gender segregation of occupations into the jobs that were women's work and the vast majority that were men's work (Kessler-Harris 1981). To this day, men and women work at separate occupations, a division under which women's work is uniformly less well-paid than men's.

To be sure, union men voiced the demand for "equal pay for equal work." But this slogan veiled the fact that most men and women have never worked at the same tasks, and thus, at best, it could apply to a fraction of women in the work force. Indeed, the slogan was raised more to protect men's standard rates than to improve women's pay.

As recently as 1970, separate and lower scales for women's work were widely accepted by unions (Cook 1968). The Equal Pay Act of 1963, hailed as a victorious cap to a long campaign, did nothing to attack gender segregation at work or the continuation of low pay for women's work; instead, it encouraged the continued segregation of women's work from men's by assigning women's jobs slightly different titles from men's.

Pay Equity/Comparable Worth

By the late 1970s, many women's organizations realized that the long-established union demand for equal pay for equal work, in addition to its other inadequacies, did not apply to women's work in fields such as nursing, clerical occupations, child care, and much of auxiliary health care, because there were few, if any, men in these occupations with whom women could claim equality. Nor was there any expectation that men would enter these fields if they could avoid them, since the pay scales were so low. In 1979 Eleanor Holmes Norton, then head of the Equal Employment Opportunity Commission (EEOC), which had recently been given the task of enforcing the Equal Pay Act, laid out the problem in her speech at a Washington, D.C., conference organized by the Women's Bureau of the Department of Labor, State Commissions on the Status of Women, and many autonomous women's organizations. She called for correcting women's low pay not only by raising it to pay levels received by men working at the same tasks, but also by comparing the worth of women's jobs to the employer with the value he places on quite different jobs held by men. The method most commonly used would be that of job evaluation, cleansed as it must be of the gender bias inherent in most such schemes. Norton concluded that improving women's wages by "comparable worth" techniques would be the major issue for women in the 1980s (Grune 1980). At the time, the last year of the Carter administration, Norton did not reckon with her successor Clarence Thomas's total opposition to supporting or even processing comparable worth claims.

In the 1980s unions with large female memberships, especially AFSCME, CWA, SEIU, NEA, and AFT, attempted to persuade the federal courts to consider equal pay demands as legitimate under Title VII through a theory of comparable worth. When that proved problematic—as it almost uniformly has—these unions began to bargain aggressively for pay equity, with the result that success in bargaining has been marked in the public sector, especially in state and local governments and in school systems (for their nonacademic staffs)[1]. Moreover, a substantial number of states adopted pay equity laws covering their own employees. In Minnesota, legislation was extended to all *local* governmental bodies within the state as well. Women have made notable

[1]These unions included most of those organized in the public sector. Exceptions are unions of police, fire fighters, and sanitation workers who have few female members, and who have on the whole been indifferent or even hostile to taking up family issues. In addition to public sector unions, some in the private sector in the recent past have also organized public workers (the UAW, CWA, HERE, ANA, and IBEW) and have taken up family issues.

gains in Washington, Iowa, Ohio, Connecticut, New York, and Oregon, and in towns, cities, counties, school districts, and public agencies across the country (Cook 1990).

What Comes First: Family or Work?

In recent years, under pressure from women's groups inside and beyond the labor movement, union attention has turned to the obligations of both men and women as parents and spouses (Golodner and Gregory 1986). The shift is reflected in the concern with child care and the impact on children of having both parents working, with care of the elderly and sick family members, with the stresses of combining homemaking and work, and with the lack of time for family life.

Nevertheless, despite concern about women's family burdens, so long as women remain subject to rigid hours and schedules at work, child care benefits and other supports can never fully meet their needs. It is not just the eight-hour day that is a problem for working women, but the exigencies of additional employer demands for overtime, time for additional training, and even occasional travel. The eight-hour day, fifty-week year, and forty-five-year working lifetime all presume that the worker puts work demands before those of family. Women have found this impossible, because they still retain responsibility for tending sick and well children; for caring for elderly relatives; for domestic chores—housecleaning, doing laundry, preparing meals, supervising children after school, scheduling doctors' and dentists' visits, preparing anniversary and holiday celebrations, and chauffering household members to their various appointments. Indeed, no quantity or quality of publicly provided family support has freed women of a critical amount of all the unequally shared family demands upon their time (Cook 1978; Hochschild 1989). Innumerable studies of time use within families and of the way in which dual-earner families face the problems of "sharing" family responsibilities reveal how little most husbands or companions contribute to household tasks. The single parent, who has no adult partner with whom to share either decisions or tasks, faces an almost insurmountable problem (Bielby and Bielby 1988; Gerkin and Gove 1983; Rothman and Marks 1987).

The United States, in contrast to many other countries with an array of family benefits built into the total social security network, sees the proper source and provider of this kind of assistance as the individual employer or as simply a matter of individual family responsibility. Thus in the 1980s, as York and Cowell recount, unions, particularly those with large numbers of women members, began to include family issues in bargaining (AFSCME 1982;

CLUW 1991). But none of these has in any known case obtained—or even asked for—*paid* maternity leave. Thus, when the issue of parental leave came before Congress, the proposed federal legislation, like the union contracts, did not provide for paid leave. Although the bill that passed the Congress in 1990 (only to be vetoed by President Bush) went beyond any program adopted abroad in that it would have extended leaves to fathers for care of sick family members as well as for newborn or newly adopted children, it nowhere included even partially paid parental ("medical") leave. Yet it is not hard to see that payment *must* be a major consideration in the ordinary working- or middle-class family. Without it, women tend to return to the workplace at the earliest opportunity and men don't leave work at all, especially if their wives are already on unpaid maternity leave.

The question is whether individual unions alone can deal with the issue of payment for parental leave. Without comprehensive legislation, the burden on unions and employers who provide this benefit represents a severe handicap for them in the competitive market. Other countries have dealt more generously with this aspect of the issue, mainly because they have already insured every family for total health care, including reimbursement for medical outlays and time lost from work. The American labor movement's growing support for national health insurance is the next logical step.

Management's Agenda

Not all the initiative on work and family issues comes from organized workers and firms. In 1983 the Bureau of National Affairs (BNA) began to make the work-family issue a subject of detailed reporting and in 1986 produced *Work and Family: A Changing Dynamic,* a study of the extent to which both organized and unorganized companies were responding to the growing needs of families. Other important management-oriented organizations, including the Commerce Clearing House, the Conference Board, *Fortune* magazine, and Catalyst (1980), have taken up the issue and initiated extensive studies (Adolf and Rose 1985; Axel 1983; Catalyst 1987, 1988; Conference Board 1990; Digital Corporation 1988; Dilkas 1984; Friedman and Gray 1989). Thus we know that IBM; Dupont; Johnson and Johnson; Hughes Aircraft; Mobil; Wilmer Cutler and Pickering; Chrysler; Aetna; and U.S. West are among the several hundred companies that have set up staff and invested substantial funds in family benefit programs to meet at least some of their workers' family needs. Cowell argues that the flexible workplace "has been defined principally by corporations seeking flexibility for their own ends, not as a way to meet the needs of the new work force." She has highlighted a major consideration, and one that also makes the unions uncomfortable about alternative schedules when espoused by corporations. But a good deal of the change has come about because of the corporations' need to retain the growing work force of women. It remains to be seen whether one positive effect of retaining women workers will also be their insistence on participation in training and promotional programs and training opportunities. All the more so, as the demographic outlook is for a growing percentage of women in a smaller work force in the 1990s and beyond. Corporations are introducing flexible schedules in the belief that such measures will result in less absenteeism, lower turnover, and higher company loyalty and job commitment (Rothman and Marks 1987; Roussakoff and Skrscki 1988).

Alternative work schedules take many forms: part-time work, compressed weeks, flextime, job sharing, homework, contracting out of specific jobs. Some, like flextime, job sharing, and compressed weeks, are rearrangements of standard full-time schedules; the others represent shorter or fewer hours of work and, in the instances of contracting out and homework, may also mean alternative places of work.

Unions and Alternative Work Arrangements

Historically, unions have expected to organize workers they regarded as fully committed to the labor force and so have framed their collective agreements to deal with the problems of full-timers. They have not considered part-time workers as eligible or very desirable for membership. Slowly, and late, unions that have had to deal with split shifts—as in the hotel and restaurant industry, and supermarkets and other sales outlets open longer than an eight-hour day—have begun to write special supplementary contracts for part-time workers (Mallier and Rosser 1983; Nulty, this volume). But, after my interviews with union officers in Sweden, Germany, and the United States, I have concluded that unions are more concerned with defending established eight-hour standards than advocating the needs of part-time workers. Contract clauses have mainly to do with prohibiting part-timers from working overtime—that is, with possibly encroaching on full-timers' work—and with opening up full-time jobs, as they become available, to part-time workers.

Agreements have been made, more often in Europe than in the United States, that protect these workers on a proportional basis, measured by the proportion of the full-time schedule worked (duRivage and Jacobs, this volume). Thus, health insurance, vacations, and holidays in Sweden (and to some degree among the unionized retail sales work force in this country) have been made available to part-timers on a proportional basis. Some unions both here and abroad have also set part-timers' dues as a proportion of the full fee.

Commissions and researchers that have studied the conditions and problems of part-time workers have recently recommended something like a Bill of Rights for part-time workers. It would include items to protect them against overtime beyond a contracted number of hours; to ensure them increases, vacations, and holidays commensurate with those of full-time workers; to acknowledge their eligibility to join trade unions; and guarantee them training and promotional opportunities (Canadian Ministry of Labour 1982).

Job sharing is much less widely available, although there are a few companies that use it on a considerable scale (Lawson 1989; "Critical Issues" *Business Link* 1990). Job sharing seems to occur most often in professional occupations and in situations where a company is located in a rural area where more women are available than men, and where few other employment opportunities exist. When job choices are restricted and child care facilities are limited or do not exist, women neighbors may alternate work and child-minding. Few cases can be cited, however, where a union has been involved in this type of arrangement (McCarthy et al. 1981; Lawson 1989).

Some unions with large female memberships have negotiated flextime clauses (SEIU 1982). Flextime does not purport to shorten hours but to make them more flexible within limited bounds. The effect is that during a period of a week or, more rarely, a month, workers must be at their stations for a core period every day but, over the whole period, work a total of the full working hours. Beyond problems of scheduling, flextime seems not to call for special concern over matters of payment, training, or promotion, perhaps precisely because it applies to both genders.

An area of considerable interest and controversy for unions is homework (Boris and Daniels 1989). Unions see homeworkers, off company property and isolated in their own homes, as virtually unorganizable and nearly impossible to represent in the handling of grievances. Other problems are the poor pay and working conditions of some homeworkers, the isolation of the worker from her coworkers, the ever-present demands of children, and the unannounced one-way monitoring by supervisors via the computer (9 to 5, National Association of Working Women 1988; essays and comments in part 4, this volume).

Unions have dealt gingerly, if at all, with these various alternative schedules and locations of work, possibly with the single exception of part-time work. Some unions that have had to deal with problems presented by split shifts— here we think of restaurant workers, bank tellers, retail sales employees, and others in customer services—have developed hourly payment with guarantees to guard against invasion of the scheduled periods of nonwork. Many such unions have large numbers of female members who accept these odd hours precisely because child or elder care can be accommodated to the periods between work.

What Remains to Be Done?

European unions have approached some of these questions of work and family from quite another direction; namely, to shorten working hours for both men and women. They have very generally cut the working year by many more days than American unions have dared hope for. Their members can count on four, five, or even six weeks of paid vacation time and from fifteen to twenty paid holidays. Moreover, they have set their goal for the near future on the 35-hour week.[2] To be sure, most of this has not been done in the name of women or of family, but of combating unemployment by providing more jobs. Trade union women who have hoped to make the shorter workday, week, or year an opportunity to include husbands in richer family life have come into sharp conflict with trade union men about how best to shorten working time. As I learned in interviews with trade union women in Sweden and Germany throughout the 1980s, women have urged that these cuts be taken in daily hours; men have preferred shorter weeks and years (Moen and Dempster-McClain 1987). Employers have also favored the latter. So far, the record unequivocally favors the men's interests and the working day tends to remain at eight hours, while gains in shorter hours are translated into lengthened vacations, more holidays, or shorter weekly hours. American trade unionists, particularly women, would do well to examine European solutions, to better understand how they might avoid a similar outcome when the issue is eventually raised in this country.

Conclusions

Title VII of the Civil Rights Act was framed to allow women and minorities access to all the opportunities of white men. Yet aside from admitting women and minorities to labor pools and training programs, employers were not admonished or even advised to change their organizational patterns and work rules so that women or men could have more time for family life and that

[2]The Summer 1990 issue of *IMF News*, the publication for members of the International Metalworkers Federation, based in Geneva, Switzerland, carried the information that the German metalworkers [IGM], in their 1990 spring negotiations, had won the agreement that their workweek will be lowered to thirty-five hours by 1995 without any reduction in pay.

men could participate in job sharing in the home. In addition, pay equity achieved through comparing women's occupations to men's has been rejected by the EEOC since the mid–1980s. Unions that *have* sought to bargain for pay equity have, more often than not, met obdurate opposition from employers, courts, and bureaucrats who administer compensation in both private and public sectors. The result is that families have been left to do what they have done ever since the industrial revolution, namely adjust their choices, functions, and schedules to those of so-called rationally organized work.

Moreover, legislators, employers, and to some extent unions, instead of establishing programs or providing incentives to encourage change in the behavior of men, have defined the problem as exclusively women's. Thus, a variety of family support programs, mainly centered on child care and "family" or medical leave, have been adopted. The aim of opening leave to men as well as women was to allow husbands to assist their overburdened wives, but the likelihood that men will be able to use unpaid leave is very slight. So the effect of unpaid leave for women, however well intentioned, remains more symbolic than real. The growing use of alternative schedules is likewise somewhat illusory, since they are mainly aimed to accommodate women and are bought at a high price. Women remain in marginal jobs. Indeed, they remain deviants in the world of work. Despite some improvements in their lot, women have failed to achieve equal treatment, and for this they are blamed. The failure, however, is not theirs. Rather, it is inherent in the man-made system that was organized to accommodate male workers who would put work ahead of family.

That unions have not led the way out of this morass is not surprising. Unions were created by men who accepted the division of labor between genders as inevitable and even right. Their early program, it must be remembered, was to insist that women should not work at all. Their solution to the problem that their own incomes could not support families and that their early breakdowns or deaths left families unprovided for, was to define themselves as heads of families and to demand—though seldom receive—a family wage to support a wife at home with children.

Times have changed. Unquestionably, two incomes are necessary to support even a small family in working- or middle-class circumstances. More than half of married women are now working for wages, and working women make up nearly half of the labor force. The question is how we can best solve the problem of women continuing to carry the bulk of the family load while also meeting the demands of an unchanging work world. The answer, to which unions could make an important contribution, is how to put family needs before those of work. In so doing, men would be restored to the family and work would be made tolerable for both genders.

References to Part II

ACTWU. 1988. "Bargaining on Women's Issues and Family Concerns: Clauses from ACTWU Contracts." New York: ACTWU Research Department. November.

Adolf, B., and K. Rose. 1985. *Employers' Guide to Child Care: Developing Programs for Working Families.* New York: Praeger.

AFL-CIO. 1955–89. *Proceedings of the AFL-CIO Constitutional Conventions.*

———. Executive Council. 1986. *Work and Family: Essentials of a Decent Life.*

AFSCME. 1982. "Negotiating about Child Care Issues and Options." Washington D.C.: AFSCME Research Department. June.

AFSCME. Research Department. 1985. "Alternative Work Schedules—It's About Time!" *Collective Bargaining Reporter* 26 (March–April):1.

———. 1988. *Leading the Way: Parental Leave Arrangements in AFSCME Contracts.* Washington, D.C.: AFSCME.

AFSCME. Women's Rights Department. 1990. *A Labor of Love: AFSCME Child Care Examples.* Washington, D.C.: AFSCME.

Axel, Helen. 1983. "Corporations and Families: Changing Practices and Perspectives." New York: Conference Board Report No. 868.

Beaumont, Dina. 1990. Interview with Carolyn York. June 22. Washington, D.C.

Bennett, Amanda, and Cathy Trost. 1989. "Benefit Package Set by AT&T Unions Shows Power of Families in Work Place." *Wall Street Journal* (May 31):A8.

Bielby, D. L., and W. T. Bielby. 1988. "She Works Hard for the Money: Household Responsibility and the Allocation of Work Effort." *Social Problems* 35:2.

Bond, James T. 1987. Statement of James T. Bond, Director, National Council of Jewish Women, Center for the Child. Submitted to the Committee on Education and Labor, Subcommittees on Labor-Management Relations and Labor Standards of the U.S. House of Representatives.

Boris, Eileen, and Cynthia R. Daniels. 1989. *Homework: Historical and Contemporary Perspectives on Paid Labor in the Home.* Urbana: University of Illinois Press.

Brandeis, Elizabeth. 1953. *History of Labor in the United States, 1896–1932: Labor Legislation.* New York: Macmillan.

BNA. 1986. *Work and Family: A Changing Dynamic.* Washington, D.C.: BNA.

———. 1989a. *The Work and Family Report.* AT&T Contract. June 9:9–10.

———. 1989b. *1989 Employer Bargaining Objectives.* A BNA Special Report: Washington, D.C.: BNA.

———. Special Projects Unit. 1989c. "Work and Family and Unions: Labor's Agenda for the 1990s. *BNA Special Report Series on Work and Family* 20 (August).

Business Link. 1990. "Critical Issues: Steelcase Offers Job Sharing to the Entire Workforce." 4:2:6–7. Berkeley Heights, N.J.: Resources for Child Care Management.

Canadian Ministry of Labor. 1982. *Part-Time Work in Canada: Report of the Commission of Inquiry into Part-Time Work.* Ottawa: Ministry of Labor.

Carr, Irene. 1990a. Interview with Carolyn York. June 27. Miami, Florida.

———. 1990b. Telephone interview with Carolyn York. July 5.

Catalyst. 1981. "Corporations and Two-Career Families." New York: Catalyst.

———. 1987. "Corporate Child Care Options." New York: Catalyst.

———. 1988. *The Corporate Guide to Parental Leave.* New York: Catalyst.

CLUW. 1977. *A Commitment to Children.* New York: Coalition of Labor Union Women.

———. 1988. Unpublished adopted resolutions.

———. 1989. "Briefly noted." *CLUW News* (November/December):5.

———. 1991. *Bargaining for Family Benefits: A Union Member's Guide.* New York: CLUW.

Cook, Alice H. 1968. "Women and American Trade Unions." *Annals of the American Academy of Political and Social Science* 375:124–32.

———. 1978. *The Working Mother: Problems and Programs in Nine Countries.* Ithaca, N.Y.: ILR Press.

———. 1990. "Current State of Comparable Worth in the United States," in Industrial Relations Research Associations. *Proceedings of the 1990 Spring Meeting.* May 2–3:525–31.

CWA. 1983. *Committee on the Future Report.* Washington, D.C.: CWA.

Digital Corporation. 1988. "Balancing Life and Homelife Survey." New York.

Dilkas, C. 1984. "Employers Who Help with the Kids." *Nations Business* (February):59–60.

Fortune. 1987. "Executive Guilt: Who's Taking Care of the Children?" February 18.

Friedman, Dana E., and Wendy Gray. 1989. "The Corporate Response to Health and Family Needs." Paper prepared for the conference, "Health and the Family." Henry J. Kaiser Foundation. Menlo Park, California. February.

Gerkin, Michael, and Walter R. Gove. 1983. *At Home and at Work: The Family's Allocation of Labor.* Beverly Hills, Calif.: Sage Publications.

Golodner, Jack, and Judith Gregory. 1986. "Unions and the Working Family." In *Work and Family, A Changing Dynamic.* A BNA Special Report. Washington, D.C.: BNA.

Grune, Joy Anne, ed. 1980. *Manual on Pay Equity Work: Conference on Alternative State and Local Policies.* Washington, D.C.: Conference on Alternative State and Local Policies.

Harvard University and Harvard Union of Clerical and Technical Workers, AFSCME, AFL-CIO. 1989–1992. *Agreement.*

Hewitt Associates. 1991. *Work and Family Benefits Provided by Major U.S. Employers in 1991.* Lincolnshire, Ill.: Hewitt Associates.

Hochschild, Arlie, with Anne Machung. 1989. *Second Shift: Working Parents and the Revolution at Home.* New York: Viking Press.

Kessler-Harris, Alice. 1981. *Women Have Always Worked.* Old Westbury, N.Y.: Feminist Press.

———. 1982. *Out to Work: A History of Wage-earning Women in the United States.* New York: Oxford University Press.

Lawson, Carol. 1989. "With Job Sharing, Time for the Family." *New York Times* (May 31).

Lozano, Beverly. 1989. *The Invisible Workforce.* New York: The Free Press.

Mallier, A. T., and M. J. Rosser. 1983. "Part-Time Working: Employment Conditions, Legislation, and the Trade Union Response." *Employee Relations* 5(2):6–11.

McCarthy, Maureen E., and Gail S. Rosenberg with Gary Lefkowitz. 1981. *Worksharing Case Studies.* Kalamazoo, Mich.: W.E. Upjohn Institute for Employment Research.

Moen, Phyllis, and Donna Dempster-McClain. 1987. "Employed Parents: Role Strain, Work Time, and Preferences for Working Less." *Journal of Marriage and the Family* (August):579–90.

9 to 5, National Association of Working Women. 1985. "9 to 5 Takes the Lead on VDT Legal Rights." Cleveland: 9 to 5.

Rosenzweig, Roy. 1983. *"Eight Hours for What We Will": Workers and Leisure in an Industrial City, 1870–1920.* New York: Cambridge University Press.

Rothman, Sheila, and Emily Menlo Marks. 1987. "Adjusting Work and Family Life: Flexible Work Schedules and Family Life." In *Families and Work,* edited by Naomi Gerstel and Harriet Engel Gross, 469–77. Philadelphia: Temple University Press.

Roussakoff, Dale, and Cindy Skrscki. 1988. "Working 9 to 2: Part-Time Employees Are Changing the Face of American Businesses." *Washington Post National Weekly* (March 21–27):6.

SEIU. 1982. "Flextime—What Local 591 Wanted and Won, Flint, Michigan." *Service Employee* 41 (9):7. Washington, D.C.

———. 1987. *SEIU Survey of Parental Leave Policies in Low-Wage Service Industries: Some Progress, Not Far Enough.* Washington, D.C.: SEIU.

SEIU. Clerical Division. 1987. "Innovative Pacts Protect Full-Timers; Benefit Part-Timers." *SEIU Clerical Division Update* (Fall):12.

SEIU. Public Policy Department. 1988. *Summary of Union Child Care Activities.* Washington, D.C.: SEIU. September.

SEIU. Research Department. 1989a. *SEIU Settlements Report: First Half 1989.* Washington, D.C.: SEIU. May.

———. 1989b. *SEIU Settlements Report: Second Half 1989.* Washington, D.C.: SEIU. December.

———. 1990. *SEIU Settlements Report: First Half 1990.* Washington, D.C.: SEIU. June.

Sermersheim, Kristy. 1990. Telephone interview with Carolyn York. July 5.

Steinberg, Ronnie J. 1982. *Wages and Hours: Labor and Reform in Twentieth-Century America.* New Brunswick, N.J.: Rutgers University Press.

TNG. 1988/1989. Excerpts from "Officers' Report to National Convention" and from 1989 Contracts on Family Policy and Contract Language. Washington, D.C.: TNG.

U.S. Supreme Court. 1908. *Muller v. Oregon.* 208 US 412. 28 Sup Ct 324.

Women's Labor Project. 1981. *Bargaining for Equality.* San Francisco: Women's Labor Project.

Part III
Temporary and Part-Time Work: Opportunity or Danger?

Most researchers now agree that the proportion of workers in the United States who hold traditional, full-time, permanent jobs is in decline. The meaning of this shift toward a contingent or flexible work force has been hotly contested, however. Many within the labor movement initially viewed these changes as motivated purely out of employer greed, without any possible benefit for workers, and to be opposed at every turn. In contrast, employers and some feminists claimed that part-time work, reduced and alternative scheduling, "mommy track" options, and other nontraditional arrangements were a product of the needs of a new work force and would, in fact, offer a solution to many of the dilemmas faced by these workers.

The essays and commentaries in this section have transcended those initial dichotomies and offer a more complex analysis. Elizabeth Engberg's interviews and case examples reveal that at least some sectors of the U.S. labor movement now recognize that the work force *is* diverse and that a single set of working conditions may not meet the needs of all workers. A majority of workers may continue to need and prefer more traditional work patterns and arrangements, but a growing number of workers will at some point in their lives—for whatever reasons—require alternatives. Engberg charts the response of the new labor movement: one that is seeking to maximize options and to protect traditional job arrangements while creating more flexible alternatives that do not sacrifice job security or penalize earnings.

Like Engberg, Virginia duRivage and David C. Jacobs argue that the "flexibility" provided by U.S. employers is inadequate and in fact destructive of workers' lives: U.S. unions must insist upon alternatives. In Western Europe and other countries where unions are strong, legislatively mandated benefits exist for all workers, and workers outside of traditional employment arrangements have secured greater parity in income, benefits, and opportunity. Leslie Nulty of the United Food and Commercial Workers shares a similar critique of the contingent work arrangements pursued by U.S. employers, noting their particular penchant toward pursuing "cheap labor" strategies for maintaining competitiveness. But given the lack of success of U.S. unions in the political arena, Nulty recommends that unions continue to focus on convincing employers of the economic drawbacks of relying on contingent employment.

Maureen Martella's research on temporary agencies confirms once again that employer versions of flexibility are not meeting the needs of most workers. Although Martella applauds the increasing responsiveness of unions toward the new heterogeneous work force, she does not see union-based solutions as adequate. Given the current weakness of unions in the United States, union solutions will at best be partial.

Nevertheless, there is reason for optimism. Taken as a whole, the essays in this section suggest that a coalition between labor and the feminist movement on policy affecting part-time and temporary workers is increasingly a possibility. Not only do the two movements share a common critique of the solutions proposed by employers, but both are moving toward developing policies that recognize the diverse needs of workers. It is the joining of these forces that has the potential to create new and better workplace options for women.

6
Union Responses to the Contingent Work Force

Elizabeth Engberg

As the year 2000 approaches, the U.S. economy is undergoing funda-mental change. Thirty years ago the United States had a manufactur-ing-based economy that produced most of the products consumed around the world. Since then, U.S. products have been replaced by those from Japan, Korea, and other developing countries. The United States has become a service-based economy, and in the past few years, the fastest-growing sectors have been clerical, health care, and retail work. The service economy has produced almost all of the new jobs, most of which are low-paying and provide few fringe benefits.

One of the most profound changes in the new economy is the decline of long-term commitment between employer and employee. Gone are the days when workers were hired as clerks and, through diligence and good service, moved up to vice president of the company. In an era of corporate restruc-turing, companies strive for higher trading prices on the stock market and a good quarterly balance sheet. The notion of a stable, long-term work force has been all but abandoned.

In place of long-term employment, the contingent work force has sprung to life. (The contingent work force includes temporary, leased, independently contracted, seasonal, and non-permanent part-time workers.) Fueled by the skyrocketing cost of health care and other employment-based benefits, em-ployers have searched, and in many cases found, a way to streamline their operating costs by creating a "flexible," or more accurately, a "disposable" or "marginal" work force. Between 1980 and 1989, the number of temporary workers more than doubled, and the number of part-time workers grew by 40 percent. Nearly half of all new jobs in the 1980s were filled by part-time or temporary workers (Sweeney and Nussbaum 1989:57). Although women account for less than half of all workers (47 percent), they are more than two-thirds of the part-time and temporary work force (U.Ŝ. Department of Labor, BLS 1990a, 1990b).

Some members of today's work force seek flexible work: those who want to combine work and family responsibilities or go to school, or those in semiretirement. But according to the Bureau of Labor Statistics, the number of involuntary part-time workers (those who would prefer full-time work) has grown more quickly over the past ten years than the voluntary part-time work force (Sweeney and Nussbaum 1989:58). Many women seek part-time or temporary work instead of full-time jobs because of the shortage of affordable child care, which makes a flexible schedule a necessity. The rate of involuntary part-time work among women is 44 percent greater than among men (Tilly 1990a:6).

Whether part-time or temporary work is a necessity or a choice, contingent workers overall receive lower hourly wages and fewer employer-paid benefits than their full-time counterparts. Less than 25 percent of all part-time workers receive health coverage on the job, whereas 75 percent of all full-time employees do. Less than one in four part-time workers are members of a pension plan and only 15 percent will ever receive any benefits. In contrast, over half of all full-time workers participate in a pension plan (Sweeney and Nussbaum 1989:59). In addition, promotional opportunities and career development are rare for part-time and temporary workers who do not accrue seniority.

Legislation that is outdated and inequitable has contributed to the plight of part-time and contingent workers. Some part-timers—many agricultural and farm workers or employees in small businesses—are excluded from federal minimum wage laws. Many more part-timers—those who piece together two or three jobs of fewer than forty hours per week—are excluded from the overtime provisions of the Fair Labor Standards Act (FLSA). In fact, the FLSA (passed in the 1930s when the average workweek was forty hours) guarantees overtime pay only to employees working more than a forty-hour week for a single employer. By 1988, the average workweek for all service-producing industries had fallen to 32.8 hours (U.S. Department of Labor, BLS 1988a).

The Employee Retirement Income Security Act (ERISA), which regulates employer pension and health plans, requires that employers who offer a pension plan include all employees working more than one thousand hours per year. Although many part-timers may work more than one thousand hours per year for a single employer, high turnover among part-timers, and especially among temporary workers, preempts the five-year vesting requirement.

At the state level, the criteria for receiving unemployment insurance vary.

In some states, the qualifying minimum wage or length of employment excludes some part-time and seasonal workers with erratic annual work schedules and earnings (UBA, Inc. 1988; U.S. Department of Labor 1988). In the public sector, many part-time and contingent workers are denied collectively bargained benefits.

In addition, the lack of a national health insurance system leaves more than thirty-seven million Americans, most of whom piece together a living with part-time or temporary work, without any form of health insurance. The passage of the Massachusetts Health Security Act of 1988 sought relief for many uninsured employees in that state. However, the law covered only employees working 20 hours per week, after a period of 180 days (6 months) or after a period of 90 days if they were a head of household, and effectively excluded most temporary workers.

The Changing Perspective of Unions

Historically, unions concentrated their organizing and representation efforts on full-time workers, in part because of the small number of part-time workers. In 1955, part-timers accounted for a fraction (4 percent) of the work force (U.S. Department of Labor, BLS 1988b: tables A21–22). In an economy driven by manufactured goods, large factories with thousands of workers offered union organizers the greatest membership growth. In these heavily unionized, male-dominated manufacturing industries, contingent workers were most often used by employers to erode the bargaining power of unions and thwart organizing efforts among workers. Because unions represented more than 35 percent of the work force, they set the standards of employment for all workers: decent wages, job security, health benefits, and a pension upon retirement.

The shift to a largely unorganized, service-based economy in which large numbers of people work shorter hours, often at several jobs, presents an enormous challenge to organized labor. More and more, unions are turning their energies toward organizing and representing the interest of *all* workers. Unions increasingly acknowledge that the changing demographics of the work force, especially the increasing number of women workers who are raising small children, make part-time employment a desirable option. In many service-based unions, women and people of color have acquired a more powerful role. Close to fifty percent of the Service Employees International Union's (SEIU) members are women, and 31 percent are people of color. Unions have taken on the fight to restore the economic status of these workers. The call is for flexible jobs—when a worker may choose to work less than full-time while maintaining her or his seniority and fringe benefits—and against contingent jobs, in which a worker has no power in her or his workplace and no representative to fight an employer driven by short-term profits.

The diversity of the part-time and contingent work force creates another challenge for organized labor. Work issues that are crucial to low-skilled, low-paid building service workers may be of less concern to registered nurses and other more highly paid professionals. In the garment and textile industry, where a flood of foreign imports has eroded a mostly unionized work force, unions face a different set of problems than in expanding industries such as health care and clerical work.

In an effort to maintain organized labor's power in the new economy, forward-thinking unionists have developed a two-pronged approach to organizing and representing part-time and contingent workers. They have attempted to stem the growth of the contingent work force while promoting flexible job structures to meet the demands of changing industries and the needs of working parents. On the one hand, unions continue to fight off employer threats to subcontract full-time jobs and to erode bargaining units with part-time and temporary workers. On the other, anticipating economic changes and the need for a flexible rather than disposable work force, many unions have bargained creative solutions that protect the economic well-being of the entire membership and guarantee business flexibility.

Union Responses in Traditionally Part-Time Industries

In some industries, such as retail, construction, textiles, and garment manufacturing, employment has always fluctuated throughout the year, and scheduling is not always on a nine-to-five basis. Unions in these industries long ago recognized the need for provisions that will protect their members during fluctuations in industry demand.

Unions in these industries pioneered the use of jointly administered (union and employer or multiemployer) or union-administered health and welfare funds, supported by employer contributions, to provide health coverage to their members. In industries such as construction and retail, where work is available on a seasonal basis, or in janitorial services, where cleaning contractors may change several times each year, health and welfare funds offer workers year-round health insurance by linking eligibility to work in the industry, rather than to employment in a particular job. In some cases—such as for members of the International Ladies' Garment Workers' Union (ILGWU) in New York City—when an entire plant closes, any worker who remains at work in the industry or is collecting unemployment or disability is eligible for coverage by the union-administered health and welfare fund for two fiscal quarters (six months) (Hoffman 1990).

The United Food and Commercial Workers (UFCW) has traditionally negotiated contracts that require employers to contribute to workers' health insurance on an hourly basis and that cover all workers, regardless of the number of hours worked. For example, professional meat cutters may work a few hours in two or more stores each week. According to a number of contracts negotiated by the UFCW, the employers must contribute toward the jointly administered health plan based upon the overall hours worked each week, not the number of hours spent in each store. Workers also accrue seniority based upon a full-time schedule. It is the union's policy to maintain and strengthen its jointly administered employee benefit plans that cover both full- and part-time workers (Nulty 1990).

In the early 1980s—the beginning of a decade of corporate raiding and restructuring—the UFCW adopted an industrywide collective bargaining policy for approximately 750,000 (60 percent) of its members working in the retail food industry. Included in the union's bargaining goals were: to incorporate minimum ratios of full-time workers to part-time workers in their contracts, to guarantee a minimum of twenty hours of work per week for all employees, to gain work preservation clauses, and to secure the maximum possible number of full-time positions (UFCW 1988).

Unions have also protected many seasonal or temporary workers by changing the way in which monthly or annual service is calculated. In a recent contract with the HSSI Distributing Company of Columbus, Ohio, the Cleveland Joint Board of the Amalgamated Clothing and Textile Workers Union (ACTWU) proposed a new structure for calculating accrued service for the company's mechanics, freight handlers, and clericals. Because most of the work is done on a seasonal basis, workers were hired for peak work loads and were laid off afterwards. According to the new contract, service will be accrued on an annual, rather than monthly or weekly, basis. Now, any member who works beyond the specified seasons or works more than five hundred hours each year has layoff rights based on seniority. In addition, these workers have guaranteed wages and receive prorated leave time. Since the new contract was ratified in March 1988, the number of bargaining unit members has increased from 100 to 128. The company has also benefited from the new structure: it has cut turnover and has sharply decreased the amount of time spent each year on training new workers (Willis 1990).

Work sharing is another response adopted by unions in seasonal and part-time industries to provide stability and job security for part-time workers. The

ILGWU contracts, for instance, covering more than one hundred thousand garment workers in New York City, include work sharing clauses. The contracts stipulate that when slowdowns in the market occur, all available work will be shared and health insurance continued (A. Hoffman 1990).

Health Care: A New Part-Time Industry

In health care, irregular hours and part-time work have always been necessary, but in the past few years employers have reduced the number of workers on their full-time payrolls and substituted temporary and casual workers. Because of the diversity among workers in various occupational groups—skill level, wages, and differences in the supply of labor—this industry exemplifies the challenge unions face in meeting the needs of a more heterogeneous work force.

Registered nurses (RNs) are among the most skilled and highest-paid health care workers. An acute shortage of RNs during the past few years has pressured many health care facilities to hire agency or registry nurses in order to meet daily work loads, an advantageous arrangement for nurses who want less than full-time work or who want to supplement their full-time salaries. Registry nurses work on an assignment basis and are paid an hourly or a per diem wage that is usually higher than the market wage in the area. Although this system may appear to be a win-win situation for health facilities and for RNs, in reality it is not. Using registry nurses as a stopgap measure has led to consistent short staffing and reduced quality of care. Registry nurses must spend some of their time being trained in the work methods of a particular facility or learning patient histories in an industry where errors can be fatal.

The Service Employees' International Union (SEIU) Local 535 in Los Angeles, California, has created an alternative to the use of registry nurses. By organizing a pool of replacement workers at Kaiser Foundation Hospital/Los Angeles Medical Center, the union has been able to meet the demands of an employer who needs registry nurses during peak work loads and the needs of nurses who don't want full-time work. The strategy provides a stable work force at the hospital, ensuring that health care is provided by the same pool of union nurses. In addition, the amount of time dedicated to training is reduced, while the time spent with patients is increased. According to the contract between SEIU Local 535 and Kaiser-Permanente that covers more than nine hundred staff and critical care nurses, the employer must maintain a pool of per diem nurses who are included in the union's membership. The nurses schedule a specific number of days each month when they are on-call. According to the contract, if one of the full-time nurses is ill or needs to take the day off, the employer must first contact a per diem nurse as a replacement. If none of the per diem nurses is available, the employer must offer overtime to a full-time nurse. As a last resort, Kaiser may hire a registry nurse to meet staffing needs (Bullock 1990).

On the opposite end of the occupational spectrum from registered nurses are nurse's aides, health care facility cleaning staff, and other less skilled workers, many of whom are part time. As health care facilities began to operate more as for-profit organizations, these workers bore the brunt of cost-cutting measures. In some cases after the union had secured health insurance and other fringe benefits for employees working half-time or more, the employer hired "casual" part-timers with irregular schedules who were not protected by the contract. As with registered nurses, employers began to understaff, and then called in casual employees to meet work load needs.

Some unions have responded to employer attempts to set "casuals" against "permanent" workers by upgrading the rights and benefits of casuals. In 1986, for example, casual employees accounted for only 10 percent of Kaiser-Permanente's northern California work force. By 1988, the number had grown to 15 to 20 percent. Historically, permanent part-time workers have been covered under all of the contract's provisions. All clerical, technical, and maintenance employees at Kaiser who work more than twenty hours per week, for example, receive 100 percent employer-paid health insurance and paid leave, and participate in the employer's pension plan. The casual, temporary, and intermittent employees, however, have not received full coverage. In order to prevent the erosion of full-time and permanent part-time work, in its 1988 contract negotiations SEIU Local 250 significantly improved the bargaining rights for casual employees. The union negotiated predetermined work schedules, with a maximum number of hours each week, for casual employees. If the scheduled work regularly exceeded twenty hours, the worker would be reclassified as a permanent part-time worker, with all the rights and benefits that status entailed. Casual employees are also now paid a wage premium of $1.00 per hour in lieu of health insurance (Kaiser-Permanente Northern California Region and SEIU Local 250 Bargaining agreement, 11/5/89–10/31/92.)[1]

---

[1]Other unions, such as the CWA, are also pushing for parity for part-time and contingent workers. The CWA has bargained prorated health benefits for part-timers, not on a straight hour-for-hour but on a staggered basis. In 1989, CWA successfully negotiated health care and paid leave time for more than three thousand part-time workers at AT&T who work between seventeen and forty hours per week. Employer-paid health insurance is staggered so that workers who work three-quarters to full-time receive 100 percent employer-paid health insurance, those who work at least half-time have 75 percent of their premium cost covered, and those who work more than sixteen hours each week have 50 percent of their cost covered. In addition,

Parity for Public Sector Contingent Workers

The move to a more contingent work force is not unique to the private sector. In the public sector, where unions represent 43.6 percent of the work force, the growth of permanent temporaries has been significant (U.S. Department of Labor, BLS 1990). With hiring freezes and budget cuts, many state and county governments have exploited loopholes in public personnel guidelines by hiring so-called temporary employees. Los Angeles County alone classifies more than ten thousand employees as temporaries, although many of them have worked at the same job for years. State and local agencies also hire and lay off the same group of "seasonal" employees year after year. A seasonal worker has no job security and in many cases the employer is not obliged to pay health insurance or offer fringe benefits.

In many cases, the terms part-time, temporary, and seasonal are misleading. So-called part-timers may work forty hours or more per week and many temporaries may spend years working for the same employer. Seasonal employment may last for nine or ten months of each year and extend for years on end.

At both Cuyahoga Community College and the Los Angeles Unified School District, the part-time and seasonal workers performed the same tasks and had the same responsibilities as the full-time staff, but the employers were able to circumvent provisions in the union contract by exploiting public personnel procedures. At the Cuyahoga Community College in Ohio, for example, workers were hired for peak work loads three times each year during registration, were paid a fraction of their full-time counterparts' wages, and were then laid off at the end of the three- or four-week period. Other employees worked half-time each week in one department and half-time in another, but because their salaries were drawn from two separate budgets, the college argued that each employee held two part-time jobs (T. Hoffman 1990).

An important union response in the public sector has been to put part-time and temporary workers on economic parity. Strategies have included securing prorated health and welfare benefits and paid leave time for all part-time workers, equal wages for full- and part-time employees, and a lower hourly threshold for inclusion in the bargaining agreement. As a result of District 925's organizing efforts at Cuyahoga Community College, for example, any employee who works more than ten hours each week is now represented by the union. Part-time employees have bargained seniority rights, tuition re-

---

because all of the part-timers are covered by the contract, they receive paid annual, sick, and parental leave (CWA and AT&T, Bargaining agreement, 5/28/89–5/30/92).

mission, and preference over outside candidates in bidding for full-time jobs, as well as prorated health insurance and paid vacation for all employees who work twenty hours or more each week.

Contracting Out Jobs

In the public sector, privatization or contracting out public work to private sector employers, has cost many union members their full-time jobs. Because the majority of the jobs that are contracted out are lower-paid, nonprofessional positions, privatization has had a disproportionate effect on women and people of color who have traditionally filled these jobs. The result has hastened the overall decline in the average wage for these groups of workers. While the popular perception is that the private sector operates more efficiently than the public, many cases of private sector contracting have resulted in worse service for more money. Public corruption and the exploitation of workers have been accomplished with taxpayer dollars (AFL-CIO Public Employee Department 1989:10–13).

Private sector employers are also subcontracting union jobs. In 1985, Bethlehem Steel decided to contract out the jobs of 138 office and technical workers at its Burns Harbor, Indiana, plant to Star Personnel. Overnight, the workers, 80 percent of whom were women, lost benefits, seniority, and as much as 42 percent of their wages. Although the workers performed the same work, at the same location, the employer argued that they were no longer employed by Bethlehem Steel and that the United Steelworkers of America contract no longer covered them. While the new Star Personnel employees immediately organized their own local of the USWA, it was not until 1989 that they were rehired by Bethlehem Steel and won higher wages and employer-paid benefits (Needleman 1990:81–88).

Union tactics against privatization have run the gamut from contract limitations, to public pressure campaigns, to organizing subcontractors. In Los Angeles County, where privatization has claimed more than four thousand union jobs in the past twelve years, SEIU Local 660 has employed public advertising and community action campaigns to dissuade private companies from bidding on public work. In an effort to contract out the three hundred jobs at El Monte Comprehensive Health Care Center, the county placed an ad in the "Bids Wanted" section of the *Los Angeles Times*. SEIU Local 660 responded by placing an ad below the county's; the local promised to investigate all financial and social records of any contracting company, to organize community opposition to the provision of services by a private contractor rather than by public employees, and to encourage and assist sister unions in organizing workers in the facility. As a result, only one bid was received and the county eventually decided against contracting out the work (McNichol 1990:37–44).

In the best cases, unions have been able to secure "no contracting out" clauses in their bargaining agreements or at least limitations on the work that can be contracted out. For example, Oregon state employees, represented by SEIU Local 503, must be notified before the state contracts out any bargaining unit work. The union then has thirty days to develop an alternate plan. If the union plan would result in greater cost savings than the state's plan to contract out, the state must implement the union plan (State of Oregon and SEIU Local 503, Bargaining agreement, 7/1/89–6/30/91). However, as long as employers recognize that subcontracting is a legal method of cutting costs, unions will be fighting an uphill battle.

Organizing the Contingent Work Force

Organizing work that is contracted out to another employer is generally tougher than organizing part-timers within a union company. AT&T, where the CWA currently represents approximately one hundred thousand workers, has made plans to subcontract the jobs of one thousand customer service representatives and telemarketers at one of its southern Florida plants to five separate temporary agencies, halving wages and providing little or no benefits. AT&T's subcontracting strategy makes this new work force difficult to organize. Any effort to organize the workers at one agency would cause AT&T to contract to another agency (Kohl 1990).

Nevertheless, some unions have successfully organized part-time, temporary, and subcontracted workers, and have then successfully bargained benefits and higher wages. In the late 1970s, SEIU Local 250, which represented more than twenty-six thousand health care workers in San Francisco, initiated an organizing drive of all the nurse registries that supplied nurses to the union-represented hospitals in the city. The union sought to prevent the erosion of their bargaining units, as well as to stop the hospitals from hiring replacement workers during a strike. After a successful campaign, the union bargained wages and other benefits for the registries, bringing their standards up to those of the unionized work force. Under the agreement, any registry worker assigned to an area hospital would pay a permit fee to the union, a prorated form of dues tied to the number of days each nurse worked in a month. In addition, Local 250's contract with the Bay Area nurse registries prohibited the registries from sending replacement workers to a hospital where Local 250 workers were on strike (Kaiser-Permanente Northern California Region and SEIU Local 250, Bargaining agreement, 11/5/89–10/31/92).

In Los Angeles, the Unified School District replaced full-time educational aides with seasonal teaching assistants (TAs). Over several years, the number of educational aides fell from eight thousand to four thousand while the number of TAs grew to ten thousand. Teaching assistants, who worked as much as six hours each day, were hired at the beginning of each school year and laid off at the end, with no guarantee that they would be rehired the following year. The TAs received no health insurance, or sick or vacation pay. Until November 1989, the TAs were the only group of employees in the school district who were not represented by a union. In Los Angeles, SEIU Local 99's organizing campaign to represent the TAs lasted almost two years. Organizers emphasized health benefits, wage parity, and job security. Realizing that the union had gathered active support from TAs at more than 500 of the 633 schools in the district, the school board voted to voluntarily recognize Local 99 as the official bargaining agent for the TAs (SEIU Public Division 1990:8–9).

Union Forms of Flexibility

Unions, in contrast to the employer option of low-pay and low-status marginal or contingent employment, have attempted to create flexible work alternatives without sacrificing pay or job security. Union solutions range from voluntary work reduction programs to job sharing programs to creating in-house pools of replacement workers. Many of these efforts have met employers' needs for flexibility and increased productivity, as well as created viable alternatives for workers.

In Santa Clara County, California, SEIU Local 715 (representing fifty-four hundred county employees) established a voluntary reduced hours program. Under the program, county employees may elect to work 5, 10, or even 20 percent fewer hours. At the University of Cincinnati, clerical workers, represented by SEIU District 925, may elect a reduced workweek and take off the equivalent of forty eight-hour days each year. Participants in both programs retain their full-time status and employer-paid benefits. In addition to its voluntary work reduction program, SEIU Local 715 has been able to protect workers who are involuntarily furloughed from full-time to part-time work. The union has negotiated full-paid health insurance for these part-timers, as well as preference in bidding on all available full-time jobs.

Job sharing refers to a situation in which two people work half-time, while maintaining their hourly wages and fringe benefits, to complete the job of a full-time worker. (Job sharing is often confused with work sharing. Work sharing is implemented as an alternative to layoffs. Two workers may have their work time reduced rather than one being laid off.) When the American Federation of State, County and Municipal Employees (AFSCME) and the Harvard Union of Clerical and Technical Workers (HUCTW) organized the thirty-eight hundred clerical and technical workers at Harvard University in 1988, the union strove to provide both flexibility and economic security for its new members. HUCTW's first contract covered all employees working 17.5 hours or more per week. If two employees wish to share a full-time job, each working half weeks or half days, they are still eligible for 80 percent employer-paid health insurance, participation in the university's pension plan, and paid leave time. In addition, part-time employees are eligible for training and skills development, including tuition remission for two courses per term at Harvard and financial aid for courses outside the university. Two part-time employees, working as a team, can also bid on a job in a higher classification (Cordt 1990).

As discussed elsewhere in this volume, unions have also negotiated flextime provisions, child care programs, and other work and family provisions that allow members to work full-time jobs rather than to involuntarily take part-time work. Flextime programs range from a four ten-hour day workweek— such as that negotiated by SEIU Local 6 and the Group Health Cooperative of Puget Sound—to flexible daily work schedules. For example, members of SEIU Local 790, who work in the city and county of San Francisco, may schedule an eight-hour workday any time within a twelve-hour period.

Although efficiency for a multibillion dollar, publicly traded corporation is too often synonymous with higher profits and trading prices for stockholders, some employers are beginning to recognize that maintaining a well-trained, experienced work force is the best way to ensure efficient and competitive operations. For city, county, and state government agencies, hospitals, retail stores, and other employers, reduced-hour programs or maintaining a pool of substitute or floating employees are some of the solutions to competitiveness that unions have offered. Unions argue that contingent work and subcontracting may cost the employer more than she or he saves. When working conditions are poor, turnover is high. The quality of service suffers and companies must pay the cost of retraining new workers.

In the 1990s, as women continue to fill most of the new jobs, unions will have to step up efforts to ensure flexibility—decent wages, seniority, affordable health insurance, and alternative work schedules—in the face of the efforts by some employers to create a contingent or disposable work force with low wages, minimal benefits, and no job security.

Organizing campaigns that target workers in the burgeoning sectors— health care, clerical, and retail—are one answer. Another is adopting strategies at the bargaining table that guarantee workers prorated health insurance, participation in a pension plan, and some form of job security and career advancement. But unions still represent a fraction of the part-time and contingent work force: fully 93 percent are without union protection (U.S. Department of Labor, BLS 1990). In response, many unions have placed legislation that would protect *all* workers—family and medical leave, universal health insurance, and pension reform—at the top of their political agendas. Changing state and federal regulations may be the only way to guarantee access to health care and other employee benefits to all workers.

7

Social Policy and Part-Time Work

Lessons from Western Europe

Virginia duRivage and David C. Jacobs

Many workers welcome part-time employment as a strategy for combining paid work and family responsibilities. But part-time work, like temporary and casual employment, subcontracting, and home-based employment (all of which are growing in the developed world), receives its primary impetus from employers' drive for flexibility in a competitive world market (Tilly 1990a). Flexibility defined in this way is a prescription for social insecurity. Particularly in the United States, part-time workers are often on the insecure margins of the enterprise, without benefits, a living wage, or any accommodation for their family responsibilities, and without union representation.

Although part-time employment as it is currently available in the United States fails to meet the needs of most workers, part-time work need not be synonymous with poor working conditions and marginality. It can and must be reformed in the interest of security, equity, and flexibility. U.S. public policy has ignored the needs of part-time workers. In contrast, Western European countries have made considerable progress in creating viable part-time options for workers while maintaining competitiveness in a global economy. An examination of social policy toward part-time workers in Western Europe reveals the feasibility of alternatives to the approaches taken in the United States and provides concrete policy options worth considering.

Social security programs and worker protections vary in Europe, but common to most is a dual social insurance system that provides basic health and income guarantees to every citizen, supplemented by such employment-related benefits as unemployment insurance. Most Western European states have enacted universal health care schemes, maternity and parental leave, family allowances, national child care programs, and guarantees of employee representation. All of these help cushion the impact of economic restructuring on workers. Similar policies implemented at a national level in the United States could act as a buffer against the vicissitudes of the economy and ensure that flexibility in the workplace benefits *all* employees. Workers should not have to sacrifice job and income security in order to work fewer hours, especially if meeting the demands of family life requires spending less time at work.

The Part-Time Work Force in Western Europe

The growth of part-time work and other atypical employment is evidence of a fundamental transformation in the arrangement of work in the industrialized world. Part-time work now accounts for more than 40 percent of the jobs held by women in Denmark, Norway, Sweden, and the Netherlands, and the vast majority of women's jobs in Great Britain, outpacing the growth of full-time employment (International Labour Office 1989).[1] International competition and the growth in services have resurrected older employment forms such as home-based work, casual or temporary employment, and work in the informal sector (Portes, Castells, and Benton 1989; Cordova 1986; 9 to 5 1986; Hartmann and Lapidus 1989). These arrangements, like part-time work, are sometimes characterized by shorter hours. Here, however, we will focus solely on the phenomenon of regular part-time work.

Part-time work is truly "women's work" in Western Europe. Women represent roughly two-thirds of the total part-time labor force in the United States, but in Western Europe the proportion of women is consistently higher. Ninety percent of part-time workers are female in (formerly) West Germany,[2] 88 percent in Austria, 87 percent in Belgium, 85 percent in Sweden, and 83 percent in France. A slightly lower percent of part-time workers are female in Great Britain and Norway (78 and 77 percent, respectively) than in other Western European countries, but only Italy has a smaller proportion of female part-timers (62 percent) than the United States. As in the United States, most of these workers are concentrated in the services and retail trade sectors of their economies (International Labour Office 1989; de Neuborg 1985). In both France and the United States, working mothers are more likely to work

[1]Official definitions of part-time employment vary from below thirty-five hours in the United States, Austria, Norway, and Sweden, to fewer than thirty hours in France and Finland. In Italy and the United Kingdom, respondents to labor force surveys determine the number of hours that define part-time work (de Neuborg 1985).

[2]Subsequent references to Germany will presuppose a united Germany in which the public policies of the former West Germany prevail.

full-time than part-time, while part-time work dominates the employment choices of working mothers in Germany, Great Britain, and Scandinavia.[3]

Working part-time may endanger women's social and economic status in both the United States and Western Europe, but there are fewer disadvantages to part-time work in many Western European nations. As trade unions and other advocates of working women in the United States struggle to improve wages and benefits for part-time workers through collective bargaining and lobbying, part-time workers in Sweden, Germany, France, and the Netherlands enjoy basic health, welfare, and family supports as a matter of citizenship, not as an earned privilege of continuous full-time employment. In many cases, workers are entitled to minimum benefits without regard to full-time or part-time work status. Much of the financial burden for subsidizing comprehensive programs falls upon general tax revenues augmented by contributions from employers for specific employment-related benefits. Taken together, these benefits significantly enhance the security of part-time workers in Western Europe (International Labour Office 1989).

Social Insurance and Part-Time Workers

In the United States, 35.7 million U.S. citizens have no health care protection (Employee Benefit Research Institute 1992). Part-time, temporary, and other casual employees in particular are likely to be without protection. But in Western Europe, and in nearly every other industrialized country, the health care of *all* citizens—regardless of work status or economic class—is guaranteed through a national health program, which is usually one element of a comprehensive social insurance system. Universal health care is highly popular wherever it is in effect.

In the United States, labor has embraced both the mandated benefits approach as well as efforts to create a universal health insurance scheme for individuals, such as part-time workers, who fall between the cracks (Jacobs 1989). Despite labor's stance, national health insurance legislation has been introduced in Congress on a yearly basis since the 1940s without success, and

---

[3]If given a variety of options, some workers, particularly women with families, would choose to work part-time. Other workers have part-time jobs but would prefer to work full-time. The relative proportions of voluntary and involuntary part-time employment are difficult to determine. Part-time workers in the United States are classified by the Department of Labor's Bureau of Labor Statistics as voluntary or involuntarily while virtually no distinction is made in the other national statistics describing part-time employment (de Neuborg 1985). In the United States, women are the fastest growing group within the involuntary part-time constituency (Nardone 1986; Tilly 1990a). It is estimated that four million workers are involuntarily employed full-time (Tilly 1990b).

bills mandating health benefits have also failed. Even these failed measures often did not guarantee health benefits to those who work fewer than 17.5 hours weekly, and thus would not have provided security for part-time employees. An exception was the 1988 bill introduced by Congresswoman Patricia Schroeder (Dem.-Colo.). It would have required employers who provide health benefits to full-time workers to offer prorated benefits to part-time employees.

Part-time workers in the United States often run the risk of losing their jobs when a personal or family illness strikes. According to one employer survey, fewer than one in four part-time workers employed in small to medium-sized private firms is entitled to paid sick leave (Hewitt Research Associates 1985). Workers and their families need not fear such injustice in Western Europe. Very few restrictions are placed on eligibility for paid sick leave under social security provisions. Only in the Republic of Ireland and Great Britain are part-time workers reported to be without sick pay coverage (Beechey and Perkins 1987). In Sweden, full- and part-time working parents are entitled to stay home with pay for up to sixty days per year, per child, to care for a sick child.

With the exception of Great Britain, most Western European workers enjoy, by law, generous amounts of paid time off for early child care, illness, and leisure. Nearly all of these governments guarantee part-time and full-time workers full pay for annual vacation periods of four to five weeks, one strategy for achieving full employment goals. Employers are required to finance annual paid leaves and are permitted very few restrictions in determining employee eligibility. By contrast, annual leave in the United States is not regulated and remains strictly under the control of individual employers except where negotiated by trade unions. A 1985 employer survey conducted by Hewitt Research Associates shows that less than half of part-time workers in small and medium-sized companies receive paid holiday or vacation leave.

However, Western European social policy, like that of the United States, does leave many part-time workers unprotected when they are laid off or unemployed. In both the United States and much of Western Europe, unemployment insurance (UI) is contingent upon the terms of employment. In Western Europe, for example, workers employed below a threshold—eighteen hours a week in Finland, Germany, and Ireland; seventeen hours in Sweden; sixteen hours in the United Kingdom; and fifteen hours in Denmark—are not entitled to receive unemployment insurance benefits (International Labour Office 1989).[4] Policies more favorable to part-time workers *are* emerging in

[4]In Great Britain, workers employed fewer than sixteen hours per week do not pay into the

Western Europe. France has adopted a dual public-private system of unemployment insurance with shorter work requirements and a national minimum
unemployment insurance benefit that is reduced according to the number of
hours worked. Additional "solidarity" benefits are available to recently widowed, divorced, separated, or single unemployed women with children.

Historically, the U.S. unemployment compensation system has protected
most full-time workers. Hours limitations are not imposed on UI eligibility,
but income thresholds and minimum years of service requirements often
disqualify part-time workers from receiving benefits. Regulations in all but six
states automatically disqualify benefit applicants who limit their availability
to part-time work (Pearce 1985).

Retirement income in the United States is provided by a dual public-private
system in which the private components play a pivotal role. Despite regulation
and special tax treatment of pension benefits, gaps in coverage remain. Just
16 percent of part-time workers are included in employer pension plans
compared with 48.5 percent of full-time workers (Woodbury 1989). Unlike
social security, private pensions are not required by federal law. Many part-
time workers in the United States are employed in industries such as retail
trade that traditionally have featured low pension coverage rates. As a result,
social security is often the sole means of retirement income for some part-time
workers. Women as well as black and Hispanic males share higher rates of
part-time employment than white males, and are more likely to earn only
social security income in old age. Moreover, formulas for determining social
security pensions in the United States favor persons with uninterrupted full-
time work patterns. As a result, long-term part-time workers often receive
inadequate monthly social security benefits.

Unlike the United States, many Western European nations offer universal
pension benefits unrelated to personal work experience. Universal benefits,
which are available in Denmark, Finland, Austria, Norway, Sweden, and the
Netherlands, are then augmented according to previous earnings. Workers
are thus served by one public pension system that does not discriminate
between "poor" and "nonpoor" workers in the way that Supplemental Security Income (SSI) and social security do in the United States. Swedish low-

national social insurance fund and are thus not covered by unemployment insurance, maternity
benefits, or sick pay (MacLennan and Fonda 1985). There is compelling evidence that employers
in Great Britain deliberately adjust part-time work hours to reduce their own liability for
national payroll taxes. Land (1986) reports that between 1979 and 1984, when employer social
security taxes increased from 6.5 percent of earnings to 9 percent, the number of part-time
workers earning too little or working too few hours increased by 22 percent, from 2.25 million
part-time workers to 2.75 million. These workers are effectively outside the social security
system and are not entitled to unemployment insurance or the basic national maternity benefit.

income workers and German part-time employees working fewer than fifteen hours a week are not required to pay into the national social security pension fund, but are still eligible for minimum pensions. In contrast, U.S. social security taxes have become especially burdensome for low-income workers, many of whom work part-time and whose effective tax rates now exceed those of higher-paid employees. Measures to reduce the payroll tax burden on low-wage part-time workers are sorely needed (International Labour Office 1989; Woodbury 1989).

In addition to state-provided benefits, private pensions are required of all private employers in many Western European countries. Such laws ensure complete private coverage of regular part-time workers, a sharp contrast to the low percentage of such workers covered in the United States, where private pensions are not mandated. Even where private pensions are not universal, as in Germany, public policy often requires that part-time workers be included in any pension benefits provided by the enterprise. There is at present no such requirement under U.S. federal law.[5]

Family Benefits

The United States lacks a national policy guaranteeing paid maternity leave. At the state level, only New Jersey, Rhode Island, Minnesota, and the District of Columbia have enacted maternity policies applying to both public and private employees within their jurisdictions (Nelson 1991). Few full-time workers in America receive paid job-guaranteed leave and even fewer part-timers enjoy these protections (York, this volume),[6] whereas national maternity leave, and in some cases, paternity leave, are government mandates throughout Western Europe. Such leaves provide a social and economic context in which parents may feel less constrained about employment choices and may opt for part-time employment, while retaining the dignity associated with full-time, full-year work.

At least half of Western European countries provide family leaves with 100 percent wage replacement with the remainder offering 66 to 99 percent of the worker's former income. On average, workers are entitled to from 12 to 14 weeks of paid leave. France, Denmark, Finland, Italy, the Republic of Ireland, and Luxembourg permit longer leaves, although sometimes unpaid. In Italy,

[5]Mandated pension schemes proposed in the United States during both the Carter and Reagan administrations met with little success. The proposed legislation actually excluded part-time workers.

[6]Information on part-time workers is unavailable although it is likely that such workers are similarly unprotected.

workers are entitled to up to one full year of job-protected leave (Congressional Research Service 1988). Great Britain, the nation with the least comprehensive program, provides workers with a lump sum maternity grant and a flat national weekly allowance (Kamerman and Kahn 1981; Congressional Research Service 1988; Stoiber 1989).

Eligibility rules for maternity leave benefits vary across nations and, unfortunately, part-timers are sometimes excluded. In Great Britain, more than half of all pregnant working women, most of whom work part-time, do not receive full maternity benefits. But no distinctions are made between full- and part-time workers for the purposes of determining eligibility in Germany and Sweden (Stoiber 1989). In these two countries, previously full-time workers have the option of working part-time without jeopardizing their family leave benefits.

Historically, only mothers have been entitled to participate in national family benefit programs, reflecting national goals to promote maternal and child health and increase population growth. Many programs embody traditional conceptions of the household rather than any notion of gender equality. But fathers are being encouraged to take leaves so they can participate more fully in home life. The Scandinavian countries and Germany provide cash benefits to fathers who stay home to care for a newborn child while the mother returns to work. Despite Sweden's attempts to promote gender equality, women are more likely to take parental leave than men and are more likely to work part-time, particularly in the public sector where pay equity and full benefits obtain (U.S. Department of Health and Human Services, Social Security Administration 1986; Stoiber 1989).

Another element of family policy in Western Europe that is beneficial to part-time workers is the family allowance, which is a government payment based upon a family's number of children. It is provided on a universal basis in the majority of Western European countries (Austria, Denmark, France, Germany, Great Britain, Luxembourg, the Netherlands, and Sweden). In Germany, for instance, women receive generous paid maternity leave, plus a $360 monthly "child raising" allowance for parents of children up to age 3 (Woodhead 1991). Tax deductions for dependents and tax credits for low-income working families with children constitute the only forms of family allowance in the United States.

Most Western European nations have established child care systems that, in many instances, are integrated with the public schools. Generous family leaves and quality child care ensure that workers are not compelled to accept part-time employment exclusively because of child care responsibilities. Germany, Finland, Italy, and Spain provide access for three- to six-year-olds to government subsidized and monitored nursery schools (Olmstead and Wei-kart 1989). In Belgium, children are able to attend free universal nursery schools at the age of two and a half. The Swedish parliament passed legislation guaranteeing child care to all children over one and a half years beginning in 1991 (Sorrentino 1990).

Many governments designed their national child care systems to advance infant and child health and to serve the human capital needs of their economies. That such programs help working parents of young children is more by coincidence than national design. In fact, the dearth of infant care, most pronounced in Great Britain but apparent also in other countries, demonstrates the persistent gap between social policy and the realities of everyday working life. In contrast to the United States, however, Western European governments are increasingly aware that providing care to the children of working parents, especially given the increasing labor force participation of women with children, meets significant family and societal needs.

In the absence of appropriate public policy in the United States, trade unions have negotiated child care benefits with a relatively small number of employers (York, this volume). In most of Western Europe, national child care policies render these efforts largely unnecessary.

Equal Pay for Part-Time Workers

By statute, part-time workers in Belgium, France, Germany, Portugal, Spain, and Sweden must receive the same rate as full-time workers performing an equivalent job. In many of the nations without such statutory mandates, labor agreements assure that part-time pay is at the same rate as full-time for many workers. Many Western European nations also have set minimum wages that provide an income floor for part-time as well as full-time workers.[7] The principle of equal pay for part-time workers is likely to be broadly reaffirmed through European Community initiative. In contrast, in the United States, the Equal Pay Act of 1963 failed to assure that part-time workers receive

[7]In general, the nations of Western Europe have set minimum wages that provide an income floor for most workers, including part-time workers, although these minimums fail to substantially redistribute income to low-paid workers. Some part-time employees, however, are not protected. The United Kingdom determines minima for some industries through tripartite negotiations in wage councils. Former Prime Minister Thatcher excluded young workers from these protections. In the Netherlands, the minimum wage applies only to those who work at least one-third the normal workweek. The French minimum wage is indexed to the national retail price index, which retards the erosion of its purchasing power. U.S. part-time workers are covered by the minimum wage, but Congress has failed to prevent a substantial decline in its value.

equitable income with regard to full-timers; equal pay is not required in situations where workers have differing work schedules even if the work being performed is equivalent.

Even the most comprehensive pay legislation, however, cannot address certain structural problems in the labor market that contribute to the economic insecurity of some working women. Beechey and Perkins (1987) argue that part-time work, particularly where it dominates the employment options for women, reinforces women's occupational segregation. Part-time workers tend to be clustered at the bottom of the pay scale in far fewer occupations than full-time working women. Comparable worth legislation and the creation of quality part-time jobs in "men's" employment are needed to equalize wages and job opportunities across the part-time/full-time boundary.

Labor Policy and Employee Representation

Unionization is an effective route to greater justice for part-time workers. In general, unionized workers receive higher rates of pay and better employment protections than do unorganized workers. Most U.S. studies indicate that the union effect on wages is especially pronounced for women and members of minority groups (Hartman and Spatter-Roth 1989). Unions can also be instrumental in improving the job quality and career opportunities of part-time workers.

Unfortunately, American unions seeking to represent part-time workers face tremendous obstacles. Much of their difficulty derives from the opportunities labor law provides for employers to oppose unionization. The National Labor Relations Board is no longer effective in guaranteeing the right to organize without employer interference. Case backlog and pro-employer bias at the NLRB have emboldened employers to display increasing hostility to unions. The high turnover and easy replacement of part-time workers pose special difficulties to organizing. As a result, in 1987, only 8 percent of part-time workers were represented by labor unions (Kornbluh 1988; U.S. Department of Labor, BLS 1990).

In most of Western Europe, unions are in a much better position to defend part-time workers. Employers in Austria, Belgium, France, Italy, the Netherlands, Switzerland, Germany, and the Scandinavian nations cannot avoid unionism, as is the case in the United States. In Western Europe, employers generally accept the leadership of centralized employers' associations that include broad agreements with unions governing particular industries. These agreements ensure that each worker, full- or part-time, is represented and protected in broad terms. They dictate wage minima and other general conditions of work. In most cases, the terms of these agreements may be extended by law to all employers in the industry even if not all participated in the negotiations (Windmuller 1987:126–44).

In addition, works councils are mandated in many nations of Western Europe. A works council is a committee of workers (and managers, in Sweden) in the enterprise who must be consulted by management or who have joint responsibility with management over specific workplace issues. Part-time workers often vote and stand for election to works councils just as do full-time employees. Employers need the agreement of the works councils in order to effect changes of work time or the reclassification of workers, among other things. Works councils provide for the local application of national agreements (Windmuller 1987:10–15, 220–21; International Labour Office 1989:86). The combination of works councils and national agreements provides an effective framework for the protection of part-time workers.

Nevertheless, a few factors limit the success of this approach. Some nations limit the participation of part-time workers in representational bodies. For example, the Netherlands excludes those who work less than one-third the standard workweek, and Norway and France limit full participation to those who work at least half-time. Also, works councils are sometimes unable to employ adversarial tactics to influence the rate and quality of part-time work. Moreover, some works councils have used their powers to sanction the dismissal of women with employed husbands or to negotiate other terms that perpetuate the inequality between men and women and between full-time and part-time employees (Cook, Lorwin, and Daniels 1984:78). Lastly, as one critic observed of the decentralized system in France, "Many of these agreements, of course, have a narrow scope and amount to little more than the employer's unilateral decision endorsed by the unions of the company committee" (Amadieu 1988:119).

Many European unions have sought better part-time work options through negotiations. For example, the Swedish LO, the blue-collar workers federation, has been particularly aggressive in this regard. In 1980, the LO made the improvement of the conditions of part-time workers a priority in its negotiations with SAF, the leading employers' federation. It sought to guarantee part-time work of at least twenty hours weekly and to assure that no one worked more than five days per week. Other LO concerns were that part-time workers be fully informed about their rights and that local unions effectively bargain about the creation of part-time jobs (International Labour Office 1989:299).

The Swedish Commercial Employees Union has hired some of its own members to work part-time organizing small shops. The union has secured premium pay for late, weekend, and holiday hours for part-time workers in organized shops. The Swedish Municipal and County Workers Union, the National Labor Market Board, and public hospital managers devised career ladders linking lower-level jobs and more advanced, substantial jobs through training programs. Many nurse's aides and nurses (some seeking training as doctors), teacher's aides, and others who participated were part-time workers (International Labour Office 1989:233; Cook, Lorwin, Daniels 1992).

Swedish employers and unions have experimented widely with job sharing programs, in which two individuals share the varied responsibilities of one full-time position. Many participants are women with small children. The Swedish Metalworkers Union and other LO affiliates have endorsed job sharing in their collective agreements. Some British banks (for example, Barclay's) and a Dutch grocery chain have also introduced job sharing (Fredriksson 1988:397–404; Olmstead and Weikart 1989).

Phased retirement is another labor-backed innovation that has emerged in many nations but is particularly prominent in Sweden. Swedish workers between the ages of sixty and sixty-five may reduce their work hours and receive assistance from the public pension system. This simultaneously eases the adjustment of senior workers and boosts demand for new hires. Similar programs exist in Belgium, Denmark, Finland, France, and elsewhere. In France, the government and an enterprise, following consultation with employees, may negotiate a "solidarity contract" requiring the hiring of additional workers at the same time that some senior workers convert to part-time status. The government provides an income supplement to the latter group (International Labour Office 1989:137–57).

The British Trade Union Congress (TUC), especially its Women's Advisory Committee, has pressed successfully for coverage of part-time workers under worker protection legislation in Britain, and has compiled a checklist of appropriate strategies for unions concerning part-time workers, including recruiting part-time members, reducing union fees, lobbying for a national minimum wage, and bargaining for equal pay and guaranteed hours (International Labour Office 1989:306–7).

Some major national collective agreements in Italy now establish standards for part-time contracts. These standards stipulate that part-time employment should be voluntary and should not be limited to women. In addition, all the privileges of full-time work should apply (Cook, Lorwin, and Daniels 1984: 205).

Unrealized Potential of European Labor

Despite the progress made in Western Europe, the full potential of the reform of part-time work and the eradication of sexual inequality has not been realized. Many Western European unionists, like their American counterparts, remain ambivalent about the benefits of part-time work and have not resolved all of the tensions between those who desire full-time jobs and those who need part-time work. The interests of the traditional male work force and those of newly employed females are not fully reconciled.

The German labor movement's inability to gain full protection of female part-time workers is one example. German unions have devoted considerable effort to reducing the standard workweek. (I. G. Metall, the German metalworkers' union, won a 38.5-hour workweek in 1984 and is seeking a further reduction to 32 hours.) A shorter workweek has also been a priority for Danish and French labor. But such reform does little to help women who want more substantial reductions in daily work hours to accommodate family responsibilities (Cook, Lorwin, and Daniels 1984:81). In addition, German law explicitly permits collective agreements to set less favorable terms for part-time work in spite of the general policy banning discrimination. This inequity may reflect not only the German unions' ambivalent attitude toward part-time work, but also insensitivity to the needs of the mostly female part-time workers. German unions have insisted that a law to ban sexual discrimination is unnecessary; one American observer found evidence of "crass sexism" in German labor (Cook, Lorwin, and Daniels 1984:83–87; International Labour Office 1989:16).

European unions have been less than enthusiastic about the proliferation of part-time options. Concerns over the difficulty of enforcing labor standards and the ebbing of union strength are central. Many trade unionists claim that part-time workers are necessarily difficult to organize and service. National unions must insist that national agreements be respected, and this is more complicated when shopfloor workers seek to sanction varied options in their enterprises. Moreover, the proliferation of unorganized part-time jobs may undermine the bargaining power of full-time workers and may perpetuate the unequal status of women. But increasing part-time employment may lessen employer use of temporary and casual workers, who are more clearly an obstacle to union organizing and effectiveness. In addition, some unionists worry that part-timers may be capable of a faster pace of work than full-timers, motivating employers to institute a speed-up among full-timers. Finally, increasing part-time work may reduce the impetus for a shorter standard workweek (International Labour Office 1989:24–26).

One of the future tasks of European labor movements will be to enhance the democratic and egalitarian thrust of employee representation. Union representation does not automatically remedy the inferior employment position of women. To the degree that men and male concerns dominate unions, women's special concerns may be downgraded. In Sweden, for example, the negotiations of the Swedish LO and SAF have shown sensitivity to part-time concerns and have advanced part-time workers' rights, but the stubborn persistence of occupational segregation in the Swedish economy demonstrates the residual conservatism of a highly centralized male-dominated regime. Occupational segregation is actually higher in Sweden than in any other Western European nation or the United States. The concentration of women in part-time employment reinforces this segregation. The comprehensive benefits and equal pay inherent in part-time employment in Sweden reduce the economic disparities between part-time and full-time employment but social disparities persist, particularly in the area of training and entry into male-dominated professions and crafts. Swedish labor should address reforms in these areas in the future, so that women can move more freely into full-time work and men can avail themselves of decent part-time options (Ruggie 1986; Stoiber 1989).

Organized women's caucuses in many countries help pressure unions for more responsive policies. For example, a women's opposition within the Norwegian labor movement has sought a six-hour workday and sexual "equality agreements" in individual firms (Cook, Lorwin, and Daniels 1984:257). The effectiveness of such campaigns is enhanced if women's organizations and unions can explicitly connect their goals to the welfare of the community. Both are strengthened by the clear articulation of a public interest.

The Role of Labor and Social Democratic Parties in Protecting Part-Time Workers

Europeans have directly confronted part-time work issues in part because of the influence of labor and social democratic parties. Although the ideologies of these parties vary significantly, on the whole they favor the extension of the welfare state and the imposition of social controls over the operation of markets.

Like trade unions, Europe's left-wing parties also vary in their sensitivity to the needs of women workers. The French Communists, historically identified with the predominantly male industrial working class, are less likely than the Socialists to focus on women's demands for more equitable part-time options.

In the last decade, these parties have had to struggle with the implications of a global economy, state fiscal constraints, and, in particular, European integration. Moreover, the growing role of multinational corporations has tended to undermine national regulation programs. Labor and social democratic parties have, in many cases, successfully defended worker protections from attack, but they have also compromised some protections under pressure from multinational capital. (The French Socialists, for example, actually facilitated temporary work contracts in the mid-eighties.)

Many activists now argue that progressive labor programs can best be reinforced by appropriate actions at the level of the European Economic Community (Brown 1988). The British Labour party and the French Socialists, in particular, have placed new emphasis on the need for a coordinated strategy among European social democrats. Increased representation of Labor, Social Democrats, and Greens in the European Parliament has stimulated initiatives on the so-called social dimension of European integration. Only the British government under Margaret Thatcher and her successor, John Major, has sought to oppose enhanced worker protection at the level of the European Community.

Even within pro-labor political parties in Europe, there is considerable debate about the virtues of increased flexibility in labor markets as an appropriate response to the demands of international competition. British economist Guy Standing, writing in the *International Labour Review* (1986), argues that flexibility has two meanings:

> The forms of flexibility that unions and workers will favor are those allowing greater autonomy, such as the ability to have greater worker control over labor power and labor time, made possible by *stable* and *secure* opportunities to adjust work time through "flex-time," options to develop flexible patterns of life cycle activities, opportunities to combine multiple work statuses, opportunities to develop skills, and so on. For employers, acceptable forms of flexibility include the ability to shift workers from site to site, have workers and jobs that are interchangeable, use flexible payment systems, and have workers who do not involve high fixed costs.

The difficult task for labor and social democratic movements is to advance the first kind of flexibility while resisting the drive by employers, under conditions of intense international competition, for the second kind of flexibility.

Conclusions

Cross-national comparisons in social welfare policy and labor law provide useful insights into the possibilities and limits of public policy-making on behalf of part-time workers. Western European nations have successfully developed, or have attempted to create, part-time worker protections for equal pay, health care coverage, pensions, child care, maternity benefits, family and personal leave, and worker representation. The programs that most effectively serve part-time workers are universal benefits, such as national health insurance, that provide coverage to all citizens as a matter of right.

In a similar fashion, broad eligibility for maternity benefits and parental leave provide employment security for practically all working women in many nations—with the notable exception of Great Britain. These benefits, in concert with universal family allowances and institutionalized preschool, suggest a collective social commitment to the well-being of women and children in a manner not found in the United States. It is important to remember, however, that these programs were not designed to increase employment equity for women but to boost population rates and conserve human capital. Linking work and family policies to issues of human capital and work force quality may be an important strategy in the fight for family leave and child care policies in the United States.

While trade unions and social democrats have been instrumental in advancing the interests of part-time workers, the scope of reform has been limited by their ambivalence toward part-time employment. In many cases, the concerns of women workers have been subordinated to the interests of working men within centralized unions and political parties. To the extent that working women in the United States are granted opportunities to fully participate in organizational and national debates over part-time work, protections for part-time workers are more likely to promote the interests of family life without sacrificing the rights and interests of individuals.

Policies that fail to consider the division of labor within the home and its effect on labor force participation will fall short of equal treatment in the paid labor force. Similarly, equal pay provisions for part-time workers will be unsuccessful in improving the economic security of part-time workers if they are not accompanied by comparable worth measures aimed at removing the profit in occupational segregation.

The prospects for implementing Western European-style reform in the United States are stymied by differences in culture, in union influence, and, ultimately, in political structure. Given the declining number of unionized workers and without any alternate form of representation, the majority of part-time workers have few means of self-defense.

Surveys indicate substantial popular support in the United States for such reforms as universal health insurance, child care programs, and family and medical leave, yet such sentiments are not being translated into new policies. Union weakness in politics, disunity among the Democrats, and a hostile

Republican administration obstructed progress in the 1980s. The United States lacks a disciplined labor party. The Democratic party is not unified on issues of workers' rights. The U.S. labor movement traditionally has stressed negotiations as the primary means to meet workers' needs with diminishing returns as the union sector has declined. It is incumbent upon labor and Democrats to coalesce on a program of legislative protections for workers in an increasingly volatile economy (Jacobs 1989, 1990).

Comments

Maureen Martella

Flexibility is the mantra of the decade, intoned by businesses as the key to being competitive in a volatile economy and proclaimed as the answer for women who need to combine employment and family responsibilities. Flexibility is a propitious word; it promises adaptability, offers the possibility of compromise, implies rationality. As Sheila Allen (1989:238) queries, "Who would choose inflexibility over flexibility?" The "flexible work force" is offered as a mutually beneficial solution to some of the problems faced by employers and workers. However, not all of the mechanisms businesses have employed to achieve flexibility merit the positive connotations evoked by the word. Nor have workers been consulted about alternative work arrangements that would meet their needs.

In the name of flexibility, businesses have been revamping the way they contract for workers. They are reducing their long-term commitment to employees, eschewing their responsibility for employees, and transferring the escalating costs of employment benefits to workers. Employers' pursuit of flexibility has contributed to the growth of the contingent work force: workers in part-time, temporary, home-based, leased, subcontracted, and independently contracted jobs.[1] Contingent jobs are "bad" jobs; they offer low wages, few or no benefits, undependable income, little or no job security, and limited opportunities for training or advancement.

---

[1]Critics of these work arrangements use the term contingent work as a corrective to the implied positive connotation of "flexible work force." But the term is not conceptually precise. It is not clear, for example, if part-time work that is stable and benefited should be considered contingent. Nevertheless, contingent work provides a useful shorthand for discussing the kinds of employment processes and conditions addressed in the essays.

Although contingent work is increasing throughout the industrial world, this trend is especially damaging to workers in the United States, where the absence of broad-based, comprehensive social programs (such as universal heath insurance) and labor policies (such as family leave) means that the welfare of individuals and families is dependent, to a great extent, upon their jobs. In their essays, Engberg and duRivage and Jacobs conclude, rightly I believe, that the best response to this reorganization is to press for social programs and labor policies that ensure for all citizens the rights and benefits that currently are accorded only to individuals (and their families) with "good" jobs. Indeed, as duRivage and Jacobs report, some European countries have policies that provide greater protection and better benefits than are available to even well-situated workers in the United States.

Engberg believes that unions must try to eliminate contingent work and, failing that, to increase the standard of living of contingent workers. She proposes that unions organize contingent workers and bargain for economic parity, prorated benefits, and lower hourly thresholds for inclusion in bargaining units, as well as negotiate limits on employers' use of contingent workers. Engberg also describes union efforts to reappropriate the term flexible work to ensure that its conditions are beneficial for workers. She offers examples of union-bargained alternatives that do not sacrifice pay or job security: voluntary work reduction, job sharing, work sharing, in-house replacement pools, flextime, and child care. These union efforts are useful and important, but how extensively are these programs being implemented? And how does that compare with the number of nonunion workers who have access to these work conditions? Engberg also needed to provide more conclusive evidence that these alternatives meet the needs of women workers.

As duRivage and Jacobs recognize, in the context of decreasing rates of unionization and the concomitant decline in union power (as illustrated by employee givebacks and cost-sharing of benefits), union-based solutions to the problems of the contingent work force are not sufficient. In fact, the contingent work force is growing in part because of the decline of unions. For example, Lapidus (1990) shows that the timing of the temporary help industry's growth is tied to the erosion of the postwar system of labor relations. Golden and Appelbaum (1990) also demonstrate that this industry's growth coincides with—and is aided by—the reduction in union power.

Both essays accept the premise that employers are developing contingent work primarily to satisfy their own needs. An alternative interpretation of the changing labor market proposes that the flexible work force is developing in response to the number of workers, especially women workers, who want jobs that provide alternatives to the standard full-day, full-week, full-year work schedule. Part-time, temporary, and home-based jobs, in particular, are proclaimed to be ideal for women workers. Flexibility in this sense is deemed benign, indeed beneficial, because it allegedly provides options for women carrying the double burden of paid work and family responsibilities.

But do women want flexibility, and how do they define it? Are there alternatives that in fact match their expectations? Too often the needs of the workers themselves are assumed rather than verified. After all, it seems self-evident that women with families need to compromise their work life to fulfill their family obligations. Furthermore, it seems reasonable that women with husbands do not really need secure jobs with benefits. Not all women workers have identical needs, however. Nor is contingent work a single category. Rather, specific groups of workers and particular forms of contingent work should be examined to understand concretely their different conditions and consequences. Recent studies of temporary workers test some common assumptions and assertions about the labor force behavior, needs, and goals of women workers and about the employment conditions of temporary work.

In my study of women secretarial and clerical temporary workers in the Philadelphia area,[2] I learned that the temporary help industry overstates the proportion of women who register with them primarily to attain flexible work schedules. For most women, the decision to work as a temporary was not systematically related to family needs. Rather, they used temporary work as a substitute for regular full-time employment while in a transient situation: as an alternative to unemployment; as a route to permanent work, especially if they were looking for clerical or secretarial work; to support themselves while looking for permanent work in another field; to work between school semesters and not have to lie about their long-term commitment to a job; and to earn income when new to an area or in an area temporarily.

To be sure, there were women who temped to achieve flexibility. But, contrary to popular perceptions, these women did not have young children. In fact, it was older, married women who were attracted to temporary work by the promise of flexibility. They wanted flexible schedules so they could participate in other activities, not so they would have time to spend with their children. They were disappointed, though, because the type of flexibility

---

[2]The study involved a mail survey of ninety-six women who worked in clerical and secretarial assignments through temporary agencies in the Philadelphia area, in-depth personal interviews with twenty-three of the survey respondents, and fifteen interviews with owners and managers of eleven temporary agencies. Analysis of the data was supported by grant number E-9-M-5-0060 from the Women's Bureau of the U.S. Department of Labor. The report on the study, " 'Just a Temp': Expectations and Experiences of Women Clerical Temporary Workers," is available from the Women's Bureau.

available from temporary work is more constrained than not. Despite the rhetoric of flexibility touted by temporary agencies, few assignments actually allowed temps to work other than a standard workweek. Women who routinely wanted to work less hours a day or less days a week found that few assignments met their needs. Flexibility, therefore, really meant time off between assignments, without pay, sometimes by the women's choice, but sometimes because there were no assignments available. Temping allowed women to move in and out of the work force as they needed or wanted, but it did not help them to integrate work and other responsibilities on a daily or weekly basis.

In their advertisements, temporary agencies highlight flexibility as a main feature of temporary work. Women are promised that they can work "as little or as much" as they want. Indeed, in my interviews with owners and managers of temporary agencies, they asserted that "temporary workers have all the control in the world" over their work schedules. But they also confessed that the more flexible (that is, available) the workers were, the more likely they were to have temporary assignments. Industry representatives conceded that women with time constraints were less likely to have assignments that met their requirements. Here we encounter an ironic twist to the concept of flexibility, one that reverses the implied benefits of flexible work: the operational definition of flexibility means workers need to be available to accept any assignment the agency wants them to take.

My results corroborate the conclusions drawn from analyses of national data that temporary work is not essentially a life cycle choice for most women temps (Golden and Appelbaum 1990; Hartmann and Lapidus 1989; Lapidus 1990). In her analysis of 1985 Current Population Survey data, Lapidus found that temporary workers were no more likely to be married, to have children, or to live in a two-earner household than other women in the work force. Nor did temporary work draw into the work force women who would otherwise not be employed (Lapidus 1990). In my study, women with children did not spend more time in temporary work than other women. Temporary work does not offer distinct advantages for women seeking to manage competing work and family demands, especially women with young or school-age children. That temporary work typically is a relatively brief hiatus from permanent work or a prelude to permanent work (for younger women) further substantiates this conclusion.

The available empirical evidence does not support the contention that labor *supply* processes (the desires of workers) rather than labor *demand* processes (the desires of employers) are responsible for the growth in temporary work. Yet, some women do actively choose to work for temporary services and many workers have legitimate needs and desires for flexibility. Both essays recognize these complexities, and thus the authors implicitly raise the dilemma of wishing to be sensitive to and supportive of women who need, or want, to work less than full-time, full-year, while wanting to ensure that standard jobs are available to everyone who needs or wants one.

Working as a temporary meets some needs of some women—as does working part-time or at home or as an independent contractor. The solution is not to ban all contingent work. Rather, as the authors of both essays conclude, we need better protection for all workers so that the need or desire for alternative forms of work does not translate into inferior work conditions.

As duRivage and Jacobs note, women are particularly vulnerable to contingent jobs. The gendered division of labor in families ensures that women will continue to "need" flexibility. Occupational segregation restricts the jobs available to women and those jobs are more likely to be constructed under contingent conditions. As theorists of an emerging perspective assert, all social relations, including those that determine labor market processes and outcomes, are gendered (Hess and Ferree 1987). Even contingent jobs are organized differently depending on the gender of the expected work force. For example, Beechey and Perkins (1987) found that part-time work tends to be used when flexibility is needed for "female" jobs but overtime and reduced work hours are used for "male" jobs.

Just as labor unions face the dilemma of supporting flexible work without impairing the availability of "good" jobs or undermining the attendant employment relations, feminists too face a dilemma implicit in the proffered alternatives. In working to obtain alternative work arrangements for women, feminists may tacitly accept the underlying gendered division of labor that assumes that it is women who must compromise in order to combine paid employment and family work. Jobs should not be organized in ways that reinforce women's role as the primary family caretakers. To create genuine alternatives, feminists and unionists alike should work toward and support national policies that redistribute responsibility for family and paid work more equitably between men and women and that guarantee protection and benefits for all people.

Comments

Leslie Nulty

The structure of employment in the United States and Western Europe is becoming increasingly complex. The essays by Engberg and du-Rivage and Jacobs call into question how well existing public and private institutional arrangements can respond to these changes, particularly in the United States.

Taken together, the essays highlight the contrast between the United States and Europe. In Europe, duRivage and Jacobs demonstrate, private sector employers must comply with more extensive nationally legislated requirements for paid leave, pensions, and other protections, but they also benefit from a higher level of publicly provided benefits such as health care. This tighter safety net cushions the most disadvantaged members of the labor force against potentially damaging but unpredictable changes in the labor market. Because these societies have set a relatively high standard below which their labor forces are not permitted to fall, there are much greater constraints on employers' ability to seek higher profits through an assault on labor standards.

But in the United States, because protection from the vicissitudes of the market is provided (or not provided) primarily from the private sector, there is greater variability in working conditions and a greater premium associated with union membership. As Engberg's article shows, in the United States, an individual's total compensation (including wages and benefits such as medical care, retirement benefits, and paid leave) is largely determined by employment status and, within that context, subject to negotiation between the employee(s) and the employer. In the nonunion setting, those standards will be set either by employer noblesse oblige or by what the market will bear. In the union setting, the outcome of negotiation is a function of the relative strength of the parties. But because union strength has been under political and judicial attack for the past ten years—above and beyond the decline of union representation attributable to our changing economic structure—moving closer to the European standard has become more difficult. Nonetheless, Engberg's extensive review of recent organizing and contract innovations demonstrates the creativity and responsiveness of U.S. labor unions in coping with dramatic changes in the organization of work.

U.S. employers also have more of an economic incentive to avoid unionism than do European employers. The reliance on private contracts in the United States (whether explicit or implicit) has a built-in bias toward greater inequality in benefits for the economy as a whole than if the socially mandated floor were higher, as in Europe. The array of fringe benefits that many European workers have as right, by virtue of public law, is provided to only a minority of U.S. workers, mainly those employed by large oligopolistic firms. Outside this group (and sometimes within it), employers have an incentive to compete primarily on the basis of labor costs set by their lowest-paying competitor. Given the lower publicly mandated minimum threshold in the United States, the distance from the bottom to the average will be greater here than in Europe.

The three authors recognize the incomplete success of the U.S. labor movement in raising the social floor through legislative efforts. In recent attempts to increase the minimum wage, guarantee the right to parental leave, and address the medical care problem, organized labor has played a leading role, but has ultimately been forced to accept political compromises that fell far short of its goals. The contrast with the continuing steady improvement in social benefits in Western Europe could not be more stark.

Nevertheless, the situation in Europe should not be idealized. Many of the European labor standards duRivage and Jacobs cite have eligibility cutoffs that exclude persons working less than some minimum number of hours per week. Presumably, those excluded constitute Europe's "contingent" labor force, which is usually identified as heavily immigrant and from the Third World. Many of the European countries that have robust social safety nets have nevertheless treated their immigrant populations quite cavalierly, with mass repatriations of a sort that would not be acceptable in the United States. It could well be that there is a sharper differential in Europe between those workers who enjoy the full benefit of the social floor and those who fall outside than occurs in the more gradual labor standards continuum in the United States.

In the United States, protection is a function of private contracts that are regulated by law, especially laws against various forms of discrimination. Any union contract that discriminates too heavily against any represented group risks legal challenge. Unionization in the United States typically eliminates many of the "internal" inequalities in wages and working conditions found in nonunion workplaces. The European national agreements cited by du Rivage and Jacobs certainly confer this measure of equality on the employees of major employers party to those agreements, but the effect on secondary employers is unclear.

In general, the major distinction between the U.S. and European economic strategies adopted in the 1980s has been the United States' choice of a "cheap labor" strategy, in which the growth of contingent employment has been a major component. In most of Europe (successive Conservative governments in Great Britain being the major exception) that strategy has been rejected, in part, perhaps, because those societies place a greater value on social stability and equality. This choice has clearly not caused them any serious disadvantage—most have enjoyed stronger economic growth than the United States.

The development of contingent employment relationships in the United States may prove to be self-defeating quick fix responses to competitive or—in the public sector—fiscal pressure. Many firms are finding that contingent employees are expensive: oil and chemical companies that have expanded their use of subcontractors for some of their more hazardous jobs have found themselves exposed to greater liability as a less experienced work force has more frequent accidents. In the retail industry, companies steadily increased the percent of part-timers, reduced their hours, and encouraged high turnover. But as customers rebelled and training and supervision costs rose, firms recognized that higher profits could be made with a *more* stable labor force. As a result the UFCW has been able successfully to negotiate increased minimum guaranteed weekly hours—a demand members had sought.

In the United States (at least for the immediate future), private contracts will continue to set terms and conditions of work, and workers' needs for a more stable job climate will continue to conflict with employers' search for maximum profits and their tendency to operate with short-term calculus. Unions must accelerate their organizing to brake the growth of contingent employment and they must continue to reveal the hidden costs of contingent employment. Companies must be made to understand that they can do better with a stable, committed, well-trained labor force than with an unreliable, embittered, and economically desperate one. As Engberg and duRivage and Jacobs show, one part of this new way of doing business has to be an increase in the social support costs borne by *all* employers—a goal the U.S. labor movement will continue to pursue unstintingly.

References to Part III

Adams, Roy J. 1985. "Should Works Councils Be Used as Industrial Relations Policy?" *Monthly Labor Review* 108(7):25–29.

AFL-CIO. Public Employee Department. 1989."America . . . Not for Sale."

AFSCME. 1989. *Public Employee*. April.

Allen, Sheila, 1989. "Flexibility and Working Time: A Gendered Approach." In *The Redesign of Working Time: Promise or Threat?* edited by Judith Agassi and Stephen Heycock, 238–48. Berlin: Edition Sigma.

Amadieu, Jean-François. 1988. "Employment Flexibility, Unions, and Companies in France." *Industrial Relations Journal* 19(2):117–23.

AT&T and CWA. Bargaining agreement. 5/28/89–5/30/92.

Beechey, Veronica, and Tessa Perkins. 1987. *A Matter of Hours: Women, Part-Time Work, and the Labour Market*. Minneapolis: University of Minnesota Press.

BNA. 1987. *Work and Family Newsletter*. October.

Bronfenbrenner, Kate. 1988. "Organizing the Contingent Work Force." Prepared for presentation to the AFL-CIO Organizing Department. September 14.

Brown, Michael K., ed. 1988. *Remaking the Welfare State*. Philadelphia: Temple University Press.

Bullock, David. 1990. Southern Regional Coordinator, Local 535, Service Employees International Union. Telephone interview with E. Engberg. July.

Congressional Research Service. 1988. *Health Insurance and the Uninsured: Background Data and Analysis*. Washington, D.C.: Congressional Research Service.

Cook, Alice H., Val R. Lorwin, and Arlene Kaplan Daniels, eds. 1984. *Women and Trade Unions in Eleven Industrialized Countries*. Philadelphia: Temple University Press.

———. 1992. *The Most Difficult Revolution: Women and Trade Unions*. Ithaca N.Y.: Cornell University Press.

Cordova, Efren. 1986. "From Full-Time Wage Employment to Atypical Employment: A Major Shift in the Evolution of Labor Relations?" *International Labour Review* 125(6):641–57.

Cordt, David. 1990. Field Representative, Harvard Union of Clerical and Technical Workers. Telephone interview with E. Engberg. May.

de Neuborg, Chris. 1985. "Part-Time Work: An International Quantitative Comparison." *International Labour Review* 124(5):559–76.

duRivage, Virginia. 1991. "New Policies for the Part-Time and Contingent Work Force." Briefing paper prepared for Economic Policy Institute. Washington, D.C.

Employee Benefit Research Institute. 1992. *EBRI Special Report SR–14.* February.

Euzeby, Alain. 1988. "Social Security and Part-Time Employment." *International Labour Review* 127(5):545–57.

Frederiksson, Ingrid. 1988. "Current Information. Job Sharing in Sweden: Some Examples." *Economic and Industrial Democracy* 9:397–404.

Gregory, Judith, and Eileen Applebaum. 1988. "Union Responses to Contingent Work: Are Win-Win Outcomes Possible?" In *Flexible Workstyles: A Look at Contingent Labor.* Washington, D.C.: U.S. Department of Labor, Women's Bureau.

Golden, Lonnie, and Eileen Appelbaum. 1990. "What Is Driving the Boom in Temporary Employment?: An Economic Analysis of the Determinants of Temporary Employment." Report prepared for the U.S. Department of Labor, Women's Bureau.

Hartmann, Heidi I., and June A. Lapidus. 1989. "Temporary Work." Paper prepared for the U.S. Department of Labor, Commission on Workforce Quality and Labor Market Efficiency.

Hartmann, Heidi I., and Roberta Spatter-Roth. 1989. *Low Wage Jobs and Workers: Trends and Options for Change.* Washington, D.C.: Institute for Women's Policy Research.

Hess, Beth B., and Myra Marx Ferree, eds. 1987. *Analyzing Gender: A Handbook of Social Science Research.* Newbury Park, Calif.: Sage Publications.

Hewitt Research Associates. 1985. *Benefits for Part-Time Employees.* Lincolnshire, Ill.: Hewitt Research Associates.

Hoffman, Ann. 1990. Director, Professional and Clerical Employees Department, International Ladies Garment Workers Union. Telephone interview with E. Engberg. July.

Hoffman, Tom. 1990. Business Agent, Local 585, Service Employees International Union. Telephone interview with E. Engberg. May.

International Labour Office. 1989. *Conditions of Work Digest: Part-Time Work.* 8(1):32–39.

Jacobs, David. 1989. "Labor and the Strategy of Mandated Health Benefits." *Labor Studies Journal* 14(3):23–33.

———. 1990. "Comment on Murray and Reshef." *Academy of Management Review* 15(4):682–87.

Kaiser-Permanente Northern California Region and SEIU Local 250. Bargaining agreement. 11/5/89–10/31/92.

Kamerman, Sheila, and Alfred Kahn. 1981. *Child Care, Family Benefits, and Working Parents: A Study in Comparative Policy.* New York: Columbia University Press.

Kohl, George. 1990. Administrative assistant to the President and Director of Research, Communications Workers of America. Telephone interview with E. Engberg. July.

Kornbluh, Joyce. 1988. "Historical Perspectives on Part-Time and Temporary Workers." In *Flexible Workstyles: A Look at Contingent Labor.* Washington, D.C.: U.S. Department of Labor, Women's Bureau.

Land, Hilary. 1986. "The Unwelcome Impact of Social Policies on Women in the Labor Market." Paper presented at the Conference on Work and Politics: The Feminization of the Labor Force, Harvard University Center for European Studies, March 14–16. Cambridge, Mass.

Lapidus, June A. 1990. "The Temporary Help Industry and the Operation of the Labor Market." Ph.D. diss., University of Massachusetts, Amherst.

MacLennan, Emma, and Nickie Fonda. 1985. "Great Britain." In *Women Workers in Fifteen Countries: Essays in Honor of Alice Hanson Cook,* edited by Jennie Farley, 90–111. Ithaca, N.Y.: ILR Press.

McNichol, Liz. 1990. "Fighting on Many Fronts: SEIU in Los Angeles." *Labor Research Review* 15:37–44.

Nardone, Thomas J. 1986. "Part-Time Workers: Who Are They?" *Monthly Labor Review* 109(2):13–19.

Needleman, Ruth. 1990. "It's Never Too Late: Office Workers at Bethlehem Steel." *Labor Research Review* 15:81–88.

Nelson, Richard. 1991. "State Labor Legislation Enacted in 1990." *Monthly Labor Review* 114(1): 41–56.

9 to 5, National Association of Working Women. 1986. *Working at the Margins: The Growth of Part-Time and Temporary Workers in the United States.* Cleveland: 9 to 5.

———. 1990. "Fact Sheet on Working Women." April.

Nulty, Leslie. 1990. Director of Research, United Food and Commercial Workers. Interview with E. Engberg. July.

Olmstead, Patricia, and David P. Weikart. 1989. *How Nations Serve Young Children: Profiles of Child Care and Education in 14 Countries.* Ypsilanti, Mich.: High/Scope Press.

Pearce, Diana. 1985. "Toil and Trouble: Women Workers and Unemployment Compensation." *Signs* 10(3):439–59.

Portes, Alejandro, Manuel Castells, and Lauren A. Benton, eds. 1989. *The Informal Economy: Studies in Advanced and Less Developed Countries.* Baltimore: Johns Hopkins University Press.

Ruggie, Mary. 1984. *The State and Working Women: A Comparative Study of Britain and Sweden.* Princeton: Princeton University Press.

SEIU. Public Division. 1990. "A Voluntary Victory." *SEIU Public Division Update.* Winter.

Sorrentino, Constance. 1990. "The Changing Family in International Perspective." *Monthly Labor Review* 113(3):41–58.

Standing, Guy. 1986. "Meshing Labour Flexibility with Security: An Answer to British Unemployment?" *International Labour Review* 125(1):87–106.

State of Oregon and SEIU Local 503. Bargaining agreement. 7/1/89–6/30/91.

Stoiber, Susanne A. 1989. *Parental Leave and "Woman's Place": The Implications and Impact of Three European Approaches to Family Leave Policy.* Washington, D.C.: Women's Research and Education Institute.

Sweeney, John, and Karen Nussbaum. 1989. *Solutions for the New Work Force.* Cabin John, Md.: Seven Locks Press.

Tilly, Chris. 1990a. *Short Hours, Short Shift: Causes and Consequences of Part-Time Work.* Washington, D.C.: Economic Policy Institute.

———. 1990b. *Part-Time Employment.* Washington, D.C.: Economic Policy Institute.

UBA, Inc. 1988. "Highlights of State Unemployment Compensation Laws." Washington, D.C.

"UFCW Retail Food Industry Collective Bargaining Policy." 1988. *UFCW Leadership Update.* September.

U.S. Bureau of the Census. 1975. *Historical Statistics of the United States: Colonial Times to 1970.* Washington, D.C.: GPO.

———. 1989. *Statistical Abstract of the United States.* Washington, D.C.: GPO.

U.S. Department of Health and Human Services. Social Security Administration. 1986. *Social Security Programs throughout the World: 1985.* Washington, D.C.: GPO.

U.S. Department of Labor. 1988. "Comparison of State Unemployment Insurance Laws." January.

U.S. Department of Labor. BLS. 1988a. Unpublished data.

———. 1988b. "Labor Force Statistics Derived from the Current Population Survey, 1948–87." August.

———. 1990a. *Employment and Earnings.* Washington, D.C.:GPO. January.

———. 1990b. *Employee Benefits: Focus on Family Concerns in 1989.* Washington, D.C.: GPO. March.

Willis, Ron. 1990. Cleveland Joint Board, Amalgamated Clothing and Textile Workers Union. Telephone interview with E. Engberg. June.

Windmuller, John P., et al. 1987. *Collective Bargaining in Industrialized Market Economies: A Reappraisal.* Geneva: International Labour Office.

Woodbury, Stephen A. 1989. "Current Economic Issues in Employee Benefits." Paper prepared for U.S. Department of Labor Commission on Workforce Quality and Labor Market Efficiency.

Woodhead, Greg. 1991. "European Worker Benefits." AFL-CIO Report no. 55:1–4. September.

Part IV
Homework: Developing a Realistic Approach

The three essays in this section provide a basis for the reappraisal of the historic union policy of banning homework and the development of a realistic and nondiscriminatory policy toward homework and homeworkers. Eileen Boris reveals the mixed and at times contradictory motivations driving union policy toward industrial homework: at once altruistic, self-interested, practical, and short-sighted. She challenges the notion that homeworkers were unorganizable; that union policy was in the best interest of homeworkers; and that unions or the state are currently capable of effectively banning or otherwise regulating homework.

Both Judith Gerson and Kathleen Christensen probe the working conditions, attitudes, and organizational and legislative needs of the increasing number of white-collar homeworkers. Gerson, by comparing clericals at home and in the office, takes issue with the conventional portrait of the homeworker as underpaid, vulnerable, and lacking control over her working conditions. There is little evidence to suggest that clericals working at home would be more resistant to unionization or logistically impossible to organize. Indeed, because of their electronic ties and their off-site status, clerical homeworkers are already linked to one another and distanced from employer interference. Christensen reinforces this portrait of a plugged-in, networking work force whose ties and identity with employers are weak. Like Gerson, she cautions against developing a single approach for blue-collar and white-collar homeworkers or even for all types of white-collar homeworkers. The truly self-employed homeworker, for example, may be quite capable of self-representation and uninterested in unionizing. Homeworkers falsely categorized as "independent contractors," however, are not only potentially organizable but require new legislation specific to their situation.

As the commentaries by Dennis Chamot and Shelley Herochik reveal, the portrayal of union ambivalence toward homeworkers and the specifics of certain policy proposals presented in these essays may meet some resistance in the labor movement, but the ineffectiveness of the older approaches can no longer be denied.

8

Organization or Prohibition?

A Historical Perspective on Trade Unions and Homework

Eileen Boris

Testifying before a government hearing in March 1989, Jay Mazur, president of the International Ladies' Garment Workers' Union (ILGWU), predicted, "Legalized industrial homework will mean a return to unchecked exploitation of desperate immigrant workers; a return to the industrial dark ages of our history when the bosses wrote their own rules, the government shrugged as if helpless, and ordinary working men and women suffered cruelly; a return to a meaner, more brutal America which all of us long ago hoped we would not see again" (Mazur 1989). He was expressing the position trade unionists have held since 1877, when Samuel Gompers blamed the loss of the cigar makers' general strike on tenement house workers.

Mazur, like Gompers, represents labor's traditional response to industrial homework, or the giving out of materials by a manufacturer or contractor to be made up in the living quarters of a worker. Organized workers found the division of production between home and factory locations a barrier to their success in forcing employers to improve working conditions. They were revolted by the exploitative hours and wages in the home. When workers found that strikes and union contracts could not force employers to end homework, they turned to the state. When unions, bound by the legal system and hampered by the economic and political strength of their opponents, could not obtain the outright prohibition of homework, they pushed for regulation as a first step toward abolition. Over time they relied on a number of tactics: organizing unions, and organizing union contract and union label campaigns;

This paper was prepared with the help of a Howard University Department of History Research Grant. I would like to thank Sue Cobble for her help in clarifying my points.

forming alliances with reformers; lobbying for laws; watching over state agencies and working with them to implement laws. Not only was homework an evil in the minds of trade unionists, but all too often the women and children laboring under its sweated conditions became adversaries as well.

But a few sought to organize homeworkers rather than eliminate their livelihood. Today some—in both highly industrialized nations like Great Britain and the Netherlands and in developing countries like India—continue the attempt to empower homeworkers and improve their working conditions. In this paper, I will not only analyze the historic responses of U.S. unions to homework, but also assess whether these approaches make sense in the 1990s.

Early Campaigns: From Strikes to State Legislation

Homework developed as an integral part of industrialization. It was essential to the production of shoes, men's clothing, braided hats, and a host of other consumer goods. Although male tailors and cigar makers worked at home, most homeworkers were women (Boris and Daniels 1989:2–3; Albrecht 1982; Dublin 1985; Stansell 1983; Blewett 1988:44–67). This situation reflected women's responsibilities for the family and their disadvantaged position in the labor market, which stemmed from their family labor and the prevalent sex-typing of jobs, which emerged as early as the 1820s and 1830s (Kessler-Harris 1982:3–72; Stansell 1986).

Organized workers initiated campaigns to end the sweated conditions of homeworkers. Intra-class conflict stymied attempts by factory or inside workers to join with homeworkers against their common enemy, the exploitative employer who attempted to play the two groups of workers against each other. Gender, ethnicity, family status, and skill divided workers from each other, impeding unionization. This was particularly true among the Lynn shoemakers during their great strike in 1860, when the homeworkers, women married to men in the trade, rejected an alliance with the factory girls in order to fight for a higher family, or male, wage (Blewett 1988:97–141). Similarly, different perceptions of self-interest impeded organization of garment workers throughout the last third of the nineteenth century. But the chaotic conditions of that industry—which encouraged the practice of homework among the undercapitalized firms that scrambled for limited profits in the growing ready-made trade—hampered unionization as much as did worker diversity (Montgomery 1987:117–23; Lorwin 1924).

The consequences of this failure to unite homeworkers with shop or factory workers had far-reaching consequences in the cigar trade because of the lesson that future AFL President Samuel Gompers derived from the New York general strike of 1877. As one employer later reflected, "At the time of the ... strike, the factory hands were idle and the workers in the tenement houses were busy. The tenement-house system thus broke the strike and the labor unions have worked ever since to break up the tenement-house system." This was a self-serving memory, for the relationship between inside and outside workers proved less problematic in 1877 than it would become after the loss of the strike (Boris 1991a).

By the 1870s, a system of tenement house production had come to dominate cigar manufacturing in New York City. Bohemian immigrants rolled cigars in their homes under a family labor system: husband, wife, children, and boarders worked at ever-lower piece rates for firms that frequently served as their landlords. Led by the tenement house workers, about three-quarters of the trade walked out in mid-October 1877. They demanded higher wages in the midst of an economic depression.

Local 144 of the Cigar Makers' International Union (CMIU), which consisted of shop, or inside, workers under Gompers' leadership, organized a multi-ethnic central strike committee. Each shop, factory, and tenement sent delegates, with women factory workers and tenement house workers (men as well as women) having equal representation. From all accounts, the homeworkers were as militant, if not more, than other workers, joining the union en masse, throwing packages of tobacco out their windows, and preventing shop workers from going to work. Yet the homeworkers' more desperate circumstances and greater vulnerability drained finances and energy from the central committee. Employers soon began evicting the tenement workers, for whom the strike committee had to find housing. By mid-December, the employers imposed a lockout; picketing of factories and confrontations with police increased with the waning of the strike's effectiveness at the beginning of the new year. Despite an effort to maintain a single organization of workers with delegates from each shop, unity—between immigrants and native-born, women and men, skilled and less skilled, shop and tenement—had ended.

Gompers later recalled that the tenement house workers "all went out on strike without organization or discipline. We union men saw our hard-earned achievements likely to vanish because of this reckless precipitate action without consultation with our union." For Gompers, the tenement house worker, like the mechanical cigar mold, female labor, and Chinese coolies, was a tool employers used to drive down the wages and undermine the working conditions of the true cigar makers, skilled Northern European men. The CMIU could have built upon the eagerness of tenement workers to improve their conditions instead of turning on them and refusing them membership in the union as long as they labored at home. It focused blame not on the manufacturers, but on the unorganized and less skilled workers, often female and immigrant. Although, given the relative power of the employers and weakness of the union, this response was not unrealistic, it was not inevitable. After the great strike, the CMIU sought to eliminate tenement work through legislation to preserve the skills and position of its members in the factories.

Regulation of homework began with the CMIU's attempt to gain from the state what it had failed to convince employers to give up through union contract. In the early 1880s, after intensive lobbying by the union and with help from an unexpected quarter—the silk-stocking assemblyman Theodore Roosevelt—New York State passed the nation's first law prohibiting cigar making in tenement houses. The New York Court of Appeals struck down this law in 1885 (*In Re Jacobs*) as a violation of a man's right to contract, thereby limiting the shape of homework regulation until the New Deal. This decision confirmed Gompers and other trade unionists in their mistrust of the state as a tool of the capitalist class. Courts eventually would permit the regulation, but not restriction, of homework as a health matter. Thus the union label replaced legislation as the cigar makers' prime weapon against homework. This symbol of organization would insure that cigars and, later, garments, came not from disease-breeding, low-waged tenements but from decent, fair-waged workrooms. But union labels were only as effective as trade unions were strong (Boris 1991a).

From the start, the representation of the home as a private place, a central tenet of a larger ideological division of the world into separate sex-linked spheres, shaped trade union arguments against homework (Levine 1984). The cigar makers not only appealed to the state to uphold the public health, but Gompers condemned homework for undermining the working-class family, robbing men of their manhood and unfitting women for domestic tasks. Skilled male workers (especially cutters) in the fledgling clothing unions used the language of violated domesticity to object to the unfair economic advantages that accrued to employers who lessened operating costs through home workshops. They described with horror "SICK BABIES . . . LYING ON UNFINISHED GOODS" and pointed to workers thrown together in a half-naked state, "degraded" by sleeping twelve to a room so "that no such thing as privacy or modesty on the part of men or women is possible" (Kaufman et al. 1986:172–87; *Labor Leader* 1889; U.S. Congress 1893:104–7, 156–57, 96–99).

In 1891, organized clothing workers in Massachusetts passed homework regulation that would serve as a model for other states at the turn of the century. The Massachusetts law prohibited unrelated persons from making up clothing in tenement homes, a formulation that legislated against the male shopworkers' home-based competitors, who brought non-relatives into their homes to sew but allowed married women and their children to finish garments in their own homes unabetted. Limited by the 1885 *Jacobs* ruling, the law reflected the sex segmentation developing within the trade, where mothers seamed pants, stitched pockets, and felled cloaks at home. Later amendments required families to be licensed as a way to guard against clothing contamination, and clothes to be tagged in an effort to stop the importation of tenement-made items into the state.

New York passed a similar law in 1892. Drawn up by the Bureau of Factory Inspection with encouragement from organized labor, the law extended the licensing system to a wider variety of goods. That same year, Chicago trade unionists, led by the socialist-dominated Trade and Labor Assembly, pushed for passage of a law in Illinois to end the making of clothes in tenements. A broad coalition, dominated by the women reformers of Hull House, linked the end of tenement work with an eight-hour day for women workers and with restrictions on child labor. (The eight-hour section of this law was quickly declared unconstitutional.) According to the leader of the cloak makers, Abraham Bisno, although the public desired to protect itself against contagious disease, the trade unionists "wanted to abolish home work because it was possible for us to organize our people much more efficiently when large numbers of them were working in the larger shops" (Boris 1989; Bisno 1967:148).

Most nineteenth-century legislation focused on the consumer of homemade goods rather than its producers. Indeed, homework became legal through a tenement licensing system that sought to ensure a clean and disease-free environment. But legislators did nothing to stem the hours, improve the working conditions, or raise the wages of the homeworkers themselves. Laws curtailed child labor, fourteen-hour working days for women, and factory night work by women and minors, but these practices remained legal if performed in the home until 1913, when child labor prohibitions extended to homework. Trade unions supported reform efforts; in fact, Gompers served on the Factory Investigating Commission that pushed for such a revision (Boris and Daniels 1989:13–32).

A mixture of motives characterized the early campaigns against homework. Trade unionists wanted to be rid of low-waged competitors. Reformers, particularly the middle-class women who formed the National Consumers' League (NCL) and the cross-class National Women's Trade Union League (NWTUL), hoped to protect vulnerable women and children. Although they deplored the working conditions of homeworkers, women reformers especially emphasized the protection of the consumer and the preservation of the home. "We not only want a fair wage for the workman . . . but sanitary quarters for them," one NCL leader declared. "We don't want the germ of disease carried from the tenements." Some middle-class supporters saw in the NCL's white label an alternative to the union label; the NCL claimed that the goods bearing it were made in sanitary conditions, not in immigrant tenement homes. The intent behind the first union labels was to denote union-made goods rather than to guarantee the quality of the physical environment of production, which could vary even with uniform wages and hours.[1]

Protecting the family lay behind the demands of trade unions and reformers. But so did the reality that homeworkers (mothers, their children, and the elderly or disabled) undercut factory workers (men, and adolescent and single women). Homeworkers were a problem because they threatened the conditions of inside workers. Because they worked in scattered sites and negotiated with employers in an isolated, individualized manner, they also appeared as casual workers who could not be organized (Boris and Daniels 1989:13–32).

But homeworkers were not isolated. They performed their labor within a rich nexus of kinship and community. Whole neighborhoods would make flowers, pins, or pants. Often women worked together and traded information on contractors and prices. They would share child care, teach the work to newcomers, and train their daughters in the work. Even if their men were in casual trades without unions, they were still aware of working-class mobilization. Although we have no evidence that homeworkers participated in food boycotts before World War I, they lived where such community actions represented a form of class protest. We do know that homeworking tenants and their landlords struggled over rents and the housing conditions that were the basis of the licenses necessary to legally engage in such labor (Boris and Daniels 1989:53–74; State of New York 1922:102–4).[2]

The first time the federal government issued homework regulations was during World War I, when Secretary of War Newton Baker prohibited the making of army uniforms in tenements. Baker, the former Progressive major of Cleveland and then-titular president of the NCL, was responding to pleas from Sidney Hillman of the Amalgamated Clothing Workers of America (ACWA). Hillman argued that government contracts to nonunion firms were lowering the wages of his membership; moreover, some firms

[1]"Tailors Get Her Aid," *The World,* November 2, 1898, clipping in Scrapbooks of Maud Nathan, vol. 2, Nathan Collection, Schlesinger Library, Radcliffe College.

[2]For examples of homeworker community, see photographs and caption cards of Lewis Hine, Tenement House Scrapbook, National Child Labor Committee Collection, Prints and Photographs Department, Library of Congress.

were sending out their finishing to homeworkers. Much to Hillman's cha-
grin, when Baker created the Board of Control of Labor Standards for
Army Clothing, he included no trade union representative. Still, the creation of this agency convinced Hillman that the state was the proper
channel to go through to gain worker's rights—though the union excluded
homeworkers from the universe of workers in need of protection (Boris
1991b).

Politicans, such as the one in Albany who told a representative from the
ACWA's New York local, "We know why you don't want the tenement
homework, it's because you want the men to get all the work," viewed union
efforts against homework as stemming from self-interest (ACWA 1919). Certainly most unions wished to end homework rather than improve the conditions of homeworkers. Even so, they hoped that by reducing exploitation they
were helping to create better jobs that could be unionized. Unionized glove
workers in Fulton County, New York, were an exception to this attitude. By
the early 1930s, wage negotiations in this well-organized area, where homework was a customary practice, included home as well as factory workers. Yet
agreements always specified a lower rate for the homeworkers although they
were highly skilled and able to make a complete glove (Skinner 1938:54–55).

Before the New Deal, most unions strove to curb homework through
collective bargaining as well as through state regulatory legislation. The
contractual end of homework was not the same as stopping the system,
however. Despite its 1921 agreement with the major manufacturers in
Rochester, the nation's fourth largest men's clothing center, the ACWA
could not eradicate homework among tenacious contractors. Similarly,
when the United Neckwear Makers Union signed its 1927 contract with
the New York City trade (120 firms in all), four manufacturers left the
city rather than gradually end their use of homeworkers, as called for by
the agreement (*Advance* 1921; *The Survey* 1926; Waldman 1944:164–
174).

The New Deal: Triumph of Prohibition

For the most part, pre-New Deal trade unions were too weak to prohibit
homework without state support, and states had their most effective regulatory
weapon removed by the Supreme Court in the 1923 *Adkins v. Children's
Hospital* decision against the Washington, D.C., minimum wage law (Lipschultz 1989). When applied to homework, the women's minimum wage
raised labor costs and thus undermined the competitive advantage for em-

ployers who sent work to the home. Not until the changed legal environment
of the late New Deal could this strategy of extending protective labor law
function as a device to curtail homework (Boris 1986).

New York took the lead. Its 1935 homework law, based on a model drawn
up by the U.S. Department of Labor, did not extend protection of the factory
to the home. Homework was prohibited when it undermined the labor standards of factory workers and harmed the health and welfare of homeworkers,
and because wages and hours could not be regulated in the home. In essence,
reformers pronounced the licensing system, which merely controlled sanitary
conditions, inadequate (Shallcross 1939:66–67, 213–17).

The New York Women's Trade Union League (NYWTUL) mounted a
strong campaign for this act. It initiated the Labor Conference for the Abolition of Industrial Homework in the fall of 1934 in response to employer
attacks on the federal National Recovery Administration (NRA) codes of fair
competition, which either prohibited or seriously restricted homework in over
one hundred industries (Boris 1985). With strong financial and political
support from the ILGWU, the NYWTUL brought together representatives
from twenty-three international and local labor bodies, including the embroidery workers, the ACWU, the hatters, the cap and millinery workers,
men's neckwear, and the glove makers. Although men dominated the leadership, together these unions represented over three hundred thousand women
workers in the industries in which homework flourished. The labor conference
conducted a publicity campaign and sent members to lobby in Albany and to
testify at NRA code hearings in New York City.[3]

WTUL leaders were in direct contact with homeworkers, but the League
envisioned helping these women give up homework, not empowering them
as homeworkers. Elsie Gluck, secretary of the labor conference, reported that
"quite a number of homeworkers had come into the office [of the NYWTUL]
to register complaints on hours and wages." She suggested that the WTUL
"form these women into some sort of group" to enable the league "to get
information on a first hand basis . . . to show that the League spoke for
homeworkers, and to educate these women to the necessity of abolishing
homework." Members of the labor conference agreed to this idea in 1935,
but the ILGWU's Frederick Umhey questioned "whether organization of
homeworkers would not be contradictory to going on record for their aboli-

[3]Press release, NYWTUL n.d., and letter from Elsie Gluck to Fred Umhey, October 15,
1934, in Umhey Papers, 53–5, ILGWU Papers, Labor-Management Documentation Center,
Cornell University. This file contains numerous letters on the labor conference.

tion."[4] Indeed, Umhey was correct. Since the 1880s trade unionists and their reform allies had juxtaposed organization and abolition as opposite strategies, had chosen the end of homework over the empowerment of homeworkers, and had accepted the goal of the family wage over a cross-gender alliance of women working at home and in the factories.

Whether the NYWTUL actually ever tried to organize homeworkers is doubtful. It seems that the NYWTUL saw the homeworker as a resource for its cause, instead of viewing itself as a resource for homeworkers. As Gluck explained to Umhey, "The possibility of getting material from stories of homeworkers seems very good just now. We have made some valuable contacts with groups of workers in Harlem and in the Lower East Side." In addition, silence in the written records after 1935 suggests that the NYWTUL either abandoned the idea of organizing homeworkers, put little effort into it, or had little success in reaching home-based laborers.[5]

After the Supreme Court declared the NRA unconstitutional in 1935, trade unionists and their reform allies focused on revising state laws and passing new ones. They played a major role in shaping the administrative orders that resulted from the 1935 New York act. Hillman supported efforts to ban homework in men's clothing to prevent any return of the practice to his industry. The remaining orders—for men's and boy's neckwear, artificial flowers and feathers, and gloves—were often hammered out at private conferences between the affected trade unions and labor administrators. A homework committee under Secretary of Labor Frances Perkins drafted a model bill, based on the New York law, that was presented to the Conference of International Union Presidents in December 1936. Local federations of labor, like those in Massachusetts where a state homework bill passed in 1937, requested the AFL "use every available resource to urge and support the enactment by states of legislation prohibiting homework as a method of industrial production, and the enactment by the U.S. Congress of legislation designed to control and limit the passage of industrial homework across state lines." Massachusetts workers, fearing a competitive disadvantage, joined with those in other northeastern states with strong anti-homework laws (New York, Connecticut, Rhode Island, and Pennsylvania) to push for interstate compacts (Boris 1990).[6]

---

[4]"Meeting of the Labor Conference on Homework," January 14, 1935; Gluck to Umhey, November 15, 1934; both in Umhey Papers.
[5]Gluck to Umhey, February 7, 1935, Umhey papers.
[6]"Memorandum for the Secretary for the use in connection with the Conference of International Union Presidents," December 18, 1936, Clara Beyer Papers, box 12, folder 185,

The trade unions' viligance was crucial to the effective functioning of these new state statutes. As New York's Frieda Miller explained in *Justice,* the journal of the ILGWU, "from their intimate knowledge of the industry, the unions can be of invaluable assistance in reporting trouble spots. The law cannot be self-administered, for it would be impossible for the State to allow the tremendous sum of money necessary to police the entire State thoroughly" (Kline 1935).

In the late 1930s, the Fair Labor Standards Act (FLSA), mandating a minimum wage, paid overtime, and child labor restrictions, became the answer to the homework problem. Within days of its introduction in 1937, the ILGWU was advising, "there should be an 'industrial Homework' definition and a provision that Industrial Homework shall be prohibited on findings of oppressive labor practices" because "much of Industrial Child Labor . . . is involved in homework, to which regulatory standards can not be practically applied." Prohibition of homework went in and out as a specified element of the bill. Although not mentioned in the final version, homework was presumed to fall under the FLSA's mandate, "since the Act contains no prescription as to the place where the employees must work." In the minds of labor law administrators, the regulation of homework and its ultimate prohibition became crucial to the wage, hour, and child labor goals of FLSA (Boris 1992).[7]

But union representatives on the industrial boards under the FLSA pushed for the prohibition, instead of the mere regulation, of homework. During World War II, with labor and materials in short supply, they succeeded in banning homework in seven garment-related industries: jewelry, gloves and mittens, knitted outerwear, buttons and buckles, women's apparel, handkerchiefs, and embroideries. These industries shared key structural conditions that encouraged homework: undercapitalized firms and low capital requirements, fierce competition, unstable markets, and hand or simple machine processes. Unions had organized the largest employers in each industry and this partial organization provided the political pressure for homework restriction. Employer misuse of existing state and federal handbook systems supplied the rationale for the prohibitions. Congress incorporated these bans as Section

Schlesinger Library, Radcliffe College; Robert J. Watt, "Resolution Adopted by the Massachusetts State Federation of Labor . . . August 2, 1937," Beyer Papers, box 3, folder 50.

[7] Merle D. Vincent to Hugo L. Black May 29, 1937, in David Dubinsky Papers, ILGWU Collection, 81–7b; "Industrial Homework Records Regulation Announced," U.S. Department of Labor, Wage and Hour Division press release, February 18, 1939, DOL Library, Washington, D.C.

11(d) of the FLSA in 1949. Homework was legal in all other industries, as long as employers abided by the provisions of FLSA.

World War II also provided a rationale for New York State to restrict homework in all remaining industries through a general homework order in 1945. In the late 1940s, the United Office and Professional Workers of America sought a homework order for the direct mail industry. Although this left-wing union succeeded with the Department of Labor, pressures from subcontractors, the larger business community, and political conservatives led to the 1953 amendment of the state homework law to exclude typing and bookkeeping from the act, thus nullifying the homework order for the direct mail industry. For the most part, the homeworking typists and bookkeepers were married women. By the early 1950s, the focus on home typing reflected both the proletarianization of some forms of clerical work and a shift to business services as the growth sector for homework. New York State amended its homework law again in 1966 to exclude inserting, collating, and similar operations from the clerical exemption. In this case, new understandings of civil rights and the political power of labor overcame any sympathy for home-working women who were taking work away from what had become a largely minority female in-plant labor force in the direct mail industry. Similarly, in 1955 the Massachusetts state AFL had the political clout to lobby the legis-lature to pass a bill that automatically revoked the homework permit of "employers who become involved in labor disputes" (Commonwealth of Massachusetts 1955; Commonwealth of Massachusetts 1960).[8] Thus, the major unions turned to the state to end the use of homework as a strikebreaking tool, a strategy that persisted as long as the government shared their position on homework. At the federal level, this manner of enforcing homework re-mained effective until the hostile administration of Ronald Reagan in the 1980s; in some states, notably New York and California, it persists into the 1990s.

[8]For a summary of the New York orders, see State of New York Department of Labor, Division of Women, Child Labor, and Minimum Wage: "Trends in Homework Industries in New York State," typescript, August 1944, New York State DOL Library, Brooklyn; Inter-Office Memorandum, "To: Supervisions; From: George Ostrow," August 17, 1953, New York DOL, Division of Labor Standards, Brooklyn. For the growth of business services, Wage and Hour and Public Contracts Divisions, Division of Regulation and Research, Branch of Research and Statistics, "Employment of Homeworkers under the Fair Labor Standards Act," July 1959, pp. 20–21, mimeographed, DOL Library. For 1960s, State of New York Department of Labor, "Public Hearing on Proposed Homework Order Governing Insertion, Collation and Similar Work in the Direct Mail Industry," October 13, 1966, in New York State DOL Library. For Massachusetts, "Industrial 'Homework' Hit By Chaikin; Asks State Bill," [Springfield] *Daily News,* December 7, 1954, in Hattie Smith Papers, box 1, folder 9, Scheslinger Library.

Organizing Homeworkers

Unions in the 1930s also sporadically attempted to involve homeworkers in organizing campaigns, all of which involved Latina or Hispanic workers, suggesting that community or ethnic identity could transcend location of labor in defining group interest.[9] Factory-employed pecan shellers in San Antonio attempted to gain the cooperation of homeworkers while calling for an end to homeworking during a 1934 walkout. A 1937 ILGWU victory at the Shirlee Frocks factory in San Antonio occurred in part because of co-operation between factory workers and homeworkers (Blackwelder 1984:96, 139–41). Puerto Rican contractors in New York City organized the Hand Drawn, Hand Embroidery, Hand Faggoting, Crochet Beaders and Appliqué Cutters Association to represent both themselves and their workers. But when outsiders tried to organize Puerto Rican homeworkers, few responded. In 1934 New York City's Local 66 of the AFL was unable to attract more than sixty of the twenty to thirty thousand mostly Italian and Spanish-speaking home embroiders to an organizing meeting.[10]

More dramatic were the organizing drives of needlewomen in Puerto Rico, where cheap labor and abundant homework threatened employers and workers on the U.S. mainland. In the early years of the depression, needlework prices declined because manufacturers could get work made up in places like rural Pennsylvania for two cents an hour and avoid freight charges and Puerto Rico's cumbersome contractor system. In August 1933, inside and outside workers in Mayagüez, the island's needlework capital, struck for higher pay; police killed and wounded strikers who had stoned the workshop of a leading woman contractor. Union organization mushroomed throughout the island, with more than three-quarters of the factory and shop workers organized and about three thousand homeworkers forming nine of their own unions by 1934 (Boris forthcoming; Dietz 1986:175; Silvestrini 1986:66–69).

Although at least seventy thousand homeworkers in Puerto Rico (or 90 percent of all needleworkers) remained unorganized, shopworkers believed that their fate was connected to that of the homeworkers. Many inside workers could draw on their own experiences as homeworkers, and as one shopworker

[9]Previous organizing by male Jewish tailors in the 1880s and early 1890s at times also united tenement house and shop workers (Boris 1989).

[10]Statements of Mr. Pedro San Miguel and Mr. A. R. Hernandez to the NRA, "The Pleating, Stitching and Bonnaz and Hand Embroidery Industry," October 3, 1933, 256–76, esp. 273, transcript 231–1–06, RG9; statement of Mr. Herman W. Berger to the NRA, "Hearings on Application for Exemption on Hours from the Code of Fair Competition for the Novelty Curtains, Draperies, Bedspreads and Novelty Pillow Industry," September 20, 1934, 22–3, box 7123, RG9, National Archives, Washington, D.C.

from San Juan testified before the NRA panel charged with drawing up a special needlework code for Puerto Rico:

> What we want is that they earn the same amount of money as we do. A Woman who works at home does as good a job as the woman who works in the shop on the same kind of work, so I do not see why she is getting less money on it . . . we do not want women who do homework to be kept out of work, but we want them to be paid just and reasonable wages so that they can live decently. Their necessities are the same as ours.[11]

The needleworkers' unions strove to raise the pay of homeworkers as well as shopworkers and viewed homeworkers as part of their constituency, an approach not considered by garment unions on the mainland. Like their mainland counterparts, Puerto Rico's union officials demanded the gradual abolition of homework. During the code hearings, Teresa Anglero, president of the Insular Council of Unions of Needleworkers, exclaimed: "This is another kind of slavery, and the cry for liberty must be raised to free us from this slavery also . . . the home work is prejudicial to the health, the life and comfort of the worker, not only in the home but in the factory." Unions suggested the community workshop, branch factories where rural women could gather to work from two to six hours a day while leaving their children with relatives or friends, as an alternative to homework. Despite support from the U.S. Women's Bureau, such centers never were implemented. Instead, the U.S. government relied upon differential rates for labor standards in Puerto Rico rather than economic restructuring of the island (Manning 1934:14).[12]

The Return of Homework

Homework surfaced as a national issue in the 1980s. A routine Wage and Hour investigation in Vermont exploded into a conservative crusade in 1980 when a Republican senatorial candidate embraced the plight of knitwear employers and their homeworkers. The Vermont knitters portrayed themselves as mothers assaulted by the state and the unions. The Reagan administration used the incident to dramatize the need for economic deregulation and began lifting the federal administrative bans against homework forged fifty years before. The ILGWU—joined by the Amalgamated Clothing and Textile Workers Union (ACTWU), the Service Employees' International Union (SEIU), the states of New York and Illinois, and some employer

[11]Testimony of Gloria Rivera, San Juan, Puerto Rico, "Hearing on Code of Fair Practice and Competition for Puerto Rico Presented by Needlework Industry Code," February 28, 1934, and March 1, 1934, 197–99, typescript, RG9.

[12]Testimony of Anglero, in ibid., 233–36.

associations—challenged the administration in court. Although the legal challenge blocked the initial attempt to end all homework bans, the administration persisted and by December 1989 only the prohibition on women's apparel remained (Boris 1987, 1992).

The conservative outcry against homework and the resulting opposition from the federal government put the trade unions on the defensive. They faced a court battle on narrow legal grounds; the battle for public opinion was no easier. Jay Mazur portrayed homeworkers as victimized, undocumented immigrants whose lack of knowledge of their rights as workers threatened labor standards. Although desirous to improve workers' lives, the ILGWU could not overcome its negative portrait of the homeworker. The 1990 "Campaign for Justice" unionization drive, which sought to organize garment sweatshops, still emphasized the vulnerability of exploited workers even as it exposed employer disregard of FLSA and OSHA.[13] Similarly, Jack Sheinkman of the ACTWU couched his opposition in terms of labor standards. The AFL-CIO spoke of abuse, citing the appalling conditions faced by homeworkers (U.S. Congress, Subcommittee on Labor Standards 1987:47–73, 147–60, 163–68).

Meanwhile, deregulators crafted a discourse that associated homework not only with freedom from state regulation but with advancement of the working mother. As Secretary of Labor Ann Dore McLaughlin declared, "The changing workforce demographics demand that we provide employment opportunities that allow workers the freedom to choose flexible alternatives including the ability to work in one's own home. Women, for example, have entered the workforce by the millions; homework adds a measure of worker flexibility and economic freedom."[14] The *Wall Street Journal* editorialized that this form of labor "increases family choices in work and child care" (1988).

Slowly, opponents of homework began to counter such claims. In the late 1980s, the ILGWU found homeworkers willing to testify during government hearings. As a Salvadoran immigrant living in Los Angeles explained, "desire to save on child care expenses" had motivated her homework, but "it hadn't worked out." Journalists reported home typists who discovered "it didn't take long before things began to unravel: The children were at [her] elbow every minute demanding a tissue or a cookie or fighting with each other; the phone would ring or someone would be at the door and usually the day ended in full-blown chaos." Finally, union spokeswomen began to assert that "home-

[13]"Dear Friend" by Jay Mazur, September 1990; ILGWU, "Campaign for Justice," brochure for organizing campaign, in possession of author. I thank Sue Cobble for providing me with these documents.
[14]U.S. Department of Labor, Office of Information, "New Industrial Homework Rules to Take Effect," *News,* for release November 10, 1988.

work is, at best, a poor solution for the lack of affordable daycare," as Jackie Ruff, executive director of District 925 of SEIU, told one government committee in 1986 (Weinstein 1989:1, 4; Howard 1989:A24; U.S. Congress Subcommittee of the Committee on Government Operations 1986:95–96).

By the late 1980s, then, trade unions were beginning to shift their discourse on homework. First, they recognized that homework belonged to the U.S.'s larger economic restructuring, which consisted of offshore production, and part-time and contingent work. Such changes were creating a more marginal labor force and undermining a welfare state in which entitlements like social security and health care benefits were tied to employment. Opposition to homework belonged to this larger protest (Boris and Daniels 1989:260–61). Second, homework opponents no longer revered women only for their mothering role or promoted the male family wage. Reflecting the rise of feminism and the importance of women within the trade union movement, union leaders called for public support of child care so that mothers could work "in decent places" instead of being forced to take work into their homes.[15] Parental leave, employer financed day care, and flextime have all been part of recent contract proposals (Milkman 1985:302–22; Cowell, York, this volume). Although the rhetoric of homework opposition has shifted, the tactics of trade unions remain constant. The majority of unions continue to rely on the government—the courts, legislatures, and administrative apparatus of departments of labor—for change.

The garment unions and SEIU have led the battle against deregulation of industrial homework. In 1983 the AFL-CIO called for "an early ban on computer homework," and the Office and Professional Employees International Union (OPEIU) also resolved against electronic homework. But the 1989 AFL-CIO Convention backed off from such an absolute; it urged "the establishment of appropriate new regulations on homework to prevent exploitation of workers in offices as well as factories" (AFL-CIO 1989). This call for regulation, rather than outright prohibition, developed out of a reassessment of the political and economic threat of homework. It also derived from the success of a number of carefully monitored pilot projects, most notably those of The Newspaper Guild (TNG) and the American Federation of State, County and Municipal Employees (AFSCME), which regulated homework through collective bargaining. Unions also called for a renewed push for state monitoring of existing laws prohibiting homework (Boris and Daniels 1989:263–69; Christensen, this volume).

---

[15]Frederick Simms, testimony, State of New York Department of Labor, "Public Hearing on Industrial Homework," transcript of proceedings, April 2, 1981, 97.

But homework prohibition has been only as effective as the amount of state resources marshalled for investigation, and allocation of those resources has occurred only with pressure from trade unions and their allies, who often initiated complaints against illegal homework. Even New York State, where inspectors in the late 1930s and 1940s scoured the tenements for homework, operated by complaint from the 1950s until 1987, when it added an Apparel Industry Task Force to search out abuses of the labor law.

In short, prohibition would work only if business and labor could police the industry, a scenario that has depended upon the strength of organized labor. Historically, homework declined only after unions had organized enough workers within an industry so that lobbying for enforcement of prohibitory bans was in the interest of employers with union contracts. Despite the bans on homework in the garment trades, by the 1980s the decline of unionization made enforcement problematic. Competitive pressures, the arrival of cheap labor from Asia and the Americas, and the concentration of the short-term spot fashion market in New York City all contributed to an increase in homework and revealed the tenuousness of legislative bans.

Effective regulation proved even more difficult, because it entailed finding homeworkers who were not registered, going to individual homes, timing homework operations, and comparing the times with those of inside workers. Yet the kind of work done by homeworkers was often not the same work that inside workers performed. Work styles and operations constantly changed, making time studies obsolete. State and federal departments of labor never had enough staff to oversee home as well as factory workers. Homeworkers were difficult to find and there was an incentive for them to lie about their hours to maintain employment. Regulation fell by the wayside as a viable strategy because it seemed impossible to check all homeworkers (Waldinger 1986; Boris and Daniels 1989:103–29).

Unions outside of the United States, however, have devised alternatives to the kind of regulation practiced here and its goal of ultimate prohibition. The English, for example, attempted both to end the exploitation of homework and improve the lives of homeworkers. Homework was included under the Trades Board Act of 1909. That law provided a living wage for all workers in industries in which sweated labor had been a problem. It established boards, now called wage councils, to come up with fair wages.[16] The 1961 Factory Act asked employers to register homeworkers, listing the number of homeworkers and providing their addresses for inspection purposes. Under the

---

[16]The British, however, lack a minimum wage law; campaigns are now underway to secure that worker protection.

Thatcher regime, this system degenerated. But in the 1980s, feminists and leftists launched a number of locally based campaigns to organize and improve the conditions of homeworkers, most notably the Leicester Outwork Campaign. The Trade Union Congress (TUC) supported these campaigns, seeing in local organizations a prerequisite for trade union initiative; only when faced with already unionized in-plant workers who moved into homework did the unions initiate homeworker organization.

In 1984, many of these local efforts combined to issue the "Homeworkers' Charter" at the first National Conference on Homeworking. Demands included free and adequate dependent care for homeworkers, resources to allow homeworkers to meet together for mutual support, the legal status of employee (as opposed to independent contractor), the end to racist and sexist practices, adoption of a national minimum wage, amendment of relevant health and safety regulations to protect homeworkers and their families, and comprehensive training and educational opportunities for homeworkers. Such demands attempted to improve the conditions of homeworkers as workers as well as to increase their opportunies to choose other labor.[17] Although unions stand in a different relation to the state in Great Britain than in the United States, and are stronger, such an approach represents a wholly different attitude toward homeworkers than exists within our labor movement. British unions recognize them as workers with specific needs and problems, not as competitors or victims (Pennington and Westover 1989:102–25, 152–70; Allen and Wolkowitz 1987:153–58, 190–200; International Labour Office 1989:204–7, 235–39).

The Self-Employed Women's Organization (SEWA) of Gujarat, India, provides still another example. It is a union of the home-based, including industrial homeworkers, vendors, and agricultural laborers. It derived from the textile Labour Association's Women's Wing, but broke away as a separate organization in the early 1970s. SEWA, a cross-class/cross-caste organization of women, strives to empower homeworkers. It lobbies and defends the rights of its members and trains them as paralegals, provides them with credit through its women's bank, creates cooperatives, and gives them decision-making powers within the organization. At the same time, SEWA has worked to gain legal recognition for homeworkers from the state and the international community, calling upon the International Labour Organization to promulgate an international convention protecting homeworkers[18] (ILO 1989:227–28; Jhabvala forthcoming).

---

[17]To date, under unsympathetic governments, such demands remain unrealized.
[18]My analysis of SEWA is based on my visit to the organization in April 1989, as a participant

These alternative strategies raise a series of questions for trade unionists and feminists in the United States. Would organizing homeworkers, if not into trade unions then into community organizations, make sense in this country? Who should take the initiative: trade unions, women's organizations, local groups? Are today's homeworkers different from those in the past? Do we merely replicate the old myths that women or immigrants are unorganizable when we claim that homeworkers can't be organized, that they are isolated, and don't have a consciousness as workers?

Although these questions cannot be resolved quickly, there are immediate measures that could benefit homeworkers and perhaps facilitate organizing. First, we need to protect the homeworker legally through strict definitions of independent contractors, so that home-based workers who are employees are covered by labor law. Second, we must plan our workplaces with parents in mind, create satellite facilities to cut down on commuting time, and put workshops in apartment complexes or suburban neighborhoods. Third, we must stop focusing exclusively on those who are homeworkers and look more closely at those who profit from homework, paying attention to the suppliers—the contractors and manufacturers—and distributors of homemade goods. We can campaign against the outlets that sell homework made under exploitative conditions, expose manufacturers who subcontract to those who send out the work, and brand those who use homeworkers. The ILGWU already has engaged in such a tactic in its exposure of fashion designers who send out their work to be sewn in homes. Perhaps the tactics of the NCL nearly a century ago were ahead of the economic and communication trends that make consumer boycotts and negative publicity more effective tools today.

We have waged a defensive campaign against homework in the United States. But legal prohibition has never adequately addressed why women do homework and so hasn't done much more than inhibit the practice. If homework is representative of larger trends in the U.S. economy, then we have to change the direction of that restructuring. That way we can create conditions under which all women, including mothers of small children and recent immigrants, can truly choose their labor and not feel that homework is their only option. We must confront the conditions that impede women in the workplace, seeking to transform the environment that makes homework seem a logical choice for some women. In the long term, that means ending the privatization of dependent care and the ex-

in the ILO-Ford Foundation Conference on Home-based Labor at the Ghandi Institute, Ahmedabad, India.

pectation that women will care for children, the elderly, the disabled. Only when women know they can raise their children with dignity and without losing present or future income, only when living wages, parental leave, and dependent care are realities, will the homework problem begin to be solved. The union agenda for homeworkers must be the agenda for all women workers.

9

Clerical Homeworkers

Are They Organizable?

Judith Gerson

U nions have been steadfast in their opposition to home-based work, maintaining that the only viable policy on homework was to ban it. In part, their position was historically rooted in the assumption that homeworkers were unorganizable because they were isolated and hidden. Union opposition also grew out of a belief that homeworkers labored under inherently substandard working conditions, thereby jeopardizing the standards for all workers in the occupation. Union policy toward home-based work and the judgments underlying that policy are now being tested by governmental deregulation and by the growth of new forms of home-based work. This chapter, by looking afresh at the validity of historic assumptions about homework for contemporary workers, contributes to the unfolding debate about whether homeworkers can be organized or not.

The Assumptions of Homework Regulations

Homework regulation began at the state, not the federal level, and particularly within the needle trades. Massachusetts, New York, and other industrial states, especially in the Northeast, first initiated regulations of sweatshop tenement house labor beginning in the 1880s (Miller 1941; Boris, this volume). Early homework regulations were framed to ensure sanitary working conditions, not simply or even primarily for the sake of workers, but for the protection of consumers (Benson 1989; Miller 1941; Women's Bureau 1935). Thus, the earliest homework regulations were

Many thanks to Sue Cobble for her insightful comments on earlier versions of this essay.

often matters of public health, not labor issues. These statewide laws were largely unsuccessful in prohibiting homework, but by the early twentieth century, anti-sweating laws, in conjunction with increasingly successful organized labor campaigns against homework, and manufacturers' needs for greater efficiency effectively decreased the number of home-based sweatshops in several industries.

But the resurgent demand for homework during the depression, when thousands of women turned to home labor to compensate for the loss of other wages, counteracted homework regulations. In 1933, as the nation struggled to regain economic stability, the federal government stepped in and banned homework in 118 industries under the National Industrial Recovery Act (NRA). Moreover, the NRA codes prohibited child labor and set minimum wages and maximum hours for all workers, including the small numbers of homeworkers laboring in the industries where no homework ban existed. The NRA transformed governmental regulation of homework from a safety issue to a labor issue and established the precedent for federal labor regulation (Miller 1941). The NRA's success in prohibiting homework, however, was directly linked to union strength.

Records suggest that federal officials recognized that not all workers were alike and that some might benefit from working at home. A 1935 Executive Order, still in effect today, stipulates that employers can apply for a certificate of homework for any worker "unable to adjust to factory work because of age or physical or mental disability; or ... unable to leave home because the worker's presence is required for an invalid in the home" (Code of Federal Regulations 1987:178). This seeming anomaly of exempting aged and disabled workers and their caregivers from the homework ban while overlooking others, such as mothers with dependent children, reflected a growing sentiment among social reformers, the Women's Bureau of the Department of Labor, and union leaders that homework actually threatened women's ability to be "good mothers" (Boris 1985). But homework had its supporters. Prominent business leaders, in coalition with the Homework Protective League, championed homework in the 1930s, maintaining that it provided the means for women both to care for their children and earn money.

A 1935 Women's Bureau bulletin, "The Commercialization of the Home through Industrial Home Work," conveys the predominant attitude that the sanctity of the home would be violated by introducing home-based work. The image of women presented is one of a helpless or unknowing object of exploitation—a woman who could not know any better. She is an "easy prey to offers of work in her home" (Women's Bureau 1935:1). The bureau also reinforced the idea that there was nothing a homemaker could do to ameliorate or modify the dangers of homework. Industry "cannot give way to normal demands of home and children upon the housewife and mother. *When a home maker becomes an industrial home worker she must subordinate all home demands to the demands of industry*" (italics in original). Homework, the bulletin continued, resulted in family neglect, child labor, late-night work, and "demoralization of home as the family shelter from the stress and strain of the outside world" (Women's Bureau 1935:33). The overall image is one in which wicked industrial forces can overtake and transform the tranquil homestead. The female homeworker's primary problem was defined in terms of her neglect of her family; her needs as an individual or as a worker were not addressed. The woman who worked at home was a hapless victim, incapable of protecting either her family or herself.

The Supreme Court struck down the NRA in 1935, but efforts initiated under the NRA provided the basis for subsequent regulatory attempts under the Fair Labor Standards Act of 1938. The FLSA presumed that the very existence of homeworkers directly threatened the ability of on-site workers to secure protection for wages, hours, and prohibitions of child labor. And, since homework was isolated, it was virtually impossible to regulate, especially given the meager resources allocated to inspection; wage, hour, and child labor infractions could persist unabated. A complete ban on homework was the only option for securing the rights of workers. Following this logic, the federal government in 1942 outlawed homework in seven garment-related industries: knitted outerwear, women's apparel, jewelry manufacturing, gloves and mittens, buttons and buckles, handkerchiefs, and embroideries. Although these industries represented the greatest concentrations of homeworkers, and ostensibly provided the strongest challenge to enforcing the FLSA, they were also industries that had relatively strong unions.

With minor exceptions, the ban on homework in these seven industries went unchallenged for almost forty years. But in 1979 a federal Department of Labor inspector found a group of Vermont outerwear knitters to be in noncompliance with the FLSA. In response, the knitters and one of their primary retailers sued the federal government, claiming that the FLSA could not be applied to their work situations. Although they eventually lost, other knitters persisted and the ban against homework in the knitted outerwear industry was rescinded in 1981. By 1984, all employers using home knitters were required to register with the Department of Labor and keep detailed records of the hours worked and wages paid. To date, homework in the knitted outerwear industry remains legal (*ILGWU v. Donovan* 1983; Johnson 1986; Mazur 1986).

Two days after the 1988 presidential elections, the Reagan administration lifted the FLSA ban on home manufacturing in five of the six remaining regulated industries: jewelry, handkerchiefs, embroidery, buttons and buckles, and gloves and mittens. Government officials decided against lifting the ban in the women's apparel industry, in part because women's apparel had the largest numbers of organized workers and hence would elicit the loudest outcry (cf. Albrecht 1982). The government considered it prudent to allow for additional study and public comment on the ban in the women's apparel industry, anticipating a gradual, rather than an immediate and comprehensive, end to the homework ban.

In explaining the decision to revoke the historic bans on homework, then Secretary of Labor Ann Dore McLaughlin revealed the current set of assumptions informing governmental policy toward homework. "The composition of the work force is changing rapidly and will include more women, and there will be an increased need for handicapped and older workers. Homework adds a measure of worker flexibility and economic freedom which responds to the changing nature of the work force" (McLaughlin 1988). Her statement collapses women, handicapped, and older workers into a single category of workers in need of sympathy because of their special circumstances. The 1935 Executive Order is still in effect today, allowing mentally and physically disabled workers and workers too old to adjust to factory work, as well as those who had to remain at home to provide for their care, the right to be exempted from a homework ban. But McLaughlin adds women to these already protected categories. According to McLaughlin's conceptualization, women, handicapped, and older workers have private lives in need of special arrangements, whereas other workers do not.

The appeal to protect older, infirm, and handicapped workers and their caregivers as well as women with young children is echoed in statements by the National Alliance of Homebased Businesswomen. Interestingly, this organization's members also argue that the impact of homework laws needs to be considered for mothers as well as for the "increasing numbers of fathers who must work to support their families but wish to do so in a manner permitting them to see their children grow up," single parents, displaced homemakers, rural women, and the aforementioned groups. Their testimony before a Congressional subcommittee investigating clerical homework argues for homework because it is convenient for the worker; it exemplifies basic values of free enterprise; and it will help the United States maintain a competitive edge in international markets (National Alliance of Homebased Businesswomen 1986).

In contrast, union demands for regulation throughout the 1980s were gender-neutral, talking only of workers and employees. The 1983 AFL-CIO Resolution on Computer Homework calls for a ban on computer home-work and asserts that leaving the fast-growing occupation unregulated will have a "devastating impact on the well-being, wages, hours, and working conditions of home workers" (AFL-CIO 1983). In supporting a ban on office homework, the Service Employees' International Union (SEIU) em-phasized the potential harm to full-time office workers. "Homework is but one of a number of ways employers are replacing fulltime office work with jobs characterized by reduced wages and benefits and eroded working con-ditions" (*Service Employee* 1986).

Thus, unions and the government, first in concert and later in opposition, evoked a variety of arguments to defend or suppress homework. Attention was seldom concentrated on the homeworkers themselves or on their working conditions. Instead, consumer safety, the need to save women from unscru-pulous employers, protection of the family, sanctity of the home, safeguarding elderly and disabled workers, and preserving the rights of on-site workers overshadowed or supplanted homeworkers in these debates. Reformers tapped into culturally appropriate sentiments, sometimes even after protection had been secured, as in the case of exempting disabled and elderly home workers. Thus, reformers, supporters, and opponents framed their demands in dis-courses infused with culturally sanctioned values. These values shaped cam-paigns for and against homework, while homeworkers' needs remained ancillary at best.

Regardless of their position on homework, state and federal governments and unions voiced assumptions based more on emotion than empirical fact. Their assumptions about either the evils or unmitigated advantages of homework were so strongly formulated that they could not consider com-promises or alternatives. They never debated the possibility of organizing homeworkers. In addition, organized labor and, initially, state and federal governments did not believe homework could be regulated, and therefore it had to be banned. They presumed that monitoring a prohibitory statute would be easier and more successful than monitoring a regulatory statute, although, historically, both homeworkers and employers have shared com-mon interests in violating prohibitions (see, for example, Shallcross 1939:197). Furthermore, critics of home-based labor maintained that dis-regard of minimum wage, maximum hour, child labor laws, and standards for adequate working conditions was inevitable in homework, and conta-gious to factory workers. Casual arguments that the use of homeworkers exacerbates the exploitation of on-site workers, while intuitively logical, have never been thoroughly tested.

In other words, unions, governments, and voluntary associations developed their claims in ways that artificially represented homework as categorically good or bad. Of course, homeworkers *have* been terribly abused—they have often worked under unsafe and unsanitary conditions; their children have had to work; they have been paid below the minimum wage; and they have worked hours exceeding reasonable standards. But there have also been homeworkers who did not have these experiences. They worked a normal numbers of hours under sanitary conditions, at or above minimum-wage levels.

This heritage of unexamined assumptions and emotion-laden rhetoric has precluded serious consideration of homeworkers' organizability. At times, labor leaders maintained that organizing homeworkers was impossible and dismissed the issue, demanding instead that homework be abolished. At other times, government officials and trade unionists framed the debate in terms of problems potentially related, but not central, to homeworkers. These positions had the net effect of turning the question of organizing homeworkers into a non-issue.

The current debate about homeworkers needs to be informed by empirical research on the homeworkers themselves. In particular, we need data comparing on-site workers in specific occupations with home-based workers in those same occupations. Such a comparison is essential to ascertain if the working conditions of one group are inferior, and what the implications of these differences may be.

How Different Are Homeworkers?

A comparison of home-based and on-site work needs to begin with an appreciation of why people work at home, which is essential to evaluating the degree of control workers exercise in deciding where they work. Do they have choice, or are they trapped by a tight labor market, unscrupulous employers, and/or personal or familial demands?

The balance between choice and constraint with respect to home-based work may be revealed through demographic and social circumstances. A distinct demographic picture of home-based on-site clerical workers emerged from a national survey of home- and office-based secretarial workers I conducted in 1985 (see table 9.1).[1] Only 6 percent of the 214 on-site workers

[1]The present study of home- and office-based clerical workers is based on data the author

Table 9.1. Mean Differences between Office and Home-based Workers

	Unadjusted $\bar{X}$			Adjusted $\bar{X}^a$		
	Office workers	Home-workers	T value	Office workers	Home-workers	F value
Sociodemographic characteristics						
Age	36.58	42.35	−3.59***	—	—	—
% Married	50.70	79.01	−4.97***	—	—	—
% with children under 6 years	12.96	27.16	−2.59***	—	—	—
% with children >18 or childless	59.26	45.68	2.11*	—	—	—
Education (years)	14.02	14.23	.45	—	—	—
Personal values						
Importance of family	4.83	4.89	− .81	4.84	4.88	.33
Importance of religion	3.52	3.85	−2.01	3.52	3.89	4.20*
Importance of work	4.44	4.28	1.48	4.45	4.31	1.86
Careerism (Z scores)	.23	− .40	2.22*	.19	− .26	2.31
Gender roles (Z scores)	.80	−1.40	4.16***	.68	−1.44	13.17***
Reasons for choosing work site						
Flexible scheduling	3.55	4.74	−10.15***	3.57	4.72	50.60***
Freedom from supervision	2.74	4.19	− 8.89***	2.82	4.22	76.03***
Reduced expenses	3.40	3.81	− 2.53*	3.43	3.76	3.57
Need for child care	2.25	3.18	− 4.48***	2.27	3.15	17.75***
Personal preference	3.92	4.47	− 3.86***	3.95	4.39	6.62*

Work characteristics						
Paid work (hrs/week)	39.03	33.06	2.68**	39.48	32.63	9.74**
Paid work (weeks/year)	42.92	42.94	.99	43.42	43.52	.97
Domestic work (hrs/week)	25.06	34.16	−3.04**	25.34	35.21	8.90**
Paid & unpaid work (hrs/week)	77.21	76.90	.89	78.85	74.87	.31
Domestic division labor	1.28	1.50	− .94	1.29	1.52	.44
Firm characteristics						
% Owners	33.18	70.00	−5.98***	36	63	22.93***
Firm size (N workers)	5.61	5.07	.44	5.46	5.61	.02
Firm age (years)[b]	7.1	6.7	− .64	7.3	6.0	1.13

Source: Gerson (forthcoming).

N = 297.

*p ≤ .05
**p ≤ .01
***p ≤ .001

[a]Means adjusted for sociodemographic covariates: respondent's age, years of education, marital status, and age of youngest child.
[b]Years in existence calculated from August 1985 as baseline date.

and 5 percent of the 83 homeworkers were sixty years or older, thereby challenging the commonly held image of senior citizens as likely recruits for homework. The mean age of homeworkers, forty-two years, was higher than the thirty-seven years for office workers, but this reflected a skewed age distribution among the latter. One-third of the office workers were relatively young—that is, less than thirty years old in contrast to 14 percent of the homeworkers. This is not surprising since young workers often lack the resources (know-how, skills, finances, occupational networks) that would facilitate working at home.

Homeworkers, in comparison with office workers, were more likely to be married and to have preschool children. Differences between home- and office workers in the proportion married persisted even after controlling for the effects of age; distinctions in the relative numbers of workers with young children remained after taking age and marital status into account. The predominance of young children among women who work at home thus provides some confirmation of the stereotypic image of homeworkers as the mothers of young children who stay home to care for their offspring. One woman reflected the comments of many others: "I work at home so that I can watch and help my children grow. Although I don't see day care as necessarily bad, I feel that there is little point in having children just to turn them over to someone else."

Indeed, homeworkers devoted more time to domestic tasks—housework, child care—than did office workers (see table 9.1). Homeworkers, according to respondent reports of the number of hours they, other family members, and paid helpers spent daily doing domestic labor, devoted approximately nine hours more per week to housework and child care duties. This result held, even after taking into account age, marital status, and number of children. The domestic division of labor (a ratio of the respondent's hours spent doing

collected with Robert E. Kraut and Ann F. Smith in 1985 using a four-step sampling procedure: selecting geographic areas, identifying secretarial firms, identifying home-based and office-based workers within firms, and contacting workers. U.S. cities with populations between 98,000 and 109,000 people in the 1980 Census formed the potential pool of study sites. We randomly selected six cities within each of the four major Census regions for a total of twenty-four cities. For each city in the sample, we identified all firms listed under "secretarial," "typing," and "word processing" services headings in the 1985 yellow pages. We contacted 453 firms, of which 241 qualified. Of these, 222 agreed to cooperate, giving a response rate of 92 percent of qualifying firms. From each cooperating firm, we obtained the names and addresses of a maximum of three home- and three on-site workers. We identified a total of 106 home-based workers, of whom 85 percent returned questionnaires, and 260 office-based workers, of whom 87 percent returned questionnaires. The present analysis is limited to only the women in our sample because so few men work in these secretarial firms. For more detailed information on the research design, see Gerson (forthcoming).

housework and child care was divided by the sum total number of hours of housework and child care performed by other family members and paid workers) did not yield a significant difference between the two groups. The child care ratio, however, revealed a persistent difference between the two groups. Homeworkers assumed a larger share of child care work and this difference remained after controlling for the demographic factors. Moreover, working at home did not result in any significant savings on child care costs, despite the increased number of hours homeworkers spent caring for children. Home- and office workers had about the same number of hours of paid child care help.[2]

Demographic data, then, provide some indication of potential reasons for wanting to work at home. The presence of young children and the higher percentage of married women among the homeworkers is suggestive of, but not determinant of, decisions to work at home. To elaborate my understanding of why workers would choose home-based work, I asked respondents to evaluate the importance in their lives of six broad domains: family, work, leisure, friends, religion, and politics (Quinn and Staines 1979). Almost all respondents considered their families very important to their lives; homeworkers were no more likely to consider their families important than were office workers (see table 9.1). Homeworkers, however, were more apt to rate religion as being very important to them than were office workers, and this association remained after taking into account demographic differences. Consistent with conventional images of home-workers, they did rate the importance of work less highly than did office workers, but this difference was not significant. But, when asked to rate the importance of economic aspects of their jobs (job advancement, money, job security), values indicative of careerist attitudes, homeworkers were significantly less likely than office workers to claim careerism was important. The distinction in careerism dissolved though, after acknowledging demographic differences between the groups.

Along with a de-emphasis on some careerist values, homeworkers espoused more traditional values regarding gender roles. Homeworkers were more likely to disagree with both general egalitarian statements about gender relations as well as ones specific to equal employment opportunities (compare Mason and Bumpass 1975; Ryder and Westoff 1970). These

[2]The fact that homeworkers spend more time on child care, but spend approximately the same amount of money as their office counterparts reflects two distinct phenomena. First, homeworkers work at home in part to care for their children. However, homework is not in and of itself an adequate baby-sitter. Thus, given that homeworkers live in households with higher incomes, many meet their child care needs by hiring child care workers and baby-sitters.

differences persisted, moreover, after controlling for demographic factors. Many women made comments similar to this respondent: "I resigned a position with a company with which I had been employed for over ten years in order to be home with my child. The personal opinions of both my husband and myself are that a child deserves his or her mother at home at least for the preschool years."

What emerges, therefore, is a picture of home- and office workers that is simultaneously disparate along some attitudinal dimensions and similar along others. Homeworkers tended to hold more traditional values, particularly with respect to gender ideology. In addition, homeworkers valued religion more highly but "get-ahead" careerist attitudes somewhat less highly than did their counterparts. Although both groups valued family life equally high, home-workers did a larger proportion of child care themselves than office workers. On other attitudinal measures, however, significant differences did not appear.

Given the relatively high proportion of married women with young children among the group of homeworkers and the evidence of traditional attitudes among homeworkers in general, it is not surprising, therefore, that scheduling flexibility emerged as one of the strongest reasons offered for working at home (see table 9.1). Having a more flexible life-style is seemingly one of the few options available to women seeking to resolve the often competing demands of domesticity and paid work. Several respondents echoed one homeworker's claim: "If it weren't for the scheduling flexibility in my job, I couldn't and wouldn't be working, period."

Freedom from supervision was the second most frequently cited reason for working at home. Homeworkers confounded common assumptions that they work at home because they are unable to find conventional employment and/ or because they had an employer who required homework. When asked directly about their choice of work location, homeworkers were more likely than office workers to state that their "place of work is based on . . . personal preference." Although homeworkers with young children did not perceive as much choice in where they worked as other homeworkers, the general perception of greater choice among homeworkers persisted whether they had young children or not.

Explanations for working at home that emphasized changes in the work process, such as the ability to get more work done, working with fewer distractions, and having a self-contained job, ranked lower in importance than scheduling flexibility and freedom from supervision. Though some home-workers reported they chose to work at home because it meant saving money on commuting, clothing, and eating out, no single cost-saving measure was statistically significant.

Even though time flexibility was a major motivation for many to work at home, homework did not always produce that flexibility. Homeworkers were more likely to stop work earlier at the end of a typical business day, but then resume work after dinner. Moreover, homeworkers did some of their household and child care work during the normal business day. For example, at 11 A.M., over 20 percent of the homeworkers but only 4 percent of the office workers were taking care of a child or performing some other household task. While homeworkers were apt to work at their jobs until late into the night, office workers often rose before dawn to complete household chores before setting off to the office. But despite these differences, when total number of hours worked, including housework, child care, and paid employment, were added together, the result was the same for both home and on-site workers— seventy hours per week. Flexibility, it seems, was often the ideal homeworkers sought, and not the reality achieved.

From an analysis of the motivations behind work site selection, workers were clearly not coerced into their situation, either by calculating employers or poor market conditions. Nonetheless, their decisions were not fully devoid of constraints either. The need for flexible scheduling, largely a reflection of the need to care for young children, emerged as the strongest motivator. Homeworkers with young children were less likely than other homeworkers to report that their work site was largely a matter of personal preference. Other reasons clustered in two sets—the ability to work relatively autonomously in a self-contained job and a set of incentives including such items as fewer expenses and no commuting.

Comparing Working Conditions and Compensation

The structure of clerical work for the two groups was noticeably dissimilar. Office workers were more likely to be full-time employees, working an average of thirty-nine hours per week, whereas homeworkers clocked thirty-three hours weekly, indicating a propensity among homeworkers to be part-time workers. Although they worked approximately the same number of weeks per year, homeworkers had a slight tendency to work for somewhat smaller and newer firms.[3] The most striking distinction in work conditions, however, involved employee status. Seventy percent of the homeworkers were either owners of their own firms or independent contractors, as compared to only 33 percent of the office workers. Thus, while only one-third of homeworkers

[3]Neither of these firm differences was statistically significant.

technically could qualify as "employees," fully two-thirds of the office workers would be considered "employees."

Being self-employed, however, did not necessarily improve overall working conditions for homeworkers. Self-employed homeworkers, like other casual waged workers, lacked control over their work processes, and received low and intermittent pay and few, if any, fringe benefits (compare Allen and Wolkowitz 1987:172–75). Indeed, interviews with self-employed homeworkers substantiated this picture; many women voiced complaints similar to the woman who said: "I thought if I was self-employed and owned my own business, I'd be my own boss. Now I realize my clients are my bosses and I have about ten different bosses. I'm almost completely dependent upon them."

Table 9.2 indicates the type of monetary compensation workers received. For homeworkers, the most common form of compensation was piece-rate pay, either by the project or by the typed page; a salary was the least common form. In contrast, office workers were much more likely to receive salaries.[4] Homeworkers were also more apt to be paid through the firm's profits but less likely to be paid hourly wages. In sum, homeworkers, regardless of other demographic or economic differences, were more apt to be paid at a piece rate, while office workers were more likely to be salaried workers.

These strong and persistent differences in type of compensation connote an underlying trend in the reliability of income. Piece-rate payment is the most erratic form of payment, dependent on flow of work from clients or employer. It is the most characteristic form among homeworkers. Conversely, salaries are the most regular method and most common among office workers. Furthermore, piece-rate payment may force workers to work faster and/or longer hours to compensate for the low rates of pay, thereby adding to the normal pressures of the job. To the extent that a steady income is important to workers, homeworkers would seem to have greater cause for concern than office workers. Numerous homeworkers made statements similar to the following: "There is really no average day or week. Sometimes jobs come in bunches, all with deadlines; perhaps the next few days there will be very little— there's no way to plan on the work or on the income."

Homeworkers earned $1,700 less from their firms than did office workers. But this income difference was not statistically significant and was further reduced after controlling for number of hours worked. Conversely, total household income was significantly greater among homeworkers and reflected

[4]Differences between home- and office workers on piece rate and salary as forms of payment persisted even after controlling for the sociodemographic covariates as well as a combination of these variables and the work covariates of size and age of firm, seniority in firm, firm ownership, weeks per year worked, and hours per week worked.

Table 9.2. Association of Homework with Economic Outcomes

	Unadjusted X̄			Adjusted X̄[a]			Adjusted X̄[b]		
	Office workers	Home-workers	T value	Office workers	Home-workers	F value	Office workers	Home-workers	F value
Method of Compensation (%)[c]									
Profits	22.01	41.56	−3.08**	23	37	5.51*	27	26	.09
Salary	38.03	7.79	6.67***	38	9	21.53***	36	17	7.62**
Hourly wages	45.02	31.65	2.07*	44	34	1.87	42	36	.61
Piece rate	17.22	55.70	−6.20***	17	56	42.87***	20	51	22.94***
Compensation (1,000s $)									
Income from firm	10.18	8.62	1.54	10.06	8.07	4.13*	10.02	8.50	1.67
Household income	31.84	37.60	−2.30*	32.89	34.97	.73	32.52	36.35	1.90
Total firm compensation	11.66	8.88	1.39**	11.81	8.75	6.90**	11.59	9.66	2.56
Fringe Benefits (%)									
Respondent's health plan	29.86	14.29	3.05**	28	20	1.69	26	22	.34
Household health plan	53.09	44.44	1.25	52	48	.33	48	54	.61
Paid vacation	49.76	6.58	9.63***	50	9	40.16***	46	20	15.91***
Overtime pay	31.07	10.67	4.22***	30	15	6.31**	26	23	.11
Unemployment compensation[d]	44.88	6.76	8.37***	46	5	38.68***	43	12	20.82***
Social security[d]	64.08	29.33	5.42***	65	28	28.61***	64	35	15.35***
Pension plan[d]	9.41	10.67	−.31	10	11	.03	7	13	1.64

*p ≤ .05
**p ≤ .01
***p ≤ .001

[a]Means adjusted for sociodemographic covariates: respondent's age, years of education, marital status, and age of youngest child.

[b]Means adjusted for the above sociodemographic covariates and the following work covariates: size and age of firm, seniority in firm, firm ownership, weeks/year worked, and hours/week worked.

[c]Percentages do not equal 100 percent because frequently workers were compensated through more than one method.

[d]Employer contribution to unemployment compensation plan, social security benefits and/or pension plan.

the fact that a larger proportion of these households were dual-earner. After adjusting for the demographic differences between home- and office workers, however, household income rose among office workers and fell among home-workers, wiping out any statistically significant differences.

One of the most important material differences between home and office clerical workers was their fringe benefits. Office workers consistently had better health insurance and vacation pay, and greater employer contributions to their unemployment compensation, social security, and overtime pay (see table 9.2). Neither group received appreciable pension plans. Both married workers and older workers were less likely on the average to receive health insurance, and thus the gap between home- and office workers on health benefits disappeared after controlling for the effects of marriage and age. But disparities in benefits in paid vacation, unemployment compensation, social security contributions, and overtime pay remained after controlling for these demographic variables.[5]

As for health insurance, homeworkers seemed to be able to rely on the family coverage provided by their husbands' plans. Some women, however, could not count on husbands for health insurance and frequently this was a problem. One respondent commented: "I now make $7.00 an hour—good pay, but no benefits. I am now looking for another job—and willing to take less money but better hospitalization. The lack of benefits is very costly to me."

Finally, using the dollar value assigned to legally required and non-mandatory benefits for nonmanufacturing workers in 1985 (U.S. Chamber of Commerce 1986), I calculated the exchange value of the benefits that home- and office workers actually received. This estimate was added to the income earned from the firm to yield the total compensation from the firm. As can be seen in table 9.2, the total compensation of homeworkers was significantly below that of office workers. This difference continued even after taking into account demographic distinctions between home- and office workers. Once worker status was considered, however, the strength of the homework effect slackened. Working at larger firms on a full-time, year-round basis increased the total compensation received.

In sum, the economic picture for homeworkers is one in which they are relatively disadvantaged, but not to the extreme some have assumed. Despite the overall similarity in the actual work they do, home-based and office-based clerical workers had clearly different work experiences and rewards. Home-workers' incomes, though competitive in dollar amounts with conventional

[5]Differences in overtime pay washed away after controlling for the work covariates.

office workers', were based on qualitatively distinct work arrangements. They were more likely to be either owners or independent contractors and were also more likely to be paid either with firm profits or by piece rate. Thus, their income was more susceptible to economic fluctuations. In addition to these qualitative differences, homeworkers appeared to be at a significant disadvantage in terms of their benefit packages. Married homeworkers compensated for this disadvantage, in part, by relying on their husbands for health benefits, but other benefits could not be similarly salvaged or as thoroughly replaced. When the dollar value of benefits received was added to income earned, homeworkers' total compensation fell significantly below that of the office workers, although this difference reflected not only the worksite location but homeworkers' greater likelihood to work part-time in small firms.

Pros and Cons of Clerical Homework

Homeworkers were more likely to be married and the mothers of young children. These demographic factors, coupled with homeworkers' predilection for a more traditional gender role ideology and a de-emphasis on careerism, suggest that working at home represented a viable compromise between the competing demands of paid work and domesticity. Although demographic factors limited the degree of choice married homeworkers with children thought they had, even this subgroup maintained a stronger perception of their ability to choose their work site than did the office workers.

The persistence of perceived choice among these women also suggests a situation of relative congruence rather than conflict between domestic and paid labor. The decision to stay at home and work was consistent with the attitudes and belief systems of homeworkers. Valuing women's responsibilities for the home and family and devaluing careerist goals, homeworkers arranged their paid work so that it did not interfere excessively with their domestic lives. Viewed from an external vantage, domesticity and paid work embody a series of structural conflicts for women in general. But, for women with more traditional values, homework facilitated an accommodation, allowing them to fulfill their primary domestic responsibilities and their secondary paid labor demands concurrently. Thus, homework represented a choice within a series of constraints, but a choice that was consonant with their attitudes.

It is also true that marriage more directly facilitated homework by providing necessary material resources. For these women, marriage inevitably meant two adult earners in the household. The higher proportion of married women among the homeworkers helps explain the higher household income among this group. In other words, being married offered an economic cushion that allowed women to be secondary earners. Marriage also subsidized homework in another way by providing health insurance coverage to secretarial workers unable to obtain it through their own work.

Family subsidization of employment expenses extended beyond health insurance coverage. Household budgets of homeworkers helped underwrite the overhead costs typically paid by conventional employers. Subsidized rent or mortgage and utilities were especially important for small business owners who would find it more difficult to survive if they paid the full overhead costs of doing business. More generally, the subsidization of expenses and the sharing of income throughout the family suggest that the material costs and benefits of homework must be calculated at the level of the household as well as the individual. At an individual level, the material disadvantages to working at home are relatively high. Yet, when these costs are recalculated at the household level or when noneconomic variables such as traditional gender ideology are entered into the equation, the costs of working at home may be lowered.

Working at home was not the ideal solution, even for women whose beliefs were in concert with their decision and whose familial situations facilitated it. Homeworkers could not smoothly integrate their paid work with their domestic work, but cycled both, often within the same hour during the normal workday, and gave precedence to one or the other during "off" hours.[6] Working at home did not result in savings on expenses of household and child care helpers either.

Homeworkers were much more likely to be either firm owners or independent contractors, paid through profits or on a piece-rate basis and much less likely to be full-time employees and paid a steady salary. The meaning of these distinctions in terms of the security of a steady income cannot be minimized. Even though the actual earnings of home-based workers were not significantly lower and disappeared after controlling for number of hours worked, the absolute difference of $1,700 should not be dismissed given a base income of approximately $10,000. Moreover, the benefits homeworkers received were consistently inferior to office workers' packages with the exception of pension plans, which were minimal for both groups. While homeworkers were able to compensate for the lack of health coverage by relying on their partner's health

---

[6]Additional analysis not included here indicates that after controlling for gender attitudes, liberal homeworkers spent the same amount of time on housework and child care as office workers (Gerson forthcoming).

plan, no such within-household substitution was possible for other job benefits. The absence of full benefit packages for homeworkers compromised their economic autonomy.

Are Clerical Homeworkers Organizable?

Traditionally, unions have been most active and most effective organizing male, full-time workers in mass production industries. The U.S. labor force is increasingly becoming more female, more part-time, and more concentrated in the service sector. Clerical homeworkers, who are largely women working part-time in the secretarial service industry, are one population we might consider as candidates for unionization. But organized labor's traditional stance against homework, which seems to be as clear today as it was fifty years ago, has precluded any serious consideration of organizing homeworkers. Historically, the question of organizing homeworkers was not adequately addressed because trade unionists assumed home-based labor was anathema to on-site work, and thereby posed a threat to organized labor. When debates about the viability of homework surfaced, labor leaders frequently responded either in categorical terms of degraded labor or in near-universal terms of exploitation of all workers. Only rarely did they focus predominantly on homework itself, and even more rarely on homeworkers.

While organized labor's stance may be reasonable given its overall goal to organize workers, a more productive approach to the issue of homework might be to start from the vantage of homeworkers themselves. The idea of a "standpoint" suggests that people who share a common social location or set of experiences share realities that shape their understanding of the world. For instance, clerical homeworkers have knowledge about the work process that is distinct from that of auto workers. Neither group's knowledge or experience is superior or inferior to the other's, but they are different (see Collins 1990; Hartsock 1985; Jaggar 1983; Yeatman 1990). When trying to answer the question of whether to organize clerical homeworkers, the workers themselves have to be brought into the debate. Without knowledge of the realities of their lives, we are left answering the query from the standpoints of other groups, each with its own needs, predilections, and biases.

The empirical evidence on clerical homeworkers suggests that, in many respects, they share much in common with office workers. Their hourly wages are equivalent, the overall number of hours worked (waged and non-waged) is the same, and both groups put a high value on family life. The overlap between the two groups suggests that organizing clerical workers in traditional office settings has many of the same goals as organizing clerical workers at home. There are comparable needs for higher wages, for instance, among home and office clericals. Moreover, some of the differences between the two groups could facilitate successful organizing as well. Homeworkers stressed freedom from supervision as one of the key elements of their decision to work at home. Without potential threats of a hostile supervisor, homeworkers may be less afraid of joining a union.

Furthermore, many clerical homeworkers know one another, and use informal networks to seek professional advice and client referrals. These networks are in many respects nascent union structures and could be used as a basis for organizing efforts. Material differences between home- and office workers also provide clues for constructive organizing tactics. The lack of fringe benefits for homeworkers is a clear incentive for them to unionize. Finally, we need to recall that not all homeworkers are equally hidden or invisible. The yellow pages provided the sample for the present study. For some occupations in certain industries, the telephone book may yield a usable list of homeworkers to be organized.

Including clerical homeworkers in the analysis as active participants will allow us to consider anew how unions might respond to diverse groups of workers in ways that simultaneously support the workers and strengthen unions. If we stop treating homework as a singular, unified category in opposition to on-site work, it is possible to envision how organizing homeworkers would be beneficial to them as well as to their counterparts in offices or factories.

Thinking about organizing clerical homeworkers also raises the question of whether expanding the parameters of unionism beyond its current emphasis on mass production workers might revitalize organized labor more generally. The needs of a part-time female labor force engaged in service work are distinct and have to be recognized for successful organization and representation (Bronfenbrenner 1988). Perhaps, because we have a changing labor force, we need several models of employee representation. One possibility is the occupational unionism waitresses successfully used from the 1900s through the 1970s. Noted for its stress on occupational identity, portable benefits and rights, union control of the labor supply, and peer determination of performance standards, occupational unionism was advantageous not only to the workers and their unions but to employers who relied on union hiring halls for dependable, well-trained, and disciplined workers (Cobble 1991).

Of course, sweated labor still exists in the garment trades, for example, and banning rather than organizing this work might well be the preferred solution. But we should be careful not to overgeneralize and assume that all home-workers are alike. There is no singular set of work experiences we can call homework. Categorical definitions that universalize homework are not valid and do not assist us in determining whether to organize homeworkers or not. Nevertheless, my data support the conclusion that for clerical homeworkers union organization is a viable option. Yes, clerical workers at home or in traditional offices can and should be organized.

10
Reevaluating Union Policy toward White-Collar Home-based Work

Kathleen E. Christensen

The realities of work at home in the 1990s are more complex and varied than often realized. Although industrial homework continues unabated, particularly in the Northeast, West, and economically depressed areas of the Midwest, the largest concentration of homeworkers are in the service sector of our economy. According to the most recent Bureau of Labor Statistics (BLS) figures, nearly 60 percent of women who worked eight or more hours at home are in the service sector (Horvath 1986). Yet these range from the high-priced telecommuter to the harassed and overworked data-entry pieceworker. The existence of these nontraditional homeworkers raises questions for organized labor. Historically, organized labor concluded that homeworkers were impossible to organize and represent. The only feasible union approach was to seek a ban on homework, as the AFL-CIO did in 1983 (See duRivage and Jacobs 1989; Boris, Gerson, this volume). This assessment now seems unwarranted for workers in the service economy, particularly those in professional or semiprofessional white-collar jobs.

Other policy options must be considered by the unions. I provide an overview of who these white-collar workers are and a proposal for policy directions, not only in the sense of how unions can organize homeworkers but also how they can best represent their interests. Specifically, I have drawn on the experiences of the American Federation of State, County and Municipal Employees (AFSCME) in what appears to be the only case of organized clerical homeworkers working with a contract that allows telecommuting.[1]

---

[1] As of 1992 Local 1923 of the American Federation of Government Employees negotiated

Female Home-based Workers: Motives and Types

Much of the public debate indicates that mothers with children under eighteen are the prime candidates for home-based work. Yet the 1985 BLS figures indicate that, of the women who work thirty-five or more hours a week at home in nonagricultural industries, approximately 259,000 have children under eighteen, but almost 198,000 are women without children (Horvath 1986). Circumstances propelling these women without children to work at home are varied. Some are trying to reenter the labor force after years out raising their children, others are approaching retirement and need supplemental income, and others find that they have increasing responsibility for elderly family members.

Within this broad group of home-based women workers, three general categories must be distinguished according to their employment status (Christensen 1986; Chamot 1988). First are *self-employed workers,* those who genuinely are in business for themselves and who have the autonomy in the marketplace to set their rates and to exercise leverage therein. Next are *independent contractors,* those who for tax purposes are also self-employed, typically as sole proprietors, but whose legal status remains ambiguous. Third are *company employees,* often called telecommuters, workers who retain the rights, as well as the privileges, of full-time, in-house employees.

Home-based Business Owners

For many women, self-employment offers more opportunity and flexibility than does the current job market. According to the U.S. Small Business Administration, women-owned businesses are the fastest growing segment of the small business population. Between 1977 and 1982, the number of female nonfarm sole proprietorships grew at an annual rate of 6.9 percent, nearly double the overall annual rate of 3.7 percent. For those women with family responsibilities, a small business appears to offer autonomy in setting a work schedule that suits their needs. For those women who have been out of the labor market, self-employment may provide more opportunities for reentry than does the conventional job market.

Indications are that the home is the workplace for many women who are in business for themselves. According to the BLS's May 1985 figures, 9 million Americans worked at least 8 hours or more a week at home as part of their primary job and were predominantly wage and salary workers, implying that

---

a plan for a demonstration (pilot) project with the Health Care Financing Agency (HCFA). In effect, they negotiated a "memorandum of understanding" that describes a one-year pilot.

most of them were doing overtime work at home (Horvath 1986). For the 1.9 million people who worked exclusively in their homes in nonfarm-related occupations, two-thirds were women who averaged a 27.7-hour workweek and were likely to be self-employed. The reality appears to be that the majority of home-based workers who work exclusively at home are women who work part-time or on a self-employed basis.

Independent Contractors

Firms in the United States underwent profound changes in the 1980s as a result of downsizing, mergers and acquisitions, and the need to stay competitive in an increasingly global economy. In fact, between the beginning of 1980 and the end of 1987, the Fortune 500 companies reduced their work forces by 3.1 million, going from an aggregate of 16.2 million employees to 13.1 million.

This type of internal labor market turbulence has prompted many companies to rethink their overall staffing attitudes and practices. The traditional attitude that firms took toward their white-collar work force entailed permanent, or at least relatively secure, employment, with some notion of career advancement. Yet current staffing practices challenge that stance. Many companies now treat their personnel in much the same manner as they do their inventories, striving for a just-in-time staffing strategy to parallel their just-in-time inventory systems, which keep supplies and materials just sufficient to meet current demand (Plewes 1988).

This desire for elasticity in staffing has resulted in an ad hoc two-tiered work force in many U.S. firms (Belous 1989; Christensen 1988b; Christensen and Murphree 1988; Freedman 1985; Polivka and Nardone 1989). The first tier comprises a core of salaried employees on the company payroll toward whom the traditional attitude still holds. These core employees are accorded a relatively high degree of job security, perquisites, health and pension benefits, and opportunities for training and skill upgrading. The second tier includes a cadre of workers, many of whom are not on the company payroll, hired as self-employed independent contractors, temporaries, or casual part-timers. These workers have weak ties to the company, are generally hired for finite periods, often in a nonsystematic fashion, and receive no health coverage or other benefits. Many in the second tier previously worked for the firm as core employees. Examples abound in the publishing, television, and advertising industries of professional and technical employees laid off from the core tier and hired back as independent contractors, euphemistically referred to as freelancers, or supplanted by temporary workers. Many of these contract workers work out of their homes (Christensen 1986).

Another major area of independent contracting is in home-based clerical work. Although the data are not systematic, my research indicates that the practice occurs across industries but is very evident in insurance claims rating, office correspondence, and medical and legal transcription. Corporations do not always directly hire the independent contractors. They often contract the work out to local clerical services which, in turn, hire women to do legal, medical, and insurance transcriptions as well as insurance coding, rating, and day-to-day office work in their homes.

In the 1980s, for example, several West Coast insurance companies contracted out claims rating to a regionally based service that in turn contracted out the work to home-based claims raters, almost all of whom were mothers of young children. Other insurance companies, Blue Cross/Blue Shield of South Carolina being the most publicly noted, contracted out the work directly to their home-based claims raters, some of whom had previously been on-site employees. Across the country, small local typing services receive overflow work from local businesses that don't want to hire their own in-house secretarial staff; these services in turn contract the work out to women who sit in their homes and transcribe office correspondence and reports. In some suburban communities, a neighborhood woman will contract out this clerical piece work to fellow neighbor women. Court reporters and medical doctors also contract out transcription work, typically to home-based typists.[2]

These home-based independent contractors are often treated like, and expected to perform as, company employees. They receive work from only one company; they work on materials provided by that company; they are given strict quotas and turn-around times; and some are required to sign contracts stating that they will not take any similar kinds of work from competing companies. These contractors have very little independence; they are expected to behave as employees but have none of the benefits.

In fact, several corporations practice a form of place discrimination, altering the status of technical and clerical workers when they move from the office to the home. They switch them from being full-time salaried employees with benefits to independent contractors. One northeastern insurance company offered home-based contracting to new mothers who might otherwise have left the company altogether. In order to maintain their "employment" and work at home, they had to become contractors. It is unclear

---

[2]Some of this home-based work may be vanishing due to automation. Women I have interviewed report that court reporting and insurance claims rating are becoming increasingly automated and that they fear that their home-based jobs will eventually be phased out.

whether or not these women could have returned to the office as regular employees, as none of them had tried to do so at the time I interviewed them (Christensen 1985).

These contractors trade the dependability of a salary for the undependability of an hourly or piece rate, often with no guarantee as to the number of hours or projects. They make less than they did when they worked in the office, doing the same work. They lose all employee benefits, including health care, pension plans, paid sick leaves, and vacations. They become responsible for paying their own social security (FICA) taxes. They operate entirely out of the mainstream of the company, so they are not in the pool of candidates considered for job advancement, skill upgrading, or retooling. They often work in both isolation and ignorance of other workers. They rapidly become second-class corporate citizens.

Not surprisingly, despite their titles as "independent contractors," these women often think of themselves as employees. Some women told me that they did not even know they were hired as self-employed contractors until it was tax time. Moreover, there are legal tax questions as to whether these home-based clerical workers are genuinely self-employed contractors (GAO 1989). The confusion over employee status for the home-based clerical workers is tied to limitations in definitions and data collection procedures regarding contractors versus employees.[3]

Although the legal status of independent contracting is ambiguous, the question of whether a worker is an employee or a self-employed independent contractor for tax purposes generally depends on the following common law criteria cited in Sec. 3121 (d)(3)(c) of the Internal Revenue Code:

- How much control does the worker have over the execution of the work?
- What is the worker's opportunity for profit and loss?
- Has the worker made a large investment in the enterprise? Does he or she have a place of business and offer services to the public?
- What is the worker's skill level?
- How permanent is the relationship?

A genuine independent contractor exercises control over the execution and timing of the work, has the opportunity to gain or lose, has made an investment in equipment or capital, has a skill that allows him or her to

[3]For further discussion of independent contracting, see K. Christensen, "Independent Contracting," in K. Christensen, ed., *The New Era of Home-based Work: Directions and Policies* (Boulder: Westview Press, 1988); Donna Sockell, "Future of Labor Law," *Boston College Law Review* 30, no. 4 (July 1989):987–1026; and Donald Elisburg, "Legalities," *Telematics and Informatics* 2, no. 2 (1985):182.

compete in the marketplace, and is not in an enduring relationship with the employer. The corollary holds true: if the worker has little control over work hours, priority, or pacing of the work, has no opportunity to gain or lose, uses materials, tools, or equipment from the employer, and has an ongoing relationship with the company, then he or she is entitled to the rights and protections accorded by law to company employees. These include the rights to unemployment insurance, workers' compensation, employers' contributions to their social security (FICA) accounts, as well as wage and hour protections under the federal Fair Labor Standards Acts (FLSA) and individual state labor code provisions.

My research reveals that, according to these common law criteria, many women doing clerical work at home are being hired fraudulently as independent contractors (Christensen 1988a). Some women themselves have come to recognize the inherent inequities of the arrangement. A case settled out of court in California illustrated and challenged the corporate practice of contracting out work to home-based workers (MacKenzie 1986). In 1982, California Western States Life Insurance Company offered some of its insurance claims processors the opportunity to work at home instead of in the office. They would become contractors, paid by a piece rate and given no benefits. The processors, most of them women with family responsibilities, saw it as an attractive option—at first. They would have more flexibility and save the money and time previously spent commuting. Most of them joined the program in 1983.

On December 1, 1985, eight of the women quit their jobs and filed a suit against the company, claiming that the independent contracting arrangement was simply a subterfuge to avoid paying them benefits. They also claimed that the company kept increasing their quotas, sometimes forcing them to work fifteen hours a day, eliminating any flexibility. Collectively, the women sought $250,000 in back benefits and at least $1 million in punitive damages. The women claimed fraud on the part of the company. California Western's position was that the plaintiffs signed the contracts, knew what they were getting, and always had the right to quit. The case was settled out of court in May 1988, with the agreement that the terms of the settlement not be made public (Christensen 1990).

Subsequent to the filing of the lawsuit, Cal-West terminated its work-at-home program and closed its office in Sacramento. Had the case gone to court, it could have become a landmark case regarding the potential abuses of contracting out homework. For the time being, however, it is a case that served to caution firms to examine the potential legal and financial consequences of hiring home-based workers and independent contractors.

Home-based Company Employees

Home-based company employees are usually paid by salary, not on a piece-rate basis; are eligible for company benefits, including health care, pension coverage, paid vacations, and paid sick leave; and typically are considered for training and retraining or promotion opportunities. As such, these telecommuters retain close ties to the employer's culture.

According to a recent survey I conducted for The Conference Board, a business research and information institute located in New York City, 29 of 521 of the nation's largest firms offer work at home, often as a way to attract and retain the best people for their remaining core positions (Christensen 1989). Changing demographics have influenced the ability of U.S. firms to recruit and retain these high-quality workers. According to a 1987 report commissioned by the U.S. Department of Labor, U.S. population growth has leveled off, particularly among the educated middle class (Johnston and Packer 1987). This means that by the end of this century, the United States will have fewer workers trained for jobs that require education and technical skills. The consequences of the changing balance between supply and demand are two-fold: a tightening of local labor markets and an increasing mismatch between available skills and new job requirements.

U.S. labor markets are feeling the pinch. A recent survey of more than seven hundred human resources executives by the American Society for Personnel Administration (ASPA) reveals that 43 percent report problems finding qualified executives; 66 percent cite difficulties finding technical help (*Wall Street Journal* 1989). In order to attract workers, the study finds, higher wages are being offered by 58 percent of these companies, tuition aid by 52 percent, and better health benefits by 31 percent. All of these recruitment incentives are costly. Some firms are turning, therefore, to less expensive incentives such as flexible schedules, which include professional part-time, job sharing, and telecommuting as effective tools for recruiting and retaining the employees they want.

When properly designed, telecommuting can meet the needs of both the employer and many employees in tight labor markets. The telecommuting programs developed by Mountain Bell, Pacific Bell, and JC Penney are examples. Although unions were not involved in developing these three programs, many of their policy features would be important to negotiate in any union contract covering telecommuting. Mountain Bell and Pacific Bell view work-at-home as a scheduling device to attract and retain valuable employees, to reduce absenteeism, and to cut the costs of office space. Home-based employees maintain their employee status, are paid exactly what they would be paid if they worked in the office, and receive all of the health and pension benefits they would get as on-site employees. In addition, they are considered for promotion and training. The company pays for all equipment and telephone costs. Further, to ensure that the home-based employee maintains a high profile in the company, Pacific Bell requires employees to come into the office at least one day a week.

These telecommunication companies are not alone in approaching home-based work as a way to attract and retain valuable employees. In 1981, JC Penney decided that hiring telephone sales associates to work in their homes would open up an untapped labor pool—women staying at home with their children—because this new work site arrangement would meet the desires of these workers. It was also a way to handle the company's needs for peak staffing. If, for example, during a half-hour, Penney had planned for only five hundred telephone calls but then got one thousand, the company needed a way to respond quickly to the unexpected surge in demand. Penney saw home-based work as a viable alternative for handling peak demand. They now hire 206 associates, all company employees, to work at home in eight U.S. cities.

After nearly ten years with the in-home associates program, the company feels that it has benefited in a number of ways. Their program has tapped a labor market of associates who would not have been able to leave their homes to come to work; it allows the company to handle a sudden surge in demand; and the productivity for individual workers has remained the same or increased, although the company has made no added demands on in-home associates.

In addition, the flexible programs of firms such as these three may augur well for the type of enlightened and strategic planning that U.S. business increasingly needs as we near the turn of the century. As previously indicated, the pool of young workers entering the labor market will shrink, and those who constitute an increasing share of the future work force may have skills ill-matched to the jobs being created. The projected work force composition is forcing some large U.S. firms to think seriously about ways to retain their own valued employees. For these firms, a move toward a work-at-home alternative may be just one of many ways to cultivate good workers who need or want flexibility.

Union Policy Directions

The critical question regarding white-collar work at home is not what can be done to stop it, but rather, for whom is it advantageous and under what conditions? My research indicates that it tends to work best for the company employee who preserves all the rights, privileges, and federal safeguards, such as workers' compensation and unemployment insurance, that are part of employee status. It can also work for people who genuinely want to be in business for themselves and who choose to incubate their business at home for a certain period of time in order to minimize the failure rate of small businesses. It works least well for workers hired under questionable independent contracting conditions. Given this, what directions can unions pursue regarding people who do white-collar work at home?

Organizability of Workers

Under current labor law, independent contractors and genuinely self-employed business owners cannot organize and bargain traditional union contracts. But this does not preclude unions from organizing and potentially representing these workers through an associate membership arrangement. This new category of union membership, endorsed by the AFL-CIO in their 1985 report, *The Changing Situation of Workers and Their Unions,* allows those who are not part of organized bargaining units or covered by a union contract to join as individuals. They are eligible for certain union benefits although the union cannot bargain in a contract on their behalf.

Unions could use an affiliate or associate membership arrangement as a way to provide education and benefits coverage to self-employed home-based workers, particularly independent contractors. Of the 1.9 million who work exclusively at home, nearly 1.5 million are self-employed. One of the biggest problems that self-employed people face in the United States is obtaining affordable health insurance. Although many women who work at home without health benefits are married, losing these benefits through divorce could put them in precarious situations. One single woman I interviewed was a mid-level computer programmer. She worked as an employee for an insurance company and made $25,000 a year plus benefits. She left the company after she gave birth. Instead of a paid maternity leave, her employer offered her the opportunity to work at home as an independent contractor, which she decided to do. She earned $7,000 a year, with no benefits. Although she currently lives with the father of her child, she is not married to him and is ineligible for coverage under his health care plan. At the time I met her she had no health care benefits and no automobile insurance. She typifies the kind of worker who would benefit from an affiliate union status in which she could obtain the health insurance she could not afford on her own. Affiliation with a union could also alleviate the isolation of working at home.

Contrary to popular belief, most self-employed home-based workers are not "loners" but are "people-oriented" and often actively involved in setting up their own advocacy organizations, which they refer to as guilds. This is often true of the genuine business owners who use local yellow pages listings and word-of-mouth contact to seek out others in the community doing similar work at home. They typically meet once a month and share information on rates as well as how to handle and negotiate with clients. Unions that offered similar services might be quite appealing.

Unions could also draw on their internal educational departments to inform home-based independent contractors about their status and their legal rights to challenge that status. The unions could pursue labor law reforms that would extend representation for these home-based contractors, as well as lobby the IRS and federal and state labor departments to move to limit and enforce the legal definition of independent contractors. An isolated individual contractor who may be in a vulnerable or highly exploitive relationship with an "employer," may feel helpless to challenge her status on her own.

The opportunity does exist for unions to meet the needs of unorganized, self-employed, home-based workers, particularly independent contractors. These workers often have ongoing relations with one "employer" and could, in fact, be more accessible through computer hook-ups than the traditional industrial homeworker.

It must be re-emphasized that the situation of independent contractors differs markedly from that of the genuinely self-employed businesswomen who have leverage and autonomy in the marketplace. Although these businesswomen could benefit from potential health or pension coverage available from an affiliate membership, they would not necessarily require the representational or bargaining support the more vulnerable contractors might need.

Representing Home-based White-Collar Workers

Once organized, the critical question becomes whether unions can effectively represent home-based white-collar workers. The only example we have so far indicates that with certain precautions the answer is yes.

Only one union local in the United States has negotiated a formal contract regarding home-based employees. (As noted previously, some internal agreements for pilot programs are beginning to appear.) Local 2412 of the Wisconsin State Employees Union, which is affiliated with Council 24 of AFSCME, negotiated a contract in 1984 with the University of Wisconsin's Hospital and Clinics in Madison, Wisconsin, to allow a small number of employees who were doing word processing to work in their homes (Highman 1990). This contract represents one of the few, if not the only, labor union contract in the United States regarding computer-based work at home. This agreement is particularly significant, since AFSCME is the largest AFL-CIO union in Wisconsin and one of the largest unions in the United States. Because AFSCME represents a large number of clerical workers, it has ongoing concerns with their work site problems. Given the potential precedent-setting nature of this contract, it is important to lay out its origins and terms.

Telecommuting was introduced at the hospital partly because of operating constraints. In the early 1980s the hospital's transcription operation had reached the limits of its physical space. But although the work load fluctuated, it continued to grow, and the hospital was having trouble recruiting and holding onto experienced, skilled transcriptionists.

The transcription department was fully staffed on two shifts but could not keep up with the work load. Overload work was contracted out to a commercial transcription service, but the amount of work continued to grow. Costs went up, quality dropped, and the time needs of physicians were not being met. It became obvious that the department had to have more staff and a far tighter handle on production and quality controls.

At the same time, several of the transcription staff expressed an interest in working at home. They viewed it as an opportunity for more flexible work hours, better working conditions, and a reduction in work-related costs, such as commuting expenses and parking fees. They thought working at home would solve the work site irritations, major and minor, they experienced. The transcribers saw the possibility of mixing their job with personal and family duties, especially their child care needs.

The union began meeting with hospital managers in mid–1984. Out of their discussions came the operation that is now in place: home-based work stations for permanent staff employees. At the outset of the discussions, both sides recognized that each had serious, deep-rooted concerns. Local 2412, like all unions, was particularly concerned with the potential for wage and compensation abuse in operating home-based work stations. The university was uneasy with the potential loss of supervision and control over the confidentiality of patient records. There was concern about the practicality of vital clerical work being performed outside the traditional office. The union and hospital worked as partners and negotiated the contract and set up the program, which ran on a pilot basis for one year. Both sides felt that a trial period would provide the time to determine if it could work, and to find out what problems would develop and whether they could be solved in a mutually agreeable fashion.

The program, which included the criteria for selecting home-based medical transcriptionists, was formalized at the end of the year. The criteria included: willingness to work as a permanent full-time employee; ability to average 110 lines per hour; ability to maintain a 2 percent or less revision rate per week;

and ability to meet work environment requirements. Final selection of the home-based transcribers was, and continues to be, based on the seniority of interested employees.

The way work is channeled to transcribers has not changed. Physicians dictate information to a centralized medical transcription department word-processing operation through a special dictation system. Physicians gain access to the system by dialing from a regular phone and entering their personal identification number. Their dictation is relayed to a recording system located in the medical transcription department. The word-processing operators then transcribe from the recording system, regardless of their work site.

The home work site requirements are critical to the success of this program. The union and management specified fifteen conditions to be met by employer and employee. The employer must provide or pay for an ergonomically correct chair and table; adequate lighting in the employee's house, if not already available; a smoke detector; phone line installation and monthly charges; and maintenance of employer-owned equipment. The employer further ensures that, for security purposes, no home-based work station has direct access to any mainframe computer or central data base; no printers are provided or connected to computers, since the employee does not need to work with hard copy; and the office assigns the work to be performed on a daily basis.

The employee, like the employer, makes certain guarantees. The employee ensures that a separate work area or work space is available in the home, typically in a separate room; humidity and temperature levels conform with equipment needs; approved electrical outlets are available; equipment is used only for work assigned by the employer; and he or she agrees to work during established hours. Furthermore, the employee transmits completed work to the office at least twice daily or after four hours of work is performed and contacts the office at the beginning and end of each shift and each time that he or she transmits finished work.

A committee consisting of the safety director, plant engineering representative, director of medical records, and a union representative was established to review the location of each home-based work site to verify that the requirements are met, and the union reserves the right to perform a general environmental inspection to ensure the safety of the employee and the equipment.

The union also recommended that, any time a new home-based employee sets up his or her work station, these additional guidelines be followed:

- Employees should be informed about the potential problems of working at home, such as isolation, family stress, legal considerations, and dead-end jobs.
- There should be a trial period, with an opportunity for full reevaluation and withdrawal of participation.

- The signing of a written agreement that covers all aspects of homework, including safe and comfortable working conditions in the home, realistic work standards, access of the union to its members, and methods by which employees may opt in or out of the homework program.

Home-based employees working full-time are paid exactly what they would receive in the office and they receive full benefits.

The program has grown since 1984, although it remains relatively small. Originally there were three home-based transcribers and in 1992 there were seven.

All participants feel that the program has been highly successful and the results of telecommuting have been positive. Perhaps most significant is that the hospital's management has found that they were able to significantly reduce their dependency on outside contractors through the work-at-home project. This in turn has allowed for increased quality control and turn-around times and a significant reduction of overall costs. A company representative reports that the people working at home are 40 to 50 percent more productive than the people in the office. The employees have benefited by reducing their commuting time and costs and by being allowed greater flexibility in work schedules. The telecommuters maintain good relations with their office-based colleagues, even joining them for potluck dinners and baby showers. The union feels it has responded to the needs of its members by letting them work at home *and* at the same time protecting their work from being contracted out.

The union local's representative, Allen Highman, concluded that the program has achieved a good balance. "Our people have exactly the same coverage and protections as they would in the office, and the company paid the full cost for the equipment, the installation, and maintenance. There are huge pitfalls in something like this from our perspective if it's not done right, but so far everything here is okay."

Conclusions and Outlook

It is clear that unions have the potential both to organize and protect people who work at home. Clearly, strategies must vary according to the employment status of workers. White-collar self-employed workers at home would benefit most from access to affiliate or associate membership. The onus of responsibility for membership would fall on the worker, although unions could use the popular press to publicize the benefits of membership for these workers.

White-collar employees whose employee status is maintained can be represented through more traditional strategies, such as those of AFSCME Local

2412 at the University of Wisconsin Hospital. Basic principles—including the protection of employee status, the equality of wage and compensation packages regardless of place of work, and the insurance that home-based workers do not incur additional costs such as telephone and home insurance as a result of working at home—must be upheld. Furthermore, the AFSCME model solves the problem of inspection by shifting the burden from the employer to a committee.

When basic principles are met, employees can be protected regardless of where they work. The biggest potential pitfall for an employee would occur when a company wants to terminate her as an employee and hire her back as an independent contractor. Unions must work forcefully to avoid that, especially now that their efforts are strengthened by the call for more rigorous enforcement by the Internal Revenue Service of the distinction between employee and self-employed contractor (GAO 1989).

Comments

Shelley Herochik

The three papers in this section address the development of union policy on clerical and industrial homework. Together, they pose several important questions: How has the labor movement viewed the organization of homeworkers historically? What were the considerations of unions in establishing policy? Have those considerations changed over time, and has union policy changed accordingly? What direction should union policy on the organization of homeworkers take in the future? Each paper makes a significant and unique contribution to the debate.

Eileen Boris analyzes the labor movement's policy on industrial homework from a historical perspective. She is critical of the assumptions and policy choices made by unions and questions their motivations in banning industrial homework. Boris charges that unions have chronically blamed the victims of industrial homework for the terms and conditions of their work. Building on assumptions about the gender-typing of jobs that was prevalent as early as the 1820s and 1830s, she believes that unions fought to ban homework rather than empower the women who were the majority of industrial homeworkers.

A mix of middle- and working-class motives—primarily the protection of the consumer and preservation of the home—fueled the drive for early homework regulation. Particularly in the garment trades, unions condemned the practice of homework for undermining the working-class family and "violating the domesticity" of the home. According to Boris, unions also viewed homeworkers as a threat to the wages of skilled white males in factories and in some cases refused homeworkers membership as long as they worked at home.

Unions in the 1980s, Boris argues, shifted their discourse on homework but have been slow to alter their strategies. In her view, union opposition to homework is better directed to the larger issues of economic restructuring and the resulting marginalization of the work force. But homeworkers—many of whom work in organized shops during the day and are threatened with the loss of their jobs unless they take work home at night—disagree. They need more immediate and certain relief. In a series of seven Department of Labor hearings held in cities across the United States in 1989, more than one hundred witnesses, including homeworkers, union members, child labor specialists and consumer advocates, testified that the effects of homework were devastating and that the bans must be retained. They presented evidence that systems of regulation and registration have failed to protect workers and their children, and that enforcement is only as effective as rapidly dwindling state funding permits. In 1990, for example, only sixty-two New York City firms were fined for violating the state's homework laws. The total of the fines was just over $71,000. Homeworkers testified that promises of flexibility have faded with the reality of caring for small children while sewing dozens of sweaters over-night. None of the rhetoric has calmed the anxiety or improved the situation of a worker forced to choose between her job and her family. Unions with experience in the failure of regulation or registration systems remain convinced that banning industrial homework is the best choice.

Boris cites examples that raise the possibility of combining traditional with newer policies. Her suggestions include improving the conditions of home-work and increasing homeworkers' chances of choosing other forms of labor. In England, homeworkers are organized into local women's groups, where they are treated as "workers with needs" and not cast as competitors or victims. In India, the Self-Employed Women's Organization strives to empower ho-meworkers and to train them in skills needed to enter other fields of work.

These examples raise critical questions for the labor movement in the United States. Given the current political climate and the loss of membership and influence of the labor movement, newer and more experimental approaches may be necessary to address the problems faced by industrial workers regardless of the location of their workplace. Much of the labor movement is now considering ways to implement Boris's agenda. Unions are working toward a legal definition of independent contractors, so that they may be covered by the law. Although an arduous and time-consuming process, it could prove to be one of keys in controlling the spread of industrial homework in the future. Union leaders have a growing awareness of the changing composition and needs of their membership, and consequently have focused opposition not on homeworkers but on the contractors, manufacturers, and distributors who profit from homework. They have made it a priority at the bargaining table and have fought to strengthen and clarify their contracts in this area. Most unions have instituted skills training and upgrading programs that encourage the development of technology to make their industries more competitive and their members an integral part of industrial growth. Unions also offer literacy programs, assistance in legalization, citizenship courses, and voter registration and education programs to empower home and factory workers.

Boris's historical perspective is selective. She is prone to view the labor movement as a monolith and quick to make assumptions about the motives of union leadership. But she is right to be impatient, and her prodding comes at an opportune time. Union membership is at its lowest point in fifty years, and it is clear that traditional policies are unable to revitalize unions or shift the balance of public opinion. Her questions may prompt new answers.

Judith Gerson focuses on the differences between home- and office-based clerical workers to build a body of evidence in response to two specific questions: What are the comparative benefits and drawbacks of home versus on-site work? Are clerical workers organizable? Her analysis is confined to workers in one occupational category, clerical secretarial service, because variations between the kinds of work and the workers themselves are too profound to make generalizations useful. Her focus is one of the great strengths of her essay, and it has led her to conclude that there is no singular set of experiences that may be defined exclusively as homework. Extending her conclusions to union policy, Gerson notes that, while banning rather than organizing industrial homework "might well be the preferred solution," clerical homeworkers can and should be organized.

Gerson finds that, in general, home-based clerical workers are older than their office-based counterparts. They are more likely to be married, have more preschool and fewer older children than office workers, and shoulder a larger share of the responsibilities for child care and domestic work. Traditional values, especially religion, are more important to home-based workers than building their careers. The majority work part-time and are more likely to be paid by piece rates than to earn a salary. Although they have few benefits and have traditionally relied on the health and benefit plans of their spouses, Gerson has found that 70 percent own their own firms.

Workers' reasons for choosing to work at home—if, in fact, they have the opportunity to choose between office-based and home work—fall into two broad categories: scheduling flexibility and freedom from supervision. Gerson finds that the persistence of perceived choice within a given set of constraints, consistent with their values and attitudes, is characteristic of homeworkers.

But the reality of their situation argues against this perception. The home-workers who Gerson surveyed worked long, late hours, with their paid workload added to their already busy child care and domestic work schedules. Homeworkers who coordinated their own schedules with those of their employer, spouse, and children felt constrained and limited. The flexibility that they had anticipated was swallowed up by greater domestic responsibility. Child care was just as time-consuming. In fact, workers at home and at the office divided time equally among paid work, domestic work, and child care: approximately seventy hours per week. Similarly, workers who sought to cut down on the expenses of commuting and eating meals out found working at home to be as costly as working in an office.

Gerson charges that unions have never seriously considered the question of organizing homeworkers because their positions are rooted in a knee-jerk assumption that homeworkers cannot be organized. In her view, both unions and the state and federal government to which they turned to solve the homework problem have painted the question of organizing homeworkers in bold black-and-white strokes. Like Boris, Gerson believes that unions have often blamed homeworkers for their situations. She offers interesting and constructive suggestions to overcome that handicap, such as the model of occupational unionism that waitresses followed, with its emphasis on occupational identity, portable benefits and rights, union control of the labor supply, and peer determination of performance standards.

One of Gerson's contributions to the debate on organizing clerical homeworkers is her argument that the homeworkers' standpoint should be considered. Without their input, most unions will not have the perspective to determine how to design a successful organizing campaign. Although then Secretary of Labor McLaughlin, in defense of the Reagan administration's move to lift the ban on homework on protected industries in 1988, combined women, handicapped, and older workers "into a single category of workers in need of sympathy because of their special circumstances," Gerson believes that each group can make a unique contribution to organizing their peers. She argues that there is a real possibility for clerical homeworkers to be used in the recruitment and organization process. Her point is well taken. Since unions have found this concept very useful in organizing factory workers when traditional approaches have failed, why not apply it to homeworkers? Organizing staffs of most major unions now reflect the composition of their industry's work force in countries of origin and languages. They should also reflect the worksites of their constituency.

Kathleen Christensen addresses union policy regarding nontraditional homeworkers, ranging from well-paid telecommuters to overworked data-entry pieceworkers. While she agrees that banning industrial homework was the most practical position for the AFL-CIO to adopt in 1983, she finds that approach less useful for homeworkers in the white-collar sector. To answer her central questions—for whom is white-collar homework advantageous and under what circumstances?—she identifies three categories of home-based white-collar workers and suggests how unions can best represent them.

Christensen's analysis focuses on independent contractors. In contrast to self-employed workers, who enjoy autonomy and flexibility, and company employees, who retain all the rights and privileges of attachment to an established business, the legal status of independent contractors is ambiguous and their rights undefined. The uncertainty of their status is often an excuse for exploitation. They are subject to "place discrimination" and the loss of status and benefits.

What is most interesting about Christensen's analysis of independent contractors is the similarity between the work lives of these home-based workers and those of industrial homeworkers. She even uses some of the same phrases to describe their conditions: independent contract clericals often work "in both isolation and ignorance" of other workers; they are "paid by a piece rate" and "lose all employee benefits," and their employers "kept increasing their quotas, sometimes forcing them to work fifteen hours a day." Like industrial homeworkers, whose families, friends, and neighbors pitch in to respond to the demands of employers, these clericals contract out work to meet production quotas. It is not surprising that Christensen concludes that clerical homework is most advantageous for self-employed workers and company employees, and creates the most serious problems for independent contractors.

Christensen's policy recommendations emerge in part from her research on AFSCME Local 2412, which represents Wisconsin state employees. AFSCME negotiated a contract establishing home-based work situations for permanent staff employees with very specific criteria and requirements for safe working conditions. Most important, these home-based workers earn exactly what they would receive in an office and are covered by full benefits.

The AFSCME experiment has proven successful. Yet the question of to what degree other unions should follow their lead remains. Local 2412's experience in representing one group of clerical homeworkers is limited. Many other unions, especially those in the industrial sector, confront industries where illegal operations are flourishing and diminishing resources have made enforcement and surveillance impossible. In those industries, including the garment trades, workers are pitted against each other to compete for the few remaining jobs. Many live in the United States illegally and are afraid to participate openly in union activities like workers' committees. Still others work several part-time jobs to support their families and cannot take the time to aid in efforts to regulate the industry. Enforcement and regulation have proved to be inadequate, at best. Other approaches are needed to organize and protect workers.

In addition to pioneering contracts tailored to workers' specific situations, Christensen suggests that associate membership programs that offer educational and health benefits for self-employed workers and independent contractors would attract these home-based workers. Experience with associate membership programs has shown that if workers are provided with benefits that meet their needs, are offered a sense of group attachment, and are required to pay only reduced, affordable dues, they are likely to become associate union members. This is a long-term union-building strategy that will aid unions in future organizing, as more organized office and factory jobs are lost and the U.S. work force is made up of more part-timers and home-based workers. Currently, the cost of providing attractive benefits is a serious obstacle to the expansion of associate membership programs.

Lastly, Christensen recommends that unions work to reform labor laws and to extend their presence in national politics, specifically by lobbying the Internal Revenue Service and federal and state departments of labor to limit who can be legally defined as an independent contractor. Unions that have fought to protect workers from the effects of homework, including the ILGWU, have tried to clarify that definition since the 1940s.

The evidence presented by Boris, Gerson, and Christensen strongly suggests that, with constructive and supportive union policy and innovative organizing strategies, clerical homeworkers can and should be organized. The growth of the service sector, and the rapid changes in the nature of work and the composition of the work force, demand that unions focus their attention on organizing efforts targeting nontraditional potential members.

If unions decide that organizing homeworkers is necessary, they must be willing to challenge outdated assumptions and policies. They must call on rank-and-file leaders and activists, whose experiences in the field are invaluable to organizing. Most important, they must listen to the opinions of members and potential members and address their needs. If not, the growing gap between membership and leadership from which some unions suffer will make it impossible for them to meet the challenges of the future.

The policy challenges in the industrial sector are even greater. Industrial homeworkers, such as the soaring number in the garment trades, present a special set of problems for organizers. Although independent contractors' descriptions of their work lives sound disturbingly like those of industrial homeworkers, the similarities soon end. Female homeworkers in the garment industry are often single heads of households with small children. Their choices of work location are limited by the lack of affordable, safe child care, and as yet there are few child care facilities funded by coalitions of unions, companies, and government available to them. They may be recent immigrants with uncertain legal status who face multiple forms of discrimination. Homework is not a choice for these workers; often, it is their only option. Even those who work in organized shops during the day are told that they must take work home or risk losing their jobs. Homework employers set production quotas in response to their orders, so that finishing twenty dozen sweaters overnight is as common as no work for two weeks.

But it is the children of homeworkers who bear the biggest burden. They suffer in unmeasureable ways, from the direct pressure of exhausting and painstaking hours of work after school to the long-term effects of losing their childhood. Homeworkers who testified during the Department of Labor's hearings on industrial homework in the women's apparel industry spoke eloquently about the abuses of child labor inherent in the system. Marie Anne, an industrial homeworker in Miami, testified that "my children work with me as well. I have six children, four under sixteen years old. They all work on the garments. The two youngest are five and ten. They work to five hours a day, cutting threads, cutting elastic, folding and bagging and other jobs. On weekends, my thirteen- and fourteen-year-old children work at the sewing machine for the day." Eda Flores, a fifteen-year-old high school sophomore, said that while in junior high, she "helped Mother with the work she was sewing at home. I would operate the sewing machine and would work with scissors, cutting and trimming. I helped Mother three hours during the week and five hours a day on the weekend. I was lucky, I did not have any accidents with the machine or scissors but the material fibers and dye particles in the air gave me sinus problems. I fell behind in my school work and would get sleepy at school" (U.S. Department of Labor Hearings, April 1989).

As Frank Banks, director of the Chicago-based Midwest Center for Labor Research, noted in his testimony: "Children, even of a very young age, are often recruited to help their parents meet the frantic production pace that is usually demanded. That's not day care, that's child labor, and it's supposed to have been illegal in the United States for several decades" (U.S. Department of Labor Hearings, March 1989).

The garment industry itself is in crisis. Flourishing sweatshops and unrestricted competition of imports from low-wage countries have driven marginal companies out of business. Systems of homework registration and regulation have failed miserably, and cutbacks in federal and state funding have decimated already inadequate enforcement programs. United States trade policy, exemplified by the Bush administration's position in the Uruguay Round of the

General Agreement on Tariffs and Trade (GATT) talks, would prevent the industry from protecting the fewer than two million jobs and the factories that still produce apparel, textiles, and footwear in this country. Likewise, the proposed free trade agreement between Canada, the United States, and Mexico would doom even the unorganized plants that operate on a crisis-management basis along the southern border of the United States.

The Bush administration's insistence on so-called free trade has heightened and intensified the crisis in industries that once were our economic backbone. As a result, the first critical step toward protecting industrial workers, regardless of the location of their work, is to reinstate the bans on homework first established in 1942. The long-range goal of the labor movement has been, and must remain, the organization of all workers. But until unions can apply the lessons learned from efforts to organize clerical homeworkers to campaigns designed to reach industrial homeworkers, banning industrial homework is the most realistic approach.

Comments

Dennis Chamot

It is confusing, and often misleading, to discuss all homeworkers as a single group, because the work situations and problems experienced by each of the subgoups differ markedly. I find it useful to divide the total population of homeworkers into several categories based upon employment status and type of work (Chamot 1987, 1988). We need to distinguish employees from self-employed entrepreneurs, blue-collar from white-collar employees, and differentiate among managers/executives, professional employees, and clericals working at home. My comments focus primarily on the needs and problems of nonmanagerial white-collar employees working at home.

Eileen Boris provides a useful historical overview of homework in the United States. Her analysis of the early conflicts between unions and homeworkers is interesting, but may be misleading for those of us trying to understand what is happening today. A century ago, labor legislation did not exist, governmental "safety nets" were yet to be developed, unions were struggling for recognition, and life was hard for all workers. At the time, the predominant union policy may have been to oppose any form of homework as direct, unfair competition to factory workers. That is not the primary guide today, at least for white-collar workers.

The unions that are most concerned about the spread of homework are precisely those with deep institutional memories about the terrible exploitation of homeworkers in the past. No one in organized labor wants to see those conditions return, on humanitarian grounds alone. In part, it is an understanding of the historical record of misery and exploitation and sympathy for the abused homeworker, rather than the antagonism Boris describes, that drives current union opposition to homework.

If the number of employees (as distinct from entrepreneurs) working exclusively at home were to increase substantially, the threat to bargained wages and working conditions could be a serious one, especially given the inadequacy and unwillingness of the Department of Labor to regulate in this area. In the clerical and office area, the threat at present is not large.

In fact, it was knowledge of the historical record of the abuse of homeworkers and the failure of regulation that led the AFL-CIO to call for a ban of electronic (computer) homework in 1983. This was later modified. Whereas the 1983 resolution called for a complete ban of computer homework, the 1989 resolution called for the restoration of the original bans on industrial homework that had been lifted by the Reagan administration and went on to "urge the establishment of appropriate new regulations on homework to prevent exploitation of workers in offices as well as factories. Special provisions should be provided for the handicapped." The details are left open, but a regulatory approach other than a complete ban falls within the scope of this most recent policy statement. The new, more flexible policy recognized several factors: the wide variation in white-collar work that could be performed in the home; the fact that some categories of homeworkers were not of concern to the unions (self-employed people, executives, and managers); and the understanding that some union members may wish to work at home under a protective union contract. (At present, those numbers are exceedingly small, and I see no great increase in demand for full-time homework from unionized office workers).

In other words, union people today are familiar with sweatshop conditions and the exploitation of children and they feel very strongly about actual and potential abuse. Their concern determines their general response to homework. There is a willingness to investigate new approaches, but union leaders must be convinced that effective protection of homeworkers can be assured. Competition, specifically in white-collar areas, is not the issue; there are more than enough unorganized, poorly paid on-site office workers to keep unions busy for a long time.

I could not agree more with Boris's comments on the need for improving the dependent care system in this country so that people can pursue employment opportunities without fear of compromising the well-being of their children or other relatives. One can choose to work at home for a variety of reasons, but "choosing" to work at home because decent alternatives do not exist is no choice at all.

Gerson's findings reinforce the importance of the dependent care issue. Overall, however, the paper's survey strategy makes it difficult to generalize beyond her sample. First, data were collected only for cities with a population of about one hundred thousand. Such a sample may not accurately reflect the problems of homeworkers in major metropolitan centers, where much of the concern about homeworker exploitation is focused. Second, only clerical service companies were contacted, through the yellow pages, thus eliminating many people who work *directly* for companies in various service industries. Many anecdotes of homeworker abuse, in fact, have come from some of these kinds of arrangements. Finally, employees and self-employed owners were both in the sample, yet the level of control exercised by members of these different groups can vary enormously. In short, Gerson's findings *understate* the problems experienced by homeworkers. Even so, the data are useful, and show that these homeworkers, as compared to office workers, are more often paid by the piece; that they are less likely to be given fringe benefits; and that some flexibility of work schedule is necessary for many because of family obligations that cannot be handled in any other way.

I agree with Gerson's conclusion that clerical homeworkers would benefit from union organization. However, I don't think I would ascribe the reluctance of unions to organize these workers to the reasons given by Gerson. She argues that unions traditionally have been composed primarily of male, full-time workers in core industries, and thus ignored the primarily female, part-time homeworkers in peripheral industries. Yet union membership today is one-half white collar and fully one-third female, with both segments continuing to increase. Women are appearing with more frequency at the level of vice-president in many unions, with a few achieving the presidency. Much is yet to be accomplished, but particularly in unions with significant white-collar memberships, the old stereotypes are not fully applicable. Certainly, clerical *employees* working at home would benefit by union representation (*self-employed* homeworkers have other needs). Any reluctance on the part of unions to organize them, I believe, is more a matter of resource allocation than a lack of understanding of their needs.

Organizing clerical employees in traditional workplaces is a major activity of several unions today, with successful campaigns having been conducted in such diverse environments as insurance companies, government agencies, and universities. The number of unorganized clerical employees working at home full-time is far exceeded by their office-based colleagues. Office workers are easier to identify, are more readily contacted, are often in larger groups, and can be more efficiently serviced. For all of these reasons, unions must set practical priorities. At present, that means putting resources into campaigns to organize *office-based* clericals.

Kathleen Christensen's paper offers a clear and useful description of the different kinds of white-collar homeworkers. She gives an excellent overview of the problems of independent contractors. This is an important discussion, because as Christensen notes, many women working at home doing clerical work are being hired fraudulently as independent contractors. Problems exist even for homeworkers properly identified as employees, because many are treated less well than their office counterparts.

Christensen's suggestion that the associate member program available through many unions offers a useful mechanism for serving at least some of the needs of homeworkers is a good one. As she recognizes, the full benefits of a formal, legally binding bargaining relationship are not available to associate members, but that option could be pursued at a later date when a sufficient number of home-based associate members are identified at a particular employer.

Christensen also describes the experiences of a group of homeworkers employed by the University of Wisconsin Hospital and Clinics and represented by AFSCME. Apparently, the experiment has been successful for all of the involved parties—the hospital has met its needs; the homeworkers are satisfied with the arrangements; and the union representatives feel that the contract they negotiated offers full protection to those employees who choose to work at home. The AFSCME experience in Madison demonstrates that homeworkers can be well represented by a union working through the traditional collective bargaining process. Even so, I might note that the program remains quite small, just a handful of people out of a 2,500-member local. Others in the local have not been demanding similar arrangements. Apparently, the majority of people who currently work in offices have no great desire to work at home.

It is important to note that modern electronic office technologies are characterized by the ease with which the work site can be moved. Just as clerical work can be moved quite readily from the office to the home, so, too, can it now be moved anywhere in the country, and, almost as easily, overseas. I do not see homework as a major threat to the working standards of office clerical workers. The numbers of homeworkers are likely to remain small because of organizational inertia and the apparent lack of desire on the part of most office employees to work out of their homes. The trend to move white-collar work to other countries is more disturbing. The technology is readily available, and the huge differences in labor costs may prove very attractive to increasingly large numbers of employers.

More than clerical jobs are at risk, because professional-level work can be exported as well. Not only has keyboarding been shifted to Jamaica, but computer programming for U.S. companies is being done in India and engineering design in Korea and Ireland. It is a simple matter to transmit electronic work via satellite to receivers in the United States, and the associated expenses may be minimal compared to saving one-third or more of payroll costs.

Blue-collar jobs have been eliminated in recent years by a combination of shifts of production work abroad and expanded automation at home. The same could happen with white-collar jobs. In this context, the number of jobs available for homeworkers may be reduced as they find themselves competing with much lower-paid counterparts from throughout the world, and as the work they do is converted to more automated systems.

Finally, I would note another phenomenon that appears to be on the increase. That is the shifting of *part* of a work schedule to the home. Spurred by employee demands for greater flexibility, as well as congestion along commuter routes, some people are finding that they can function at home with the assistance of personal computers, modems, Fax machines, and telephones. Thus far, this situation appears to be very different from that of the full-time or exclusive homeworker who is usually discussed. The hybrid worker has a formal place in an office that is used regularly, and in all ways is treated as a regular employee and member of the group. The part-time work at home is primarily for convenience rather than a transition to full-time homework. I believe that an increasing number of professional-level employees and managers will make use of a hybrid arrangement.

References to Part IV

Advance. 1921. "Ridding All Rochester of Home Work." (June 24): 1–2.

AFL-CIO. 1983. "Resolutions on Computer Homework." In *Office Workstations in the Home,* National Research Council. Washington, D.C.: National Academy Press.

———. 1989. *Proceedings of the AFL-CIO Constitutional Convention:* 427.

———. Committee on the Evolution of Work. 1985. *The Changing Situation of Workers and Their Unions.* Washington, D.C.: AFL-CIO.

Albrecht, Sandra L. 1982. "Industrial Home Work in the United States: Historical Dimensions and Contemporary Perspective." *Economic and Industrial Democracy* 3(4):413–30.

Allen, Sheila, and Carol Wolkowitz. 1987. *Homeworking: Myths and Realities.* London: Macmillan Education.

Amalgamated Clothing Workers of America. 1919. *Proceedings.*

Belous, Richard. 1989. *The Contingent Economy: The Growth of the Temporary, Part-Time, and Subcontracted Workforce.* NPA Report 239. Washington, D.C.: National Planning Association.

Benson, Susan Porter. 1989. "Women, Work, and the Family Economy: Industrial Homework in Rhode Island in 1934." In *Homework: Historical and Contemporary Perspectives on Paid Labor at Home,* edited by Eileen Boris and Cynthia R. Daniels, 53–74. Urbana: University of Illinois Press.

Bisno, Abraham. 1967. *Abraham Bisno: Union Pioneer.* Madison: University of Wisconsin Press.

Blackwelder, Julia Kirk. 1984. *Women of the Depression: Caste and Culture in San Antonio, 1929–1939.* College Station: Texas A & M Press.

Blewett, Mary. 1988. *Men, Women, and Work: Class, Gender, and Protest in the New England Shoe Industry, 1780–1910.* Urbana: University of Illinois Press.

Boris, Eileen. 1985. "Regulating Industrial Homework: The Triumph of 'Sacred Motherhood.'" *Journal of American History* 71(40):745–63.

———. 1986. "The Quest for Labor Standards in the Era of Eleanor Roosevelt: The

Case of Industrial Homework." *Wisconsin Journal of Law and Feminism* 2 (Spring):53–74.

———. 1987. "Homework and Women's Rights: The Case of the Vermont Knitters, 1980–85." *Signs: A Journal of Women in Culture and Society* 13 (Autumn):98–120.

———. 1989. " 'White Slaves of the Cities'; Rhetoric and Reality in the History of Industrial Homework." Colloquium paper presented at the Woodrow Wilson International Center for Scholars, Washington, D.C.

———. 1990. "Women's Networks and the Enactment of Legislation: Homework Laws in Depression America." Unpublished paper, the Berkshire Conference of Women's Historians. Rutgers University.

———. 1991a. " 'A Man's Dwelling Is His Castle': Tenement House Cigar Making and the Judicial Imperative." In *Work Engendered: Toward a New History of American Labor,* edited by Ava Baron, 114–41. Ithaca: Cornell University Press.

———. 1991b. "Tenement Homework on Army Uniforms: The Gendering of Industrial Democracy during World War I." *Labor History* 32 (Spring):231–52

———. 1992. "Homework Regulation and the Devolution of the Post-War Labor Standards Regime: Beyond Dichotomy." In *Labor Law in America: Historical and Critical Perspectives,* edited by Christopher Tomlins and Andrew King. Baltimore: Johns Hopkins University Press.

———. Forthcoming. "Puerto Rican Needlewomen under the NRA." In *Puerto Rican Women and Work,* edited by Palmira Rios and Altagracia Ortiz. Philadelphia: Temple University Press.

Boris, Eileen, and Cynthia R. Daniels, eds. 1989. *Homework: Historical and Contemporary Perspectives on Paid Labor at Home.* Urbana: University of Illinois Press.

Bronfenbrenner, Kate. 1988. "Organizing and Representing the Contingent Work Force." Paper presented to the AFL-CIO Organizing Department, September 14.

Chamot, Dennis. 1987. "Electronic Work and the White-Collar Employee." In *Technology and the Transformation of White-Collar Work,* edited by Robert E. Kraut. Hillsdale, N.J.: Lawrence Erlbaum Associates.

———. 1988. "Blue Collar, White Collar: Homeworker Problems." In *The New Era of Home-based Work: Directions and Policies,* edited by Kathleen E. Christensen. Boulder, Colo.: Westview Press.

Christensen, Kathleen. 1985. *Impacts of Computer-Mediated Home-based Work on Women and Their Families.* New York: Center for Human Environments, Graduate Center, City University of New York.

———. 1986. *Pros and Cons of Home-based Clerical Work.* Testimony before the House Committee on Government Operations, U.S. Congress. 27–36. Washington, D.C.: GPO.

———. 1988a. "Independent Contracting." In *The New Era of Home-based Work: Directions and Policies,* edited by Kathleen Christensen, 79–91. Boulder, Colo.: Westview Press.

———. 1988b. *Rising Use of Part-Time and Temporary Workers: Who Benefits and Who Loses?* Testimony before the House Committee on Government Operations, U.S. Congress, 82–83. Washington, D.C.: GPO.

———. 1989. *Flexible Staffing and Scheduling in U.S. Corporations.* Research Bulletin 240. New York: The Conference Board.

———. 1990. "Case Studies of Telecommuting Arrangements in U.S. Corporations and Public Agencies." In *Conditions of Work Digest: On Telework* (Fall): 49–62, 89–92, 95–98, 108–10, 125–27. Geneva, Switzerland: International Labour Organization.

Christensen, Kathleen, and M. Murphree. 1988. "Introduction." In *Flexible Workstyles: A Look at Contingent Labor,* 1–4. Washington, D.C.: U.S. Department of Labor, Women's Bureau.

Cobble, Dorothy Sue. 1991. "Organizing the Postindustrial Work Force: Lessons from the History of Waitress Unionism." *Industrial and Labor Relations Review* 44 (April):419–36.

Code of Federal Regulations, Parts 500 to 899. 1987. Washington, D.C.: Office of the Federal Register. National Archives and Administration. Revised July 1.

Collins, Patricia Hill. 1990. *Black Feminist Thought: Knowledge, Consciousness, and the Politics of Empowerment.* Boston: Unwin Hyman.

Commonwealth of Massachusetts. 1955. *Report of the Commission Established to Study and Revise the Laws Relating to Industrial Homework.* August 15. Boston: Wright & Potter.

———. 1960. *Industrial Bulletin* no. 20. Boston: Wright & Potter.

Dietz, James. 1986. *Economic History of Puerto Rico: Institutional Change and Capitalist Development.* Princeton: Princeton University Press.

Dublin, Thomas. 1985. "Women and Outwork in a Nineteenth-Century New England Town: Fitzwilliam, New Hampshire, 1830–1850." In *The Countryside in the Age of Capitalist Transformation: Essays in the Social History of Rural America,* edited by Steven Hahn and Jonathan Prude, 51–69. Chapel Hill: University of North Carolina Press.

duRivage, Virginia and David Jacobs. 1989. "Home-based Work: Labor's Choices." In *Homework: Historical and Contemporary Perspectives on Paid Labor at Home,* edited by Eileen Boris and Cynthia Daniels. Urbana: University of Illinois Press.

Elisburg, Donald. 1985. "Legalities." In *Telematics and Informatics* 2(2):181–185.

Freedman, Audrey. 1985. *The New Look in Wage Policy and Employee Relations.* Report 865. New York: The Conference Board.

———. 1988. *Rising Use of Part-Time and Temporary Workers: Who Benefits and Who Loses?* Testimony before the Committee on Government Operations, U.S. Congress, House of Representatives, 35. Washington, D.C.: GPO.

General Accounting Office (GAO). 1989. *Tax Administration: Information Returns Can Be Used to Identify Employers Who Misclassify Workers.* September 25. Gaithersburg, Md.: GAO.

Gerson, Judith M. Forthcoming. *At Home and in the Office: A Comparison of Home- and Office-Based Clerical Workers.* Chapel Hill: University of North Carolina Press.

Hartsock, Nancy C. M. 1985. *Money, Sex, and Power: Toward a Feminist Historical Materialism.* Boston: Northeastern University Press.

Highman, Allen. 1990. Telephone conversation with Kathleen Christensen. April.

———. Undated. "University of Wisconsin Hospital and Clinics Agreement with Local 2412 of the Wisconsin State Employees Union, AFSCME, on Work at Home." Unpublished manuscript in possession of Kathleen Christensen.

Horvath, F. 1986. "Work at home: New Findings from the Current Population Survey." *Monthly Labor Review* 109(11):31–35.

Howard, Marjorie. 1989. "Home Work: Escape from Office Means Stress Can Hit You Where You Live." *Boston Herald* (January 29):A24.

International Labour Office. 1989. "Home Work." *Conditions of Work Digest* 8(2):

International Ladies' Garment Workers' Union et al., Appellants, v. Raymond J. Donovan et al. 1983. 722 Federal Reporter, 2d Series:795–828.

Jaggar, Alison M. 1983. *Feminist Politics and Human Nature.* Totowa, N.J.: Rowman and Allanheld.

Jensen, Joan. 1980. "Cloth, Butter, and Boarders: Women's Household Production for the Market." *The Review of Radical Political Economics* 12(2):14–24.

Jhabvala, Renanta. Forthcoming. "Self-Employed Women's Association: Organising Women by Struggle and Development." In *Dignity and Daily Bread: New Forms of Economic Organising among Poor Women in the Third World and the First,* edited by Swasti Mitter and Sheila Rowbotham. Boston: Routledge & Kegan Paul.

Johnson, Candice. 1986. "Homework Proposal Hit as Return to Sweatshops." *AFL-CIO News* 31(34):1, 4.

Johnston, William, and Arnold Packer. 1987. *Workforce 2000: Work and Workers for the Twenty-first Century.* Indianapolis: Hudson Institute.

Kaufman, Stuart B., et al., eds. 1986. *The Samuel Gompers Papers: The Making of a Union Leader, 1850–86,* vol. 1. Urbana: University of Illinois Press.

Kessler-Harris, Alice. 1982. *Out to Work: A History of Wage-Earning Women in the United States.* New York: Oxford University Press.

Kine, Edith. 1935. "Standout Women on the American Labor Scene: Frieda Miller, Head of Women in Industry Division, Guards against Homework Violations and Enforces Minimum Wages." *Justice* (October 15):14.

Labor Leader. 1889. "Slop Shops. What Is to be Found in New York Tenements." Boston, September 14.

Levine, Susan. 1984. *Labor's True Woman: Carpet Weavers, Industrialization, and Labor Reform in the Gilded Age.* Philadelphia: Temple University Press.

Lipschultz, Sybil. 1989. "Social Feminism and Legal Discourse, 1908–1923." *Yale Journal of Law and Feminism* 2 (Fall):131–60.

Lorwin, Louis. 1924. *The Women's Garment Workers: A History of the International Ladies' Garment Workers' Union.* New York: B.W. Huebsch, Inc.

MacKenzie, Roderick. 1986. *Pros and Cons of Home-based Clerical Work.* Testimony before the House Committee on Government Operations, U.S. Congress, 70–82. Washington, D.C.: GPO.

Manning, Caroline. 1934. "The Employment of Women in Puerto Rico." U.S. Department of Labor, Women's Bureau. *Bulletin of the Women's Bureau* no. 118. Washington, D.C.: GPO.

Mason, Karen Oppenheim, and Larry L. Bumpass. 1975. "U.S. Women's Sex-role Ideology, 1970." *American Journal of Sociology* 80:1212–19.

Mazur, Jay. 1986. "Homework: A Return to the Industrial Dark Ages of Sweatshops and No Protections." *AFL-CIO News* 31(31):10–11.

———. 1989. "Testimony by Jay Mazur, President, International Ladies' Garment Workers' Union, before the U.S. Department of Labor Hearings on Industrial Homework in the Women's Apparel Industry, New York City, March 29." Photocopy.

McLaughlin, Ann Dore. 1988. *New York Times* (November 11):A26.

Milkman, Ruth. 1985. "Women Workers, Feminism and the Labor Movement since the 1960s." In *Women, Work & Protest, A Century of U.S. Women's Labor History*, edited by Ruth Milkman, 302–22. Boston: Routledge & Kegan Paul.

Miller, Frieda S. 1941. "Industrial Home Work in the United States." *International Labour Review* 43:1–50.

Montgomery, David. 1987. *The Fall of the House of Labor.* New York: Cambridge University Press.

National Alliance of Homebased Businesswomen. 1986. Prepared statement read before the Subcommittee of the House Committee on Government Operations. 99th Cong., 1st sess., February 26.

Pennington, Shelley, and Belinda Westover. 1989. *A Hidden Workforce: Homeworkers in England, 1850–1985.* London: Macmillan Education.

Plewes, Thomas. 1988. "Understanding the Data on Part-Time and Temporary Employment." In *Flexible Workstyles: A Look at Contingent Labor,* 9–13. Washington, D.C.: U.S. Department of Labor, Women's Bureau.

Polivka, Anne, and Thomas Nardone. 1989. "On the Definition of Contingent Work." *Monthly Labor Review* 112(12):9–16.

Quinn, Robert, and Graham Staines. 1979. *Quality of Employment Survey, 1977: Cross-Section.* Ann Arbor, Mich.: Inter-University Consortium for Political and Social Research.

Ryder, Norman, and Charles B. Westoff. 1970. "National Fertility Study." Philadelphia: Temple University Institute for Survey Research.

SEIU. 1986. "SEIU Says 'No' to Homework." *Service Employee* (April/May):4.

Shallcross, Ruth Enalda. 1939. *Industrial Homework: An Analysis of Homework Regulation, Here and Abroad.* New York: Industrial Affairs.

Silvestrini, Blanca. 1986. "Women as Workers: The Experience of the Puerto Rican Woman in the 1930s." In *The Puerto Rican Woman: Perspectives on Culture, History and Society,* 2d ed., edited by Edna Acosta-Belen. New York: Praeger.

Skinner, Mary. 1938. "Prohibition of Industrial Home Work in Selected Industries Under the National Recovery Administration." Children's Bureau. *Bulletin* no. 244. Washington, D.C.: GPO.

Sockell, Donna. 1989. "Future of Labor Law." *Boston College Law Review* (30) 4 (July): 987–1026.

Stansell, Christine. 1983. "The Origins of the Sweatshop: Women and Early Industrialization in New York City." In *Working-Class America: Essays on Labor, Community, and American Society,* edited by Michael Frisch and Daniel Walkowitz. Urbana: University of Illinois Press.

———. 1986. *City of Women: Sex and Class in New York, 1789–1860.* New York: Knopf.

State of New York. 1922. *Annual Report of the Industrial Commissioner for the Twelve Months Ended June 30, 1921.* Albany: J. B. Lyon Company.

The Survey. 1926. "The Outworkers." (January 15): 499.

U.S. Chamber of Commerce. 1986. *Employee Benefits, 1985.* Washington, D.C.: U.S. Chamber of Commerce.

U.S. Congress. House. Subcommittee of the Committee on Government Operations. 1986. *Pros and Cons of Home-based Clerical Work.* 99th Cong., 2d. sess. Washington, D.C.: GPO.

U.S. Congress. House. Subcommittee on Labor Standards of the Committee on Education and Labor. 1987. *Oversight Hearings on the Department of Labor's Proposal to Lift the Ban on Industrial Homework.* 99th Cong., 2d sess. Washington, D.C.: GPO.

U.S. Department of Labor. Hearings on Homework in the Garment Industry. April 1989. Miami, Florida.

———. March 1989. Chicago, Illinois.

Waldinger, Roger. 1986. *Through the Eye of the Needle: Immigrants and Enterprise in New York's Garment Trades.* New York: New York University Press.

Waldman, Louis. 1944. *Labor Lawyer.* New York: E. P. Dutton.

Wall Street Journal. 1988. "Help for Homeworkers." November 14.

———. 1989. "Labor Shortages Are Getting Tighter and Tighter, Companies Say." In "Labor Letter," February 7:1.

Weinstein, Harry. 1989. "Witnesses Describe the Misery of Home–Based Garment Work." *Los Angeles Times,* March 24:1, 4.

Yeatman, Anna. 1990. "A Feminist Theory of Social Differentiation." In *Feminism and Postmodernism,* edited by Linda J. Nicholson, 281–99. New York: Routledge.

Part V
New Directions in Organizing and Representing Women

Katie Quan's account of the 1982 uprising of Chinese garment workers in New York, as Ruth Milkman suggests, reveals both the possibilities and limits of current union efforts to organize and represent women. These immigrant women demonstrated an enormous capacity and need for collective mobilization. But solidarity and desire for unionization cannot guarantee success in the 1990s. Unionization in the garment industry is stymied in part by a reliance on union tactics ill-suited to match the global organization and mobility of employers. Perhaps Quan is representative of a new generation of labor leader—one who can respond imaginatively to these disconcerting new economic and structural realities without losing a grasp of the timeless fundamentals of building a grass-roots movement.

The essay by Patricia Gwartney-Gibbs and Denise Lach, as well as the concluding piece by Richard Hurd, raise equally fundamental questions regarding union representational structures and practices. Gwartney-Gibbs and Lach contend that many unions rely on traditional problem-solving mechanisms that are gender-biased in conception and execution. Common problems experienced by women workers are not defined as "grievable" under the union contract or are viewed as unresolvable through the union dispute resolution process. According to Gwartney-Gibbs and Lach, women also felt uncomfortable with the formal, adversarial nature of the traditional union procedures.

The Harvard model described by Richard Hurd appears to be almost a direct response to the concerns raised by Gwartney-Gibbs and Lach. Clericals at Harvard consciously created union structures that enfranchised and empowered them. Building on a workplace culture that probably reflected specific occupational as well as gendered concerns, Harvard unionists fashioned an inclusive organizing process that ultimately transformed the union's representational mechanisms. Collective bargaining at Harvard involved dozens of working committees; the problem-solving processes they negotiated demanded rank-and-file participation, defined workplace problems in the broadest possible fashion, and relied on a consensual, "win-win" approach to conflict resolution.

Both Gloria Busman and Jessica Govea argue that the Harvard emphasis on giving authority and responsibility to the workers themselves is essential to any successful organizing, whether with men or women, farmworkers or clericals, immigrant or native-born workers. For Govea, however, unions must also be willing to make organizing a priority. Factory workers were organized in the 1930s in part because the CIO committed enormous resources and launched campaigns targeting entire industries and occupations. A similarly ambitious assault is required if the white-collar and service sector is to be unionized.

The CIO succeeded because they responded to the needs of a new constituency. In the 1990s, that new constituency undeniably is female and, as Susan Josephs concludes, will require a unionism attentive to gender differences. The essays in this section, however, also indicate that the new work force defines its identity along ethnic, racial, occupational, and sexual lines. Patti Roberts argues, for example, that lesbians and gay men face particular kinds of workplace-based discrimination. If the labor movement is to uphold its claim to represent all workers then it must not only acknowledge but champion the needs of all workers as they themselves define those needs.

11

Organizing Immigrant Women in New York's Chinatown

An Interview with Katie Quan

Ruth Milkman

O ne of the most celebrated events in women's labor history is the "Uprising of the 20,000," the huge garment workers' strike that took place during 1909 and 1910 in New York City. This legendary "girls' strike," which transformed the International Ladies' Garment Workers' Union (ILGWU) into a modern industrial union, demonstrated the previously untapped potential for militancy among young female Jewish and Italian immigrant workers, and dramatically challenged the conventional stereotypes of the era, which constructed women workers as passive and uninterested in unionism. As Samuel Gompers said in 1910: "The strike . . . brought to the consciousness of the nation a recognition of . . . the extent to which women are taking up with industrial life, their consequent tendency to stand together in the struggle to protect their common interests as wage earners, the readiness of people in all classes to approve of trade-union methods in behalf of working women, and the capacity of women as strikers to suffer, to do, and to dare in support of their rights."[1]

In 1982, another labor struggle shook the New York garment industry. Once again, twenty thousand women workers took to the streets to defend their rights. As in 1909, the strike leaders were young immigrant women—

---

[1] This is from Gompers' report to the 1910 convention of the American Federation of Labor, cited in Louis Levine's classic history of the ILGWU, *The Women's Garment Workers: A History of the International Ladies' Garment Workers' Union* (New York: B. W. Huebsch, 1924), p. 166. Most later accounts of the strike rely heavily on Levine's work. Among the feminist reconstructions of this event are Barbara Wertheimer, *We Were There! The Story of Working Women in America* (New York: Pantheon, 1977), chap. 16; Meredith Tax, *The Rising of the Women* (New York: Monthly Review Press, 1980), chapter 8; and Alice Kessler-Harris, " 'Where Are the Organized Women Workers?' " *Feminist Studies* 3, no. 1–2 (Fall 1975):92–110.

always the bulk of the garment industry's work force. This time, however, they were not Jewish and Italian, but Chinese women. In contrast to the situation in 1909, at the start of the 1982 strike, the workers involved were already union members. They belonged to Sportswear Local 23–25 of the ILGWU, whose membership was made up overwhelmingly of Chinese women.[2]

The crisis began in June, when the industry's Chinese contractors balked at signing a new labor agreement. They did so at a time when unions were in decline nationwide, losing members and frequently acceding to employer demands for "givebacks" and concessions of past gains. Although in China-town itself the garment industry was thriving, skyrocketing imports and the globalization of production by "American" clothing manufacturers had led to huge job losses in the industry nationally, further weakening the ILGWU. Despite these adverse conditions, in the summer of 1982 Chinatown's women workers took to the streets to defend their union. Their resistance proved triumphant, giving a new lease on life to garment worker unionism in New York.[3] Jay Mazur, Local 23–25's manager at the time, has since gone on to become the ILGWU's International president, and his rise to power in the union was due at least in part to the successful outcome of the 1982 Chinatown strike.

Although just as large as its forerunner seven decades before, the Chinatown strike garnered much less outside attention or support, reflecting the social isolation of organized labor generally in the late twentieth century. Today, only a decade after the strike, it has been virtually obliterated from public memory. Yet it offers lessons just as important for today's labor movement as the 1909–10 "Uprising" did for its contemporaries. Most importantly, it illustrates the potential for effective organizing among immigrant women workers. This rapidly growing segment of the U.S. work force is viewed by many commentators today (and even by some labor union officials) in much the same way that women workers generally were regarded early in this century: as passive, vulnerable workers with little capacity for militancy and minimal interest in unionism.

The following interview with Katie Quan was conducted on July 14, 1990, at her home in Berkeley, California. Quan, a key leader of the Chinatown

[2]Peter Kwong states that in the early 1980s 85 percent of Local 23–25 members were Chinese. See his book, *The New Chinatown* (New York: Hill and Wang, 1987), p. 153. This is one of the few published accounts of the events of 1982, although Kwong's perspective differs in some respects from Quan's.

[3]For the union's official account of the strike victory, see "6-Week '23–25' Struggle Obtains 100% Pact Signup," *Justice* 64, no. 7 (July–August 1982):5.

strike who was involved in both workplace and community organizing in New York's Chinatown during the late 1970s and early 1980s, recounts the history of the strike as well as the many obstacles that had to be overcome to make its success possible. While this is a success story, and a rather exceptional one in this period of union defeats, it suggests both the possibilities and limits of current efforts to organize immigrant women.

Quan had worked in garment factories in Chinatown for seven years before the strike, and among other efforts, was involved in the Chinese restaurant workers' successful unionization drive in the late 1970s. When the 1982 crisis erupted, she was organizing a campaign among Chinatown garment workers for a day care center. As Quan explains in the interview, the day care campaign ultimately benefited from the successful resolution of the strike. In late 1983 the Garment Industry Day Care Center of Chinatown opened, with a mixture of private and public subsidies so that Local 23–25 members paid only $6 per week on average for the child care.[4]

Quan, originally from the San Francisco Bay Area, became a full-time staff member of the ILGWU in 1984. Her first position was in the research department of Local 23–25. She went on to hold a variety of posts in New York City, including assistant director of the ILGWU's New York Metro Organizing Department, before returning to the West Coast in 1990 as the manager of the union's Pacific Northwest District Council, whose offices are in San Francisco.[5]

RM: How did you first become involved in organizing Chinese garment workers?

KQ: Both my grandmothers were garment workers. One was an ILG member who worked at Koret of California in San Francisco for many, many years. The other was a hand ironer in Oakland Chinatown in a small, typical sewing factory, and she was not a union member. My mom always said to me, "You see, there's a big difference between your grandma who works at Koret and your grandma who works in the nonunion sewing factory." And indeed, when my grandma who worked at Koret retired, she was able to collect a pension. It wasn't so much, but at least she was able to get something. My other grandmother didn't have a pension coming to her, although she had worked

[4]The center served seventy children. See "Peace of Mind for Working Mothers," *Justice* 64, no. 2 (February 1984): 8–9.
[5]"Homecoming for ILGWU's Quan," *California AFL-CIO News* 33, no. 1 (January 12, 1990): 3.

just as many years in sewing factories and in fact had to work into her seventies, until basically she couldn't stand up any longer. So, this is what I grew up with. And then, in the late 1960s and early 1970s, like many other young people in the San Francisco Bay Area, I was affected by the anti-Vietnam War scene, the struggle for black liberation, and the rights of minorities in general. I became involved in community work in San Francisco and Oakland. I worked in a youth center in Oakland Chinatown called East Bay Asians for Community Action, and it was right next door to a nonunion garment factory. I can still remember going to meetings at the youth center and staying until ten or eleven at night, and when I left, women were still working in the garment factory next door. The conditions there were really bad. That guy must have never swept in a month—garbage was piled almost a foot high! That's when I decided that if garment workers organized, it could really have some long-term, deep meaning for the Chinese community.

I had some friends who were going to work in garment factories to see if they couldn't do some organizing, and I decided to try it. I got a job in Oakland Chinatown as a seamstress. Although I already knew how to sew, because I sewed my own clothes at home, I learned how to use a factory machine and how to work on piece rate. The boss taught me. It was a nine-person shop, and it wasn't such a terrible work environment, it was very nice and bright and clean. I worked there a couple of months, and after that my husband and I moved to New York. We had heard about some of the things that they had been doing there in the Chinese community. There had just been big, community-wide protests against racism in the construction trades. The community people were demanding jobs and they were being told they were too short and stuff like that. We wanted to go check out the scene. Well, we ended up staying in New York fourteen years! I started working in Chinatown garment factories when I got there, in 1975, and I continued doing that for the next eight years.

RM: Were the factories you worked in unionized?

KQ: Yes, even at that time more than 90 percent of the shops in New York Chinatown were union shops. Until recently, we really didn't have too much of a problem with nonunion contractors there. The shops had been organized back in the 1950s, at a time when there were very few imports, and when the union represented workers in maybe 70 percent of the industry in New York City. In sportswear, which is what the Chinatown shops produced, quite a high percentage of the manufacturers were unionized. Just about all the factories in Chinatown were doing work at that time for union manufacturers. To some extent they were organized from the top down. The union would approach the manufacturer, and say, "What's this? You've got some nonunion contractors down in Chinatown working for you? Well, your contract says that you've got to use union contractors. If you want to use them they've got to be union." Meanwhile, the workers were also organizing. Cards were passed out to people and the union had to bring in people who spoke Chinese to talk to the workers and so forth. But there weren't a whole lot of garment factories in Chinatown in the late fifties—ten maybe—and there was never a large nonunion sector there. As long as most of the sportswear manufacturers were union, anyone who opened up a factory would want to be union so that they could get work.

When I first started working there, in the mid–1970s, there were about 200 garment factories in Chinatown and a lot of the workers had been there a long time. I was almost the only young person around. But as time went on and immigration picked up, people of all ages got into the garment factories, and the industry boomed in Chinatown. By the early 1980s, there were 450 shops—the number had more than doubled in only five years. I think, too, that there was a difference in the way people of different generations understood the union. A lot of the old-timers actually had more knowledge and concern about what the union is all about. But at the same time we had this phenomenon of newly arrived workers just dying to get into the union, because of the benefits. Local 23–25 used to have new membership meetings with seventy-five to a hundred workers every week joining the union—and these were people who had already waited months. They were already qualifying for their medical benefits when they were having their induction into the union! The first thing they wanted to do after they got off the plane and got a job in a factory was to join the union so that their benefits would start right away.

But most of the women—it was almost all women—who worked in Chinatown didn't really participate actively in the union. They didn't go to union meetings because they didn't understand English. The workers were 99 percent Chinese, though in every shop you'd find one or two Hispanic workers. And at that time, the union meetings were only in English.

RM: I suppose in the Chinese community the issue which often arises in organizing other immigrants, namely whether people are legally documented, is not such a problem. It's often argued that fear of the government keeps undocumented workers out of unions and out of anything that's at all risky politically.

KQ: In the Chinese community, there aren't many people here without documents; they're mainly legal. Actually, in the restaurants that we organized in New York there were always a couple of people who were undocumented, but the bosses never used it against them. But I have to say that, over the years of working in New York, I organized a great many factories where a lot of the workers were from various Latin American countries and didn't have papers, and now here in San Francisco we're doing the same. And these people are not afraid. I have never seen a situation where the people's legal or nonlegal status with regard to immigration has really been the main thing setting back the struggle. I've never seen that. And I've seen some people who are here without documents take some very big risks on a picket line. I think that this issue is totally blown out of proportion. I'm not saying that it wouldn't have some effect on some people, but I've really never seen it to be a significant factor in any organizing drive.

The real problems were in other areas. In my first shop in New York, which I worked in for a year, I remember how very difficult it was to organize even on the most basic level. For example, organizing the workers to fight for higher piece rates was really hard. The boss would always give us piece rates which were too low. We didn't have a real good system set up for dealing with it in our factory. Basically when the boss gave a piece rate that was too low, everybody would just grumble, "This is cheap," but nobody would really confront the boss and try to negotiate a higher piece rate. But there were a couple of women who sewed faster than the rest and who were more respected by the rest, and eventually I got them to agree that they should represent other workers by negotiating better piece rates with the boss. And I got the others to agree that we would all stop working while they were negotiating. That wasn't easy, because with piece work the lost time costs people money. Also, they didn't want to stand up to the boss, they didn't want to be looked upon as being uncooperative. We had to go around and talk to everybody—there were about twenty-five of us—and they didn't all want to do it. We had to call people at home, we had to walk home with them and so on. Just to pull off a simple work stoppage around the piece rates took an immense amount of organizing.

After a few months of doing this I understood that organizing the rank-and-file workers in Chinatown wasn't going to be that easy. I had had these visions of—you know, I'll work in one factory and maybe I'll have a friend in another factory, and our jobs will be really organized and we'll go out, and just one by one by one we'll be able to do it. It didn't take me too long to understand that that was never going to be the way that it was going to happen. Our shop was actually a little bit easier to organize than some others, because all of the workers had been there for ten or fifteen years, and they really didn't want to leave the shop. Over the years working, we had developed a lot of personal ties with each other. We were also a very strong shop as far as making sure that we got paid what we were supposed to, and on time. We got all the benefits that we ever were supposed to get. It's not like we were the only shop in town that was like that. There were others too. But eventually I worked in ten or eleven other garment factories after I left that one, and I found that while often we were able to develop this sort of organization within the factory, in some cases we just weren't. Sometimes, the chemistry just wasn't there. People didn't get along with each other, they never would have worked together, and there was just nothing you could do about a situation like that.

RM: In the academic literature on the garment industry, there's a lot of discussion of the phenomenon of immigrant workers who aspire to become entrepreneurs themselves. They work, save their money slowly, borrow more money, and eventually open a small shop—living out the classic American Dream. This is often seen as a dampening influence on class consciousness. How does it affect organizing garment workers?

KQ: Class consciousness is a strange thing in the Chinese context because there's nobody who's Chinese that doesn't know that labor and management are in contradiction to each other. It's like yin and yang. In Chinese, the term "management-labor dispute" is much more common than in English. Everybody knows if you're a worker, where your place is, and if you're a boss, where your place is. It has something to do with the rigidity of the Chinese notion of identity.

But sure, a lot of people do aspire to go into business on their own. It's the American Dream, or the dream of the Golden Mountain—that's what the Chinese call the United States. I think it's because they first came over during the gold rush, and also they mostly came to California in the summer, when the hills turn golden brown. And the dream comes true sometimes. In that last shop where I worked in New York, the boss was formerly a person who did buttonholes. I worked there for five years, and we just watched her get rich. In the beginning, okay, she moved to the suburbs, to New Jersey. Then, she'd come to work in a fancy car. Pretty soon, next thing you know, it was a chauffeured car. Then the next thing you know she was building a swimming pool in her backyard. We just watched ourselves just staying the same year in and year out, while she was just getting richer and richer and richer.

But relatively few people actually manage to do this. And it's not that easy to stay there once you're there. So many businesses fail that, often, people are right back working again. There is a lot of movement back and forth between being a worker and a small businessperson. It's not like the coal miners versus Rockefeller!

RM: When you were first organizing in New York in the seventies, were you active in the union? Did the union have any relationship to what you were doing?

KQ: Well, they told me not to do work stoppages, because that would violate the contract. On the other hand, the contract also says that workers will not be required to start work if the piece rate is not settled. So I always felt that I had an out there. But I really didn't become active in the union until much later, in 1981, when we started organizing for the day care center. As immigration picked up and more and more young women entered the work force, day care became a glaring issue. I'd be sitting around with some friends and suddenly kids would be running around all over the place, with nobody to take care of them. People would say how they put their kids on a day care center waiting list the day they were born and now the kid's five years old, about to go into kindergarten and they still haven't gotten into day care. Chinatown only had about three day care centers with a capacity of serving five hundred or six hundred children, and with the increased immigration that was not even close to the level that was needed.

RM: So what did women with children do?

KQ: Some women didn't work at all. But that wasn't really a good alternative because most of their husbands were Chinese restaurant workers earning $10,000 a year or less. Some people brought work home—industrial home-work, which is illegal, and dangerous. I heard a story about a toy getting caught under the treadle of the machine and the woman didn't know it, so it gave her foot extra leverage and when she pushed down she nearly sewed right through her whole hand. So she barricaded the sewing machine by putting up those baby crib fences around herself. It was like a prison, she said. Nobody *wanted* to work at home, that I ever met. They would get out of the situation as soon as they could find somebody to take care of their kids.

RM: Did people ever bring their children to the factories?

KQ: Yes, that was another alternative. It was also pretty dangerous and more than once we heard of kids falling out of the windows of the lofts. When we were starting our day care organizing, we went to this one building and workers on several floors told us in a very hushed voice that just the week before a kid had fallen out of a window. Other women arranged private baby-sitting, but you know in the New York tenements, private baby-sitting's often not the best. For instance, I had a girlfriend who took her kid to this old lady who had nine cribs in her tenement apartment. My friend says, "God, if there's a fire, which one does she take first?" Sometimes also the parents would just lock up the kids at home, where they could get into all kinds of mischief. There were no really good alternatives. So we decided to organize around the issue.

It wasn't so easy to do. In the beginning, I really wasn't prepared for organizing women with young children. I had organized in my shop, I had organized tenants, I had organized Chinese restaurant workers, but I still wasn't prepared for the experiences that I had then. Organizing young women with kids turned out to be real different from organizing men. With the Chinese restaurant workers, who had unionized just before this, and who were all men, if you'd have a meeting, they'd basically come on time. Of course, you'd have to hold the meeting where they wanted it, and at the times they wanted to meet. I had meetings at my house at one o'clock in the morning because that's when all the waiters get off work. Also you couldn't interfere with them going to the racetrack—and in fact if you wanted cards signed you went to the racetrack to look for them on their off days. But still, the men were much more used to dealing with matters outside of household matters. They didn't do the kinds of things that would happen routinely in day care organizing.

With the women, you'd set a meeting for one o'clock, and people would come in at two, three, whenever the kids got up from naps. And they brought the kids with them. They didn't want to meet when it was a cold season, because the kids would catch each other's colds. They didn't want to meet, obviously, when it was raining and snowing because they didn't want to bring their kids in on the subway in bad weather. And when we finally managed to have a meeting, it was hard to keep it focused. They'd talk in one sentence about day care and then, in the same sentence, they'd start talking about their kids, about changing diapers and all that stuff. I'd always have to drag the discussion back to day care. It was so frustrating in the beginning because you'd set out to accomplish something for a certain meeting and you'd just feel like you'd never get there. So I started calling people up the night before, after the kids were asleep, and basically going through the whole meeting, you know, when I could just talk to them one-on-one. I had to go through the whole meeting ahead of time with each person. Then by the time we got together, we could just agree upon what was going on. But I'd never had to do that before in mixed situations or with men only.

Also, besides myself, there was just one other person who spoke English. The others didn't, and they weren't really educated that well even in Chinese. Most of them had just a couple years of schooling. So things that you needed for an organizing campaign, like writing press releases and stuff like that—we didn't do much of it in the beginning. In the end, yes, we learned how to do it, but this was a huge effort. Also, we were not used to going and talking with union officials, or day care experts, both of whom were very intimidating to us. We were a different class of person and we weren't used to talking with big shots. Basic things like language and knowledge of the system make a big difference. I'm thinking about a group of women we're organizing right now who are all English-speaking. Some of them are black, some are Hispanic, and some are white. One or two are immigrants, but mostly they're not. And they're so much more able to do things for themselves. If I just say, "Write a letter to the Board," they come up with a letter. They'd say, "Okay, we're going to have this demonstration, we've got to get so-and-so to support us." So they'd write down which organizations they wanted to get support from and then they'd go out and get it. Whereas with the immigrant women you would have to basically go with them each time. It gets into a whole lot of things—like transportation, for instance, often they don't know how to get around.

With the day care organizing, our whole idea was that, well, we are Chinese members and Chinese members contribute $3.5 million in dues to the union each year. So the union should do this for us. But none of us were active members of the union, none of the people in the union knew who we were. I used to go to union meetings and say some things in the meetings sometimes, but I was never a shop steward, I was never active in the union in any way. And I didn't know anybody who was.

We decided that they were not going to take us seriously unless we proved the need for day care. We had a press conference to launch the whole thing. It was big news, all over the newspapers. We had babies in our arms crying and stuff. Then we circulated a petition and we got about three thousand signatures in ten days. We went up and down the factories using the bosses' P.A. systems to say what we were there for, and about 99 percent of the people in every shop signed. After we got people to sign the petition, we took it to the union. The union's response was that we didn't have to go around and have a petition signed, because the union is for day care. "Why couldn't you've just come talk to us?" they said. And in fact Local 23–25, the local that most of the Chinese belong to, had looked into day care earlier. They even sent a couple of people down to Philadelphia to look at the day care center down there, but they had figured out that there wasn't enough money and so they just dropped the idea. But once we made it a very pressing issue, Jay Mazur, then the manager of Local 23–25, formed a committee composed of civic leaders and people who were knowledgeable about day care. Susan Cowell was the union staff person assigned to it. She made it happen as far as the administrative side went. She found out that the city agency that administered the city child care centers was looking for models other than just strictly government-financed day care. And because of what we had done, all the community hype that we had gotten over this thing, the employers wanted to show that they were good guys, too. So they had a fundraising banquet and raised about $30,000. The union got this put aside as seed money for the day care center, and it became a cooperative effort between the union and the employers. We found out that there was a day care center that had been built in Chinatown in the mid–1970s, but it had never opened because of lack of funding. The building was occupied by some city department, but it had all these day care facilities. So the site was there. The pieces came together very well. The center opened in late 1983 and had its formal dedication in January 1984, about three years after we started our campaign.

RM: This is basically a story of cooperation between the union and the employers. Yet right in the middle of it came the 1982 strike, which was a dramatic example of exactly the opposite. How did the strike come about? How could the two take place at the same time?

KQ: In 1982, the union contracts were up for renewal. In New York they have master agreements, so everybody's contract is up at the same time. The union negotiated a contract with the manufacturers and then went on to negotiate a contract with the contractors' association. All the Chinatown sportswear contractors belonged to the association, they made up about 70 percent of the contractors in it. At some point, the Chinese contractors balked because they said the contract was negotiated without representation from them. They said it was discriminatory, and they refused to sign the contract. So the workers were faced with the possibility of losing their union benefits. The contractors had assumed that they could get the workers to side with them, both being Chinese. They thought that the Chinese workers would stick with the Chinese bosses, but it didn't work like that. The Chinese workers were not that dumb! They said, "You're talking about—here go my medical benefits, what's my family supposed to do? I've worked nineteen years and next year I get to retire. You're saying I can't collect my pension? Forget this!" At the same time, they wanted to reduce holidays by three and to do some other outrageous things.

The response of the workers destroyed the myth that Chinese workers don't stand up for their rights because they work for Chinese bosses or because they're from the same part of China, or related in some way—the idea that national interests prevail over class interests. I really don't think that it's too helpful to make overly broad generalizations. There are situations where national interests are more important than class interests, but it depends on the issue and on the way it's organized. You can appeal to either interest to promote whatever you want to promote. I think that it's possible to use issues of ethnicity in organizing workers as workers. And probably in some cases, where ethnic identity is very strong, it's just about essential to do it. But that doesn't mean that ethnicity is overridingly more powerful than class under all circumstances.

Anyway, after the contractors refused to sign, the union sent out letters to workers asking if they wanted to be on a committee to fight for the contract, and they got five thousand postcards back. But then they never put the committee together. They never had a meeting until I forced the issue by saying, "Well, we have this committee. When did you have a meeting?" So on the spot, they set up a meeting for us. I brought my whole shop and that was a really big shock at that time. It was all the seamstresses, fifty of us. We all went up to the union office. This was no small feat because we worked in Chinatown, we had to take the subway and walk a couple of long blocks to get to the union office on Twenty-eighth Street. There were another four or five other people there from other shops, but it was mainly us. They went through the list of demands and said what the union was doing, and the workers in my shop wanted to know what we could do. Someone came up with the idea that we should help leaflet. So at five o'clock the next day, everybody put down what they were working on and left their seats. We all went to the corner where the leaflets were supposed to be distributed, took the leaflets and started handing them out. It was great! I had a girlfriend who worked in Chinatown who passed by and was handed a leaflet by this middle-aged Chinese lady. Later she says to me, "My, God, it's so different! Usually, it's us giving leaflets to them. Now, they're giving leaflets to us!" And so everybody in my shop did this.

The next day, the union called up on the telephone and they said, "Over at the radio station they need somebody to talk on the radio as to why the workers want a union." I told a couple of the key people in our unit and they said, "Well, let's all go." So, at two o'clock in the afternoon, we just all left and went to the radio station. It was on the Bowery, two or three stories up, and the staircase was only about three feet wide, and you've got fifty people just crowding, lining the stairways and down on the street. The head of the radio station got really upset at first, he thought we were having a demonstration against him. And you know, it was the first time any of us had been on the radio. It was funny, they had this big mike on a boom, and it was very intimidating. We got all nervous, but it was good, we did it, and then we went back to work.

Everybody was talking about the strike. It was on the radio that's piped into the factories, and it was being debated in the Chinese newspapers and everything. The whole community was talking about it. People were calling each other at night to talk about it on the phone. You would meet people in the stores shopping for vegetables and you'd hear about it. People would be talking about it on the subways. It was really the talk of the town. And overwhelmingly the workers were pissed off at the bosses and wanted the union contract. Our shop was no exception, we'd talk about it. And they told me that I should go call Jay Mazur and I should tell him we want a union contract and we want a strike and we don't care if we don't have strike benefits. We've got to have a union contract. So I would call Jay and I would tell him what the workers were saying and he would just listen very intently; this happened for days on end. I was telling him we should strike.

At that time I went to work for the union to prepare for a strike for a couple of weeks. The union was doing some things to try to bring forward some of the more active people. They put a number of people on staff who were active, and we had meetings in the Chinatown office and in the Roosevelt Auditorium in Union Square. To think about organizing twenty thousand people was not an easy task, especially if you start from ground zero. But you know, everybody was galvanized. Some people even went on wildcats. They walked out when their boss said they weren't going to sign the contract and they came up to the union office. Meanwhile, we were preparing frantically. We were making picket signs and banners and all this. And the union had a big rally in the heart of Chinatown, in Columbus Park. Fifteen to twenty thousand people were at that rally. It was just huge, and it was all these Chinese garment workers. There they were with their picket signs and their hats and everything. We got some militant women up there from some of the shops to give some really dynamite speeches and it was really, really inspiring. It was something that all of us were proud to be a part of. And after that, the union began to go around and sign individual contracts with individual employers. Instead of dealing with the contractors' association, the union decided to try to get them to sign individual contracts, which most of them did. But by the deadline that the union had set, there were still 75 to 100 employers who had not signed, out of 450 in Chinatown. So we had another big rally and a march through Chinatown and then we set up picket lines in front of shops that hadn't signed. The workers were told, "If the name of your shop is on that sign, then your shop is on strike and don't go up there." It only took a morning; by one o'clock all the rest had signed up. This was really, really fantastic!

Everybody learned a lot from the strike. The bosses learned, well, you can't mess with the garment workers. As the Chinese say, "When the fire burns to the hairs on your skin, then they'll really move." And the union leaders saw that the Chinese workers do fight, whereas they may have had their doubts because maybe they thought that the bosses' appeal based on ethnicity may have worked, or that they're women, they don't speak English, so therefore they won't fight—all these myths. But this really showed the union leaders that the Chinese women do fight and that they have to be much more responsive to what the Chinese workers need. As far as the Chinese workers are concerned, we stunned ourselves as well, you know. Remember how I was telling you how difficult it is just to put one piece-rate struggle together? You face an awful lot of that in your everyday life and you think, "Well, god, I can't even get these people together to sit down and wait for a few pennies more on a piece rate—how are we going to be able to do this?" But people really came out and came forward.

All this happened the summer after we had presented petitions about day care to the union. And it was after the strike that we started to get great response on the day care issue. It wasn't a straight connection, but the idea that the Chinese workers were important to the union and the union really had to do what it could to look after the welfare of the Chinese workers was made obvious by that whole struggle. At the same time, the employers were looking for some way to make themselves look good under those circumstances. And so the whole idea of cooperating with the union to provide funding for this day care center came up when both sides were looking for ways to mend the fences.

RM: What was the impact of all this on the garment workers' union itself, and on the composition of its leadership? For a long time the ILGWU leadership has been dominated by native-born males, even though the membership is made up mainly of immigrant women. Has that changed?

KQ: Well, the successful outcome of the 1982 strike really showed that the union could and would fight in the interests of Chinese garment workers. To that extent, it gained renewed respect among the members and also in the community at large. More people began to turn to the union as spokesperson for the garment workers and began to include the union in all kinds of community coalitions. Also, a number of women joined the staff of the union at about this time. And over the years they have provided leadership to the Chinese rank-and-file members.

Immediately after the strike, we were looking for some vehicle to keep some of these marvelous people who had come forward during the strike and who were there every night to do phone banking, and who were there every night to do poster making and so forth. We wanted to find some way to keep in touch and we formed the Chinese Chorus of the ILGWU. A couple of us really had wanted to form a women's committee within the union, but that had met with some disapproval in some sectors of the local leadership, so we decided to go easy for a while. Eventually, Kathy Andrade, who had been on the Hispanic Committee of the Coalition of Labor Union Women for many years, pressed us to form a Chinese committee of CLUW, which we did. The Chinese Committee of CLUW became a training ground for a number of rank-and-file activists, and it was really formed to promote the idea of Chinese women workers as being strong and a force to be reckoned with, vis-à-vis the larger labor community, vis-à-vis the Chinese community, and also vis-à-vis the women's movement. We had very big contingents on Labor Day, we had women's health seminars, we had cooking classes. We'd go to City Hall and protest against gentrification and get petitions signed against police brutality, and participate in peace marches in Washington—just a variety of things. I could really see a big difference between somebody who'd been in CLUW for awhile and somebody who hadn't. There's just so much more they knew about trade unionism, about other broader issues—there was almost no comparison. We had this core of twenty people who had put themselves out in many different areas, in political areas and community-wide areas, going beyond just the day-to-day thing of sewing in the factories. At the same time, CLUW helped these women become leaders in the factory. Some of them became shop stewards, about five or six of them are now on the Executive Board of Local 23–25, and out of that group one or two became staff people later on, after the first batch of us did. And down the road I think we'll see some more promoting of leadership out of this group of women.

RM: How is the situation of garment workers in California, where you're working now, different from the one in New York?

KQ: Well, we're starting out from a much weaker position in the market. It's been a very long time since the union had such a corner on the manufacturers on the West Coast like it did in New York even in the 1970s. In San Francisco too, at one time, all the shops were unionized. My grandmother was working in a factory in 1930 and she first joined the ILG then, and she said that at that time all the shops in Chinatown in San Francisco were unionized. When I asked her how that came about, though, she really didn't know. Now there are very few union shops. And even in the union shops, conditions are much worse than they used to be. In the old days, the contract was more strictly adhered to. Since I left the factories in the early 1980s, it's been a very big struggle just to enforce the provisions of the contract. When I was working in the garment factories, it was really unheard of that people should work Sunday and holidays. Saturday, maybe yes, and you should get some overtime for it, but Sunday and holidays almost nobody ever worked. But now, they're just like any other day of the week. Also, we used to get yearly increases on the piece rates and there used to be a whole system set up where you could just add on a certain percentage to your wages and you would see some sort of increase in your take-home pay. But in the past ten to fifteen years, the employers have done away with the old piece-rate formula and have just given people a completely new piece rate every time they have a new style in. So you don't really see increases in your wages.

RM: What's behind this deterioration of conditions? Is it just the increased global competition in the industry?

KQ: It's partly because the union has really not organized enough in the past twenty years. We didn't spend a lot of effort in organizing the nonunion manufacturers and so we lost our grip slowly. In trying to organize today, we're faced with the problem that if we get a group of twenty people who want to join the union from a certain factory, well, that's fine and great, but where are they going to get union manufacturers' work? They're having a tough time trying to keep alive back East, they can't send any more work from back East over here. And we don't have any other manufacturers here who can give out work. So organizing in today's West Coast context is going to have to be a little bit different.

In the next couple years I want my organizers to try organizing medium-sized, self-contained manufacturing concerns, with about a hundred people, but with at the most one or two contractors. If we could pick up a few of those, great. And we're going to have to look at organizing on a more comprehensive scale, because to just go after the ones and twos is really not going to be able to do it. Suppose you go out and organize a small shop of ten people. Okay, you go to the boss and say you want union recognition. He might say no, in which case, you'd be stuck, you'd have to strike against him, but you really wouldn't have that much leverage. If he says yes—well, great, but then, the manufacturer may pull out the work and he wouldn't be able to get work from anybody else and he might close up overnight. So you might want to go after all the contractors of one certain manufacturer and get that manufacturer at the same time. But you know, some of these manufacturers are very large. They have a couple of hundred contractors from San Jose to Sacramento and San Francisco and Oakland and every place in between. So you're talking about a very large-scale, several-year effort. Then of course, the manufacturer could say, "Well, to hell with you! We're just going to do everything overseas."

The globalization of the industry has meant that there are a lot of competing pressures on labor. As Koret of California so articulately pointed out to us this year, when they closed down their plant here, when you can produce a woolen jacket overseas for $8.50 less than what it costs you to produce in the United States, you are of course going to do it overseas. This has forced us into a situation where in order to just retain the jobs and the work in the United States, not just the union, but also the American employers or contractors, have had to swallow some of the gains that people had made earlier and say,

"All right, if that's the case, let's work forty hours a week rather than thirty-five hours a week and maybe I can make up some of the cost difference and I can accept a lower price from the manufacturer."

But I don't think that protectionism or strictly limiting imports is really going to be the total long-range answer to the question of jobs for garment workers in the United States. To say we should cut off job boundaries at national borders, while the manufacturers are going worldwide without any borders, is sort of missing the point. I think that trade unions have to look at the industry in a global sense, just as the manufacturers do. For them, there are no borders, they'll just go anywhere. Koret says that even Hong Kong's too expensive for them now. So only their brokers are in Hong Kong, but they broker for China, for Macau, maybe for some of the smaller islands of Polynesia. They really chase after where it's most profitable. They say that the maquiladora factories on the Mexican border are too expensive for them. They want to go into the hinterlands of Mexico, like Mérida, which is the capital of the Yucatán. It's very far away, and there's not too much industry there, and they could really pay people very little. Or they want to go to places where there's all kinds of gross human rights violations, like El Salvador. Clearly they see their production resources as without national boundaries. And I really think that it behooves the labor movement to make ties among workers of different countries much stronger. The ILGWU actually spends quite a bit of effort and money in building international relations with labor unions in other countries. Well, this is fine and good, but I've seen over and over that whenever we've had an organizing campaign that involves work being shipped to another country and therefore we're losing our jobs here, we are never able to get something concrete hooked up whereby the workers of this country and the workers of the other countries have a concerted effort to put unified pressure on the manufacturer at the same time. The only example that I know of where this happened was when the 3M workers in South Africa walked out in support of the 3M workers in New Jersey some years ago. In the case of Koret, I found myself hit with the plant closure and then all of a sudden discovering that we should have built up relations with people in Guatemala, with people in the Philippines, with people in Korea, a long time ago. If we had done that we would have had a much stronger way to fight Koret in its plant closure. During this struggle, I brought a Guatemalan trade unionist to one of the meetings of the Koret workers. This guy is an exile in Washington, but he still has contacts in Guatemala. And he pledged to the Koret workers that he would get down and start organizing the Koret plant in Guatemala. He said it may not be in time to really affect the struggle here, but in the future it's going to mean that Koret's going to have to respond to the pressures of the workers in

Guatemala as well as the workers in the United States. I think that's an example
of the way that we should go. And I purposely did that also because I really
didn't want our American workers to think that people in these poor countries
of the Third World are stealing our jobs, as if they don't care if they work for
slave wages or anything like that. Bringing this guy to talk to them was really
an eye-opener for our members. I'm hoping that they will begin to understand
that the Guatemalan workers are extremely exploited, even more so than we
are here, and that they are very concerned about fighting for their rights as
well and in fact we should help them. I'm hoping that kind of strategy can
really prevail in the longer run.

There are some other new directions to go in, too. Maybe we should think
more about the fact that 75 percent of the garment industry work force in the
Bay Area is either Chinese or Vietnamese or Chinese-Vietnamese, and involve
the union more in the community. In the Koret campaign, the union had a
press conference in Chinatown—the first in recent memory held in San
Francisco. But we had to struggle over it among the staff when we got back.
Some people said it was divisive. Yet 75 to 80 percent of the Koret workers
were Chinese. And the community responded in a terrific way, sending letters
of protest and all kinds of stuff. It was an amazing show of support.

RM: What else would you like to do in the coming years as an ILGWU
manager?

KQ: Well, in my office, I'm going to really need a whole lot more staff,
although it's difficult to justify spending a lot more money when you just lost
a big base of membership. But I think that you can't look at it as a budget
balancing thing when you're in our position. If you don't invest in something
and try to get some returns out of it, you're not going to be able to get
anything. And you know, despite all the difficulties in organizing, I really
think that it *is* possible to, you know, dig some roots in the community and
get down there and know the people and know how to organize them. It
might take a long time. You know, it was really from 1975 till the early
1980s—I was already in the industry for seven or eight years before I was
really able to use some of the knowledge I had and to be effective. And then
you have the chances of history, too, which may not come along for a while.
But I think that if we have a little money and a little time we'll be able to get
there.

12
Gender Differences in Grievance Processing and the Implications for Rethinking Shopfloor Practices

Patricia A. Gwartney-Gibbs and Denise H. Lach

nions are important to women workers. Women who are covered by
a collective bargaining agreement generally earn higher wages compared to similar workers who do not have union representation.
Indeed, the slow erosion of the sex-wage gap in the United States is likely to be associated with gradually increasing union membership among women workers, particularly in the public sector (Freeman and Leonard 1987).

Besides better wages, unions also offer protections against arbitrary and unjust treatment. Unions provide an environment of bilateral negotiation between employers and employees. Union contracts provide regularized and well-exercised mechanisms of protecting employee rights and resolving employment disputes. But do union contracts protect women employees as well as they protect men?

The grievance procedure is key to the union contract. Union-negotiated grievance procedures have been widely regarded as the most systematic and effective means of dispute resolution in workplaces. The union grievance procedure has often served as a model for resolving worker disputes in non-union firms, despite criticism in recent years of its sometimes adversarial nature. There have been numerous studies of union grievance procedures (see, for example, Lewin and Peterson 1988), but how effective they are for women workers remains unexplored. In 1975, Wertheimer and Nelson urged re-

Our research was supported in part by a grant from the Fund for Research on Dispute Resolution and the facilities of the Center for the Study of Women in Society, University of Oregon. Research assistance by Chris Blint, Susanne Bohmer, Andrea Higgins-Everson, and Becky Medler is gratefully acknowledged. A version of this paper was presented at the 1991 American Sociological Association annual meeting.

searchers to examine how grievance procedures may operate differentially for women than for men (1975:151–52). To our knowledge, this is the first research to do so.

Drawing upon in-depth interview data with seventeen women and thirteen men workers (including eight union stewards and activists), we show that conflicts originate and dispute processing operates differentially for women and men in "Firm A," a unionized public sector agency.[1] We will focus upon three dimensions of dispute processing.

First, we examine the sources of women's problems and disputes in the workplace. We focus upon certain "female-typed" conflicts, that is, those associated with family and household responsibilities and subtle, difficult to name "personality conflicts" that our women interviewees experienced differently than men. Even though the union contract with Firm A has provisions sensitive to the needs of women workers, their implementation is left to personal negotiation between workers and supervisors, which, our interviews show, creates additional problems of favoritism. Our interviews also show how everyday personality conflicts in the workplace rarely escalate to a level that is grievable (that is, harassment), but can nevertheless make women's work lives miserable and less productive than they would be if there was a way to resolve the conflicts.

Second, we examine barriers women experience in taking workplace problems and disputes to the union. These barriers include: female-typed conflicts being less often covered by the union contract; paternalism and disbelief on the part of some stewards toward female-typed conflicts; workplace legends that create distrust of both union and management; and a generalized aversion among women to confrontation and adversarial action.

Third, we show that women who use the union grievance process report instrumental support (for example, explanation of the steps involved) and emotional support, even if they are unsuccessful in resolving their disputes to

[1]Firm A employs about three thousand workers distributed across many small work units serving several thousand clients. Interviews were conducted with both women and men, but here we focus on women's experiences. Interviewees were selected from a highly female-concentrated occupation (clerical) and a highly male-concentrated occupation (maintenance), including a small number of tokens (male clerical and female maintenance workers). Each interviewee was asked to describe the history of her or his workplace problems and disputes, from beginning to end, including both grievable (according to the union contract) and non-grievable disputes. Firm A employees are racially homogeneous (92 percent white), as in the state of Oregon where Firm A is located (95 percent white). Our interviewees reflect this homogeneity: three of the thirty were nonwhite (two Hispanic and one American Indian). (For a further description of our methods as well as information on the larger, ongoing project see Gwartney-Gibbs and Lach 1991.)

their liking. Moreover, many women who use the union grievance procedure experience empowerment from the process.

In our interpretation of these findings, we speculate on how gender differences in conflict origins, in grievance processing, and in outcomes may underlie broader patterns of employment inequality between women and men. We also examine the implications for union policies and recommend educational efforts unions may consider. Finally, we conclude with a statement explaining how both unions and women workers will benefit from further research on gender and grievance processing.

Sources of Women's Workplace Problems and Disputes

We hypothesized that women and men would experience different sources of workplace conflict, due to different gender roles, but our findings contained some surprises.[2] Several women, and some men, experienced workplace problems and disputes associated with family issues, particularly leaves and scheduling. One might expect these conflicts would arise over a *lack* of union contract provisions sensitive to working women's family obligations, but that was not the case, for the union contract with Firm A contains several such provisions. Rather, conflicts arose over how the provisions were implemented. Beverly, for example, recalled an instance

> "when my father was ill in the hospital in [a large city one thousand miles away] and I needed to go there to help my mother. While I didn't have any trouble getting the time off [using sick leave], which I'm entitled to, I heard about it several times from my boss after I returned—about how inconvenient it had been and what a strain it had put on the department. The general attitude was that they had done me a favor by letting me do it."

Her supervisor knew he could not forbid her to use sick leave for a family illness, but he let her know of his disapproval when she arranged for the days off and when she returned. This places normative pressure on Beverly, as well as her coworkers, to avoid future uses of sick leave in this manner. The same supervisor admonished a new mother to "shape up and get your child care situation fixed so that you didn't have to take so much sick leave."

Along with many other companies, Firm A has adopted a flextime policy as part of an attempt to be sensitive to the needs of women workers. But the

---

[2]A note on terminology: We use "problem" and "dispute" to describe workplace conflicts in varying stages of resolution. We think of problems as being any difficulty in the employment relationship. We think of disputes, more actively, as any and all efforts made to resolve the problem. We use "conflict" as a general term encompassing the range of problems and disputes.

particular arrangements for flextime are worked out individually between an employee and her supervisor. This places the burden of implementing "family friendly" policies on women workers. Moreover, we found that implementing "family friendly" policies in this way invites favoritism and particularism. For example, in several interviews, one clerical worker in an office was allowed to leave a bit early for the lunch hour to take a class or play sports and stay a bit late to make it up, or arrive ten minutes early in the morning and leave ten minutes early in the evening to avoid traffic at the child care center; but another clerical worker in the same office was not allowed to do the same because "the office has to be covered." Some offices allowed a little slack, for example, by putting an answering machine on the telephone for a few minutes, but in other offices, "You're on the clock. You're supposed to be there from eight to five. You need to be. If you're not, you've got a problem." We found that job sharing, another policy designed to be friendly to women workers, was another potential minefield of conflicts over favoritism, for it allowed supervisors to blame the less-favored member of the job sharing pair for tasks that slipped through the cracks.

Sick leave, flextime, and job sharing, as well as other benefits and protections, are explicitly detailed in the union contract. Therefore, when conflicts arise in relation to these matters, there is a basis for problem solving within the context of the grievance procedure. We found, however, that some of the most difficult and frequent everyday problems in women's work lives—what they often called "personality conflicts"—were not grievable issues under the union contract, unless they reached unusual extremes, such as "mental harassment." Tensions in work groups are not uncommon, of course, among men or women, but the women we interviewed spoke more often of such problems and they seemed to be more upset and derailed in their work by them than men. While some union stewards try to resolve such problems whether or not they can technically be called grievances, this was not the case in Firm A.

Examples of personality conflicts include clerical workers' reports of intense surveillance by their supervisors, who watched over their shoulders as they typed, listened in on telephone calls, and peered into their work areas at the beginning and end of the day to check on their arrival and departure times. In the extreme, these behaviors can be called harassment, which is grievable. But more often, the experiences are subtle—a meaningful look or a snide comment.

"My supervisor would do things like come into the office and acknowledge everybody else who was there, but not me. He just totally ignored me."
"She would say things out loud to the temporary worker—'Oh, you do

such beautiful work. You typed this so nice. It's so nice to have *someone* here who can type so well!' Little jabs."

Such conflicts are often difficult to label or prove. As a union steward said:

"I've talked to people who've told me 'My supervisor's driving me nuts because they're doing this and doing that.' And it's really hard to prove any of that stuff. And yet they tell me lots of times that *they* come across as being the terrible person. If it's really an out-and-out illegal thing that the supervisor is doing, then you can get 'em for it. But if it's just subtle little things, it's really hard."

A frequent source of personality conflicts seems to be how work should be accomplished in settings where there are few rules. One woman said:

"A global thing about clerical jobs is there are a million details with no training. You can't train a clerk to cover all the details that are not written down anywhere and can't be written down anywhere."

An example of how this can develop into conflict:

"My supervisor feels personally that I should be doing and feeling and thinking things in her way. She's the kind of person that needs to make copies of everything, and she even has set up some kind of system that actually makes more work for her. But that's just the way she is. She likes to be very organized. I don't like to work that way. I feel like there's a lot of steps that can be cut to get our work done."

Karen's supervisor was less tactful. "She treated me as a lowlife—demanding that I do this and that, not saying 'Would you' or 'Could you' do this, but 'You are going to. . . . ' I had to worship the ground she walked on."

Wendy described what she called mental abuse by her supervisor, which she felt "You just have to absorb; secretaries cannot talk back."

"When I'm typing, I might be asked, 'Are you sure that's right?' and then it brings doubts to my mind. Or my supervisor says 'Well, I gave you that report; where is it?' I search all over the office and then he says 'Oh well, I've got it right here.' But it doesn't seem like there's apologies. Supervisors have raised their voice at me, but if I used the same tone of voice, I was called unprofessional."

But harassment isn't limited to supervisors. Jean, a new custodian in a group of old-timers, described how coworkers made her life miserable:

"They would send me on wild-goose chases. I went down to the first floor to Fran and said I needed a vacuum, and she said to go look on the fourth floor. So I went and looked and there was no vacuum. I went and looked all over the third floor and the second floor, and there was no vacuum. Finally, I went back and said 'Fran, I still can't find a vacuum,' and she said 'Well, you'll just have to look around for one.' She wanted me to fail."

Jean went on to explain that, in retrospect, it was not just pettiness causing these problems. When she came into the group, as the first new employee in several years, Jean's supervisor assigned her almost twice as much square feet to clean as the old-timers. At the same time management was talking about streamlining the custodial team. Jean surmised that her coworkers feared if she could do the job, they too would be required to increase their workload. Instead, they set her up to fail.

Coworkers, like supervisors, can also exert more subtle pressures than the vacuum chase. A clerical worker described tension with a coworker:

> "It was impossible for me to interact with her. All the interaction was with other people, sort of skipping around her. It didn't feel right, but she refused to be part of what was happening."

When personality conflicts are multiplied over hours and days, workers' situations can become personally intolerable and the situations can interfere with the work that is supposed to be done. Rarely, however, does a personality conflict escalate to the point that it is covered by the union-negotiated grievance procedure at Firm A. A union steward we interviewed even dismissed a hot case involving accusations of racism because "basically it's about personality conflicts." He felt he could do little other than listen: "Maybe these people spilling their guts diffused it."

Personality conflicts seem to generate a great deal of emotional work for women. One said "I thought maybe I could change myself" to resolve the office tensions. Another woman said:

> "I couldn't allow myself to relax at all. I couldn't allow myself to operate the way I normally would. I held myself in check very carefully. I was careful to be very calm, to not ever complain. It was very hard on me."

Needless to say, "excessive emotional work" is not a disputable claim under the union contract.

Sexual harassment is, of course, covered by the union contract, but defining it and doing something about it also proved difficult for women in Firm A. It was hard, for example, for one interviewee—a young woman who supervised a temporary crew of all-male laborers—to "name" her subordinates' mocking and insolence as sexual harassment. When they hooted out of a work truck to another woman, "Hey baby! I like what I see!," she was able to name it, but she couldn't pin down her own experiences. Similarly, an office worker said of a coworker: "That kind of thing is hard to describe. He made comments and had certain body language, and I think he was dating some of the clients. I think it was sexual harassment on a limited scale." A union steward said, "There may be a grievance here in the making, but it's very, very difficult, because our contract isn't real strong on what we can do" about sexual harassment.[3]

Barriers to Taking Workplace Problems and Disputes to the Union

Given that the types of workplace conflicts women experience are less often specifically covered by the union contract at Firm A and given that there is no policy or consistent effort to address noncovered conflicts, it is no wonder that women feel discouraged in taking their problems to the union. Karen, who experienced severe mental harassment in a clerical job, said, "If you break a leg, you can see the effect. But if it's mental, how can you really prove it?" Another woman said, "Who's going to believe me?" Nora, a custodian, wanted to discuss personality conflicts, but:

> "Our particular union representative, I don't think he would be a good one to take [my case] to. He's kind of a negative person. He has his views and he doesn't leave room for anybody else's opinion. I get along fine with the guy. But I think I would probably call the union office and go that route rather than go through him. I can't say that he would misrepresent it, because I don't think he would misrepresent the union, but if he didn't think my ideas were particularly worthy, then he wouldn't show any interest as far as supporting me."

Nora added, "One of the other ladies I work with asked him [to talk about the personality situation in the work group], and he didn't have time." For these reasons, she has not yet approached the union.

By chance, we also interviewed Nora's union steward and he described how he sees his role:

> "When workers come to me, they want to know what can be done. But I'm usually more like a sounding board, kind of a father confessor."

This statement and his attitude toward women's personality conflicts seemed patronizing and paternalistic to us. About the personality situation that concerns Nora, he said:

> "All three of the women involved came to me and they all told me different stories. I tried to get information out of it, but the stories were so lacking in any real concrete detail that I couldn't think of anything. I talked with other bargaining unit members about it and they said 'Yes, it's terrible—can't do anything about it.' The union hasn't said so in so many words, but the process

[3]Sexual and other types of harassment are grievable under Firm A's contract. This steward is referring to the difficulty of "proving" harassment cases at Firm A.

required to do something is long and involved and gathering the evidence is so iffy."

We found such paternalism and disbelief rare among the stewards with whom we spoke. But it is important to know that some workers become permanently disaffected after feeling rebuffed by a union representative. Cheryl, a custodian, attended one big union meeting and from the floor raised her concerns about inequities in union-negotiated insurance premiums. Nothing happened. She has never attended another meeting since, saying "They don't pay any attention to us," and she has become a self-conscious free rider: "I thought 'Well, I'm okay. They're taking care of me. Why should I kick about it?' So I didn't."

Some workers do approach the union, but are dissatisfied with the help they receive. Jean, whose vacuum chase was described earlier, tried to take her case to the union, but "The union said there was nothing they could do about it because Fran was my coworker, my equal, not my supervisor." In another case, the union filed a grievance but the interviewee said, "I'm frustrated, because this started in April and here we are in November and we're barely above step two [of the grievance procedure]." Others described talking about issues with their stewards, but the stewards didn't do anything or didn't know what to do. Not surprisingly, such dissatisfactions with stewards were not limited to our interviews with women at Firm A; men expressed similar issues.

The experiences of coworkers can also inhibit the decision to go to the union, as one of Nora's statements above suggests. In Firm A, stories of workers' experiences in pursuing disputes sometimes developed into workplace legends passed on from one worker to another. Negative stories, in particular, deterred workers with grievable disputes from acting upon them. When we asked Lynda why she didn't file a grievance that her steward thought she could win, she replied:

> "The main reason I didn't was I'd heard from another clerical specialist that [a top administrator] is the person that eventually reviews them. She's strictly for management anyway and it would be real hard to win any kind of grievance with her."

Another clerical worker said:

> "I'm afraid of filing a grievance because it brands you. I'm a little bit nervous about that. I worked in a different section for five and a half years, and one of the workers there filed a grievance because he was put on a shift that he didn't want. He won the grievance and he was put on day shift again, but he was very heavily harassed, very heavily, by management."

The chief union steward knows that stories get passed around.

"If we've lost a case for somebody, or if we can't defend somebody, coworkers will say 'I sure wouldn't go to them. The union will just screw up.' "

Even Karen, who grieved and won her mental harassment case, fears that her grueling and humiliating experience will trickle through the grapevine and discourage others, rather than show the power of the grievance procedure.

Other reasons that women gave for not pursuing their workplace problems and disputes show more generalized aversion to confrontation. In part of her interview, Lynda's statements illustrate her fear of filing a grievance:

"I didn't go that far. I felt I may be digging myself a bigger hole with management if I did that. I felt if I did go farther, what was I getting myself into? I just assumed that I might be creating more problems for myself. Maybe if I just kind of let it go, it would all smooth over and wouldn't be such a big problem."

A woman steward spoke similarly of women's apprehensions in going to the union:

"A lot of women were afraid to speak up. It's like they're so grateful to have a job and they're helping their husbands out. And a lot of women are used to having an authority figure tell them what to do—they go from their fathers to their husbands. I talk to women all the time. Most of them didn't know what we did. We don't file a lot of grievances; a lot of it is mediation. When they were comfortable enough to know that I wasn't going to go in and file a grievance and drag them through arbitration, they felt better about it."

A laborer's explanation of her unease in pursuing a grievance shows her paralysis in the face of possible adversarial action:

"It was really strongly suggested [by friends]. But I was so, kind of immobilized by it. I tend to get immobilized when things aren't going right."

Similarly, a custodian said, "When I get into conflict, I back down. I'm not conflict-oriented at all."

Fear of retribution was another factor voiced by some women for not going to the union. One reported: "A lot of clerks are afraid to go to the union with their true feelings. They're afraid of punishment." A steward notes:

"They are intimidated. Sometimes there's some real solid grievances and people go 'Well, even if I win it, I still have to work here. I'm gonna pay for it later, so I think I'll just let it go.' There's a lot of that. We have three or four supervisors who are just notorious for being nasty to you if you do [file a grievance]."

Perhaps for these reasons, many women we spoke with wanted to try to work things out informally with their supervisors before approaching the union. As a bookkeeper said: "I was hoping I could work things out person-to-person with my boss rather than going to the union and filing a big grievance." Often, however, supervisors were not helpful. We heard many stories of canceled appointments, misunderstandings, gossip, and misleading information. A laborer's boss misled her about reclassification:

> "He told me that if I pushed for a reclass to grounds keeper and if I went to the union, that they could change my position to grounds keeper, but they might not hire me for it."

Believing she could lose her job, she has not talked with the union. A custodian having conflicts with a coworker cannot talk to her boss because the coworker and the boss are friends. Scuttlebutt, she believes, sabotaged her effort to move up in her job, to the lowest level of management:

> "I wanted to talk to my boss's boss, and I had an appointment to talk to her. But she canceled the appointment and said she didn't want to talk to me."

In another instance, a worker spoke with her boss's boss but

> "She resented me asking about it. She felt like I was out of the chain of command. She told me I was boxing her in. I really didn't understand."

Support and Empowerment from the Union

When women overcome their fears and hesitancies and actually go to the union, they report finding both instrumental and emotional support. Indeed, their views of the union seem to take on almost a rosy glow.

Karen had never been involved in the union before, because "I never thought I would need a union. I just sit down and do my work and expect harmony, you know?" She described the things her steward did in pursuing her mental harassment grievance against her supervisor and coworkers:

> "She heard my story. She would have lunch with me and try to get details from me. A lot of times when I talked with her, I was in tears; I was just beside myself. She said 'There is no question, Karen, that you are being railroaded, that you are the victim, that they wanted to get you out any way they could.' She said she had not ever seen a case like this. This was after she talked with my department to see exactly what was going on. Then she said 'You definitely need to file a grievance.' She arranged meetings, she contacted my doctor, and she contacted Personnel. She knew exactly what to do, and if she wasn't sure, she would check it out. She really kept on the ball, because if we missed one little meeting or one little thing, they could throw it out.
> When I was in that frame of mind, so distraught, it would be easy to mix up a meeting time. She was really good as far as helping me with whatever paperwork needed to be done. When I had to go see a psychiatrist, she came with me to be like a comforting board. I felt very much in violation then; they go back to the day you were born trying to find anything along your life

pattern that might have triggered [the harassment]. At the end she said, which
I thought was really good, 'I feel that the other people involved should have to
go through what you had to go through.' "

These themes are echoed in other women workers' reports of their experiences with union stewards willing to take on their complaints: affirmation of
workplace problems, even those subtle, hard-to-document personality conflicts; emotional relief; explanation of rules and procedures; negotiation with
various other players in the grievance process; and a step-by-step escort through
it all, at a time when they could not do it on their own.

Several clerical workers described how their attachment to and belief in the
union grew, particularly after they had relied on the union for help in resolving
difficulties.

"I wasn't a union member for years. I was raised Republican, nonunion. I've
changed over the last couple of years because of different things in my life—
work problems is one of them. I can really see the benefit of a union now."

Wanda said that she would not have thought of going to the union for support
in dealing with her substance abuse problem until coworkers suggested it.
After winning a grievance to get her treatment covered under terms of the
union contract, she says:

"I would tell others to use the union to the maximum, to use the grievance
procedure if they need to, and to try for support. I'd never used the union
before. Its been twenty years and I really never did bother with it, except to
complain about union dues! I would say to use it. I mean, even if you've never
done it before and wouldn't expect any help, I'd give them a try. Try the
union process."

Interestingly, even when the union was not instrumentally helpful, some
women workers' attitudes become more positive after the contact. As Jean,
the custodian, said:

"I've never worked for a union before and I like it, in spite of the fact that they
haven't done much for me (laughs). I like working with the union involved,
because you don't get as put-upon as you would otherwise."

Barbara, a secretary on a disciplinary work plan to improve her attitude and
work quality, grudgingly acknowledged the union's support. Even though the
union was unwilling to file a grievance or negotiate a lesser punishment for
her (indeed, Barbara believed the union agreed with her supervisor that she
was insubordinate and deserved discipline), the union stewards attended numerous meetings with her.

"The union representatives had nothing to offer me except to try to deal with
my supervisor and try to make sense of the nonsense that came out of her

mouth. They would come to the meetings and they would talk to me after. A union representative is there as an arbiter of common sense, to witness what I had to put up with, a reality check. That helped me to deal with the stress."

This sense of the union as a neutral party, "a witness," was important to Barbara (and many other interviewees) even though it was clear that the union would not back her one hundred percent.

Several women found the experience of union involvement empowering. "When the union steward told me it was preferential treatment, I was enforced by that. I felt some power." One woman described how her supervisor changed after a meeting with the steward present: "She felt the power, not just of this man, but of the union."

All the women stewards we interviewed became stewards after the union assisted them in resolving workplace problems and disputes. One described other unionists with whom she came into contact as "real strong people; strong women. It's really good to be around them." She continued: "Being a shop steward and being involved in union business and going to a lot of workshops, conferences, listening to other women and reading and just self-discipline, I've come a long way."

Summary and Interpretation

The interviews with women workers in Firm A suggest several things about women's experiences in grievances and grievance processing. First, the *origins* of workplace problems and disputes may be different for women than for men. Women's greater household and familial responsibilities may impinge upon the workplace more for them than for men, which can create difficulties in accomplishing work. Moreover, our interviews suggest that provisions negotiated by the union to ease these burdens, such as flextime, family leave and job sharing, may inadvertently provoke new conflicts by leaving their implementation to individuals' negotiation with supervisors.

Perhaps more important, however, is that many women workers report difficulties in the workplace—often loosely called personality conflicts—that are not covered by the union contract at Firm A. Rarely do personality conflicts with supervisors and coworkers escalate to a point that they can be labeled or proven as harassment cases, which are grievable. Rather, these everyday, subtle occurrences in work settings eat away at women workers, causing them intense "emotional labor" that can interfere with their main tasks (Hochschild 1983). Yet such problems are not recognized by the contract in Firm A, and, indeed, they are sometimes summarily dismissed by union stewards.[4]

Our research suggests that women's workplace problems and disputes are different from men's and are less likely to be covered by the provisions of union contracts. To the extent that this is proven true in more representative studies in the future, women workers may be systematically, although perhaps inadvertently, disenfranchised from the union-negotiated grievance procedure. Moreover, to the extent that the union contract does not address problems that women face in the workplace, the less likely it is that women will approach the union for assistance, enter the dispute resolution process, or consider the possibility of becoming a union steward or activist. This point underlies our second major observation: that there are gender differences in the *processes* of dispute resolution in the workplace.

We found that women are sometimes uneasy approaching stewards with personality conflicts and related employment problems that are difficult for them to name. We also found that this unease is justified, for at least some stewards appear unsympathetic, unhelpful, and patronizing about such problems. Other women showed varying amounts of fear, aversion, and uneasiness with the idea of confrontation and going to the union for assistance in conflict resolution. But trying to work things out with their supervisors on their own was not reported as a successful alternative. Importantly, we also found that those who had used the grievance process—even unsuccessfully—were happy with, and felt empowered by, the experience.

To the extent that women workers enter formal dispute resolution processes established by the union less often than men, there are likely to be gender differences in the *outcomes* of workplace conflicts. On one hand, fewer female-typed conflicts, like personality conflicts and family-related problems, will show up in formal settlements, such as arbitration, litigation, and government agency action. Moreover, those that do show up are likely to be nonrepresentative of women's daily problems and unusual in strength of case.[5] On the other hand, when their workplace conflicts go unresolved, women may exhibit lower job satisfaction, poorer performance evaluations, and greater turnover. Repeated across time, place, and circumstance, these gender differences in

[4]Some unions have policies that allow stewards to take up nongrievable issues, but the effectiveness and extensiveness of these informal opportunities for resolving women's, and men's, workplace difficulties is not known.

[5]As evidence for this, see Marmo (1980). Marmo reviewed all sexual harassment arbitration cases published between 1958 and 1978. He found that eighteen of the nineteen cases had nothing to do with the victim; rather, they involved reinstatement of the male perpetrator.

conflict resolution in the workplace may be associated with aggregate patterns of gender differences in earnings, promotions, and other features of employment, as well as gender differences in union leadership.[6]

Where Do We Go from Here?

What do these findings suggest for unions? Our in-depth interviews suggest that changes are needed in both perception and practice of the grievance procedure to make it possible for women workers to resolve their workplace problems and disputes without undue trauma. Educational efforts and modest innovations in union organization will make the grievance procedure user-friendly for women.

First, unionists must recognize that at least some workplace conflicts experienced by women may differ in nature from those experienced by men. "Female-typed" conflicts include (but are not limited to) those related to household and family (child care, family leave, scheduling) and personality conflicts, with either coworkers or supervisors. Union recognition of gender differences in conflict origins would help to legitimate female-typed conflicts with union members, union stewards, and management. This acknowledgement, in turn, should make it easier for women to use the grievance procedure to solve their workplace disputes. Recognition of female-typed conflicts in the labor contract is a step toward legitimating them. But because it would be impossible to specify all female-typed conflicts, we suggest a broad definition or statement of what is grievable combined with education of stewards on women workers' issues.

Even though the Firm A contract provided family leave policies and alternative scheduling options, many women workers spoke of difficulty implementing those policies because the implementation arrangements were left to the individual employee. When a union negotiates these types of provisions, sensitivity must be used to create language that removes the burden of responsibility from the employee. The union can take an active role in mediating implementation of these policies in the workplace.

To facilitate recognition of female-typed conflicts, we recommend educational efforts by the union that aim to help stewards and union members identify the differential workplace experiences of women and men workers, including gender differences in conflict origins noted above. A union could also undertake a survey or analysis of members' conflicts to examine the

---

[6]A more elaborate theoretical framework examining gender differences in the origins, processes, and outcomes of workplace disputes may be found in Gwartney-Gibbs and Lach 1990.

different origins of women's and men's (and other subgroups') workplace conflicts. Even if no female-typed grievances have been filed by women members, it is not necessarily an indication that they don't exist. Women members may have difficulty naming the problems they are experiencing, but an astute steward should be able to uncover the underlying components of a personality conflict to ensure that the member is protected from any grievable mistreatment and to perhaps act as a mediator.

Another educational effort could involve heightening awareness among stewards of women members' hesitancy in approaching them and filing grievances. Women may perceive that their specific workplace problems will not be well received by stewards or the union and, thus, be hesitant to speak with them or file a grievance. Many women we talked with also expressed repulsion and fear of involving themselves in the grievance procedure because they perceived it to be a traumatic experience. Workplace culture and mythology in any organization probably includes some "horror stories" of women who entered the "twilight zone" of the grievance process and were never heard from again. It is important for union stewards to be aware of workplace culture and women members' aversion to what may be perceived as adversarial action, to help overcome resistance to engagement in the grievance process.

"Empowered" was how many women with whom we spoke described their experiences with the grievance procedure once they had made the difficult decision to file a grievance. Grievance-filing women described newfound self-confidence in having union advocacy and improved self-esteem as a result of successfully resolving disputes through an institutional process. This is very important for unions and for women workers. The challenge is to make the sense of empowerment part of normative work culture, so that workplace dispute resolution via the union-negotiated grievance procedure is viewed as a potentially positive experience.

A union-sponsored educational effort for members could help create an "empowered" workplace culture for women members. Women grievance filers could tell their stories, serving as role models for their peers and reinforcing the image of women successfully using the grievance procedure.[7] Unions could also provide specific information on how the grievance procedure works, what is in the contract, how to describe conflicts in terms of the labor contract, when to notify a steward of conflicts occurring in the workplace, and how to approach a steward. Such an educational effort should be part of orientation for new members or of negotiated release time for all new workers, to reach

---

[7]Aside from an educational campaign, women who have these empowering experiences could be recruited as new union stewards.

them before the workplace culture has a chance to discourage problem-solving. Reading the contract, approaching a steward or supervisor, and practice in filing a grievance may be beneficial to all new union members and workers, but especially to women members apprehensive about the process.

Besides educational efforts, certain innovations in union organization may encourage greater membership and involvement by women. Many women we talked with had difficulty participating in their union as fully as they would have liked due to family responsibilities. Many women cannot attend union meetings after work; in addition, women who work on swing or graveyard shifts are often unable to participate. Lunch-hour meetings or other alternative times could help women participate more fully in the union organization. Providing child care during meetings (a benefit currently offered by some unions) would also facilitate women's attendance and participation.

Some women with whom we talked expressed little desire to participate in, or even to learn more about, the union because they perceived it to be extra "work" for which they didn't have time. Internships or apprenticeships with experienced union stewards may be one way to simultaneously encourage participation and reduce the amount of work involved. Such partnerships could introduce union processes to members at a slower pace, but allow them to take on more responsibility as their skills develop. Union stewards could also "job share" a stewardship so that each member takes on one-half the job—a somewhat less intimidating amount of union work.

Finally, many women union members expressed fear of the grievance process, which they perceived as highly adversarial, and great reluctance to follow a grievance through to arbitration. If educational efforts, designed to demonstrate the power and promise of the union grievance procedure, do not effectively change women's apprehensions in confronting management, unions may want to consider an alternative to the traditional grievance procedure. Some unions already offer the mediation or negotiation services of third-party neutrals (to either the union or management). Although success is mixed when third-party neutrals have no final authority, these alternative problem-solving forums may be less threatening than engaging directly with management through the grievance procedure.

Conclusions

Previous empirical research on women's experiences with union grievance procedures has focused almost exclusively on arbitration awards and proceedings, which is the final step in the grievance process. Over fifteen years ago, Wertheimer and Nelson (1975) called for research on how workers perceive the grievance process, particularly why workers seem to fear it, and whether there may be gender differences in possible fear of retribution; whether supervisors are harder on women who actively pursue their disputes than on men who do the same; whether there are patterns to women's grievances that are not seen in men's; and whether such differences are job-related or gender-related. But still, virtually nothing is known about how woman employees fare relative to men in the processes of resolving disputes through union-negotiated grievance procedures. We have explored some of these questions.

The topic of gender and grievance processing warrants further study because the labor movement needs women workers. Unions, justly or not, have had a reputation for discouraging, or even restricting, female membership. Women workers, however, are no more averse to unionism than men (Kochan 1979; Fiorito and Greer 1986). This finding implies that unions can gain strength by designing and offering women workers employment protections that they cannot obtain in a nonunionized firm. Both women and unions will benefit by grievance procedures that effectively address women's workplace problems and disputes.

13
Organizing and Representing Clerical Workers

The Harvard Model

Richard W. Hurd

The private sector clerical work force is largely nonunion, simultaneously offering the labor movement a major source of potential membership growth and an extremely difficult challenge. Based on December 1990 data, there are eighteen million workers employed in office clerical, administrative support, and related occupations. Eighty percent of these employees are women, accounting for 30 percent of all women in the labor force. Among private sector office workers, 57 percent work in the low-union-density industry groups of services (only 5.7 percent union) and finance, insurance, and real estate (only 2.5 percent union). With barely over ten million total private sector union members, the labor movement can ill afford to overlook the thirteen million nonunion women who work in private sector clerical occupations (BLS 1991).

Concerned trade unionists are now searching for appropriate models for organizing and representing these workers. Two schools of thought have emerged. Some believe that clericals are like other workers and can be organized when job-related concerns predispose them to action. According to this view, private sector clerical organizing can proceed if and when unions devote sufficient attention and resources to the endeavor using conventional organizing techniques. Other unionists argue that clericals are different. Not only are they primarily women, but they also tend to be traditionally feminine and turned off by macho blue-collar unionism. According to this interpretation, a special approach is required regarding style, tactics, and/or issues to be addressed.

I will focus on one highly visible private sector clerical organizing victory: the 1988 union win among Harvard University clerical and technical employees. The Harvard case is, in many ways, representative of the success unions have experienced among university-based clerical workers in recent years using rank-and-file grassroots oriented campaigns. And, as a private sector campaign that confronted intense management opposition, it also offers tactical lessons that are relevant beyond the confines of academia. Perhaps most important, the Harvard case presents us with a distinct organizing and bargaining model whose relevance to other organizing efforts deserves careful evaluation: the Harvard Union of Clerical and Technical Workers (HUCTW) not only employed a grassroots *organizing* approach, but also devised a unique bargaining strategy that succeeded in institutionalizing and preserving rank-and-file involvement.

How Organizable Are Clerical Workers?

The available evidence suggests that clericals are just as likely to be pro-union as other workers. This conclusion is based in part on recent opinion polls and union-sponsored surveys that have consistently disclosed that unrepresented women workers are more positively disposed toward unionization than are unrepresented men. Reinforcing evidence is offered by Ruth Milkman, who has uncovered a secondary phenomenon: the propensity of women to support unionization increases as the proportion of women in the work unit grows (Milkman forthcoming). In other words, women in gender homogeneous work groups offer the most congenial target for union organizers. Because clerical work is predominantly staffed by women, this information should be encouraging to unions interested in organizing clericals.

Additional support for this optimistic assessment is offered by Phil Comstock, of the Wilson Center for Public Research, and Cynthia Costello. Based on thirty-eight thousand responses from nonunion women to Wilson Center surveys between 1982 and 1989, Comstock concludes that women workers are increasingly attracted to unions because the majority now work out of economic necessity and have a long-term attachment to the labor force (BNA 1990b:C-2). Costello's research demonstrates that women clerical workers are potentially as oppositional and militant as unionized male workers (Costello 1987).

Although there is general agreement among trade unionists on organizing potential, there is considerable disagreement about the best strategy for reaching clericals. Many concur with Comstock that organizing women clericals is not substantially different from organizing other workers. Comstock argues that the concerns of the "new women workers" are converging with those of their male counterparts. He points specifically to low-paid office workers who are responsive to organizing because they "have job related complaints, [and] believe that 'something needs to be done' to improve their earnings, treatment and opportunities" (Comstock 1989:10). Comstock offers an optimistic assessment of the potential for traditional unions to organize clericals with standard approaches emphasizing issues of pay, benefits, and working conditions.

Others are skeptical of the ability of male-dominated unions to effectively address the concerns of women clericals. Milkman (forthcoming) and Costello (1987) see clericals organizing, in part, on the basis of gender ties. Similarly, Naomi Baden argues that unions must use approaches that are sensitive to gender differences. Female office workers are most likely to respond positively to women organizers who develop collective workplace leadership and emphasize the emotional and personal rewards of unionization (Baden 1986). Ruth Needleman adds that women expect more from unions than men, and they respond best to organizers who pay attention to the complexity of workplace relationships and who facilitate rank-and-file participation (Needleman 1988).

Even among those who agree that standard union approaches are inappropriate for women clericals, there is some disagreement over whether the work culture and values of clericals promote or hinder unionization. In a case study of a strike by clerical employees at a Wisconsin insurance company, Costello concludes that the women's willingness to fight management's sex discrimination practices reflects a more militant style than is usually attributed to clerical workers (Costello 1987). But Roberta Lynch of AFSCME disagrees. She views the "female" culture of clerical work as a hindrance to unionization. Clericals tend to be passive and traditionally feminine, and thus averse to strikes and other forms of direct action. Furthermore, they value their close working relationship with professionals and managers, and worry that a third-party union might create an uncomfortable adversarial environment (Lynch 1986).

Karen Nussbaum of 9 to 5, the National Association of Working Women, partially reconciles these apparently contradictory views. She notes that organizers must be patient because most clericals have no experience with unions. Trust must be cultivated in order to help clericals overcome their fear: of the unknown, of being ostracized by their boss or coworkers, of being mistreated or fired, of strikes, of unions as impersonal third-party intruders, and so on. Once clericals resolve to support a union, their commitment is firm because the process has been painful and they have exercised such great care in reaching the decision. When challenged, this commitment readily transforms into militance (Nussbaum 1986).

Clerical Organizing in Higher Education

One of the clearest indications of the potential for clerical organizing is the success unions have experienced among the employees of colleges and universities. Although many of the victories in this arena have resulted from a natural extension of the growth in public sector unions in the 1970s, unionization has also spread to clericals at private institutions. While precise figures are not available, it is probable that unionization levels among clericals at public universities are comparable to those of other state and local government employees. It is also clear that the clerical employees of private universities are more likely to be union members than are other private sector white-collar workers. Roughly half of the bargaining units were first certified in the 1980s, with very few university clericals represented prior to 1970. Remarkably, clerical workers now have union representation on 70 percent of the campuses where organizing campaigns were conducted in the 1970s and 1980s (Hurd 1989b).

Although on a broad scale unionization has spread rapidly among clerical workers in higher education, specific campaigns tend to move slowly. These workers are initially skeptical of unions and carefully evaluate the decision to support an organizing campaign. In response, most unions have adopted a grassroots approach in which the union staff member helps build a large representative internal committee; the committee then does the actual organizing. Most of the organizing is one-on-one, worker to worker. Although time-consuming, grassroots organizing builds a base of highly dedicated activists. Two successful examples of this style are the Columbia University campaign by United Auto Workers District 65 and the Yale University campaign by the Hotel Employees and Restaurant Employees (Hurd 1989a, 1986; Ladd-Taylor 1985).[1]

If leaders of a preexisting staff association support union affiliation, a win is more likely. At Vassar College, for example, a staff association was formed in 1975 by clerical, technical, and professional employees to organize social events and, on occasion, to present concerns to the college's administration. By 1985 the association's leaders had become frustrated with the administration's lack of responsiveness and invited six unions to make presentations at

---

[1]It is not uncommon for a union to lose a first election, maintain a presence, then eventually win bargaining rights. This scenario is especially likely where management aggressively opposes unionization. At the University of Cincinnati, for example, SEIU District 925 began organizing in 1984, losing its initial representation election in 1986 by fifty votes in a unit of 1,400. The union filed for a second election in 1988 and won by 170 votes (Schneider 1990).

open lunchtime meetings. The leaders then decided to seek collective bargaining rights with the assistance of the Communications Workers of America (CWA). In a subsequent National Labor Relations Board (NLRB) election, the membership voted 76 percent in favor of joining the CWA (Beluardo 1986).

Where a substantial portion of the work force is familiar with unions, reticence diminishes and organizing proceeds more quickly. Cuyahoga Community College is located in heavily unionized Cleveland, Ohio. When SEIU District 925 decided to organize the college's clerical workers in 1982, two bargaining units, representing the blue-collar workers and the faculty, already existed on the campus. Because of the heightened familiarity with unions there was less fear, and District 925 distributed union authorization cards only two months after its initial contact, quickly signing up 65 percent of the workers (Hill 1985).

Although diverse in many ways, most successful college and university campaigns share one important element: the clericals involved come to view the union as their own organization. At Vassar and Cuyahoga Community College, the organizing efforts were initiated and controlled by the clerical workers themselves, with the parent unions providing technical and legal support. At Yale, Columbia, and Cincinnati, the campaigns were based on the grassroots organizing philosophy, and the workers "assumed ownership" of their locals. College and university clericals are more likely to support unionization if they are convinced that the bargaining agent will be controlled by the membership. The specific parent union is largely irrelevant, with at least sixteen national unions and many independent locals serving as bargaining agents at campuses across the country. Although there are some cases where clericals view the union as a service organization and have neither demanded control nor asserted ownership, the typical university clerical union is created and thrives because of rank-and-file activism.

The Early Stages of Organizing at Harvard

Harvard University's clerical campaign, the first in which a grassroots approach was fully institutionalized into the ongoing representational activities of a union, confirms the importance of the grassroots organizing approach.

Union organizing among white-collar workers at Harvard spanned nearly two decades. Early organizing led to elections in 1977 and again in 1981 at Harvard Medical School, both resulting in narrow defeats for District 65. District 65 affiliated with the United Automobile Workers (UAW) in 1981, and the UAW then assumed responsibility for the organizing efforts at Harvard. In 1984, the UAW filed for a third election at the medical school, but the university challenged the unit definition and the NLRB agreed, expanding the bargaining unit to include all of Harvard's clerical and technical employees (Golden 1988:40–41).

Kristine Rondeau went to work as a research assistant at the Harvard School of Public Health in 1976, and was a volunteer in the 1977 District 65 campaign. During the 1981 election she worked full-time as a member of the union's organizing staff. After the 1981 defeat she stayed with the UAW and became the lead organizer at Harvard. In 1985 Rondeau and six other staff members left to form the independent Harvard Union of Clerical and Technical Workers (HUCTW) (Golden 1988:41).

For a year and a half the seven organizers (all former Harvard employees) operated on a shoestring budget funded primarily by donations. The HUCTW's perseverance during this difficult period was instrumental in winning respect from a broad cross-section of the clerical and technical employees and dissolving concerns that the union was an outside force (Solomon 1990). Although the HUCTW affiliated with the American Federation of State, County and Municipal Employees (AFSCME) in January 1987, it had established itself as the grassroots domain of Harvard clerical workers. AFSCME provided much-needed financial support, but the local was allowed almost complete autonomy (Golden 1988:40–42, 45).

Rondeau and her fellow organizers developed HUCTW's strategy, borrowing some tactics from the successful clerical campaigns at Yale and Columbia. Virtually all organizing was conducted one-on-one, usually over lunch. In these discussions, HUCTW's staff members and rank-and-file activists emphasized how a union could help individual workers confront their powerlessness. As Rondeau said, "You have to strengthen people as individuals, and you have to find a way for them to develop their own self-confidence. You have to find a way for them to express anger at being powerless yet somehow represent themselves in a positive way that works for them" (Green 1988:6). Each worker was encouraged to define her own issues, while the union provided the support and sense of community necessary to overcome isolation.

The organizing task at Harvard was enormous: thirty-seven hundred employees working in two thousand isolated offices and laboratories scattered among four hundred buildings. With AFSCME's financial support, the local's organizing staff was increased in 1987 to sixteen. Eight were former Harvard employees and the other eight continued to hold part-time jobs at the university. The organizers divided the campus into twenty-two areas, each with its own organizing committee. These area organizing committees met weekly over lunch with a staff member to discuss progress and strategy and to identify potential recruits for a campus-wide organizing committee. Eventually, the larger campus-wide organizing committee included 450 members, with at least one from each building (J. Diamond 1988).

The organizers worked with the committee members to help them develop basic interpersonal skills, concentrating on how to form a relationship and how to listen. Committee members had to overcome their own fears and approach other workers to discuss the union one-to-one. Workers were not pressured, but were encouraged to support the union and to become involved to the degree that they were comfortable (Leavitt 1990). Member Donene Williams said, "There was a strong emphasis on doing it ourselves, and doing it our way" (Williams 1990a).

The 1988 Victory

In December 1987, HUCTW staff and rank-and-file leaders decided that support was sufficiently broad and solid to initiate a card campaign. Members of the campus-wide organizing committee were given cards and went back to the workers in another series of one-on-one meetings to collect signatures. In March 1988 HUCTW filed for an election with the NLRB after signing up a majority of the unit (V. Diamond 1988).

The union's reliance on face-to-face organizing by Harvard workers was designed to build commitment prior to filing for the election and to provide the best possible defense against management's inevitable resistance efforts. Rondeau described the reasoning behind the philosophy: "They have to be intellectually and emotionally committed. Otherwise, when there's an anti-union campaign, you lose them" (Golden 1988:41). The preelection organizing merely reinforced the earlier attention to individual worker concerns. Organizing committee members kept track of all union supporters. Anyone who was wavering received diligent one-on-one attention at home, at lunch, and at work in a process one organizer called "polite yet ruthless" (Golden 1988:44).

The union's campaign encouraged workers to stand together to gain power. Its central theme was the "philosophy of voice." By emphasizing worker empowerment and involvement in determining the conditions of their employment in order to improve quality of life on the job, HUCTW was able to avoid confronting management on specifics. With democratic decision making as the key issue, stronger group identity was also facilitated (Leavitt 1990; Byrne 1990a).

This is not to say that specific issues did not arouse the ire of workers. Susan Manning identified pay as her key concern, while Bertha Ezell expressed frustration that personnel rules had blocked her career advancement because she did not have the correct credentials (Weinstein 1988). For those with young children, affordable day care was a primary need and the union made a special effort to highlight this concern (Noble 1988). The union also focused on matters important to older long-term employees, such as pensions and health care (Feinberg 1987). The campaign was never limited to these specific issues, however. HUCTW's focus on empowerment offered each worker a potential solution to the problem most important to her or him.

HUCTW also emphasized how needs were interrelated and helped individuals realize that they were not just unionizing for themselves but for their coworkers as well. Pauline Solomon, for instance, said "From the beginning [the organizers] took the approach that if I wanted someone to support my issue then I should support their issue" (Solomon 1990).

Group support and cooperation was facilitated, in part, by the workers' common identity as women. Women made up over 80 percent of the unit and many viewed their job-related difficulties from a feminist perspective. Barbara Horell supported HUCTW because she did not want "to be relegated to undervalued 'women's work' " (*Chicago Tribune* 1988). Pauline Solomon's involvement was precipitated by concern for pay equity: "If you compared our skills with men doing work that required a similar level of education and training, we would be making much more money" (Solomon 1990).

The way pro-feminist union organizers defined certain issues also fostered gender consciousness among workers. The union focused on the affordability of child care, a major burden for low-wage clericals but a minor irritation for the mostly male faculty. Similarly, pension deficiencies were discerned as particularly severe because of the blocked upward mobility and substandard pay typically associated with the clerical and technical jobs held mostly by women. At union rallies organizer Joie Gelband would hop on a piano and sing to the tune of "Diamonds Are a Girl's Best Friend": "A pat on the head can be quite condescending, but unions are a girl's best friend" (Warren 1988).

Because specific issues were secondary, it was possible to forego traditional campaign literature. Instead the organizers and committee members concentrated on building relationships among supporters to strengthen the feeling of community. Newspaper articles about the campaign *were* copied by the union and circulated to reinforce the notion that the HUCTW was doing something important. Newspaper articles, however, never substituted for personal contact.

Although traditional campaign literature was scarce, posters, bumper stickers, and buttons were integral to the campaign. This paraphernalia helped popularize two slogans that became central to the organizing effort: "It's not

Anti-Harvard To Be Pro-Union" and "You Can't Eat Prestige." The prestige associated with university employment is a barrier to organizing university clericals, and was especially noticeable at internationally renowned Harvard. The union slogans attacked this issue head-on, pointing out that on the one hand, to be rewarding a job must offer more than prestige alone, and on the other, that unionization need not undermine the institution itself. The HUCTW went to great lengths to convince workers that they could use the union to increase their influence, improve their work environment, *and* make Harvard a better university in the process (Golden 1988:47).

From the beginning of the organizing process, the HUCTW reached out to the broader university community and to potentially sympathetic organizations and individuals outside of Harvard, informing them of the clerical workers' concerns and updating them on campaign developments. In 1988, when the university unleashed a sophisticated anti-union campaign in response to the union's card-signing effort, the HUCTW was prepared and called on students, faculty, and community supporters to urge Harvard president Derek Bok to refrain from engaging in an anti-union campaign (Rondeau and Manna 1988). Bok received hundreds of letters and phone calls imploring him to permit a fair vote.

Shortly after filing, the union's "neutrality campaign" went into high gear. Twenty-seven distinguished Harvard professors (many holding endowed chairs) issued a public statement urging "that the University management remain scrupulously neutral during the organizing drive" (Adams et al. 1988). The Boston City Council passed a resolution requesting that Harvard "refrain from anti-union campaigns and further attempts to delay a representation election" (Boston City Council 1988). Students signed petitions; church, civil rights, women's, and labor organizations sent representatives to visit Bok; and hundreds attended a candlelight vigil outside of Bok's home (J. Diamond 1988). Although Harvard continued to wage war on the union, the "neutrality campaign" clearly put the university on the defensive.

Harvard's carefully crafted anti-union campaign balanced on a fine line between academic free speech and union busting, as the university attacked the union with what the *Chicago Tribune* called a "velvet scalpel" (Warren 1988). The university emphasized Harvard's record as a "progressive, responsive employer," one that paid competitive salaries with good benefits, and offered quality child care (Weinstein 1988). The administration attempted to appear objective, factual, and academic. Four booklets titled "Consider the Facts" and numerous letters stating management's case were sent to each employee. Throughout, union representation was portrayed as inappropriate for Harvard's white-collar workers because of the rigidity and needless conflict that would result (J. Diamond 1988).

The university held 120 "captive audience" meetings on work time. Although attendance was technically voluntary, recalcitrant employees frequently received notices of meetings with an added message that their supervisors "have been made aware of the day and time of these meetings and join [the administration] in encouraging you to attend" (*Harvard Crimson* 1988b). Clerical and technical employees opposed to the union joined together as the "Staff Support Action Committee" to assist management's campaign (Weinstein 1988).

The administration relied heavily on supervisors to assist their effort. A 104-page briefing book, full of such information as lists of legal anti-union statements (and their unlawful counterparts); strikes at other universities; examples of restrictive and undesirable clauses from "representative" AFSCME contracts; and the positive aspects of pay, benefits, and working conditions at Harvard, was prepared for supervisors (BNA 1988). Supervisors were informed that the university had the right to fire those supervisors who were uncooperative (*Harvard Crimson* 1988a).

President Bok attempted to remain above the fray. He had established his own academic reputation in the field of labor-management relations, writing books and articles that in some cases were explicitly critical of management efforts to resist unions. But as an administrator facing an organizing campaign, Bok saw the situation in a different light. A few weeks before the election he sent a four-page letter to each employee, using somewhat tortured reasoning to explain his position:

> [Unions are] a good thing for America and for working people. . . . However, I am not at all persuaded in this case that union representation and collective bargaining will improve the working environment at Harvard. . . . [Unions have] resisted efforts to allow supervisors and employees to vary the way they work in response to their special needs and capabilities (BNA 1988).

The union did not wither under management's onslaught. Hundreds of copies of the university's briefing book for supervisors were printed by the union and distributed to its members. A video was produced simulating an anti-union meeting to prepare members for the captive audience events (Hart 1988). The anti-union propaganda was undermined by HUCTW's grassroots strategy: organizing committee members talked individually with coworkers about the administration's intimidation efforts (Williams 1990a).

In the end, the HUCTW prevailed. The final tally in the May election was 1,520 "yes," 1,486 "no," with 41 challenged ballots, only 3 less than required to overturn the election. The union was ecstatic. Kristine Rondeau proclaimed, "We want to make this a model for women everywhere" (J. Diamond 1988). Ecstasy did not cloud reality, however. HUCTW representatives declared they would take one day off and then resume organizing the people who voted no (BNA 1990a).

Management interpreted the union's get-out-the-vote tactics as "harassment," "threats," and "systematic interrogation," and seven days after the election they (management) filed technical objections to the vote with the NLRB (Fatsis 1988). The union responded by staging a protest at Harvard's June 9 commencement (United Press International 1988) and by requesting that supporters call or write Derek Bok and ask him to "reconsider this intentionally divisive behavior" (HUCTW 1988).

Although the administration persisted with its appeal, NLRB Administrative Law Judge Joel Harmatz dismissed all charges against the union on October 21 (Harvard College JD (BOS)–257–88). Harvard decided to halt its legal challenge at this stage and forego appeals. On November 4 President Bok announced that the university would recognize the union. He also promised to pursue a "constructive and harmonious" relationship with the HUCTW (Butterfield 1988).

The HUCTW Contract

With the election outcome settled, the HUCTW was determined that its emphasis on grassroots participation would continue. The union's commitment to the philosophy of voice influenced its bargaining strategy, and its goal of worker empowerment eventually produced an agreement that incorporated innovative models of democratic decision making. Union certification was followed by a burst of organizing and the addition of many new members. HUCTW leaders adopted a cautiously conciliatory posture, reminding the university that they desired to work cooperatively to improve Harvard. President Bok's appointment of Harvard professor emeritus and former U.S. Secretary of Labor John Dunlop as chief negotiator signaled a softening on management's side as well. The two sides agreed to forego formal negotiations for ninety days. Instead, they established two eight-member transition teams (one for each side) that held regular meetings. This allowed the two parties to learn about each other, while simultaneously permitting the animosity created during the election and appeal process to cool (Bureau of National Affairs 1990a).

During the ninety days, the union surveyed members and prepared contract goals and objectives. In February 1989, the HUCTW distributed a list of bargaining objectives to all of the clerical and technical workers. Included were standard union concerns such as an improved salary structure, expanded benefits, fair transfer and promotion policies, and health and safety protection, as well as less common objectives such as a family policy, employee participation, and mutual respect and cooperation. To handle negotiations, the union held an election to choose sixty-five negotiating team members (HUCTW 1989; Williams 1990a).

The first set of discussions focused on devising a unique participatory structure for the formal bargaining. Nine separate bargaining tables were established to deal with separate sets of key issues: salaries and job classifications; pensions and retirement; family policy, child care, and elder care; affirmative action; health and safety; health and disability benefits; personnel practices; education and career development; and employee participation. The elected members of the union negotiating team each served on only one table. Each table met at least once a week, although some tables met more frequently as the two sides approached final agreement (Williams 1990a; BNA 1989a).

The bargaining format was also unusual. The typical adversarial approach of offer and counteroffer was shunned, and lawyers were excluded from the negotiations. At each table general discussion of the issues under consideration was followed by a review of various options for dealing with the concerns of both sides. Specific contract proposals were debated only after a reasonably thorough understanding of mutual interests and conflicting objectives had been achieved. This approach was possible because of the union members' commitment to Harvard, and because John Dunlop recognized that the union was interested in constructive changes (BNA 1989a).

Although negotiations proceeded amicably, the HUCTW did not abandon its aggressive side. The union continued to organize nonmembers, and the rank and file actively participated in a contract campaign that culminated in a series of rallies workers enthusiastically supported (average attendance was nine hundred) (Williams 1990a).

Negotiations were a resounding success. The two sides reached agreement on June 25, 1989, and the contract was ratified June 29 with 94 percent voting in favor (Bureau of National Affairs 1989c). The contract itself was remarkable. It not only offered sizeable economic gains to the members, but also dramatically altered workplace relations by giving workers more of a voice.

The HUCTW estimated that members would receive average pay increases of 32.5 percent over the life of the three-year agreement.[2] More astonishing

[2]Calculated from data included in HUCTW 1989; Harvard Vice-President for Finance

than the substantial wage gains were the considerable improvements in a broad range of fringe benefits, including health insurance, dental insurance, disability, and pensions. Nonmonetary protections were also achieved, including an agency shop, strong affirmative action and equal opportunity language, and health and safety protections (HUCTW 1989). As the *AFL-CIO News* pointed out, the contract broke "important new ground in a number of key areas" (AFL-CIO 1989). Harvard agreed to scholarships for child care, a cooperative effort to expand affordable child care options, a thirteen-week maternity leave period, an extensive family leave program, and a referral service for elder care (Harvard University and HUCTW 1989a:16–17).

But the contract's most unusual feature was its extensive reliance on joint labor-management teams. The family policy section included a union/university committee to administer the child care scholarship program. Health and safety committees were called for in each school or administrative unit. A joint committee was established to promote affirmative action and antidiscrimination programs. Three separate committees were set up to study and implement changes in the job classification system. And, the first substantive section of the contract outlined an extensive employee involvement program (HUCTW 1989).

The contract established a participatory system featuring the Joint Council (JC), "intended to be a forum for the discussion of all workplace matters which have a significant impact on staff" (Harvard University and HUCTW 1989a:4). Each school and administrative unit was required to set up at least one JC. In essence the JCs were designed to provide forums for ongoing discussion and to resolve concerns that normally would be processed through contract provisions with specific work rules. The Harvard contract was devoid of such rules.

Each JC was required to have equal representation from the bargaining unit and management and a cochair selected by each side. Either side would be allowed to raise issues for consideration and every effort would be made to reach consensus on these matters. Consensus recommendations would then be passed on to the dean of the school or a top management official of the administrative unit. If consensus could not be reached or the relevant dean or administrator failed to act, the issue would be referred to the University JC (UJC). The UJC was empowered to seek the assistance of a mediator. In no case would the individual JCs or the UJC have the authority to modify the

---

Robert Scott estimated that the cost of pay hikes would total less than 25 percent due to turnover (BNA 1989b).

collective bargaining agreement (Harvard University and HUCTW 1989a: 5–6).

The HUCTW-Harvard agreement also set up a separate system to address specific contract violations normally handled through standard grievance procedures. The agreement also defined a dispute much more broadly than in most contracts, thus allowing for subtle issues of "harassment" or "personality problems" to be resolved under this procedure. A worker (or workers) experiencing workplace-related difficulties would first be required to attempt to resolve the situation informally with the supervisor. The HUCTW and the personnel office would assist if necessary. If informal resolution proved impossible, the case would move to the Local Problem Solving Team (LPST), made up of an equal number of management and union representatives from each school or administrative unit. The LPST would attempt to reach a consensus solution. If *it* failed, it would refer the case to the University Problem Solving Team (UPST). If the UPST was also unsuccessful, it could choose to select a mediator. The mediator would attempt to facilitate an agreement, and if this were not possible she or he could make a final decision. However, this arbitration power was limited to disputes that involved interpretation or application of the contract (Harvard University and HUCTW 1989a:7–8).

A final remarkable aspect of negotiations was a cooperative effort to rewrite the personnel manual. After deleting all sections of the old manual that would be covered in the contract, the personnel practices negotiators discussed a variety of preexisting rules and regulations for possible changes. Among the topics considered were hours of work, holidays, vacation, sick pay, layoffs, breaks, and disciplinary policy. In most cases, reaching agreement on specific rules was reasonably easy and policy changes were undramatic. More difficult and especially important to the union was integrating flexibility throughout. Ultimately, the introduction to the negotiated manual made clear that it was "not intended as a rigid rule book applicable to every situation and workplace in a highly diversified University" (Harvard University and HUCTW 1989b: 2). According to Joie Gelband, who represented the HUCTW at the personnel practices table, "The whole purpose of the manual is to promote flexibility and the whole issue of mutuality—that it's in the best interest of everyone for the employee and supervision to reach agreements" (Gelband 1990).

Both sides praised the agreement. Derek Bok declared, "We look forward with increasing confidence to a positive relationship between Harvard and the union." Kristine Rondeau was ebullient: "It's the prettiest contract you've ever seen. It's got great economics and cooperative labor-management relations, and it addresses the concerns of working women" (Cooperman 1988).

The tone of the language in the contract and personnel manual reflected the harmony evident in the public statements from former antagonists. The contract preamble stated:

> It is our common purpose . . . to work together to advance the long-term role of Harvard University as a premier center of learning. . . . We have learned that we share a commitment to the processes of reasoned discourse in resolving problems and issues that may arise. . . . We are optimistic about [the] future" (Harvard University and HUCTW 1989a:2).

Similarly, the personnel manual proclaimed: "The University and HUCTW share the view . . . that participation and creative problem-solving are basic features of the relationship" (Harvard University and HUCTW 1989b:2).

Among the union leaders and rank-and-file activists, the most important contract provisions were about employee involvement. As Kristine Rondeau said when the agreement was announced: "From our first step in organizing Harvard back in the seventies . . . our union's goal has been to get our members on the other side of Harvard's doors into the rooms where decisions affecting workers' lives are made. We stand on the verge of making that goal a reality" (PR Newswire 1989). While the joint councils and other committees were viewed as pivotal by local leaders, they conceded that most rank-and-file members placed higher value on the wage and benefit improvements (Williams 1990a; Leavitt 1990; Byrne 1990a).

Both the union and Harvard's administration praised the contract's flexibility, which was achieved in three ways. First, the contract established a decentralized employee involvement plan allowing each school or administrative unit to retain its own autonomy and focus on its own problems. Second, many aspects of the relationship between management and workers (such as discipline) were omitted from the contract and consigned to the personnel manual, with the qualification accepted by the HUCTW that the manual offer only guidelines that might not be applicable to every situation. Third, the contract was largely devoid of work rules, a feature that was the university's highest priority. Vice-President Scott noted:

> The deans indicated that the highest priority in negotiations should be given to retaining flexibility of administration by avoiding work rules such as seniority, bumping, limitations on hiring, transfer rights, job guarantees, prohibitions of layoffs, etc. (BNA 1989b).

Another aspect of the contract that appealed to both management and labor was the absence of a standard grievance and arbitration system. As noted, individual workplace problems were to be handled by joint labor-management teams rather than by individuals; the definition of a grievance was broadened, and the procedure encouraged consensus by its reliance on mediation in combination with arbitration.

In essence, the management assessment of the contract was remarkably similar to that of the union's leadership. According to John Dunlop, Harvard decided to pursue "a long-term vision rather than any short-term advantage" and to promote "employee participation and individual initiative in a spirit of trust and open communication" (Bureau of National Affairs 1989b).

Implementing the Contract

After three years under the contract, the union retains its commitment to the participatory system. The UJC has been constructed and twenty-seven JCs have been formed by schools and administrative units. The JCs meet biweekly and, in effect, continually negotiate over working conditions. In addition, the UPST and nineteen LPSTs have been set up, although they typically meet only when there is a specific complaint requiring attention.

The JCs have proven to be the most important component of the participatory system. The experience to date has been mixed, with "one-third doing great . . . , one-third making progress . . . , and one-third requiring close attention" (Williams 1990b). In most cases union representatives have been better prepared than management for JC meetings and have initiated topics for discussion. How effectively a JC functions tends to be determined by the attitudes of the management representatives. The successful JCs share a common characteristic: management representatives and the dean or administrator involved are self-confident managers who do not view sharing power as a threat (Williams 1990b). In instances where management still believes that it should be fighting the union, the JCs are making very little progress. James Healey, a professor of industrial relations at Harvard selected to mediate HUCTW contract disputes, concedes that "there are islands of unspoken resistance, where administrators give lip service to the concept but then act in a way which subverts the process" (BNA 1990c:C-5).

Even where JCs are staffed by recalcitrant management representatives or where communication is poor, the HUCTW retains its commitment to the process. HUCTW activist Marilyn Byrne observes, "A lot of what the JCs have accomplished is subtle, in the realm of gaining credibility by showing management that we are committed, are reasonably intelligent, have initiative, and can contribute to the decision-making process" (Byrne 1990b).

The successes offer the union cause for optimism. Among the improvements initiated by JCs are new or refurbished staff lounges in individual schools, more desirable summer and holiday leave policies for library employees, better work sharing when vacancies arise, steps to reduce workplace inconveniences during construction, and revised hiring procedures (Gelband 1990; BNA 1990c:C-3). The HUCTW views the University Health Services JC as a model; barriers have been broken down between doctors and support staff and a positive atmosphere has been created by focusing on the mutual goal of providing high-quality health care. A specific innovation developed by the Health Services JC is an orientation program for new physicians coordinated and delivered by support staff who are HUCTW members (Williams 1990b).

So far, the LPSTs have played an auxiliary role. Each LPST has been involved in only a few formal cases. The university-wide UPST has recommended solutions or assisted in about twenty-five individual cases, three of which eventually went to mediation before being resolved (BNA 1990c:C-4). The HUCTW, however, believes that the greatest measure of success in the problem-solving process is that 350 complaints have been resolved *informally,* either directly by the employee and supervisor or with the assistance of a union representative and personnel officer (Williams 1990b).

In sum, the participatory system is considered to be a qualified success by the union. That the problem-solving process is working is evidenced by the limited reliance on the LPSTs, resulting from the resolution of difficulties at the lowest levels. The experience with employee involvement in decision making through the JCs has been uneven due to pockets of management resistance. Nonetheless, much has been accomplished, partly because the union has taken advantage of the relatively open system and undefined nature of the process to set the agenda for many JCs. As a result, specific improvements have been achieved that would normally be possible only during contract negotiations. Given the unit-specific nature of these gains, it legitimately could be argued that many never would have occurred under a traditional bargaining relationship.

In explaining the HUCTW's ongoing commitment to the participatory system, local president Donene Williams notes that "JC work is slow, the consensus decision making process is slow . . . [But] the flexibility to reach a consensus decision together gives our contract its strength" (Williams 1990b). Marilyn Byrne adds, "I don't know if it's the kind of process that can work in every environment. For union members it requires a large obligation" (Byrne 1990b). Because extensive rank-and-file involvement is required, HUCTW leaders view continued union diligence as essential. Kristine Rondeau warns that "a union that's not well organized shouldn't even think about doing this" (Bureau of National Affairs 1990c:C-5).

Significantly, the participatory system negotiated at Harvard actually has served to foster union involvement. Union membership has expanded and commitment has remained remarkably high. Seventy-three percent of the unit now belong to the local, and nearly 15 percent of members actively participate in union affairs. Approximately one hundred serve on JCs, sixty on LPSTs, and forty on special joint labor-management committees (BNA 1990c:C-5). As of 1992, many of the union representatives to the JCs also serve on HUCTW organizing committees. There are five organizing committees with twenty to thirty members each who attempt to organize new employees and long-term employees who have not yet joined. Organizing committee members also serve as a communication link to the membership as the HUCTW continues to eschew literature in favor of one-on-one contact. In addition to the organizing committees, the union structure includes 4 officers, 13 executive board members, and 108 elected union representatives. The elected representatives' primary duties are to assist informally in the problem-solving processes, and to meet one-to-one with members to answer questions concerning rights under the contract (Williams 1990a; Leavitt 1990).

The extensive member involvement explains local leaders' confidence that the HUCTW is prepared to meet all challenges. If management's commitment to meaningful participation wanes, the union is ready to respond. According to Rondeau, "If we ever really need [contract guarantees], we'll fight hard. . . . If they fight us, we'll fight; if we have to do it the old-fashioned way, we'll do it as well as anyone" (BNA 1990c:C-5). But it is clear that the HUCTW does not want to do it the old-fashioned way. The union eschewed a rule-based relationship because of its conviction that no one set of rules would apply to all of Harvard's workers and workplaces (Williams 1990b). The members are convinced that the system is working because "employees and supervisors are talking, and using moral reasoning rather than rules to solve their problems" (Gelband 1990).

Learning from Harvard Clerical Workers

The labor movement has cause to celebrate the Harvard organizing victory, but was it any more than just an isolated NLRB election win? The HUCTW contract has some appealing features, but what difference should this make to workers not employed at Harvard? Although the case is exceptional in some ways,[3] and the clerical work force will not unionize en masse because of what

---

[3]The prestige of Harvard and the lure of Cambridge (a mecca for leftists) combine to attract a relatively young, well-educated group of clerical workers who are highly mobile and politically progressive (*Chicago Tribune* 1988; Weinstein 1988). Furthermore, Harvard is not a typical employer. Even prior to unionization it offered its employees relatively good pay, benefits, and working conditions. Harvard's liberal traditions and contacts with the labor movement made it more susceptible to outside pressures than many private sector employers.

happened in Cambridge, an evaluation of the experience reveals several important lessons for unions.

The Harvard case confirms that clerical workers generally and university clericals in particular respond favorably to a grassroots organizing approach. The clerical and technical workers at Harvard clearly wanted a union that encouraged their full participation. Specific tactical aspects of the campaign helped to reinforce the union's philosophy of voice. The HUCTW focus on empowerment allowed workers to define their own issues, and offered them a credible *process* for solving problems, achieving fair treatment, and attaining influence. Similarly, the decision not to use traditional campaign literature served to reinforce the grassroots campaign since committee members themselves became the conduit of information.

Because of the skepticism clerical workers feel toward unions, it is essential that organizing campaigns reflect a clear understanding of the concerns of the workers. At Harvard this meant emphasizing voice and building an extensive grassroots structure. Workers responded positively when they could embrace the union as their own. In contrast to organizing constructed upon worker dissatisfaction, the process at Harvard created a positive environment from which worker empowerment evolved. The organizers did not sell the union to the workers, but rather sold the workers on their own potential. The HUCTW broke new ground by taking the logical next step and institutionalizing participation through the bargaining process and the contract itself. The experience demonstrates that the grassroots approach can produce not just a union victory, but an excellent first contract.

The union built power through its enduring attention to organizing, which continued even after the contract was ratified. The ability to be both adversarial in certain instances and nonadversarial in others meant that the HUCTW could bargain from a position of strength and also maintain its commitment to worker involvement. Those portions of the contract that institutionalize participation through JCs, LPSTs and other joint labor-management committees will undoubtedly appeal to clericals (and other white-collar workers) who are seeking respect and influence through their unions. The participatory system enhances the clericals' close association with professionals and managers, whereas a *purely* adversarial union could interfere with workplace relationships. The model of labor-management cooperation propagated by the agreement could prove to be an effective organizing tool in other campaigns. The desire of clericals to seek justice while preserving harmony in the workplace has at last been fashioned into a contract that can serve as a prototype. The example of the HUCTW agreement lays bare management's claim that unionization necessarily creates a rigid, rules-based, adversarial environment poisoned by third-party interlopers.

To return to the debate raised early in the chapter regarding the appropriate strategy for organizing clerical workers, the Harvard case also lends support to those who argue that special approaches are required. The women at Harvard responded to a campaign that displayed female leadership and what Kristine Rondeau has referred to as the "feminine model of organizing" (BNA 1990b:C-1). Most of the organizers were women, a collective rank-and-file leadership system was developed based on interpersonal bonds, and the self-empowering rewards of unionization were emphasized.

The Harvard experience could be interpreted as consistent with the views of those who describe clericals as traditionally feminine and concerned with maintaining good relations with their supervisors as well as those who argue that the clerical work culture is conducive to the expression of militance. This seeming contradiction was best reflected in the way that the HUCTW dealt with the prestige issue. Rather than allowing the close working relationship between clericals and professors to become an impediment to organizing, the HUCTW attacked the issue head-on. Status concerns were turned into an advantage as the workers embraced the concept that "It's not anti-Harvard to be pro-union." This slogan also sent the message that the HUCTW was not a typical adversarial union.[4] Although the work culture was not oppositional, this model created an environment that allowed women clericals to become strong union advocates.

Although the Harvard case may be most relevant to organizing and representing university clerical workers, key aspects are generalizable to other workplaces. Particularly instructive is the tactical response of the union to the university's sophisticated union resistance activities. Reprinting and distributing Harvard's supervisors' manual, for example, served to demystify management's campaign. Even more important was the union's reliance on regular one-to-one contact with supporters as its primary response to management's efforts. This grassroots approach helped resolve doubts before they got blown out of proportion. In addition, the effort to reach out to the broader community of women's organizations, labor unions, religious groups, and political allies served two functions: It put management's anti-unionism in the limelight

---

[4]Similarly, the union handled the faculty skillfully. By reaching out to the faculty and asking *only* for neutrality so that a reasoned choice could be exercised in the best tradition of the academy, the HUCTW persuaded faculty to remain silent and thus largely defused this potential barrier. On campuses where the faculty are unionized, more openly courting their active support can be quite helpful.

and put Harvard on the defensive. Simultaneously, it helped tie the clerical workers into the broader labor and social movement, diminishing the feeling of isolation that can be so debilitating in the face of management's anti-union onslaught.

Clearly, no one model is appropriate for every union and every group of workers, and the Harvard case does not prove that traditional organizing and representation methods cannot be successful. Nonetheless, unions would be well served to consider the innovations reported here. The HUCTW's success in institutionalizing participation after the organizing phase ended, and its flexibility in pursuing cooperation with management while maintaining tenacious membership commitment to the union are especially noteworthy.

It would be a mistake to conclude that the participatory model of organizing and representing workers followed at Harvard should only be implemented in clerical campaigns or in other settings where women workers predominate. In fact, the HUCTW success presents a serious challenge to traditional union methods. It is increasingly difficult to "sell" unions today, and most would benefit from certain aspects of the HUCTW model, regardless of the occupations or demographics of their constituencies. Developing rank-and-file involvement and collective leadership, letting workers define the issues, and promoting worker empowerment are all essential to a long-term strategy to outlast management and fulfill the goal of organizing the unorganized.

Comments

Gloria Busman

In an era of nearly pervasive gloom regarding the future of the U.S. labor movement, it's exciting that two of the three chapters in this section focus on instances where working women, through collective action, have demonstrated courage, strength, and determination, and have succeeded in improving conditions for themselves and their coworkers. I suspect these case studies are not atypical; I am confident that they need not be.

The common thread in Richard Hurd's examination of the Harvard University collective bargaining victory and Ruth Milkman's interview with Katie Quan is that of the union as a tool for empowerment. In both instances, rank-and-file women developed their own leadership, defined their own issues, built support around those issues, and achieved their goals. In both situations, an established union eventually offered advice and support, but the impetus came from within the group itself.

In the Gwartney-Gibbs and Lach study of two bargaining units that share the same public sector employer, we seem to have encountered a different type of woman worker and a different sort of union. Here we find women whose domestic responsibilities make it difficult or impossible for them to attend union meetings (but what about the immigrant Chinese women we met through Katie Quan?). Both the clerical and maintenance workers Gwartney-Gibbs and Lach interviewed find conflict difficult, so they are reluctant to use the grievance procedure. Moreover, problems of favoritism and personality conflicts seriously affect the quality of their work life, and they are frustrated that the union contract does not seem to deal effectively with these problems. But those women who have "bitten the bullet" and used the grievance procedure, or even become stewards, have experienced a sense of empowerment and are much more committed to the union.

To correct the lack of involvement and the dissatisfaction of many of the women in the bargaining units, Gwartney-Gibbs and Lach propose solutions that focus on "the union" (as distinct from the membership) taking steps to deal more sensitively with women workers' concerns. No distinction is made between the maintenance unit, where women are a minority, and the clerical unit, where women compose 80 percent of the bargaining unit. The women members in both units are viewed (and undoubtedly view themselves) as passive recipients of a system over which they can exert little control or influence. The authors' solutions reinforce the concept of union women as a group for whom something should be done, rather than as (in one of the two units) a powerful majority who can propose contract language changes; elect new, more sensitive stewards; and use the collective bargaining process as a tool for empowerment. For the maintenance unit, where women are a minority, no suggestions are made for using strategies that others in a minority situation have found effective to encourage or effectively demand consideration of their needs.

The problems of these union members are not unique to these bargaining units, nor to the public sector, nor to women workers. The apathy and alienation described have been of concern to many union leaders and members. Workers of both sexes are often reluctant to file grievances because they don't want to make waves or be branded a troublemaker. Supervisors can and do make life difficult for a worker who uses the grievance procedure. And no contract ever written can guarantee every worker will be liked equally well or that union brothers and sisters will not give a bad time to a new worker they perceive as breaking down conditions the group is struggling to maintain.

The circumstances described by Gwartney-Gibbs and Lach, and the solutions they propose, reflect the "service" model of unionism, in vogue since after World War II. This pattern of union organizing and representation has reinforced the concept of "the union" as an entity separate from the membership and which therefore receives the credit and blame for working conditions. Workers are invited to join the union with assurances that "the union" will take care of their problems at work in exchange for a "yes" vote and later for the payment of dues. Since most present-day union members were offered this definition of "the union" when they joined, it is not surprising that few groups perceive their union as an organization whose success or failure depends on them and their initiative.

For women, and men, such as those described by Gwartney-Gibbs and Lach, finding the imagination, courage, or will to realize the potential of collective bargaining in their own workplace will not be easy. But one of the major benefits of union organization *should* be the sense of empowerment that comes with action, rather than passive acceptance of unsatisfactory conditions.

The more positive examples of union activism reported in the other chapters in this section reflect the advantages of the "organizing model," a different method of union representation advocated by a growing number of union leaders (*LRR* 1991). In the "organizing model," union staff and administration assist work groups in defining their own goals and developing strategies for achieving them. Union representatives and organizers stress the importance of involving members directly in shaping their own work destiny and that of their union.

The Harvard campaign is perhaps the ultimate recent example of the "organizing model." The time lapse from the first show of interest to the election victory and subsequent agreement was long, but I would argue that the slow pace of the campaign, where support was built one by one and in depth, may well be more cost-effective for the union as an institution and result in more permanent gains for the affected employees than the method many unions have used in the past: targeting an employer, pushing for a quick 30 percent to file, going to an election, losing it, waiting a year, trying again, and quite possibly losing again.

One of the first private sector organizing campaigns in which I was involved was for a bargaining unit of several thousand manufacturing employees of both sexes. The union had made six prior attempts, but all had failed. Yet a hard-core group of workers remained determined, and they approached the union for one more try. This time, union staff used a different approach. The existing pro-union leaders were encouraged to quietly build support and understanding of the potential advantages to be achieved with a union contract. Initial contacts were one-on-one, followed by small group gatherings of workers who knew and trusted each other. Staff worked with rank-and-file leadership to develop other leadership, in other departments. No one stood outside the plant gate indiscriminantly handbilling with a canned message. Instead, small groups of workers discussed workplace problems and possible solutions. They were shown examples of contract language that had worked well for other bargaining units, and they gradually developed a consensus on goals. They developed a commitment to those goals, and to their union, that would withstand the employer's attempt to conquer by dividing the group. A lot of time and money was spent on this campaign, but it resulted in a victory and left in place a bargaining unit that was in a strong position to negotiate effectively.

This effort preceded the Harvard clerical campaign by more than twenty years, but even then the grassroots methods were not "new." Instead, they were a return to the way men and women had built their unions in the 1930s. This grassroots approach has been repeated successfully in numerous settings over the past couple of decades, and an increasing number of national union leaders are persuaded that the model is the one to follow. There may be exceptions, but in today's climate they will be rare. Without the slow, careful building of understanding and commitment; without an awareness of what is involved in not just winning the election, but negotiating an agreement in which workers can take pride, there are not likely to be meaningful victories for workers and their unions.

Is the Harvard approach more likely to meet with success where the workplace is female-dominated? Researchers have found substantial variances between women and men regarding perceived needs and the value system each sex brings to work issues. Women are reported by some researchers to place a higher value than their brothers on personal relationships at work; this characteristic may have influenced both the emphasis placed during organizing on the one-on-one contacts and the development of a bargaining structure allowing for departmental differences and flexibility. Nevertheless, since many Harvard bargaining unit members work closely with faculty and administrators, the value placed on personal relationships could also have made the negotiators more open to searching for innovative "win/win" solutions that would meet the needs of both groups.

Some research has shown, as Gwartney-Gibbs and Lach report, that women are less comfortable than men with conflict and confrontation. My own experience with a variety of union women has convinced me, however, that women workers can be every bit as militant as men, and as willing to accelerate the level of conflict when they are convinced it is warranted. Many women do exhibit a willingness to explore a range of problem-solving techniques before resorting to direct confrontation, but it is possible that, because women as a group have lacked the physical and institutional power of men, they have developed alternative methods of achieving their goals. The women at Harvard certainly brought to the bargaining process an admirable mix of flexibility and militance.

Of course there are women (and men too) who are culturalized to welcome a strong authoritarian union leadership which will take care of things at work. But strong leaders alone can't do it today, if they ever could. Successful organizers and union representatives cannot settle for that approach. They must find ways to assist the workers with whom they work to develop the confidence and determination to take control of their working lives, and to do so in concert with one another.

If, in fact, women are more reluctant than men to work in an environment of continual conflict, they may be in an ideal position (as at Harvard) to encourage management to support a problem-solving, rather than a confrontational, approach to labor relations. The present U.S. system of labor relations is not carved in stone. It has evolved over the years and can continue to change, in directions that I hope will strengthen the rights of all working people. Women workers who have a strong sense of self may be the very ones to adapt our traditional system of collective bargaining to cope more effectively with the subtle nuances of today's quality of work life. If there are different issues of significant importance to working women, union women must be prepared and trained to articulate those concerns and participate in developing strategies to achieve solutions at bargaining tables and through grievance machinery.

Work in the United States has changed, and so have the workers. Milkman's interview with Quan is valuable not merely as an exciting example of women workers achieving meaningful change through their union, but as a reminder of the need to respect and accommodate cultural differences among women. My first union job was with Quan's union, the International Ladies' Garment Workers' Union. At that time, the membership in southern California was shifting from the traditional Jewish and Italian base to a Hispanic majority. These Hispanic women, emerging as leaders, first introduced me to union women unafraid of confrontation and conflict. Like the Hispanic women who have achieved leadership more recently in California's hotel and restaurant industry and in SEIU's Justice for Janitors Campaign, they defy the stereotype of Latinas as docile, traditional women reluctant to challenge male authority. I hope a newly formed Asian-American Labor Committee will provide the union movement with new insights and leadership helpful in effectively representing women from that ethnic group.

Not every woman who works is going to be a union leader; neither is every man. But if women are encouraged to value themselves and the work they do, to have respect for their own as well as others' ideas and values, and are exposed to examples of empowerment by women like themselves, I believe workplaces and union halls will find more leaders like Katie Quan and the Chinese-American garment workers, like Kristine Rondeau and her colleagues at Harvard. As this happens, women such as those in the Gwartney-Gibbs and Lach study who are still functioning in a "service model" union setting will find a way to build a stronger, more participatory, sensitive, and effective local union.

Comments

Jessica Govea

T he common thread in the three chapters of this section is that women workers want—and are most effective when they have—a say. This is not unique to women workers. I am a first-generation woman of color and I have been a professional organizer since 1966. I began my work as a founding organizer with the United Farm Workers' union, with whom I worked for sixteen years, and my responsibilities included serving as the union's national director of organizing and being elected to the national executive board. In my years of organizing, I have found a similar desire for power and voice in men, women, and children of all colors and of all economic levels. The most successful organizing I have been involved in or witnessed is where people take real ownership of their organization by exercising *both* authority and responsibility.

We hear a lot of reasons for the diminishing numbers of unionized workers: runaway shops, plant closings, a hostile government administration, aggressive anti-union campaigns by the company, a work force that is different in terms of gender and racial or ethnic composition. Each of these may have a degree of validity, but the bottom line is that *there are fewer organized workers because the labor movement is organizing less.* There is a direct correlation between the degree of organizing success and the priority given to and resources committed to organizing.

I was excited to read about the organizing of the clerical workers at Harvard University. Their story and parts of the Chinatown story reaffirm many of the basic principles and tactics that make for effective organizing.

It is critical to identify and develop leadership from among the workers and train them to organize their fellow workers. When this happens, the workers take ownership of their organizing campaign from the very beginning and develop relationships with their coworkers that are based on workplace organization needs, making it possible for them to effectively address those needs once the battle is "won."

"Selling" the workers on their own potential is much more important and effective than "selling the union" to the workers. If a campaign is undertaken with the goal of getting a contract and the union approaches the workers with all kinds of promises about the benefits they will receive if they "sign the card and vote," then the victory—if there is one—will be thin and short-term. The workers become consumers, the union becomes the seller, unrealistic expectations are established, and an unequal relationship evolves. But if the goal and accompanying plan depend on *collective* power, the result will be an organization where the workers and the union are partners. As partners, they own and learn from their successes and failures.

Because union membership is dropping, unions and organizers too often feel tremendous pressure to sign up cards fast and file for an election. This approach can result in compromise and lost elections. It may take time building leadership and organization and take longer to achieve a successful election or a completed contract, but the process is more likely to create a lasting organization.

If the broader community is involved in your struggle, it provides the protection of public visibility and reinforces with the general public the positive value and importance of worker organization. The classic example of community involvement in a labor struggle is the United Farm Workers' first grape boycott, which began in 1966 and ended in 1970, when it was recognized by California's grape growers. Although the farm workers themselves took principal responsibility for organizing and for developing and implementing the boycott strategy in North America and parts of Europe, hundreds of thousands of people participated in the effort and made victory possible.

Now that there is a focus on the numbers of women and immigrants in the workplace, unions and organizers must be careful not to romanticize or patronize either group. I have too often heard excuses made for workers, especially minority and women workers: they can't come to meetings, they have too many other things to worry about, they might get fired, *fill in the blank— Mexicans, Dominicans, Haitians, women*—are never on time, don't speak up, won't come to a meeting unless you have food, drink, and entertainment. If an organizer works closely with the worker leadership to develop an effective plan for the organizing campaign, workers will usually make intelligent choices about what they are prepared to do to build their union.

It is important to recognize each worker's unique needs and concerns, but don't over emphasize how "different" people are. A clerical worker or garment worker may dress, look, speak, and act differently from a factory worker or a farm worker, but, if they are not organized, they generally share fears about job security, frustration with inadequate wages and job-condition protections, and the inability to move themselves and their families forward.

Organizers must demonstrate leadership, clarity of vision, courage, and respect for the people they are seeking to organize. This means being punctual and prepared, following up on all commitments, training and developing the worker leadership, helping people think through what their options are, and being prepared to take calculated risks.

Finally, the best protection for organized workers is for them to commit to organize the unorganized in their industry, their community, and/or their region.

In 1975, state legislation was signed into existence by then Governor Jerry Brown that provided—for the first time in history—California's farm workers the right to secret-ballot representation elections. It was an exciting time for a community that had been engaged in a ten-year struggle, and many parts of rural California were swept by the farm workers' desire to be represented by the United Farm Workers' Union. Among the most enthusiastic were the vegetable industry workers of California's Salinas and Imperial valleys who had gone through a major strike to rid themselves of the sweetheart contracts the growers had signed—without the workers' knowledge—with another union in 1970. As union officials, we coordinated the election campaign. The worker leadership organized their fellow workers and very few elections were lost. In December 1979, the hard-won contracts in the vegetable industry expired and it soon became clear that the companies were determined to not renew them. We engaged in an eighteen-month, six hundred-mile, two-state strike for several thousand workers, which I codirected. This strike was powerful, effective, and successful *only* because the workers and the worker leadership were involved from the very beginning in shaping the demands, strategies, and negotiating positions.

The elected strike leaders from each company met together every morning to fine-tune strategy and assignments. They did not act as representatives of individual striking companies but as coordinators of an industrywide effort. Because they learned to work with each other, they were able to keep their people together through some very difficult times. The strike leaders succeeded in negotiating a contract that dramatically increased wages, tripled contributions into the medical plan, and created full-time union representative positions on the job and from the work force. The gains were tremendous. The sacrifices, including the murder of one striker by a management person, also had been tremendous.

After this success, the leadership began to look beyond the workplace to other areas of their lives that needed improvement, such as health care and the education that their children were receiving. They also decided that in order to protect their hard-won improvements, they needed to organize unorganized farm workers in their industry and region.

Joining a union is not a sacrifice—it is a decision. If belonging addresses the interests and needs of workers and provides them a role and a voice, then they will respond positively. Sometimes organizers fall into the trap of thinking that they have to come up with all of the answers or are timid about getting people to commit significant amounts of their "off" time to union work. I have found that as long as people have real authority and responsibility for something that is important to them, they will rearrange their schedules and their lives to do the necessary work.

Organizing is hard because it's about agitation and change. We are all made uncomfortable by agitation and we all resist change—even when it is in our interest. But if the labor movement chooses to make organizing the unorganized a priority and matches that commitment with the necessary resources—hiring talented, gutsy, and thoughtful organizers, investing in well-planned organizing drives that won't necessarily show immediate results, reshaping budget allocations—then there are tremendous opportunities all over this country.

Comments

Susan Josephs

Researchers looking for the sources of apparent gender differences have spurned biological determinism as the sole cause, but are still left with unanswered questions. How do gender differences affect organizing, grievance filing, and the determination of goals and priorities? Are discernible gender differences the result of a "female ethic" or are they the behaviors one would expect from any excluded or disempowered group? Are differences more workplace-determined than gender-specific? The three articles in this section attempt to answer some of these persistent and central questions.

The organizing campaign at Harvard University clearly reveals the effectiveness of a grassroots approach in organizing women clerical workers. The Chinese garment workers of New York in Ruth Milkman's study may not have needed the same consciously structured, one-on-one consultation as the Harvard clerical workers, but they also needed a gradual coming together—the "ganging up" at radio stations and the frequent meetings—to overcome their isolated living situations and to organize collectively.

But is it only women who need a participatory "bottom-up" one-on-one experience? If members of a group feel part of the hierarchy and, by identification, part of the process, aren't they more likely to accept positions emanating from above and to trust that their interests are being protected? Aren't men more likely to accept hierarchical structures in part because these structures are led and dominated by men? Perhaps men who also feel excluded—members of minority or dissident groups, or male workers in unionized industries that have suffered reversals of fortune and who, therefore, have had their trust betrayed and complacency destroyed—will act in similar fashion to the women in these case studies. It may be that when the existing structure and bureaucracy is working well for a group, that structure is safe, but when that group fails to deliver, the system is open to change. One difference between men and women may be that union bureaucracies have never really worked for women as a group. If the number of men and women who are disaffected with traditional unionism continues to increase, organizers will need to learn from and apply the organizing methods used at Harvard to win workers and gain their trust.

Innovations in union problem solving and representation emerge as a fascinating aspect in both the Hurd and Gwartney-Gibbs and Lach articles. As Hurd reports, there are no work rules in the Harvard contract and individual workplace problems are handled by joint labor-management teams rather than a traditional grievance and arbitration system. Informal problem solving rather than formal grievance filing is a basic and long-standing concept practiced by some unions, and many unions also act on the principle that, regardless of whether a specific contractual provision has been violated, a "grievance" exists *whenever* the work force is sufficiently unhappy and united in purpose. But to be able to transfer the kind of systematically created grassroots support achieved in an organizing campaign to grievance solving by instituting more participatory problem-solving procedures would indeed be a major advance and one from which all unions could benefit.

But to what extent is this approach particularly appropriate for women workers? Female employees in prestigious academic institutions may find a flexible joint approach more appropriate than women factory workers; similarly, male professionals may respond better to the Harvard model than either men or women in industry. Yet as Gwartney-Gibbs and Lach suggest in their essay, the specific issue of gender may also be pivotal.

Gwartney-Gibbs and Lach find differences in the attitudes of men and women toward the grievance process. The women in their study filed fewer grievances and were more alienated from, or intimidated by, the grievance process. They also seemed to express a need for a less rigid structure, perceiving the present system as overly combative or nonresponsive to their particular needs. But is this a function of gender or, as was suggested earlier, the reaction of individuals who belong to an excluded and disaffected group? Male workers may trust a system more because they believe the male-dominated system reflects them and their interests, whereas disaffected women workers may be reacting more to their feelings of exclusion than to the nature of the system. In my study of carpenter apprentices, I found that both male and female apprentices were disaffected with the existing union structure, which did not seem responsive to, or inclusive of, them as apprentices (Josephs et al. 1988). It would be illuminating to study a work site where the traditional grievance procedure is handled by a female-dominated stewardship and leadership to see if it is the grievance process itself that marginalizes women or the gender-bias of the union representatives.

Overall, while I would argue that structural and situational circumstances are more important than gender, both in organizing and representation, it is impossible to totally disclaim differences due to gender. Psychological and sociological research has found that gender differences exist, even if they are culturally rather than biologically determined. Hurd, Milkman, and Gwartney-Gibbs and Lach present further evidence of this phenomenon. Women workers *did* rely on different approaches and *did* react in different ways. They showed a greater grassroots spirit, an increased alienation from present structures, an empowerment through action rather than through identification with hierarchy, and a desire for less rigid and combative problem-solving methods.

It is difficult to assess, however, whether these differences will remain as women become more of a dominant force in labor unions. Moreover, what is now perceived as a style or approach peculiar to women may be the precursor of a less gender-specific grassroots model of unionism necessitated by changing societal circumstances that in fact will be the form best-suited for the majority of workers, male and female. It may be that the institutional style of 1930s industrial unionism is no longer an adequate model.

The essays in this section demonstrate that we are in a period when the impact of women workers on unions is of vital importance. The grassroots activist approach and broader vision of the women workers discussed in these articles may forge not only a new partnership, but also a new direction for the labor movement as a whole.

Comments

Patti R. Roberts

The articles in this section thoughtfully describe innovative approaches in organizing women. Particularly compelling is the suggestion that the strategies and tactics that get results with women are not necessarily the same as those used in the past with male workers. It is clear from these articles that not only are many of the successful methods different, but also that the issues women respond to are different.

But lesbians and gay men make up another group of workers who have not yet had the necessary organizing energy and resources directed toward them. Perhaps because they, like women, have historically been the victims of stereotypical assumptions, few unions have sought to address their particular needs. Stereotypes abound: you can't organize them; all lesbians, and gay men especially, have money; they're only working in a few fields; they're only interested in sex; there aren't any where I work. My comments recount some of the preliminary efforts by lesbians and gay men to refute these stereotypes. I also will provide an overview of some of the workplace issues of lesbians and gay men.

The Stonewall Rebellion of June 1969 heralded the beginning of the modern lesbian and gay movement, the full impact of which has yet to be explored by the union movement. The Stonewall Rebellion marked the first time that gay men and lesbians resisted police harassment. It signaled the public coming out of a closeted minority, the awakening of a powerful new consciousness, and the development of a significant political presence. Inextricably linked with the emerging women's movement, lesbian and gay organizing has since been visible in many areas, including protecting lesbian mothers' custody rights, abolishing laws limiting consensual adult sexuality, and exposing hate violence directed at lesbians and gay men. Although unions are increasingly aware of the importance of organizing the women in their midst, the union movement has been slow to recognize this other important constituency. The gay liberation movement, now over twenty years old, has yet to be embraced by much of the labor movement.

Similarly, gays and lesbians have not yet fully recognized the importance of the labor movement in their efforts to change consciousness and obtain greater civil and political rights. Even when the focus of change is on workplace issues, such as benefits for domestic partners, organizing efforts by gay men and lesbians often occur without union backing. The links between these movements are still to be forged.

In the 1970s we witnessed the first signs of the emerging gay and lesbian presence within the union movement. As a result, "sexual orientation" or "sexual preference" was added to the language of many collective bargaining agreements prohibiting discrimination based on race, sex, and national origin. Additionally, "just cause" disciplinary protections were interpreted to include protection against firings based on sexual orientation.

As the 1980s unfolded, lesbians and gays in unions joined together to form union caucuses; sought representation on civil rights or human rights committees; published newsletters; and expanded their demands to include more affirmative protections, such as bereavement leave, and other benefits. It may be during the 1990s, however, that this group's organizing potential will be acknowledged and its activism and energy utilized. In part, because of the growth of the gay and lesbian movement and in part as a response to the AIDS crisis, there is a greater willingness of lesbians and gay men to be "out" in the workplace. Being "out" is a necessary prerequisite for union activism: it is far more difficult for people to be politically active and take a leadership role when they are unable to talk honestly to their coworkers about their lives, feelings, and issues, or when they are fearful of being "outed."[1] As a result, the number of union activists and leaders who are both "out" and willing to organize for gay and lesbian issues has grown dramatically. Consequently, gay and lesbian brothers and sisters are making more insistent demands at the bargaining table for recognition of their key issues.

Of course, an increasingly vocal minority demanding union acceptance and representation may well engender antagonism and opposition within the work arena as homophobic attitudes surface in reaction. But the reaction of union

---

[1]"Being outed" refers to the controversial tactic of publicizing the fact that someone is gay or lesbian. Usually the person "outed" has been a politician, athlete, or other public figure who has been identified with homophobic policies or remarks.

leaders to the active presence of lesbians and gay men most likely will vary, just as it has varied in response to women's demands. Some unions will resist change; others will make it a top priority and will welcome this new constituency into their ranks. To be successful in incorporating this minority group, the labor movement must make room for it and welcome it in a far more positive way than it has to date, and must be responsive to its needs and issues. How union leadership reacts to this internal pressure will play an important role in determining whether the energy of lesbians and gay men is activated within unions, and whether industries and work sites with a large gay constituency are organized.

What Issues Have Been Raised by Gay and Lesbian Workplace Activists?

The recognition of their domestic partnerships or same-sex relationships has been one of the most important for workplace activists and has arisen in a number of different contexts. The first example in which an employer publicly extended benefits to domestic partners occurred in a union shop. In 1982, employees at the *Village Voice*, a weekly newspaper in New York City that is represented by UAW District 65, pushed for and won expanded benefits at the bargaining table. That early victory involved extending health benefits provided through a self-insured plan to both heterosexual and homosexual partners of unmarried employees. Since then, many public sector employers and, more recently, some private sector companies, such as Lotus in Cambridge, Mass., and Levi-Strauss in San Francisco, have adopted versions of domestic-partner benefit coverage for their unionized and nonunionized employees.

Although unions and unionized workplaces have been actively involved in the effort to win health-care benefits for domestic partners, lesbian and gay community activists have led the efforts, especially in Berkeley, San Francisco, Seattle, and Los Angeles. Lesbian and gay activists approach the issue in terms of equity. They argue that their benefits are less, their protections fewer, and their paychecks diminished when their relationships are not recognized, and their partner or partner's children are not provided with medical or dental benefits. By contrast, a coworker's spouse and children are entitled to these benefits. As fringe benefits are an increasingly large part of a worker's compensation, sometimes equivalent to 30 percent or more of wages, these demands have a strong economic as well as moral component.

During a contract-negotiation period, one public sector union, Local 616 of the Service Employees' International Union (SEIU), which represents county workers in Alameda County in northern California, put out a flyer that emphasized the economics of domestic-partner discrimination. Andrea Davis, then president of the local, believes this flyer was one of the most effective in educating members.

WANTED—ACCOUNT CLERK
Starting wage of homosexual or unmarried worker $9.02 per hour. For married worker $10.33 per hour. Apply at the County Personnel Office. Alameda County is An Equal Opportunity Employer.

Arguing that equal opportunity would give the same benefits to all couples, married or unmarried, gay or straight, the union negotiated successfully the first part of their goal, a domestic partner registration system and bereavement leave. They postponed negotiating health benefits to future bargaining years, although members and staff have supported revised health programs. Local 616 was successful in part because the president was an open lesbian who, along with the union's lesbian/gay caucus, had worked hard to educate the membership about the issue. If "out" leadership is lacking, gay/lesbian demands are often abandoned so early in the bargaining process that they are never taken seriously by either the rank and file or management.

Coming Out on the Job: Collectively and Individually

Union activists' growing awareness of lesbian and gay issues has been spurred in part by the large number of workers coming out on the job and in the union. Increasingly, we hear of union leaders who not only are openly gay or lesbian, but are also willing to talk about lesbian and gay union issues. One lesbian, Greyhound bus driver Janis Borchardt of the Amalgamated Transit Union, ran for office for the first time in 1987 after being a strike leader and steward. During the campaign, she faced an opponent who tried to use her sexual orientation as a tactic to defeat her. He charged, "We don't need a dyke in the office." Borchardt responded openly, saying her ability to do the job, not her orientation, was the issue. Ultimately, she won the election by a close vote, receiving strong support from people of color and minorities. Since then, she has won reelection by a large margin. Having an officer directly acknowledge her sexual orientation had several major positive repercussions in that union. Since her first election, Greyhound bus drivers have marched with their union banner at the Gay Pride March. Others in the union have come out as well, feeling safer and therefore more able to be an active force in the union. Gays and lesbians have been disproportionately active in the union, forming a large percentage of working committees to focus on general union issues. As a result of the union's acceptance, the gay and lesbian members are now an enormous asset for the union.

Lesbian and Gay Employee Associations

Lesbians and gay men have increasingly joined together in employee organizations in nonunionized settings, demonstrating the openness of the lesbian and gay male community to workplace organization. This phenomenon is especially common in the computer industry and other high-tech fields. These groups are primarily oriented toward building a social network, but they also provide an educational forum and a nucleus for raising workplace demands. This coming together of lesbian and gay employees often inspires the formation of other minority employee groups and presents many opportunities for labor organizing. Just as many AFL-CIO unions now seek "associate" members as a first step toward reaching beyond their own membership, unions may want to work with these groups as a way to connect with an organizing effort currently underway.

In some industries, lesbian and gay employee groups include both union and management employees; for example, LEAGUE, a national coalition of AT&T groups across the country, claims more than four hundred members and eight chapters.[2] In addition to providing counseling and EEO information, LEAGUE chapters have sponsored a Lesbian and Gay Awareness Week and have begun preliminary discussions about the domestic-partner benefits issues. As a result of a suggestion by a lesbian/gay employee association, Levi-Strauss, with over thirty thousand employees worldwide (only a portion of whom are unionized), looked at the domestic partner issue and subsequently expanded benefits to unmarried partners of employees. It is too early to determine how the mixture of union and management members will work, or if they will be able to unify around workplace issues. A conference for members of these various groups held in San Francisco in 1991 brought together over one hundred representatives of gay employee associations, and plans are underway for future events with even greater participation. For example, the American Federation of Teachers (AFT) has an active national caucus, Lesbian and Gay Teachers Association, that puts out a regular newsletter.[3] Recently, it has persuaded the New York City United Federation of Teachers to join in a lawsuit filed against the city's Board of Education in an

[2]LEAGUE can be reached at: AT&T Bell Labs, Rm. #A-351, 67 Whippany St., Whippany, NJ 07981.
[3]American Federation of Teachers, National Gay and Lesbian Caucus, can be reached at: P.O. Box 19856, Cincinnati, Ohio 45219.

effort to get domestic partner benefits. In the San Francisco Bay Area, Gay and Lesbian United Educators (GLUE) grew out of an organization originally formed in response to an anti-gay ballot measure of the 1970s.[4] One of their recent projects, the publication "Legal Rights of Lesbian and Gay Educators," explains lesbian and gay teachers' rights under the collective bargaining contract and under local and state laws. The pamphlet describes the group's purpose:

> GLUE hopes this pamphlet will empower all gay and lesbian teachers to demand equal treatment in the face of discrimination or harassment. GLUE's ultimate goal is to create a workplace free of all homophobia and discrimination.

GLUE has been influential in changing public attitudes and policies, lending a strong gay presence to the school district and the city as a whole. One GLUE member, Tom Ammiano, a gay teacher and a comedian, recently won a seat on the San Francisco Board of Education, receiving the highest voting percentage of all the candidates. Though teachers are certainly not the only workers who have organized within their union, they are an illuminating example of the significant role that active gay and lesbian committees can play.

Labor Caucuses and Labor Networks

Lesbian and gay workers increasingly have organized caucuses within unions as well as across union lines. The strengthening and broadening of these cross-union gay and lesbian labor networks in different parts of the country, such as New York, Boston, and the San Francisco Bay Area, will be critical to the support that gay and lesbian activists often need within their own union.[5]

The activities of these cross-union gay and lesbian labor-oriented groups vary. Directed both toward educating the gay and lesbian community about unions and the labor community about gay and lesbian issues, they are breaking new ground and are creating an environment receptive to future organizing.

Herneen Chernow, a labor activist with SEIU in Boston and one of the founders of Gay and Lesbian Labor Activist Network (GALLAN), explains her group's role:

> GALLAN provides an organization where we can be out, but not be isolated. It's also a place where people can come out. Some folks are not comfortable

[4]GLUE can be reached at: 655 Fourteenth St., San Francisco, CA 94114.

[5]Gay and Lesbian Labor Activist Network of New York can be reached at: P.O. Box 1159, New York, NY 10009; (212) 923–8690. GALLAN can be reached at: P.O. Box 1450, Jamaica Plain, MA 02130.

being out at work, and they can use GALLAN as a bridge to coming out. It sometimes helps to have a way to bring up and talk about our issues. Perhaps it makes it a little less personal and therefore less threatening.

GALLAN, in addition to putting out a newsletter for labor activists, has held several community forums. Forum topics have included the need to use union labor to build a gay community center and the impact of AIDS on health care workers. These community meetings, which provide a way for gay and lesbian activists to learn more about the labor movement, have been well attended and well received.

Organizations such as GALLAN help to strengthen their members' commitment to labor, since members share a common language, not just as lesbians and gay men but as union members. Interestingly, Chernow points out that many of Boston's local labor leaders, both elected and staff, are lesbians. Although not crediting this fact exclusively to GALLAN, she says that such a "lesbian presence in the labor movement would have been unheard of just two years ago . . . GALLAN strengthens our commitment to labor."

In the spring of 1991, a group of lesbian and gay labor activists came together at a national labor conference sponsored by *Labor Notes* magazine to form Lavender Labor, an international support network.[6] At the plenary session, the group addressed fellow unionists with this powerful statement:

We are here to make a statement for the people who met last night at the lesbian/gay caucus. First, we would like to invite any other gay brothers or lesbian sisters out there who would like to do so, to please stand up. [a few people stood up] Now if all the lesbians and gays here stood up, it would be the equivalent of ten tables, as at least 10 percent of the population is gay or lesbian.

The fact that so few people stood up shows how pervasive homophobia and discrimination against lesbians and gays is in our society. It just doesn't feel safe to come out even at a progressive conference. To be publicly identified as gay could cost us our job, our children, our lives.

Even within our unions we are faced with ostracism, ridicule and marginalization. We are everywhere. We are in health care, the building trades and the Teamsters, textile mills and schools. We are of all races and cultures and all countries.

When the union fails to defend the rights of gay and lesbian workers, the only winner is the Boss. When lesbian and gay families don't get the same benefits that other families get, the Union that bargained and worked so hard is the loser.

We offer you a challenge. . . . Here are some suggestions, for how YOU can help make your union safer for its lesbian and gay members:

[6]Lavender Labor can be reached in care of the author, Patti R. Roberts, 407 North Street, Oakland, CA 94609; (510) 655–3634.

- participate in your city's Gay Pride March
- confront co-workers when they make anti-gay jokes
- include gay and lesbian issues in your local's Civil Rights Committee
- talk to lesbian and gay co-workers and find out what issues they think the union should take up
- wear a gay or lesbian button to work, just for a day, and see how people react to you
- start up or participate in a committee to gain Domestic Partner Rights in your union
- participate in AIDS education programs
- support getting Lavender Labor, the newly formed International Network of Lesbian and Gay Labor Activists, which already has members from three countries, onto a plenary at the next Labor Notes Conference
- help distribute the Lavender Labor Newsletter

Lavender Labor, functioning as a national support network, will publish a quarterly newsletter. The group hopes to provide a national focus for many of the local efforts now going on.

Although it may be too early to determine how successful the efforts of individual lesbian and gay labor activists, lesbian and gay union caucuses, employee associations, and labor networks will be in educating the lesbian and gay community about the importance of unions, and conversely, educating the more established union leadership and rank-and-file members about the need to embrace their lesbian and gay coworkers, the level of activity is definitely increasing. I predict significant development and organizing in the upcoming period.

References to Part V

Adams, James Luther, et al. 1988. "A Message from Members of the Harvard Faculty." Leaflet.

AFL-CIO. 1989. "First Contract Seals Big Victory at Harvard." *AFL-CIO News* 34(14):1.

Baden, Naomi. 1986. "Developing an Agenda: Expanding the Role of Women in Unions." *Labor Studies Journal* 10(3):229–60.

Beluardo, Paula. 1986. Business Agent, Communications Workers of America. Telephone interview with Jill Kriesky. February 19.

Bernstein, Harry. 1988. "Elite Harvard Has a Sophisticated Style of Union Bashing." *Los Angeles Times* (June 14) 4:1.

BLS. 1991. *Employment and Earnings* 38(1):37, 40, 229.

BNA. 1988. "Harvard Workers Choose Representation by AFSCME Affiliate in Close NLRB Vote." *Daily Labor Report* (May 19): No. 97:A–1.

———. 1989a. "Union That Won Harvard Vote Said to Be Near Settlement on Initial Pact." *Daily Labor Report* (May 19): No. 96:A–3.

———. 1989b. "Top Harvard Negotiators Describe Union Pact." *Daily Labor Report* (July 12): No. 132:A–2.

———. 1989c. "Agreement on First Contract Reached for 3,500 Clerical Workers at Harvard." *Pension Reporter* No. 28:1232.

———. 1990a. "Harvard University Union, Management Have Working Relationship." *Daily Labor Report* (April 5): No. 66:A–2.

———. 1990b. "Women Seen as Source of Growth for American Labor Movement." *Daily Labor Report* (September 21): No. 184:C–1–C–3.

———. 1990c. "Harvard Now Shares Management Role with Clerical Union It Once Fought." *Daily Labor Report* (November 6): No. 215:C–1–C–5.

Boston City Council. 1988. Resolution of Councillor Scondras. March 23.

Butterfield, Bruce. 1988. "Harvard Union Wins Long Battle for Recognition." *Boston Globe* (November 5): 2:1.

Byrne, Marilyn. 1990a. Harvard Union of Clerical and Technical Workers. Telephone interview with William Rose. May 18.

———. 1990b. Harvard Union of Clerical and Technical Workers. Telephone interview with Kathy Mooney. December 18.

Comstock, Phil. 1989. "The Future of Unions in America: The View from the Shop Floor." Presented at AFL-CIO/Cornell University Conference on Changing Challenges for Unions. October.

Cooperman, Alan. 1988. "How Union Won at Harvard." *Chicago Tribune* (May 19): 1:17.

———. 1989. "Harvard, Union Reach Tentative Contract." *Associated Press,* June 27. Domestic News.

Costello, Cynthia. 1987. "Working Women's Consciousness: Traditional or Oppositional?" In *To Toil the Live Long Day,* edited by Carol Groneman and Mary Beth Norton, 284–302. Ithaca, N.Y.: Cornell University Press.

Diamond, John. 1988. "Harvard Workers Vote to Unionize in Narrow Margin." *Associated Press,* May 18. Business News.

Diamond, Virginia, ed. 1988. "Lessons of the Harvard Union Drive." *Statistical and Tactical Information Report* 38:1–2. Washington, D.C.: AFL-CIO National Organizing Committee.

Fatsis, Stefan. 1988. "Harvard Charges Union Violations as Hearing on Vote Opens." *Associated Press,* August 15. Business News.

Feinberg, Mark. 1987. "Long-Timers Join Fray at 'McHarvard.' " *In These Times* 2(30).

Fiorito, Jack, and Charles R. Greer. 1986. "Gender Differences in Union Membership, Preferences and Beliefs." *Journal of Labor Research* 7: 145–64.

Flynn, Barry. 1988. "Unions Use Ad Campaigns to Help in Membership Drives." *Boston Business Journal* (September 19):1:8.

Frazier, Rodger. 1986. American Federation of State, County and Municipal Employees, Iowa. Telephone interview with Jill Kriesky. May 7.

Freeman, Richard B., and Jonathan S. Leonard. 1987. "Union Maids: Unions and the Female Work Force." In *Gender in the Workplace,* edited by Clair Brown and Joseph A. Pechman, 189–216. Washington, D.C.: Brookings Institution.

Gelband, Joie. 1990. Harvard Union of Clerical and Technical Workers, University Problem-Solving Team. Telephone interview with Kathy Mooney. December 19.

Golden, Daniel. 1988. "Taking on Harvard." *Boston Globe Magazine* (August 7): 21–48.

Green, James. 1988. "Union Victory: An Interview with Kristine Rondeau." *Democratic Left* (September–October):4–6.

Gwartney-Gibbs, Patricia A., and Denise H. Lach. 1990. "Gender and Workplace Jurisprudence." Working Paper no. 35, Center for the Study of Women in Society, University of Oregon.

———. 1991. "Workplace Dispute Resolution and Gender Inequality." *Negotiation Journal* 7(2):187–200.

Hart, Melissa R. 1988. "Union Stages Support Rally." *The Harvard Crimson* (February 23).

———. 1988a. "Towing the Line." *The Harvard Crimson* (February 22).

———. 1988b. "Stand Back, Harvard." *The Harvard Crimson* (April 12).

Harvard University and HUCTW. 1989a. *Agreement* July 1, 1989–June 30, 1992.
———. 1989b. *Personnel Manual* July 1.
Hill, Ann. 1985. SEIU, District 925 Regional Director, Cleveland office. Telephone interview with Richard Hurd. March 4.
Hochschild, Arlie R. 1983. *The Managed Heart: The Commercialization of Human Feeling.* Berkeley, Calif.: University of California Press.
HUCTW. 1988. Campaign materials.
———. 1989. Expanded contract outline.
Hurd, Richard W. 1986. "Bottom-up Organizing: HERE in New Haven and Boston." *Labor Research Review* 8:5–19.
———. 1989a. "Learning from Clerical Unions: Two Cases of Organizing Success." *Labor Studies Journal* 14(1):30–51.
———. 1989b. "The Unionization of Clerical Workers in Colleges and Universities." In *Power Relationships on the Unionized Campus,* edited by Joel M. Douglas, 40–49. New York: National Center for the Study of Collective Bargaining in Higher Education and the Professions.
Hurd, Richard W., and Adrienne M. McElwain. 1989. "Organizing Activity among University Clerical Workers." *Proceedings of the Forty-first Annual Meeting* (New York, December 28–30, 1988), 515–22. Madison, Wis.: Industrial Relations Research Association.
Josephs, Susan L., et al. 1988. "The Union as Help or Hindrance: The Experiences of Women Apprentices in the Construction Trades." *Labor Studies Journal* 13 (Spring):3–18.
Kochan, Thomas A. 1979. "How American Workers View Labor Unions." *Monthly Labor Review* 102:23–31.
Kuttner, Robert. 1989. "A Beachhead for the Beleaguered Labor Movement." *Business Week* (July 17) :14.
Labor Research Review. 1991. "An Organizing Model of Unionism." 10 (1).
Ladd-Taylor, Molly. 1985. "Women Workers and the Yale Strike." *Feminist Studies* 11(3):465–89.
Landau, Adrienne. 1990. Harvard Union of Clerical and Technical Workers, University Health Services Joint Committee. Telephone interview with Kathy Mooney. December 19.
Leavitt, Sue. 1990. Harvard Union of Clerical and Technical Workers. Telephone interview with William Rouse. May 10.
Lewin, David, and Richard Peterson. 1988. *The Modern Grievance Procedure in the United States.* New York: Quorum.
Lynch, Roberta. 1986. "Organizing Clericals: Problems and Prospects." *Labor Research Review* 8:91–101.
Marmo, Michael. 1980. "Arbitrating Sex Harassment Cases." *The Arbitration Journal* 35:35–40.
Milkman, Ruth. Forthcoming. "Union Responses to Workforce Feminization in the U.S." In *The Challenge of Restructuring: North American Labor Movements Respond,* edited by Jane Jenson and Rianne Mahon. Philadelphia: Temple University Press.
Needleman, Ruth. 1988. "Women Workers: A Force for Rebuilding Unionism." *Labor Research Review* 11:1–6.

Noble, Kenneth. 1988. "Broader Day Care Is Aim of Harvard Union Drive." *New York Times* (February 28) 1:24.

Nussbaum, Karen. 1986. 9 to 5, National Association of Working Women, President. Personal interview with Richard Hurd, Whitefield, N. H. October 3.

PR Newswire. 1989. "Harvard Union of Clerical and Technical Workers Settles First Contract with Harvard University." *PR Newswire,* June 26. Business Desk.

Rathbun, Jennie. 1990. Harvard Union of Clerical and Technical Workers. Telephone interview with Kathy Mooney. December 19.

Rondeau, Kris, and Marie Manna. 1988. Letters to clerical and technical workers, February 8 and March 2.

Schneider, Debbie. 1990. Service Employees International Union District 925 organizer. Telephone interview with Richard Hurd. April 12.

Soloman, Pauline. 1990. Harvard Union of Clerical and Technical Workers. Telephone interview with William Rouse. May 18.

United Press International. 1988. "Harvard Union Demonstrates at Commencement. *United Press International,* June 9. Regional News.

Warren, James. 1988. "Union Tries to Pass Test at Harvard." *Chicago Tribune* (May 15):23.

Weinstein, Harry. 1988. "Harvard Campus. A Textbook Labor Union Campaign." *Los Angeles Times* (May 17):1.

Wertheimer, Barbara M., and Anne Nelson, eds. 1975. *Trade Union Women: A Study of Their Participation in New York City Locals.* New York: Praeger.

Williams, Donene. 1990a. Harvard Union of Clerical and Technical Workers, President. Telephone interview with William Rouse. May 5.

———. 1990b. Harvard Union of Clerical and Technical Workers, President. Telephone interview with Richard Hurd. December 11.

Working Women Education Fund. 1990. "Stories of Mistrust and Manipulation: The Electronic Monitoring of the American Workplace." February. Cleveland, Ohio.

Part VI
Female Leadership and Union Cultures: Feminizing the Labor Movement?

Undoubtedly, the labor movement is feminizing. The question is, what difference will it make? Is the labor movement transforming as women enter it or are women simply adopting and perpetuating the current status quo? What about the women themselves? Are they empowered or defeated by their battles to participate in and lead union organizations?

Pamela Roby and Lynet Uttal have interviewed men and women rank-and-file union activists, the unsung army of union stewards who, every day in countless shop floors across the country, choose to spend their time and sometimes their money in helping their fellow workers. Roby and Uttal ask how these workers' individual strategies for balancing work, family, and union demands vary and how unions can help encourage the shop floor activism of those with family responsibilities. Their research suggests that unions have become more "family-friendly," and that for most of these women, the rewards of union activism outweigh the sacrifices. Union activism appears to transform women more than men: requiring nontraditional gender behavior and at times, nontraditional family and social support structures.

Lois Gray describes the slow but steady progress of women into the higher union offices, with the exception of the top elected positions, which remain resolutely male. She recounts the adjustments required of these pioneering women, and the individual strategies they adopted to succeed. Unions may be appointing more women leaders but they may also be doing less to accommodate and adjust to female leadership at the top than at the bottom. Like Roby and Uttal's union stewards, Gray's female interlopers confront pressure to circumscribe their family lives. Unlike many female rank-and-file activists, however, these tokens must function primarily within male-dominated work cultures that reflect the needs and values of men. The heartaches this minority status creates for women is confirmed dramatically in many of the commentaries in this section.

The commentators, three union activists and one academic, offer collective, not individual, solutions to the dilemmas of female activists. For Kim Fellner, the problems of women integrating public institutions will never be solved until men share equal responsibility for the private sphere and until women have enough power to transform the public institutions created by men into organizations that "respect women's needs and accept their value." Ruth Needleman agrees, arguing that this kind of transformative feminization will occur when women "tell the truth" about their experiences in groups to each other, when they validate their own lives and experiences and explore alternative models collectively.

Diane Harriford and Roberta Lynch take us beyond gender. The integration of women into leadership and the transformation of union culture is, as Lynch sums up, "necessary but not sufficient." Both remind us that women are diverse and that not only family, but that feminism, work, and even unionism may mean different things to different women. Harriford details the particular "ways of doing" and "ways of knowing" she observed among black women unionists in the New York City CLUW chapter. Lynch asks what difference would it make if women succeeded in winning seats of power in an institution that no longer has the ability to change women's lives? For feminization to be anything other than a pyrrhic victory, women must lead in the true sense, that is, they must remake the labor movement not only for themselves, but for men as well.

14
Putting It All Together
The Dilemmas of Rank-and-File Union Leaders

Pamela Roby and Lynet Uttal

U nions and other worker organizations have become increasingly important to women as more and more women have entered the labor force and as women have assumed increasing financial responsibilities for their families. As union stewards, women shape the quality of their own and others' working conditions by carrying out formal grievance procedures and informally handling daily problems. Stewards may also affect workers' take-home wages by educating coworkers about collective bargaining and unions, and by uniting workers in seeking better wages. As growing numbers of workers, union members, and stewards have considerable family responsibilities, union practices that enable members and rank-and-file leaders to integrate their families into union activities and otherwise assist them in integrating union and family activities have become increasingly important to the health and survival of unions and to the condition of workers.

This is a revised version of a paper presented to the Thirty-sixth Annual Meeting of the Society for the Study of Social Problems held in New York City on August 28, 1986, and of an article published as "Trade Union Stewards: Handling Union, Family, and Employment Responsibilities" in *Women and Work: An Annual Review*, vol. 3 (1988):215–48. For a description of the methodology used in this study and further reading on subjects discussed in this chapter, see the earlier article and Roby 1987. We thank each of the 159 trade union stewards whom we interviewed for her or his perspectives and time. We also thank the Academic Senate, the Feminist Studies ORA, the Graduate Opportunity Mentorship Program, and the Social Science Division of the University of California, Santa Cruz; and the Women and Work Research Center of the University of Texas–Arlington, for financial assistance. We appreciate the generous advice and other assistance of Sue Cobble, Alice Cook, Arlene Daniels, Barbara Gutek, Marcy Howe, Joyce Miller, James Mulherin, Jim Potterton, Patricia Sexton, George Strauss, Mike Webber, Barbara Wertheimer, and the principle officers of the union locals where we did our research.

This chapter reports on one part of a larger study of women and men rank-and-file labor union leaders.[1] Here we examine three major questions concerning the relationship of stewards' family and union responsibilities: How have family responsibilities affected women's as compared with men's handling of union responsibilities? How do these women and men, all of whom are full-time employees, manage union responsibilities in addition to family and employment responsibilities? How do unions assist stewards in simultaneously managing their family and union responsibilities?

Women and Union Leadership

When we began to study women's leadership in unions, we decided for several reasons to focus on the conditions and perspectives of trade union stewards. Over the past decade, women have constituted an increasing proportion of most union stewards.[2] Trade union stewards occupy an influential position in the workplace. Stewards are union members and employees of private enterprises or government agencies who are elected by union members in their unit (office or shop) or appointed by the union to represent their coworkers and the union. In many unions, a steward's primary role is to handle the initial step or steps of worker grievances.[3] In most unions, stewards also have political, educational, and organizational responsibilities. Working side by side with others in the steno pool, warehouse, or factory, stewards represent their coworkers before management, communicate between the members and the union, serve as relatively independent leaders of their con-

[1] This chapter is based on what 124 women and men shop stewards told us in individual interviews. The stewards, whom we interviewed for an average of a little over three hours each in 1985 and 1986, are from ten major trade unions that represent wage-earning industrial and service workers, that is, nonprofessional employees. The women stewards in our sample had been employed full-time for an average of seventeen years or slightly less that the average of twenty years for the men stewards whom we interviewed. The female stewards' lengthy employment records demonstrate that they are not intermittent or temporary employees as is often assumed for women. Both female and male stewards reported working on the job over forty hours a week on the average, but the men worked about four more hours of overtime than their female counterparts. Twenty-nine percent of the women, as compared with 53 percent of the men, reported working over forty hours the week prior to our interview.

[2] Comprehensive data have never been gathered on the numbers of women who hold local union posts across the country, and union locals do not calculate the percentage of their members or stewards who are female. It is generally agreed, however, that, over the past decade, women have constituted an increasing proportion of most unions' stewards. Nevertheless, for those northern California locals from which we have obtained lists of stewards, female members continue to be underrepresented among stewards.

[3] In some unions, the steward watches for company violations of the contract but a business agent or higher-level union staff member, not the steward, actually handles the grievances. For descriptions of the historical roots of the union steward, see Nash 1983 and Peck 1963.

stituents, and, in handling grievances, interpret and extend the negotiating process and contract (Cook 1962).

Stewards' understanding of workers' problems, their decisions to act or not act, and their ability to represent workers effectively can significantly affect women's everyday employment experiences. A good steward can make a difference in areas of particular interest to female employees, such as termination practices related to workers' absences involving the care of sick children, the distribution of overtime, the allocation of promotions and special job assignments, the scheduling of workdays, and sexual harassment. In addition, service as a steward is a step toward higher-level positions in unions and workplaces (Cook, Lorwin, and Daniels 1984). Furthermore, by working as stewards, women gain leadership skills, which they may use in reshaping their workplaces and unions, developing new workplace organizations, and attaining other employment goals of their choosing.

In contrast to the considerable research and writing on stewards in Great Britain over the last twenty years, little attention has been devoted to the study of union stewards in the United States since the 1940s and 1950s. Women were largely ignored in the earlier U.S. studies, as well as in the more recent British research on union stewards (Mills 1948; Peck 1963; Batstone, Boraston, and Frenkel 1977; Robertson and Schuller 1982). Now changing labor market and union conditions call for new studies of the leadership and attitudes of trade union stewards, both men and women.

Not only has women's involvement in the labor force increased dramatically since the end of World War II, but a sharply increasing percentage of mothers have joined the labor force. Today the *majority* of mothers, including mothers with young children, are employed or looking for work. Moreover, 39 percent of all working women are now mothers with children under age eighteen (Bureau of Labor Statistics 1990). If the underrepresentation of women among union officers and staff is to be overcome, the question of how women and husbands of working women are to handle both family and union responsibilities in addition to full-time jobs must be addressed.

Our work is among the first to ask how women and men in the United States handle union, family, and employment responsibilities. It builds on the research literature concerning the interface of work and family (Berheide 1984). Our study allows us to examine whether and how these findings apply to trade union stewards. In addition, most of the research on the employment/family topic examines how women are affected by and how they responded to employment/work conflicts rather than how male spouses or employers, unions, and other public institutions adapt or might adapt to families. In contrast, our research examines how both men and women union stewards

experience and cope with the triad of family, union, and employment responsibilities. It includes men and women's reports on ways their spouses assist
them and ways their unions support and might support their handling of
family as well as union responsibilities.

Are Women Less Active Than Men?

Women workers have long been described as hard to organize and, once
organized, less likely to participate in their unions than men. Their lack of
participation conventionally has been attributed to their primary responsibilities being in the home. Recently, feminist scholars have challenged this
characterization of working women.

Our research confirms this feminist challenge. In comparing female and
male stewards' levels of union activity, we found that the women we interviewed had similar rates of participation as the men on three indicators: they
attended the same proportion of union meetings, held a similar number of
other union positions, and participated in a similar number of other union
activities.[4] The women, however, unlike the men, rarely reported doing steward work outside of working hours.

Because we also wanted to learn how family responsibilities affected these
stewards' levels of union activity, we divided stewards according to four categories of domestic living situations. We categorized stewards as (a) living
with a partner and children; (b) living only with children; (c) living only with
a partner; or (d) single (never married, divorced, separated, or widowed persons
without children). We found that male stewards were much more likely than
female stewards to be living with a partner and children (66 percent as compared with 25 percent) and less likely to have any other kind of arrangement:
5 percent lived only with children, 11 percent lived only with a partner, and
18 percent were single. In contrast, 25 percent of the female stewards were
living with a partner and children, 27 percent were living only with children,
21 percent were living only with partners, and 27 percent were single (see
table 14.1).[5]

When we examined the relationship of stewards' domestic living situations
to union activity, we found clear variations. Single female stewards had higher
participation rates than female stewards with partners and children. Surpris-

---

[4] The data in this and the next section are examined in greater detail in Uttal 1987.

[5] The distribution of workers in the total U.S. population among household types was similar
to that among stewards: among full-time, year-round workers in the total U.S. population, 52
percent of the men were in traditional families with a spouse and children under age eighteen,
as compared with 32 percent of the women (U.S. Bureau of the Census 1980).

Table 14.1. Distribution of Stewards by Domestic Living Status
and Gender

| | Domestic living status | | | | |
Gender	Living with partner and children %	Living only with children %	Living only with partner %	Single %	Total %
Male	66 (n = 40)	5 (n = 3)	11 (n = 7)	18 (n = 11)	100 (n = 61)*
Female	25 (n = 14)	27 (n = 15)	21 (n = 12)	27 (n = 15)	100 (n = 56)

*The total n is based on 117 couples. Five homosexual cohabitating couples and two male stewards whose domestic living status is missing data are not included.

ingly, however, single female stewards also had higher participation rates than single male stewards, and as high a rate as male stewards with partners and children. Male stewards with partners and children had higher participation rates than either single male or female stewards with partners and/or children. These findings show in sum that the presence of a partner and children affects stewards' levels of participation in union activities, but does so inversely for men and women. For women, the presence of a partner and/or children lowers their level of participation in union activities. For men, the presence of a partner and children boosts their level of union participation. Interestingly, however, women with no family responsibilities were more active than similarly situated men and almost as active as men who had wives who (presumably) took on much of the domestic responsibility.

Family or Union?

How do these women and men, all of whom are full-time employees, adjust their family lives so as to handle union responsibilities in addition to family and full-time employment responsibilities? Clearly, not all of the female or male stewards in this sample have to handle traditional family responsibilities such as raising and caring for children or managing households for families. More women than men did not have such responsibilities: 56 percent of the female stewards and 23 percent of the male stewards reported living without partners. Female stewards were also less likely than male stewards to be living with children of any age (49 percent as compared with 69 percent) and less likely than male stewards to be living with children under age twelve (29 percent as compared with 42 percent).

The finding that a relatively small percentage of female stewards lived with partners and/or children does not mean that our question concerning how they adjusted their family lives so as to handle union responsibilities does not apply to them. Rather, female stewards in particular reported that living without partners or children was one of the ways that they had adjusted their personal lives so as to be able to handle union responsibilities and employment and personal responsibilities.[6] Carole, a thirty-one-year-old gas company serviceperson, was especially aware of these competing demands.[7]

> For a long time, it was a big conflict to me how often I could see family, friends, or lover when I was involved in the union. A constant source of stress—when will I get out to see Mom? I was always explaining to my lover why I had meetings four nights a week. Ultimately, I became less involved in the union. But then I'm always cutting away big stressful parts. Like the conflict with my lover about time. [The solution was] I just don't be in the relationship. [Note: Carole is currently on two committees and attended forty steward meetings in the last twelve months plus eight general union meetings. This represents a very high activity rate. She now lives alone].

Joyce, a thirty-six-year-old billing specialist divorced from her husband, reported that independent living was the best strategy to allow her to continue her level of union activity: "My boyfriend and I would probably be living together if it weren't for the union. But because I need the time in the evening to do phone calls and paperwork, I've hesitated to set up that arrangement. I need my solitude."

Another way of reducing family-union conflicts in order to handle union responsibilities was to dissolve traditional marital arrangements. Of the female stewards, 34 percent were partnerless because of divorce or separation. An additional 14 percent of the female stewards were divorced and remarried. In comparison, fewer male stewards reported currently being partnerless because of divorce or separation (13 percent) and fewer had remarried (11 percent).

Dorothy, who had been a steward for over eight years, resolved her conflict by divorcing her partner:

> The union is not the only reason our marriage broke up, but when I told [my husband] that I was thinking about running for vice-president [of the union], he said, "I thought you might be . . . , let me tell you something now. If you decide to run for vice-president, you also decide to terminate our marriage." It was not an easy decision. . . . It was three months of hard soul-searching. I

[6] Similarly, groups of professional women are much less likely than professional men to be married with a spouse present. For discussions of gender similarities and differences in marriage and parenthood among academics, physicians, and lawyers see Simeone 1987; Lorber 1984; and Epstein 1983.

[7] All names have been changed to protect the anonymity of those we interviewed.

finally said, I'm running. It didn't matter whether I won or lost. I have to live, and I have to live with myself as a person.

Several other women who were divorced also volunteered that not only was their spouse's lack of support for their union work a factor in their decision to divorce, but that if they were not involved in the union, they would be involved in "something else." Rosemarie recalled that her ex-husband had asked her, "Who comes first, me or the union?" and that she replied, "It's something I enjoy and need. If I wasn't active in the union, I'd be active in the PTA or something else."

Some who divorced later found partners who effectively support their union work and goals. Dale, who was divorced, said of her present partner, who is also a member of her local, "My man's not only my total support but the recipient of all my anxieties when I come home. He's a little jealous when I go out of town [on union business], but he never tries to talk me out of it. If he did, it would destroy our relationship." Patricia, one of the remarried respondents, reported that her first husband

> was very jealous of any outside interest. My present husband gives me drive. I pull him in and ask for his input. We were married when I ran for office. After I was nominated, I had some doubts as to whether I could perform the duties and thought of dropping out of the race. He was the one who kept encouraging me. He told me, "You're ready for it."

Several female stewards explained how they were able to do union activities by having their children live with other people. Mary, a thirty-four-year-old supply clerk, is in her second marriage. After she left her first husband, she altered her life again to do union work: "I let my youngest daughter stay with my sister and my son stayed with my older sister. I stopped seeing the guy I was seeing." Currently, Mary's two children live with her six months a year and live the rest of the year with her mother. Gloria, a forty-seven-year-old food service worker, said she did not have to change her personal life to do union work because "I didn't have a family. My two children lived with their dad from fifteen years old on."

Adding union activities to employment and family responsibilities was not conflict-free for either men or women who were living with a partner and children in traditional family living situations. Both men and women reported that they had experienced conflicts in the last twelve months. In fact, more male stewards (58 percent) than female stewards (43 percent) reported that they had experienced a family-union conflict in the preceding year.

Women and men, however, reported qualitatively different types, and resolutions, of union-family conflicts. Generally, women said that their main conflict was how to keep union responsibilities from interfering with or subtracting from family time. Their resolutions involved keeping union responsibilities from impinging on or invading their family time. In contrast, male stewards typically experienced conflict over simultaneous union and family responsibilities; they usually gave priority to the union responsibility and missed the family event.

Rebecca, a forty-seven-year-old health insurance specialist, told us that she helped her husband with his business in the evenings. She felt her monthly union meetings cut into this family responsibility. Her solution was to do union work only during work hours and while riding public transportation home so that she was available to help him in the evenings. Other women reported that they kept their union responsibilities out of their family time by cutting back on their own personal needs, such as sleep.

Several female stewards noted that it was especially difficult to integrate their domestic responsibilities with the nature, timing, and location of union meetings. Pamela, a twenty-six-year-old customer service representative who is married and lives with her seven-year-old son and her second husband, observed:

> Things are not set up for working women. Meetings last a long time with everyone [telling their] complaints so I don't go. If they were only a few hours ... but they're too long to be away from the family. If I leave early I feel embarrassed because people want to know why [I'm leaving early].

Cheryl, a forty-one-year-old customer representative, married but with no children, also had problems with the way the union scheduled its meetings:

> The majority, but not all, in charge of the union are men. They don't worry about holidays. Invariably they schedule workshops the weekend before Thanksgiving. Some of this planning is off kilter. But more women are getting involved. I [guess they] figure if you're dedicated enough you'll make other arrangements.

In contrast, male stewards did not indicate that the timing of union meetings was problematic for them because of competing family responsibilities.

Women reported that when they confronted union-family scheduling conflicts, they were faced with the likelihood that the family activity would not be taken care of at all if they did not do it or if they did not begin preparatory work ahead of time for someone else to complete. Women either skipped union meetings or made arrangements ahead of time so that things could be easily taken care of by others at home in their absence. Marie, who is forty-eight years old, commented, "If I know ahead of time that I have a meeting, I leave some food that my husband can heat up."

Men, however, could be late to or absent from family events and their absence did not jeopardize the occurrence of the event. Several male stewards with partners and children said they frequently solved family-union conflicts by missing family events, which simply went on without them. Jack, a fifty-year-old truck driver, said: "There was a union meeting and one of the kid's birthdays. We had [the kids] over. I went to the meeting." Mike, a forty-six-year-old business systems technician, had missed a unique family event: "During a strike, my youngest daughter was born and I was out picketing. [My wife] was in the hospital and . . . she wanted me to be there and I went to picket duty."

Male stewards justified family members' hurt feelings by explaining the seriousness of union responsibilities. Ralph, a forty-six-year-old truck driver, recalled:

> An employee was going to be discharged on my daughter's birthday last year. I stuck around to circumvent termination. I got chewed out. There were hurt feelings from my little girl. I explained to her the price of a job to a family if I hadn't taken the time.

Male stewards seemed comfortable with attending to union responsibilities outside of working hours. Family members changed their schedules to accommodate the stewards' union responsibilities. The men did not perceive this as problematic or inconvenient for others. A typical response was, "There is no clash between my family life and job. I just have to tell them, 'Tonight I have a meeting,' so they know when to start dinner."

Many male stewards could put family responsibilities second to union work because their female partners took up the slack. Male stewards with partners and children did 21 percent of the cooking, 21 percent of meal cleanup, 29 percent of grocery shopping, 19 percent of general housecleaning, 20 percent of the laundry, and 56 percent of bill paying as compared to 61 percent, 51 percent, 67 percent, 51 percent, 61 percent, and 78 percent, respectively, reported by female stewards with partners and children. Sixty-five percent of the male stewards with partners and children had partners who were also employed.

Although female stewards, on average, do a much higher percentage of household chores than male stewards, a few women have fully employed spouses who do most of the household's tasks. For several, this division of labor occurred because their partners arrive home from work several hours earlier than they do. For others, "discussion and struggle" shifted their family's housework ratio. Janice, an SEIU steward, explained, "We had a lot of family meetings for a while about how everything is to be divided. Hopefully, they are over." Another, a Teamster steward married for twenty-one years, said her husband did half the grocery shopping, most of the housecleaning, and 99 percent of the cooking. She added that this arrangement came about because "he's a better housekeeper than I am. I don't do it. He does it, and I'm glad. I think it's great."

Only a minority of female and male stewards reported that their partners did not support their union work. Most partners encouraged the stewards' union work, did not complain about the amount of time spent doing union work, and helped with thinking through union-related problems. Cherise, an IBEW steward, told us: "He dialogues with me about [my steward work]. . . . He asks me questions. He's excited when I'm excited!" Sharon, a UAW steward, noted, "He's understanding when I attend classes or meetings for the union, and he takes care of our son." Another UAW steward related that her husband is "real glad I'm there doing some good."

There was, however, a difference in the *type* of support received by male and female stewards. A few more women than men reported that their spouses taxied them to meetings, but a sizable number of male stewards and no female stewards received secretarial and editorial support, such as typing and writing. Men were freed from domestic concerns so they could participate in union activities: "She'll assume total responsibility for child care to free me to attend meetings." In addition to concrete services, men were more frequently accompanied by their partners' to union activities. "She goes to picnics, labor parades, joins along with me."

When female stewards *did* report getting concrete support services from others, it was usually help with domestic, rather than union, responsibilities. Generally, this support came not from partners, but from older children or mothers. Claudine, a thirty-four-year-old account clerk, maintained responsibility for household work, but shifted the actual performance of domestic responsibilities to her daughter. She observed:

> During negotiations, I was gone constantly. My family and I talked a lot on the phone. This was discussed with my family before I started. I said, "This is what I want to do," and they said, "Go for it!" Luckily, I have a thirteen-year-old daughter who can cook and do laundry.

Some female stewards (but no male stewards) in nontraditional living arrangements handled the combined load of union, family, and employment responsibilities by cutting back on housework, organizing their time better, and buying more convenience foods.

> I organize my personal time and work time differently than before. I used to be pretty lazy. Now I'm more organized. My housework and personal life are more organized due to my scheduling time. Too bad it took the union involvement to do that. It helps.

Men typically cut back on recreational activities, an option no female steward used.

Both male and female stewards had to decide how to prioritize domestic and union responsibilities. Female stewards with partners and children placed family responsibilities above union responsibilities. In contrast, for single female stewards, like most male stewards, union responsibilities took precedence. Women, however, unlike men, limited or eliminated their involvement in personal relationships. Men with families also placed union responsibilities first. When faced with a union-family conflict, male stewards asked their families to excuse their absences, apologized to their children for missing significant events like birthday parties, and told their wives not to delay dinner for them. Women were less likely than men to even have partners or children to whom they made these excuses, but women with partners and children took special care to keep union responsibilities from impinging upon family time. Unlike men who depended heavily on their partners for all types of support services, female stewards generally either handled matters by themselves or relied upon people other than their spouses for support.

Union Responses to the Work, Family, Activism Crunch

When asked, "Has the union done anything that has made it easier for you to participate or be active in the union?," stewards often cited factors that can be called "family-respecting practices."[8] Most frequently, they noted the sensitivity of unions in scheduling or locating meetings and in encouraging family integration with union functions. The time that was considered "especially convenient" was right after work, sometimes in the evening. Other stewards said their unions rotate times and locations so that members with families can attend at least some meetings that fit in with their family and work schedules. CWA and UFCW locals held their monthly membership meetings at two different times on the same day so the stewards could choose the time that best fit their family and work schedules, an option the stewards appreciated. Scheduling meetings far in advance was also cited as helpful, for it allowed stewards to plan family activities around meetings rather than forcing them to choose between a family activity or a union meeting. Delores, an SEIU steward who was actively involved in union negotiations and was the mother of three teenagers, noted the importance of breaks during union work: "We had breaks of an hour or two during negotiations when I could run home and check with the kids on surprise visits."

[8]Some of the ways in which unions accommodate families are a matter of union policy. Others are a matter of individual decision and practice on the part of union business agents and officers. While some unions are more supportive of stewards' family responsibilities than others, no single union offers all of the supports mentioned below (see CLUW 1990).

In a few cases, union staff made special provisions for stewards with family responsibilities. Chuck, a HERE steward who had full responsibility for his infant and toddler daughters when his wife was at work, told us that he was able to be a steward only because a business agent had given him special on-the-job training for his steward work, thus making it unnecessary for him to attend the steward training classes that were held during his parenting time. Union staff gave him their home phone numbers so he could call them whenever he needed more information. Other stewards reported that the understanding that business agents and union officers showed them and the care with which they filled them in on activities they missed when their family members were in the hospital or having difficulties made a big difference to them.

Stewards were appreciative of union officers and business agents who were receptive to children attending union meetings and who allowed for mild disruptions. The stewards also liked having other union stewards and officers get acquainted with their children, and having their children feel a part of their union. Ruth, a CWA steward, said the San Francisco Central Labor Council-sponsored lectures by Chicago's late mayor, Harold Washington, and Jesse Jackson provided her children with valuable black role models, education, and perspectives they could not receive at school. A forty-two-year-old CWA mother of three observed: "I've involved my family in what I do. Every time I get a chance to take them with me, like the two picket lines and the 1984 campaign, I do. . . . My kids are like partners." Now her oldest daughter is also employed with the telephone company and, not surprisingly, is a CWA steward too.

Union family picnics and softball games are popular with some stewards. Others, especially those without cars, appreciate the union's willingness to arrange transportation to meetings. Another much-appreciated service is union-catered meals at steward meetings.

The second most frequently cited support was paid release time from employment for union activities. Stewards are paid their regular wages for this time either by their union or by their employer, depending on the terms of their contract. The UAW union coordinators (stewards) at the New United Motors Manufacturing (NUMMI) plant have two hours a week of company-provided time for union work. The CWA stewards' release time is paid for by the union itself. Although the Machinists do not have a formal release-time policy, Claudia, an IAM steward who was also an officer of the local Coalition of Labor Union Women (CLUW) chapter, reported, "Whenever I need time off for a CLUW function, if the company will let me off, the union will pay for my lost time, hotels, travel, and other expenses." These stewards have to do less or none of their steward work on family time.

Some unions reimburse stewards for expenses so that they do not place a burden on family budgets. The money stewards spend while fulfilling their steward responsibilities is often significant when considered in relation to their salaries. Dennis, a Teamster who has served as a steward intermittently for thirteen years, finds it helpful when the union reimburses him for union calls. Margaret, a sixty-year-old ILGWU steward who earns under $5,000 a year as a buttonholer in the garment industry, told us, "Sometimes they pay for my gas for coming over there for meetings because I have to go twenty-five miles both ways." Shirley, an IBEW steward, noted that when there is a "joint grievance, we meet for breakfast and they buy breakfast. They pay mileage and buy lunch for stewards' conferences too."

What Could Unions Do?

Stewards, when asked, "What *could* your union do to make your participation easier?," most frequently responded that their union could schedule meetings at more convenient times. A number also wanted more advance warning for steward meetings and more convenient meeting sites. Of course, what a convenient meeting place and a convenient meeting time mean vary from family to family. Surveys might be helpful when determining the best time for union meetings.

Members noted that meetings should be shorter and/or kept to the length of time promised. When discussing meeting length, Ann winced and said she would consider staying on as a steward if the meetings kept to their schedules. "I could understand a few exceptions but not going over the promised time at every meeting." Steve, a member of another union, observed, they could "save time by not having so much confusion at meetings. [They could] put out written information that would be beneficial to stewards."

Union release time for steward work and meetings was the second most frequently cited request. Third was the provision of child care and hot meals for members and their children during union meetings.

Interestingly, more men than women with young children requested child care services. Perhaps this finding reflects the higher percentage of stewards with young children, or it may indicate that men are more likely to expect external support for their child care responsibilities. George responded promptly to our question: "Have a baby-sitting service! It would be a help if you could bring children and put them in a room while you're in the meeting instead of having them in the meeting." Sam wanted child care to be more than just baby-sitting: "Provide meaningful child care with activities for meetings. Have classes for parents and kids, activities, baseball games, that kind of thing."

Several stewards whose unions do not reimburse their expenses, thought their union should. Marcy noted, "I have to pay for parking and the baby-sitter [when I have a union meeting]. The union should pay something when stewards have families."

In sum, unions assist stewards with family responsibilities in numerous and varied ways. But, no one union offers all of the varied types of support described above. Also, except for providing meaningful child care during steward and membership meetings, all the forms of support that stewards suggested for families are already being offered by at least one union local in our sample. These findings suggest that it would be possible for unions to implement a greater variety of supports than currently exist, but that the support currently offered is making a difference. More progress, however, is needed on the child care front. As Susan Eaton, SEIU's Western Regional Coordinator for Programs and Services, has recognized, "While providing quality child care at meetings, conferences, and training sessions can be expensive, it also communicates to women workers that their participation is welcome, and it makes it possible for working mothers to attend" (Eaton 1990:45).

Conclusions and Implications

In this study we examined how family responsibilities affect men and women stewards' handling of union responsibilities, the ways stewards have managed union responsibilities in addition to family and employment responsibilities, and the ways unions have and might assist rank-and-file leaders in coordinating their union, family, and work responsibilities. One of the most striking findings is the considerable gender difference in the personal living arrangements of female and male stewards. The concentration of male stewards in households with both partners and children as compared with the even distribution of female stewards in households with and without partners, and with and without children, suggests that the combination of employment, public activity, and home life is experienced differently by men and women and results in different family organizations. The second major finding is that although both women and men experience union-family conflicts, they have qualitatively different types of conflicts and resolutions for these conflicts. When male stewards had such conflicts, they generally put the union activity first and relied on their wives to take care of the family event. In contrast, female stewards with partners and children generally prioritized family activities over union activities and insisted that the family event, such as children's birthdays, would not happen without them. We also found that the unequal division of housework and parenting persists. Male stewards, whether their spouses are employed or not, do considerably less housework than female stewards. Female stewards, if living with partners, are more likely to be living with an employed spouse and do much more housework than their male coworkers. We found that unions have developed a variety of policies and practices that support the integration of family and union activities. Many individual unions, however, have as yet failed to offer the full range of family supports.

We hope our research findings and future research will enable women workers to participate more fully in unions and other worker organizations. Women's full participation in such organizations could potentially transform not only the labor movement but the workplace itself.

15

The Route to the Top

Female Union Leaders and Union Policy

Lois S. Gray

Although women now constitute about one third of the members of labor unions in the United States, they are still barely visible in top leadership. To what extent are women currently making inroads in union leadership and what types of union responsibilities do they hold? Is there a glass ceiling? How do the career patterns of women unionists compare with those of men? What can unions do to facilitate their recognition? These are the key questions I examine in this article, drawing on past research supplemented by insights from union leaders I interviewed.[1]

Much of what has been written about the gender gap in union leadership focuses on what stands in the way—the barriers. This article will also look at the roadblocks to leadership. My emphasis, however, will be on the positive— what can and is being done to overcome these barriers. Lastly, I will assess the possible impact of increased representation of women on union policies and leadership styles.

Where Are the Women in Unions?

Women are not new to labor leadership. Of the countless numbers who played key roles in local labor struggles during the past century, many rose to

[1] For a study of union administration, I interviewed sixty-one national union presidents (four of whom were women) about their career patterns, goals, accomplishments, and leadership styles. For this essay, I interviewed twenty-three women who hold leadership positions at various levels—national, regional, and local—and collected data about membership, policies, and practices from all of the national unions in which women constitute 50 percent or more of the membership as well as those which have sponsored women's departments or special activities for women.

national prominence. Agnes Nestor, for example, was elected president of the Glove Workers in 1907, becoming the first female to head a national union, and the following year the American Federation of Labor appointed its first woman to national staff (P. Foner 1980; Wertheimer 1977). Nevertheless, in 1968 Alice Cook observed that women:

> are rarely found as officers of the intermediate bodies, the joint boards, and district councils, and almost never appear on major negotiating teams or on national executive boards, national staffs, and among the national officers . . . even when they are in a majority, women play the role, and are assigned to the status, of a minority—moreover, a minority still in that state of political self-consciousness where tokenism suffices to meet its demands (p. 132).

Available statistics confirm Cook's assessment.[2] The proportion of women in top elected leadership posts was less than 5 percent in the 1950s and 1960s. In the 1970s the numbers increased, reaching 11 percent in 1978[3] (Bergquist 1974; Needleman and Tanner 1987).

This proportion remains the same today. According to my calculations, women on executive boards of national and international unions listed in the 1990–91 *BNA Directory* (Gifford 1991) total 11 percent when independents are included and 9 percent if only AFL-CIO affiliates are counted, the same percentages reported in 1978. One in five AFL-CIO unions has at least one woman on its governing board; but women are generally underrepresented in relation to their proportion of the membership. In seven out of eight unions, women constitute less than one-fourth of the executive board membership, including some, but not all, of the unions in which women make up fifty percent or more of the membership.

In 1975, none of the AFL-CIO unions was headed by a woman (*U.S. News & World Report* 1975). In 1992, women are presidents of three national unions affiliated with the AFL-CIO: Lenore Miller, who heads the Retail, Wholesale and Department Store Union (RWDSU); Dee Maki, Association of Flight Attendants (AFA); and Nedda Cassei, American Guild of Musical Artists (AGMA). Among national independent unions, the American Nurses' Association (ANA) is also headed by a woman. Five women hold the title of

---

[2]Unfortunately, statistics about women in union leadership have been hard to come by. Few unions publish or even collect these figures. The U.S. Department of Labor discontinued this type of data collection in 1978, leaving the Bureau of National Affairs listings for national officers as the sole source.

[3]After 1970, published statistics included employee associations along with the earlier reported AFL-CIO unions. These independent organizations, representing mainly teachers, nurses, and public employees, have significantly higher percentages of women members and leaders.

secretary-treasurer in national unions, a position usually carrying authority second only to the president.

In 1980, the national AFL-CIO elected the first woman to its executive council. In 1992, two women sit on the council (down from three in 1991), a somewhat lower percentage of governing board representation than the average affiliated union.

All current AFL-CIO federation presidents at the state level are male. Almost all of the state federations, however, have at least one female member on their executive boards. Eighty-seven women served as principal officers of local central labor councils (CLC) and altogether women account for 12 percent of total CLC offices held in 1991 (Gifford 1991).

Although the increase of women as national and regional elected officers has proceeded at a "snail's pace" (Baden 1986), union women have been more successful in achieving leadership recognition through appointment. This phenomenon suggests a growing commitment on the part of the still mostly male leadership. In 1991, approximately half of the national unions affiliated with the AFL-CIO had one or more female department heads in their head-quarters staff and women accounted for one out of eight of these supervisory positions, up sharply from earlier years (Le Grande 1978). Overall, women are estimated to hold one-third of all staff positions in national unions, a proportion that doubled in a decade. In a few unions, notably those with strong organizing outreach to women workers, the proportion of females on national staff reached approximately 50 percent, registering a dramatic increase in recent years (Needleman and Tanner 1987). In 1980 the AFL-CIO ap-pointed its first female department head; the number increased to three in 1990 when its first female regional director was also appointed.

The greatest change appears to be at the grassroots level. Among those unions that have actually counted the number of women local leaders, the American Federation of State, County and Municipal Employees (AFSCME), the American Federation of Teachers (AFT), and the National Education Association (NEA) report that approximately one-half of their current local officers are female; the Communications Workers Association (CWA), 35 percent; Service Employees' International Union (SEIU), 40 percent; and International Union of Electrical Workers (IUE), 12 percent. In the Office and Professional Employees International Union (OPEIU) and the NEA, more than 50 percent of local union presidents are female.

Even in unions with predominantly male membership, the percentage of women in key local positions has gone up. For example, one in ten local United Auto Workers (UAW) presidents is female (*UAW Solidarity* 1989) and female local union presidents have recently come to the fore in such formerly all-male domains as the steelworkers, mineworkers, and machinists (P. Foner 1980: 545–48; Baden 1986). In addition, knowledgeable observers report increasing numbers of women in the local union leadership pipeline. Growing recognition in local office augers well for the future since this is the pool from which future leaders will be drawn.

Gender stereotyping is also beginning to change. Historically, union women disproportionately carried the duties of recording secretaries and served mainly on women's committees. They were rarely elected to negotiating committees or other roles that constitute launching pads for union power and recognition (Gray 1988). More recently, women elected as vice-presidents and union executive board members are being assigned to a broader range of responsibilities, including collective bargaining. In 1991, women directed organizing departments in three unions, including the largest AFL-CIO affiliate, the Teamsters (IBT). Research, which focuses on preparation for collective bargaining; legislation, which deals with key policy issues; and public relations, which involves interpreting the union to the media, are currently the most frequently held responsibilities of females who direct union staff departments. These nontraditional functions reinforce the impression that women are breaking out of the molds of the past.

The discrepancy between women as a proportion of membership and their representation in leadership is roughly similar in unions to other political institutions in our society and shows the same tendency to change at the grass roots (Schwartz and Hoyman 1984:71; R. Foner 1991).

Breaking In and Moving Up

In sharp contrast to other professions, the careers of union leaders are rarely planned. Becoming a leader in a union tends to be an accidental vocational choice that grows out of complex patterns of experiences and relationships in the trade or occupation in which one is employed. Studies of local (Sayles and Strauss 1967) and national union officials report that individuals initially take on leadership responsibilities because of appeals from fellow employees who urged them to speak up to management; because they are motivated by the challenge of learning and using their abilities; and/or because of their commitment to the social egalitarian appeal of unionism (Quaglieri 1988). Few think of seeking office in the union as a step toward a full-time career. The accidental character and political dynamic of the personnel selection process in unions help explain why so few women have emerged as top leaders.

Biographies from the past and interviews with present leaders reveal four routes to the top of the union hierarchy and illustrate the difficulties women face. Historically, national leaders were founders. Such labor pioneers as Samuel Gompers, Eugene Debs, and Philip Murray are examples. Among today's labor leaders, this path to leadership is increasingly rare. One of the few living labor leaders who organized a new union is Cesar Chavez, president of the United Farm Workers of America (UFWA). Another path to top leadership, now rare and perhaps disappearing, is inheritance. Numerous union presidencies have been passed from father to son: the Rafterys in the Painters, the Hutchinsons in the Carpenters; the Foscos in the Laborers, and the Carloughs in the Sheet Metal Workers.

A third union career path, the technical expertise route, is of recent origin but is regarded by some as the wave of the future (Schwartz and Hoyman 1984). The technical expertise route involves entering the union as a specialist and becoming recognized as a leader. Lane Kirkland, president, and Tom Donahue, secretary-treasurer of the AFL-CIO, took this route to top leadership positions. Both are college graduates who were initially hired for specialized functions and worked their way to the top through demonstrated administrative ability. Other examples include Jack Sheinkman, president of the Amalgamated Clothing and Textile Workers Union (ACTWU), and his predecessor, Murray Finley. Both originally joined the union as attorneys.

The majority of national union presidents and other top officers, however, have followed the elective route up from the rank and file. This is a long and tortuous path that begins with activism in the local union and winds through rising levels of responsibilities to regional and national office. Typically, leaders become active in local union affairs and run for office at an early age. Working their way up "through the chairs," as some describe the process, they eventually reach top positions twenty to thirty years later (Quaglieri 1988). This career path has not changed for decades (Mills 1948) and continues to be the expected route for those aspiring to national leadership.

Women are disadvantaged in relation to all but one of these career patterns. Women have not been the beneficiaries of family connections to the same degree as men. John L. Lewis *did* appoint his daughter to head District 50 of the United Mine Workers, but that was the rare exception. There are women founders who have risen to top leadership—Karen Nussbaum, who organized 9 to 5, a clerical organization that subsequently affiliated with SEIU; Delores Huerta, who helped Cesar Chavez form the UFWA; and current and former presidents of the AFA who were key players in the move to break away from the Airline Pilots Association to found a separate union of flight attendants—but few new unions are currently being founded. Hence, the opportunities for women to use the founders route are slim indeed. Since the mass influx of women into unions is a relatively recent phenomenon, the time investment required to advance to top-level positions through the elective route is also lacking for most of today's women.

The most readily available avenue to recognition for women is that of technical expertise, which is, in fact, the route many have taken to achieve top-level staff and department head appointments. These top-level appointments have in turn led to election as vice-presidents and executive board members of national unions. The vast majority of unions today staff their pension, public relations, occupational safety and health, research, education, and legal departments with individuals recruited from outside the membership. Many even turn to the outside in their search for organizers and the field staff who service contracts. A recent survey of national union headquarters found that only one in three require previous union membership as a precondition for professional staff employment (Clark and Gray 1992). Women in particular have been able to take advantage of these expanding staff openings in national union headquarters and in some large local unions. Examples of women who made it to top office through technical expertise include Joyce Miller, who was originally employed as education director of the ACTWU and advanced to its vice-presidency; she became the first woman elected to the Executive Council of the AFL-CIO.

A variation on the technical expertise route that is almost exclusively female consists of hiring in as a clerical. Currently only one male president started his union career this way. Jay Mazur worked for a local union pension and welfare fund in a clerical capacity and eventually rose to be national president of the International Ladies' Garment Workers' Union (ILGWU). But a great many women have achieved leadership positions through the clerical route. For example, Lenore Miller, the president of Retail, Wholesale and Department Store Workers, started working for that union as a secretary in the national headquarters, and Mary Crayton, the first woman to become regional director of the AFL-CIO, began her union career as a clerical for a local union.

Many women are currently in the pipeline pursuing the elective path to union leadership, but it remains to be seen how they will fare.

Roadblocks

Regardless of the route to national prominence followed by women leaders, those I interviewed faced roadblocks in every stage of their climb to leadership.

The major roadblocks are societal, work- and union-related, and personal, all influenced by gender stereotyping and discrimination. Women who go to work and join a union are seriously handicapped as a result of their societally proscribed roles as homemakers with responsibilities for child raising and homemaking. Scholars consistently rate this dual role as the most important barrier to female involvement in union activities (Cook 1968; Wertheimer and Nelson 1975; Koziara and Pierson 1980; Needleman and Tanner 1987; Andriappan and Chaison 1989). Reinforcing this point, Roby and Uttal's study of local union stewards in this volume found that family relationships are much more time-consuming for women and that women take special care to keep union responsibilities from impinging on their family time, in contrast to men, who place union responsibilities over family responsibilities. Women's family responsibilities constrain them from attending meetings, volunteering for committees, staying out late after work, and travelling, all of which are essential to union orientation, training, and advancement. Traditional attitudes of husbands who see women's place in the home often add a further barrier; and time out for childbearing results in a late start in catching up on knowledge about the job and the union.

Work- and union-related barriers include sexual stereotyping and male bonding both on the job and in the union. At work, employer notions about the type of work women can perform (unskilled or clerical) succeeds in steering them away from the high-prestige, skilled jobs from which local union leaders are usually drawn (Sayles and Strauss 1967), and prejudice or even harassment from male supervisors discourages union activism (Wertheimer and Nelson 1975; Andriappan and Chaison 1989). Women are still a minority in the unions and even those unions that are predominantly female in membership have traditionally been led by men. Thus, women tend to be seen or see themselves as "outsiders." They are often not invited to caucus meetings or social gatherings where union issues are discussed. There are few, if any, female role models to inspire emulation. Furthermore, women are not usually given the opportunity to represent their fellow employees in negotiations with employers, the most prestigious of all union leadership responsibilities, in part because the American tradition of adversarial labor relations calls for "tough leaders" and women are considered "too emotional" or too soft to bargain with "tough" employers (Cook 1968). These traditions, which define what is expected both in union-management relations and male and female behavior, get in the way of selecting female spokespersons to bargain with management and relegate those women who are willing to be active to dead-end assignments or to functions that are important but not linked to upward mobility in a union.

Women are also handicapped in access to training and support networks. Informal mentoring is the key to learning the ropes in any organization and male leaders tend to select persons like themselves—that is, other males—as possible successors. According to leaders I interviewed, many women who have achieved recognition in a male-dominated power structure may also feel less secure and hence do not reach out to mentor other women. Perhaps the most pervasive barrier women union leaders face (all of those interviewed mentioned it) is *underestimation*. On the job and in the union they are often ignored or overlooked and almost always regarded as less able to achieve than men.

Gender discrimination is pervasive. Women in unions, as in other organizations, report incidents of sexist remarks, sexual harassment, and overt discrimination (Fellner 1990). For example, in 1986 then New York City mayor Ed Koch commented to the press that Sandra Feldman, president of the United Federation of Teachers (UFT) had "nice legs" and reporters besieged her for pictures. Those few women who are encouraged, mentored, or sponsored by male officials are often falsely accused of sexual involvement, a charge that would not be made against their male colleagues.

Not only are women expected to be smarter, work harder, and achieve more than their male counterparts, but at the same time they are expected to lead exemplary personal lives, a double standard when compared with men.

Personal barriers reinforce these societal and organizational roadblocks. Women tend to lack self-confidence (Cook 1968; Wertheimer and Nelson 1975; Koziara and Pierson 1980; and Needleman and Tanner 1987) and internalize negative concepts about their capacity for leadership roles (Kanter 1977), fear failure and generally believe that men can handle these responsibilities better than women (Koziara and Pierson 1980; Wertheimer and Nelson 1975). Other personal limitations cited by observers are tendencies to accept passive roles (Chaison and Andriappan 1982) and lack of knowledge of union procedures (Wertheimer and Nelson 1975; Needleman 1988). The implication of this research is that women, as a result of societal, job, union and personal barriers, are less likely than men to feel comfortable and involved in union activities and, therefore, do not compete for leadership recognition to the same extent as their male colleagues.

Strategies for Success

For advice on overcoming barriers we look to women who have "made it" to major union leadership roles. The interviews I conducted with twenty-three women leaders reveal a number of common themes or patterns: they work hard, study intensively, make sacrifices, take risks, demonstrate results, build a constituency and/or acquire a sponsor, set goals, and undertake strategic planning.

The Horatio Alger maxim of working hard to get ahead is one of the keys to success for women in unions as elsewhere. As one put it, "You have to start at the bottom to get to the top." The elective route requires that women as well as men start at the grass roots in the local union and volunteer for all kinds of assignments, including serving on committees, marching in picket lines, and writing for the local union newspaper. Ida Torres, now secretary-treasurer of Local 1, RWDSU in New York City, recounts the innumerable hours she spent as a volunteer counseling workers with problems, telephoning members to remind them to vote, and keeping track of strike benefits. Women following the expertise route also find that volunteering for extra duty—organizing, researching issues, writing position papers—eventually pays off in recognition and promotion.

Personal sacrifice is expected. The higher the position, the greater the demands on the individual. Linda Puchala had to persuade her husband and twin daughters to relocate to Washington, D.C., when she was elected president of the AFA; and Gwen Martin, when appointed as an international representative in the SEIU, found herself commuting hundreds of miles on weekends in order to be with her family.

In-depth knowledge is another essential. Women who aspire to union offices need to know a great deal about industrial relations practices, including the content of their collective bargaining agreements, how the contract has been interpreted in arbitration decisions, and the types of collective bargaining issues that might arise in the future (Koziara and Pierson 1980). In addition, they must master negotiating, speaking, and writing skills in order to represent their members in grievance procedures and at the bargaining table. They have to understand the intricacies of union structure and practices in order to get things done.

The most difficult knowledge to acquire, according to the women I interviewed, is political know-how: how to build coalitions and elicit grassroots support. These skills are acquired through the equivalent of an apprenticeship, a combination of formal education and job experience. The formal education often means enrolling in union- and university-sponsored labor education courses. "Job know-how" requires finding a mentor or hooking up with a knowledgeable person who is willing to share desired inside information. All of the women interviewed acknowledge a debt to mentors, in almost every case male, who took the time and interest to break them into the trade of union leadership.

Becoming visible is another component of the game plan for achieving recognition. Olga Madar, who was the first elected woman vice-president of the UAW, reports that she was initially hired for a nontraditional job in a plant partly because she was an expert softball player; later, the union appointed her to a full-time job as recreation director. Each of the national leaders cites turning points that occurred as a result of successful and highly visible accomplishments. They report that, in their early roles as local union activists, their first recognition came when they spoke up to management about grievances that were important to their coworkers and when they employed innovative tactics to win them. Some mobilized membership support by focusing attention on issues of specific interest to other women, such as equal pay and child care. Whatever the task, however, interviewees agree that women "have to be better than men."

After graduating from Cornell University's School of Industrial and Labor Relations, Vicki Saporta was hired as an organizer for the IBT's Western Conference and gained visibility through repeatedly winning elections. Her impressive record of union wins brought her to the attention of the national union and ultimately resulted in her appointment as the first woman to head the national organizing department. Susan Cowell, vice-president of the ILGWU, was initially hired as an organizer but attained recognition when her knowledge of Asian language and culture (her college major was Asian studies) was urgently needed for the union's drive to organize garment workers in New York City's Chinatown. Dramatic and visible accomplishments are needed to break the stereotype that women are not "tough" enough to meet the demands of leadership.

Whether running for office or serving as appointed staff members, women leaders agree that it is essential to build constituencies whether they be mixed gender or women only. According to successful women leaders, each woman who seeks recognition has to build her own constituencies and networks of support within the unique political structure of her own union. Women in national staff positions talk about having a "fan club," supporters and networks of staff and local leaders to whom they relate. Overt political caucuses, however, are viewed with alarm by incumbent union officials (usually male); thus, female networks, at least for those in appointive positions, must be circumspect—not necessarily covert but neutral in tone.

Strategic planning is important for all potential leaders and essential for women. Strategic planning involves setting goals, assessing the environment and developing a long-term road map for overcoming barriers and reaching desired objectives. Since union leaders normally "fall into" their roles, career planning is rare. Nonetheless, in contrast to male leaders, many of the women interviewed reported that they set out on a deliberate course of action to reach their goals. An outstanding example of achieving success through carefully calculated planning was the ascent to power of Shirley Carr, president of the Canadian Congress of Labour (CCL), the counterpart to Lane Kirkland, president of the AFL-CIO in the United States. When she was first elected steward, she "had a process in my own mind" (Larson 1986). After her election to a regional office in the public sector division of Canadian labor, she found her rise to a top position blocked by incumbents and so turned her attention to the broader CCL, persuading her union to back her run for vice-president. From there, she threatened to run against the president of CCL, who, in turn, offered her the interim position of secretary-treasurer, promising to retire after one more term. Shirley Carr kept the pressure on until she triumphed as the first woman to head the two-million-member CCL.[4]

In sum, the experiences of women who have achieved top office in unions demonstrate how barriers can be overcome. In comparison with their male counterparts, they must work harder, make more personal sacrifices, be more goal-oriented, do more planning, and make up for political and organizational inexperience through intensive study. To achieve the same goals, women must excel.

What Unions Can Do

Thus, although a few exceptional women have made it to the top, the path is clearly harder for women than for men. Equal opportunity will not be truly realized unless unions adopt policies to facilitate and support aspiring women leaders.[5] As Pat Scarcelli, vice-president of the United Food and Commercial Workers, says "Unions must become 'women friendly.' "

Already, a number of changes are occurring that will tend to move more women into leadership. Increasingly, union organizing drives targeting women workers, as dramatically illustrated at Yale and Harvard universities, give women the necessary experience and visibility to compete for union office while rendering unions more receptive to recognizing their contributions (Kautzer 1985). As noted before, founding a union or at least a piece of one is a tried-and-true path to leadership.

At one time, organizing, which requires travel, long hours, and endurance, was considered a "man's" job. Now an increasing number of women are being hired as organizers. Half of the first graduating class of the AFL-CIO's newly formed Organizing Institute, for example, were women. "If you want to

[4]Shirley Carr resigned from this position in 1992.

[5]A 1986 survey of fifteen national unions found only five that were rated as "affirmatively committed" to addressing women's concerns through convention actions, budget allocations, standing departments, and committees, conferences and training materials, with another five deemed "somewhat committed" to providing resources for their women members (Baden 1986).

organize women, you need to use women," says Richard Bensinger, the institute's director (BNA 1990a). According to the AFL-CIO, women organizers currently have a better track record in number of election wins than their male counterparts (AFL-CIO 1990). The appointment of women as union organizers may be expected to increase in the years ahead, reflecting increased organizational efforts on the part of unions and emphasis on recruiting women in the occupations and industries in which women predominate, as well as the success women have demonstrated as organizers.

Unions that emphasize "women's issues" help to create a climate that encourages their female members to play a more active role. Gender equality in pay and job classification has been the focus of collective bargaining negotiations and grievance enforcement for many unions. The UAW, for example, in 1949 began negotiations to eliminate separate seniority lists that were grouped by gender and to open the skilled trades to women in automobile manufacturing (Kates 1989; *UAW Solidarity* 1989). With the number of women in formerly all-male jobs increasing, the UAW more recently has turned its attention to sexual harassment at work, utilizing collective bargaining clout to protect members' rights, and has sponsored training programs on sexual harassment. As detailed in earlier chapters in this volume, unions have been instrumental in the drive for equal pay for jobs of comparable worth and have provided the troops for political action on family leave and child care benefits, which are being negotiated into many collective bargaining contracts.

Union promotion of women's issues not only encourages female activism but provides opportunities for women to showcase their leadership abilities when they are selected to serve as expert witnesses in hearings and to participate in negotiations, grievance handling, membership education, and political and legal action. In addition, interest in women's issues often leads unions to form alliances with women's organizations, further highlighting the importance of women's contributions to union goals and providing women leaders with increased political leverage.

Many unions allocate resources for special programs for women and create structures for women's activities. Women's departments and committees, while controversial among some feminists who seek a gender-free environment (O'Cleireacain 1986), are considered important by others, who point to their value in providing opportunities for women to "network" and to learn from each other how the union functions. As described by Addie Wyatt, former vice-president of the UFCW, women's committees are the means by which women "find strength in each other and the courage to press these issues in the union" (P. Foner 1980). The UAW constitution requires the establishment of a women's committee in every local union. Such committees have proliferated on a voluntary basis in many other unions, along with women's departments and special activities for women members. The nationwide Coalition for Labor Union Women (CLUW), when first formed in 1975, appeared threatening to some established male leaders. Its eventual acceptance is indicated by the financial support CLUW now receives from unions and the appointment of its president to the AFL-CIO Executive Council.

The availability of special outreach training has been credited as a major force in the increasing number of women in local union leadership. Training and education programs for women unionists have spread rapidly throughout the United States. Almost half the universities with labor education programs and unions with education departments reported in a recent labor education survey that they offer special programs for women (Gray and Kornbluh 1990). Regional women's summer schools, initiated in 1975 with backing from the University and College Labor Education Association (UCLEA) and the AFL-CIO, have attracted thousands of participants over the years. The first participants paid for most of their expenses and less than half held union office. Acceptance of the summer programs is demonstrated by the fact that, fifteen years later, almost all participants were supported by their local unions and close to 90 percent held some union office (Needleman 1988).

Like women's departments and committees, however, segregated training experiences are criticized by those who seek the immediate integration of women to leadership. Even supporters have certain reservations. The authors of the CLUW booklet, *Absent from the Agenda,* for example, note the value of special structures for women, but caution that separation may result in isolation from the mainstream of union activities (Glassberg, Baden, and Gerstel 1980; Baden 1986). Others fear that separation, while admittedly building self-confidence and networks for self-help, leads to divisive, counterproductive "antimale attitudes." The AFL-CIO considered and rejected the idea of a women's department, deciding instead to pass a resolution calling for appointment of a coordinator of women's activities in its civil rights department. At the same time, the federation pledged to address the concerns of women in all departments and to initiate an affirmative effort to appoint and promote women staff.

All interviewees agree that affirmative action in union personnel selection, recruitment, and training is essential to achieving the goal of a gender-integrated leadership. Yet relatively few unions have formalized personnel policies with explicit affirmative action policies and procedures (Clark and Gray 1992). Initiating positive steps to recruit and appoint women to staff and/or to groom women for elective positions still depends on the voluntary commitment of incumbent officers who are mostly male.

Although many unions have rejected in principle the concept of "quotas," in fact some of these same unions have set aside certain key positions for female representation. The AFL-CIO, for example, opened its executive council (EC) ranks to the president of CLUW, even though she did not meet the long-standing practice that EC members be presidents of national unions.[6] In a similar spirit of affirmative action, a number of unions have set aside a spot on their national executive boards for female representation. The SEIU, one of the few unions with a formalized affirmative action policy, recently established and carried out a goal of recruiting qualified women to fill 50 percent of the union's national staff positions.

Lessons from Abroad

The experience of women in the United States is not unique. There is no country in which women are represented in leadership in proportion to their share of the membership. Unions in Western Europe have experimented with various policies to ensure the representation of women. In Denmark, women are organized into a separate union. At the other end of the spectrum, several German unions enacted constitutional provisions establishing quotas for proportionate representation in leadership. Women's departments and women's committees are widespread throughout Sweden, but after many years of experience, Swedish unions abolished these special structures, opting for "simple justice," which is interpreted to mean "spontaneously" choosing women for elected positions. The CCL designates six places for women on its executive board. The National Union of Public Employees in Great Britain established the Working Party on Women's Involvement, which recommended drastic structural changes to correct the gender disparity between membership and leadership, including a "rotating chair" for meetings so as to give women an opportunity to acquire leadership experience and demonstrate their abilities (Till-Retz 1986).

Several international trade secretariats, struggling with the issue of gender equality, are requiring national delegations to set aside places for women. The International Confederation of Free Trade Unions, while not requiring representation of women, recently sent out a plea to its affiliates that women be included in their delegations and took the affirmative action step of calling a special meeting of women delegates prior to the convention to ensure that they were informed on the issues and encouraged to participate.

Counterparts of these international experiments may be found in the United

[6]There had been only one exception to this practice before the appointment of Joyce Miller.

States in one form or another but have not, to date, been organized into a planned program for women's involvement in leadership.

What Difference Does Female Leadership Make?

There is a running debate in the voluminous literature about women as business executives about whether their leadership styles differ from that of their male counterparts. The traditional view is that women, in order to succeed in a "man's world," have to adopt the "male" approach to leadership, which is described as "tough, self-centered and enormously aggressive" (Rudolph 1990). In contrast, recent studies of successful women executives report a distinctive, more "feminine" style which is described as "caring and helping" (Helgesen 1990) and "encouraging participation" as well as amenable to "sharing power and information." Stylistic differences are attributed to the differing life experiences of men and women in which the former are expected to be competitive and the latter, cooperative. Although there have been no studies of women's leadership styles in the union context, participant-observer comments divide along the lines expressed in the business literature with a minority contending that those who make it to top positions, particularly in the collective bargaining arena, have to adopt the "tough" style of male union leaders. For example, Sandra Feldman, a prominent union leader, was described as having "a spine of steel" by the man who faced her at the bargaining table (Rohter 1986). She, however, described herself as evincing a softer and "more accepting" style as compared with her male predecessor.

According to some, women leaders' evaluation of men may be a generational phenomenon, a characteristic only of those who are first to achieve recognition in their organizations but one that tends to disappear as more women occupy these roles; also less evident among younger women who feel comfortable with their own styles as a result of confidence built by the women's movement and the growing networking among union women. Many of the women I interviewed describe themselves and their female colleagues as generally showing more tenderness and caring, less ego involved, more results oriented, and more democratic with their staff, including clerical workers. Clayola Brown, vice-president of ACTWU and manager of a joint board in New York City, describes herself as "more consultative" than most male managers, a style acquired through her prior experience as the union's education director.

Warren Bennis, a leading writer on leadership theory in business settings, projects a future that will reflect changing demographics and organizational structures, leading to a shift in leadership requirements from an emphasis on "ability to command" to "ability to persuade" (*Working Woman* 1990). Similarly, according to Ruth Needleman, if unions must "involve more members" and project an image "less bureaucratic and more democratic" to survive and grow, it is women leaders who will be effective (Needleman 1988). If these projections of future organizational needs are valid and women's strengths correctly assessed, women may be expected to break through the "glass ceiling" and be sought out for leadership positions in the years ahead.

Comments

Kim Fellner

Union women inhabit the territory where the cultures of the labor movement and the women's movement collide. In those unsettled regions, misunderstanding and injustice are among the most common consequences—though with mutual effort and good will, compromises can be reached and richer hybrid societies created.

Although the two essays in this section deal with quantifiable patterns rather than with spiritual context, the collision between union culture and the ideals of the women's movement are at the heart of the issues they raise. One piece discusses how women trade union stewards compare with their male counterparts in balancing personal lives with union obligations; the other traces some key components in how women move into the ranks of union leadership. Yet both implicitly (and rather too politely) build on the conflict between the aspirations of women to make the most of their talents and skills and the inhospitability of many unions to those desires.

Of course it shouldn't be that way. Never were two movements more meant for each other—or more necessary for both the economic and social liberation of women workers. But despite goals that would appear to be symbiotic, a comfortable equilibrium between the two has been difficult for many union women to achieve.

The two articles in this section demonstrate, if not explicate, how these dissonances have affected the move of women into union leadership. Pamela Roby and Lynet Uttal's article on union stewards highlights the differences in living situations between male and female stewards. While two-thirds of the men live with a partner and children, only a quarter of the women live in that traditional configuration; another quarter (27 percent) of the women are single, as compared to 18 percent of the men; 21 percent of the women, versus only 11 percent of the men, live with partners but no children. Not as surprising—but equally significant—27 percent of the women live alone with children, as opposed to only 5 percent of the men.

Roby and Uttal also note that, for the most part, women stewards with partners continue to have major responsibility for household maintenance. Despite their full-time jobs and union obligations, they still do far more than half the domestic chores (cooking, housecleaning, laundry, etc.). Perhaps more important, women put the general welfare of their children before their union responsibilities, while their male counterparts put their union obligations first, leaving primary responsibility for children to their spouses—*even though 65 percent of the men had partners who were themselves employed!*

The significance of these findings has been greatly illuminated by Arlie Hochschild's 1989 book, *The Second Shift: Working Parents and the Revolution at Home.* Hochschild describes the tensions produced in marriages and in society when working women are still expected to do the majority of household and family maintenance—thereby working one shift on their paying job and a "second shift" at home. Many marriages do not survive the pressures.

We live in a time, Hochschild suggests, of tension "between faster-changing women and slower-changing men. . . . The old way of being a woman in a patriarchal but stable family system is fading. But a new equal relationship with men at work and at home is not yet in reach." These observations are as true for union shop stewards as for most American working women, and they enrich and complement Roby and Uttal's findings.

If, for example, a working woman with a partner and/or children is also a union activist, she is being asked to work a *third* shift on top of the other two. While men may take on union steward work as their second shift and suffer some additional domestic strains because of it, we can extrapolate that women stewards diminish their chances for marital survival—let alone tranquility— even further. In this light, it is not surprising to find that 54 percent of women stewards—twice as many as their male counterparts—live without partners.

We might conjecture that at least some of the large proportion of women stewards who remain single and without children, perceiving the severe difficulties of success on both the public and private front, have opted to seek advancement on the job or in the union, in lieu of building a family. No one should be surprised that many women are unwilling to make this sacrifice— or wonder why women are not proportionately represented in the leaderships of their unions.

While these issues come into play for women at all levels of union leadership, stewards have two additional handicaps not generally shared by female staff and higher-ranking officers. First, for the steward, union work is indeed a third sphere of obligation, while for staff, and frequently (though not always) for officers, the union becomes primary employment. Second, in many cases, stewards employed on the shop floor earn less than the union's professional staff or officers; hence, they have limited access to child care and other benefits and conveniences that can ameliorate the inequities of the second shift.

These issues play a critical role in how women pursue the "Route to the Top" discussed by Lois Gray—and whether they succeed. The remedies stewards recommend to enhance and encourage participation by women, such as family-respecting scheduling of meetings, released time for union duties, and reimbursement of expenses, help offset these impediments at the steward and lower elective levels. But they are clearly not enough to help women follow the traditional male route to leadership, which Gray describes as "moving through the chairs"—because women leaving the shop floor hit the glass ceiling before they reach labor's executive suite.

One impediment to their progress, of course, is garden-variety sexism—a hard weed to uproot. "I encountered horrible sexism most of the time I was organizing," one staffer told me in a set of interviews several years ago. "You need support out there in those isolated areas, but when I called my boss, he told me, 'I know what's wrong with you, you turn off the guys.' It took my feminist friends to tell me, 'I hope you told him you didn't know you were hired to turn *on* the guys.' I had forgotten that stuff, and some of the passion of my initial organizing experiences was mired."

But advancement also succumbs to subtler systemic hazards. As in Hochschild's case studies of women who are successfully promoted and discover they no longer have enough time for their personal lives, union officers—and staff—may find themselves not just working long days but effectively married to the job! One of our colleagues, Madeleine Janover, recalls having to choose between a decertification election and her parents' fortieth wedding anniversary. "We were right down to the final days," she says, "and my mentor said, 'Look, it's your choice, you just have to figure out how you're going to feel if we lose the election because you were away and didn't get to make those extra house calls. You're going to have to live with that down the road.' So I opted not to go. Well, my father died shortly after that. There was never a forty-fifth. And I live with that instead. It was a wrong choice, and that had something to do with my eventually leaving union work, because when the commitment is so total, we just get things out of perspective."

Or as SEIU organizing director Andrew Stern notes, "It's hard to keep organizers if they have to travel all the time. Those I do keep are heavily single or divorced or, in the case of male organizers, in traditional relationships with a wife who takes care of the kids." This observation echoes some of the devastating quotes from the Roby and Uttal interviews: the male steward who missed his daughter's birthday party (knowing he could count on his wife to make sure it happened anyway!), the one who chose a picket line over the birth of his child. How much more extreme the options are for women—to let one's daughter suffer the cancellation of a long-awaited celebration, to opt against childbearing.

Most women rightly rebel at these masculine norms—and may well sacrifice their union careers in the process. In the style of the business world, unions are filled with men who place work before family, who socialize and politick long hours to achieve and retain their positions.

Roughly two-thirds of the union leaders interviewed by Gray are men—and the bias of the article seems to be like that of Henry Higgins in *My Fair Lady*—"Why can't a woman be more like a man?" If only women put the union first, and modeled their behavior on that of successful men, more of them would get ahead. Yet those critical years of leadership positioning—let us say twenty-five to forty-five—are exactly the years in which most women face their most intensive family demands. That might account for the overwhelming number of women leaders, be they staff or elected, who are at the lower or upper end of the age spectrum, or single, or childless. Only the fortunate few have simply been lucky in their choice of partner.

Indeed, what is described here is a unique form of selection process that clears the union leadership track of all but a few unusual women—women who are some mix of strong, ambitious, bright, dogged, aggressive, charismatic, ruthless, shrewd, politic, unconventional in their self-confidence and life expectations—and very, very patient!

As Lois Gray's interviews show, despite the odds, we of the labor movement have been blessed with some remarkable female leadership at all levels. However, Gray's work also suggests, if somewhat obliquely, that there is a less desirable "underbelly" to leadership success. Not only do women who aspire to leadership have to know the rules of the game, they sometimes have to play by them. In a male-dominated environment, that generally means finding a male mentor. But for the least secure or most ambitious, it can also mean conforming to the norms of a macho culture, adopting an unemotional or callous management style or refusing to risk outspokenness on controversial issues within the labor hierarchy—even when one of those controversial issues is the role of women.

"What I have found most disappointing," a union staffer at a progressive union relates, "is that the women on the staff have bought into this corporate 'I'm trying to be a manager, a professional, defined by the dress-for-success look.' I have women friends who came up through the ranks with me, who even considered me something of a mentor, who have achieved good positions in the union hierarchy and don't talk to me any more because it just isn't done. It's very upsetting and hurtful. Here, no woman over forty who wants to be promoted should have hair below her shoulders—and no upper-level union administrator does. I could do it if I really put my mind to it, but I'd have to give up a big piece of myself. I don't need another $5,000 a year that badly."

More than twenty years ago, women's movement leader Charlotte Bunch noted, "There is no private domain of a person's life that is not political and there is no political issue that is not ultimately personal." And so it is for us in the labor movement. In her book *Personal Politics,* published more than a decade ago, Sara Evans notes that much of the impetus for the women's movement came out of the contradictions between the ideals of the civil rights movement and the New Left and the day-to-day lives of women working in those movements. In the labor movement, we struggle with the same contradictions.

Under the skillful prodding of women leaders at all levels, unions have adopted some goals of the women's rights movement, supporting legislation like the ill-fated Family and Medical Leave Act of 1990, establishing women's committees and training programs, grudgingly acknowledging that equal opportunity and compensation ought to be part of the union's agenda, internally as well as in society.

But the goals of women's liberation—transforming society so women are free to choose the roles and endeavors that best fulfill their needs and potentials—are much farther from realization. Even though child care is officially on labor's agenda, no national union yet provides it for its own staff and officers. And bowing to pressure from the Catholic church and the National Right-to-Life Committee, the overwhelming white, male AFL-CIO Executive Council resoundingly refused to support reproductive choice. Saddest of all, two of the three women on the council voted with the majority.

Underlying this concrete withholding of resources and support is a culture that winks at the diminution of women. A 1989 AFL-CIO Executive Council meeting in Bal Harbour is a case in point. "Two young showgirls, appropriately nicknamed 'Postage Stamp Girls' by some, have provoked a fierce debate among convention goers," the *New York Times* reported in one of its rare fits of labor coverage. "At issue is whether young women in skimpy black bikinis with sequins are beneficial to labor's drive to improve its relations with women, who account for an increasingly large chunk of the workforce. . . . The National [Association of] Letter Carriers hired them to pass out small gift bags at its lavish cocktail party the other night. Men lined up to pose for photos with the women . . . 'I think it enhanced the image of labor,' said Vincent R. Sombrotto, President of the letter carriers union." The article adds that AFL-CIO president Lane Kirkland "brushed off the criticism, saying 'Don't you take some things too seriously?' "

I think of Carolyn Jacobson of the Bakery, Confectionery and Tobacco Workers. As president of the International Labor Communications Association, she tried every year—in vain—to halt distribution of the Paperworkers' Union calendar, which shows a woman in a tennis outfit scratching her bare butt. Its message: "Don't forget to look for the union label."

And almost every union woman has a more personal anecdote of culture shock. "The culture of my local included a weekly visit to the airport strip joints by my male coworkers," reports SEIU staffer Susan Eaton. "I argued that strip joints were exploitative of women. They hooted and hollered and made a point of describing the strip joint experiences in even more detail. They even regularly left cards from the various strip joints on my desk with the 'tryout times' inked in."

This inherently hostile culture presents perhaps the greatest challenge to change. It has, I believe, generally produced one of two contradictory responses in women. Either she will understand, and feel deeply, that she is not wanted and will walk away to seek friendlier environs. Or she will bury her discomfort and anger, striving to become "one of the guys," joining in the laughter and adopting a macho attitude to distinguish herself from the "sissies" of her sex.

I cringe as I write this, knowing myself guilty of these responses on more than one occasion. Yet both these reactions are inadequate, the first ceding male power without a struggle, the second adopting the male model to attain power. Both ultimately beg the real heart of the problem: tempering the male organizational model of unions, and society at large, to respect women's needs and accept their value. The willingness of the male establishment to do so depends certainly on power—recognizing the critical importance of organizing women workers if the labor movement is going to survive, with dire consequences for failure. It also requires the strength of numbers within, enough women at various levels of the organization willing to fight for change and harass obstructionists. Finally, it requires a self-respect for the contributions that women bring, a recognition and pride in the spiritual and humanitarian qualities that define feminist leadership at its best: a greater sharing of power, different intuitions, more nurturing perspectives.

This, of course, forms the basis for the richer hybrid society: one where women need not renounce power or ambition to practice nonhierarchical leadership and respond to emotional concerns. And one where men can have the same opportunity!

But even these transformations, both desirable and necessary, will not change the requirements for extraordinary achievement. I suspect that, regardless of ideology, some successes demand a single-mindedness and determination beyond the norm. It will always take a few uncommon souls, male or female, willing to sacrifice all else, to perform certain heroic feats of organizing or other superior accomplishments. That too is a legitimate choice. We must, however, eradicate the mythology that makes this unique demand the criterion for normal organizational advancement for women (or other less empowered groups). Union men will espouse, or may even live out, the lifestyle of the all-sacrificing hero, even where there is no real, task-related necessity to do so. It is in these, the most prevalent situations, where the restructuring of union life to permit equal participation by women must be vigorously pursued and won.

After eighteen years as a union staff person, I am in the process of sifting through my own experience for lessons and guideposts. I realize I have received power from male mentors—who had it to give. And I have received strength from the women who blazed trails of endurance and triumph to lighten my path. I think especially of my "home union," SEIU, where I was mentored by a one-of-a-kind organizing director, John Geagan. He was a maniac, loud and lewd. But he lived to organize, and he loved those of us who loved the labor movement. Being an eccentric himself, he did not demand conformity; rather, he accepted talent and effectiveness in a myriad of styles. He harassed and leered ceaselessly, he'd suddenly be lying on the carpet gazing up your dress—but I forgive him everything and laugh when I think of him. Because beneath that exasperating, sexist nonsense was a man who helped dozens of women move up the union hierarchy—and I have yet to meet the woman who took his blandishments seriously (although many understandably took offense).

SEIU also offered a wonderful role model in the person of Elinor Glenn, retired president of Los Angeles Local 434. Ellie Glenn has been a source of inspiration and strength to successive generations of union women. She herself was mentored in the 1930s by former SEIU president George Hardy, a crusty and canny janitor with a legendary foul mouth. Ellie, who started out as an actor with the National Theater Project during the Depression, will proudly tell you she was the real-life model for Marjorie Morningstar. While she learned to play the union game and acquired an impressive diplomacy, she never lost her sparkle, her individuality, her zeal to help other women survive and thrive. Matchmaker and surrogate mom, no-nonsense yet nurturing, she has helped dozens of us live to fight another day.

What I remember as well is that John Geagan and Elinor Glenn adored each other. They were united, not only by their unique and vivid personae, but by their devotion to a vision of the labor movement. Not as a bureaucracy that forces everyone into a neat cubbyhole, not as an empty shell of platitudes about solidarity and equity, but as a living vehicle to bring out the best in each person and forge justice in the land. In that goal, labor and feminism are one. It's a vision worth fighting for.

Comments

Diane Harriford

Pamela Roby and Lynet Uttal make a noteworthy contribution to our understanding of the conflict between union leadership and family responsibilities. The union stewards' first-person accounts provide an immediacy and relevance lacking in much research of this sort. Lois Gray's research is a worthy companion to the Roby and Uttal essay. Yet our understanding of the particularities of the conflicts and barriers women face could have been enhanced if the researchers had chosen to examine race and ethnicity as well as gender.

For example, Roby and Uttal seem to suggest that living alone is an unsuitable alternative to the traditional family. But a traditional family—as well as gender, work, and union participation—mean different things to different women. For a black woman, the "traditional" family may not be highly normative. Living in extended households, living only with her children, or living alone may be viable options for her. Most important, organizational participation can be seen as a part of a black woman's gender role expectations. She is expected to assume a public role in her community. Managing conflict between family and union leadership is a different event for her than for a woman whose gender expectation does not include organizational participation outside of the family. In some cases, union activity for this woman may cause severe conflict because leadership participation is proscribed by her community.

Gray describes the structural and personal barriers to women's participation in leadership positions and tells us what unions are doing to help reduce these barriers. According to Gray, women are making slow but steady gains and some unions are actively encouraging female leadership. Women are being groomed for leadership positions and appointed to various union offices. The particular structural barriers to formal leadership for black women may not be the same, however, and black women may not be receiving the same degree of encouragement, mentoring, and grooming as white women.

Gray also notes that women in leadership positions may bring a different "way of doing" to union organizations. She finds that women are often more concerned than men with process and other people's feelings and are more likely to encourage communication and cooperation.

Her observations resonate with my own research on the New York City chapter of the Coalition of Labor Union Women, a primarily black-led organization. I spent over a year observing meetings and other CLUW chapter functions and found that women did bring different leadership styles to the organization. The toughness, rigidity, and competitiveness usually associated with union activity were replaced by greater warmth, flexibility, and cooperation. A sense of community, of sisterly concern, was most important to the members of the organization and was transmitted and reinforced whenever possible. Potluck dinners, bus trips, and theater parties were activities used to develop a sense of community.

The leaders were determined to make CLUW meetings harmonious affairs and wanted everyone to feel comfortable enough to participate. Bickering and a sense of hierarchy, while not completely absent, were modulated as much as possible. Instead of running meetings as though they were military endeavors, the leaders often ran them like family discussions. The credo seemed to be "we can disagree without becoming disagreeable."

If serious disagreements arose during meetings, CLUW members would usually postpone the discussion until the next meeting so that the individuals or groups of individuals who were disagreeing could have time to work out some compromises. Postponing the discussion also provided time for other members to talk with the disagreeing parties informally and help resolve the conflict before the next meeting. The leadership believed that efficiency was important, but managing conflict and encouraging cooperation were more important. Decisions could wait until the next meeting if they could not be made agreeably at the current meeting.

These CLUW women I observed also had a different "way of knowing." Their standing as working-class black women gave them a particular epistemological frame or standpoint that enabled them to define issues differently than either the traditional white male union leadership or their white union sisters. They formulated issues differently. Sexual harassment in the workplace, for example, was of great concern to them because of the high rate at which black women are harassed. At the same time, however, they were sensitive to the ways in which sexual harassment charges against black men can be used to control and delegitimize black men. They had a grasp of the complex relationship between race and gender and framed issues within that context.

In addition, their particular understanding of race and gender made it possible for the black leadership to constitute CLUW as a black-led but multiracial organization. Their interest in racial issues did not cause them to lose sight of the need to make non-black CLUW women comfortable, to make them full members of the family. One black CLUW leader maintained, for instance, that "unity (between women) is important for women in the labor movement since the men, even those that talk differently, don't want women to get ahead of them." It would seem that their different "way of knowing" coupled with a different "way of doing" made it possible for the black women in CLUW to embrace a racially and ethnically diverse group of women.

The elected CLUW leadership depended upon several groups of informal leaders among the predominantly black rank and file in order to sustain CLUW as a highly cohesive and effective organization. The women in the organization with the most authority were the retirees. They were informal leaders to whom many of the formal CLUW leadership went for counsel. They had "seen it all" and were wise in ways that the members of the organization respected, plus they had a historical perspective that deepened their understanding of current issues. The retirees had the last word in any discussion. The other CLUW sisters believed that wisdom comes with age and thus granted them a special place in CLUW. They can be viewed as the "mothers" of the organization.

Another informal group of influential members were those who could get along with everyone. These women were people with a collectivist vision who put the needs of the organization before their own personal ambition. They could be counted on to do what was best for CLUW and not simply think of their individual careers. Their opinions on organizational policy were given high credibility.

Women who, despite overwhelming odds, had made it on their own were also influential and well-respected by the other CLUW members. They were survivors who were looked to for direction. If a CLUW sister had been able to take care of her own life, many believed that she could understand what was best for the organization. She knew how to get things done.

Many of these informal leaders (as well as the elected leadership) brought to their union work an impressive degree of political sophistication gained from their activity in the Civil Rights Movement, in their communities, and in their churches. They not only had a clear grasp of the political nuances and complexity of issues, but they also, as one CLUW member said, were not "afraid to stand up and let people know where they stand." Yet despite their skills and credentials, these black leaders tend not to be groomed for union leadership. One could assume that those being groomed for leadership positions possess attributes the current leadership defines as "leadership material" and that the more organic leaders described here are thought to be less suitable. In addition to being black these leaders may be deemed too old, or be seen as lacking proper educational credentials or personal ambition, or they may simply not be "agreeable" enough to those in power.

Union leadership among women takes many faces and finds much of its power in informal structures. To look simply at the women who take formal positions may overlook those women who wield the most power and influence among their sisters.

I hope that future research will analyze the particular experiences of black women and illuminate the contribution they can and have made to the labor movement.

Comments

Ruth Needleman

oth chapters in this section document the compromises and hardships
that characterize women's experiences as they assume roles of leadership within unions. The breakthroughs have been important but in no
way overshadow the injuries encountered on the way. Fortunately, the work
of female pioneers in union leadership has been worth it; their efforts have
brought significant changes and cleared a path for many more. After all, it was
not that many years ago that sexual harassment was not acknowledged; that
child care and parental leave were unknown at the bargaining table; or that
top leadership gatherings took place without a female presence.

Lois Gray summarizes the demographics of this slow transition. More
frequently appointed than elected, women have nonetheless moved into top
staff and national leadership positions. Women's committees, women's conferences, so-called women's issues and "family" concerns are no longer
exceptional. Most unions search in earnest for women organizers representative of the new work force and for women leaders to give voice and
visibility to the growing percentage of female union members. But like
Gray, Pam Roby and Lynet Uttal examine the problems and obstacles
women encounter: the stereotypes, the conflicts with time and family, the

Many women union leaders contributed to this article, knowingly and unknowingly. Among
those whose experiences and ideas figure in the text are: Cathy Collette, director of AFSCME's
Women's Rights Department; Dottie Jones, assistant director of the UAW's Women's Department; Cynthia McCaughan, coordinator of women's affairs, AFL-CIO Civil Rights Department; Josie Mooney, staff director, SEIU Local 790; Karen Nussbaum, executive director,
9 to 5, National Association of Working Women, and President, District 925, SEIU; Anna
Samick, Directing Business Representative, International Association of Machinists; and Margaret Shelleda, Deputy Executive Director, SEIU Local 790.

accepted patterns and models that favor men and discourage women along the path to leadership.

The data collected on stewards by Roby and Uttal are, in fact, among the most vivid and persuasive evidence available on gender differences. This study (one wonders why it has not received more attention!) dramatizes the contrasts in life experiences between men and women working as stewards. That men with wives and children can choose union responsibilities more easily than women with husbands and families is not surprising information. That men with families do not feel torn between union and family while women experience tremendous conflict between the two is equally predictable. But the percentages and numbers outlined by Roby and Uttal convey a much stronger message: they show that in order to assume a steward's responsibilities, women give up families, take on extra workloads, give up sleep and recreation, and become scrupulous planners and delegators.

The job of the steward—what it entails and how it is done—weighs differently on women's personal and work lives than on men's. Similarly, the paths to union leadership so accurately described by Gray require of women greater exertion and more detours. In one sense, you could say women take that path without compasses, maps, and often without company. Underlying the findings in both studies is the troublesome realization that women's work lives are inextricably tied to their home lives, and that to achieve equal status, change must occur at home, as well as on the job and in the union.[1]

Although both chapters provide us with important suggestions for accommodating women better and for strengthening support systems within unions, neither explores the need or possibilities for effecting change outside the union, within the family. Roby and Uttal refer to family-respecting practices (scheduling of meetings, on-the-job training, child care and meals at union events); release time; family-oriented social activities; and better reimbursement policies. Gray points to greater organizing efforts among women; emphasis on gender equality and family issues; greater commitment of resources to training and building support networks for women; and affirmative action policies for recruitment, selection of staff, and leadership development. These recommendations are far-reaching and will make a major difference for women, precisely because the assumption (and the reality!) is that women will continue to carry

---

[1] "For women to escape subordination to men," writes Cynthia Cockburn in *In the Way of Women*, "the relationship of home to work has to change beyond anything yet envisaged in the name of equality policy. Men have to be domesticated and in the workplace (to use Joan Acker's phrase) the rhythm and timing of work must be adapted to the rhythms of life outside" (p. 97). Cockburn, along with Joan Acker among others, provides an analysis of patriarchy to frame the discussion of obstacles women face in unions.

the main, if not full, responsibility for children and family. Without sharing parenting and family responsibilities equally, women unionists will continue to sacrifice more personal time in order to stand beside men in trade union leadership, and they will lack the kind of support Roby and Uttal identified as available to married male stewards.

Initiating Change

Nonetheless, the union provides one of the best vehicles for moving, even initiating, change in women's role and status in society. Unions are the main organization working to change the economic position of working women, and economic security, the ability to survive financially, is the cornerstone for securing equal rights and opportunities. There is a reason why more women than men are joining unions and that proportionately more women of color favor unions. Unions provide a good arena for implementing change because they are limited in size, democratic in structure, and generally promote or are compelled to endorse a progressive social agenda.

Still, within unions as within society, what makes change so slow and difficult for women is that they are dealing not with individual barriers or obstacles but with a culture, a long-established union culture. It has been shaped over decades and encompasses customs, attitudes, expectations, and behaviors more characteristic of the white men who have led the unions than of the women (especially women and men of color) who are increasingly their members.

What is needed to make unions a more comfortable place for women and to enable more women to assume leadership positions is a change in culture. Reshaping a culture, however, is a long-term process that involves many smaller, incremental changes in policies and practices. In most unions, it has proven difficult to institute such changes in policies and practices, precisely because they are rooted in established custom or culture. The attempt to change where and when union meetings are held, for example, often meets resistance because it is *part* of the culture, shaped in response to the needs and schedules of members who were traditionally male and white. Men set evening meetings and welcomed the convenience of nearby bars or taverns. Women have family chores in the evening and also think primarily about personal safety. So even though the members have changed and their needs and schedules are different, the old culture persists. Some leaders and members cling to the old ways because they are familiar and comfortable, not because they want to exclude a new generation of workers.

In reality, most unions want to be responsive to the new work force, to be able to organize and involve more women and people of color. The AFL-CIO has shifted resources toward family issues and supported initiatives addressing diversity. The April 1991 AFL-CIO Education Conference focused a day of workshops and activities around diversity. The AFL-CIO has contributed directly to the regional summer schools for union women since they were initiated in 1975. The George Meany Center for Labor Education provides training programs on women and women's issues, hosts a school for African-American and other minority workers, and is exploring ways to increase the numbers of African-American and minority trade unionists in all their programs. It is efforts like these that support the forces for change and help open the way for a transition to a different culture.

Understanding and Changing Union Culture

How can union culture be transformed? What is a union culture? Every union, even every local union, has its own culture, shaped by the surrounding society but more particularly by the people who founded it, led it, participated in it, and dominated it. Culture includes attitudes, behaviors, practices, events, rituals, and customs.

The history a union tells about itself defines what is valued within that culture. Most of the venerated heroes, for example, are white men of various ethnic backgrounds, and the legendary and key events usually date to a period when few women had visibility. Buildings, scholarships, and awards are named after the male heroes. It is the faces of male unionists which line the walls.

In the past decade, however, women historians, filmmakers, and labor pioneers have lifted the veil on working women's past and brought forward the stories of uncommemorated heroines. The film *With Babies and Banners* documents the importance of women in the great battles during the Flint sit-down strikes at General Motors. Likewise, *Union Maids* and *Rosie the Riveter,* also films, offer further insight into women's role in building unions. Over the past two decades, a treasure of history books has highlighted events and heroines, and created new legends.[2]

Labor studies programs and women's leadership schools have brought this new history to a whole generation of women workers, and now these women want to see the lives and contributions of their mothers and grandmothers

[2]Too many books have been published to list them all here. Historians Barbara Mayer Wertheimer, Alice Kessler-Harris, Rosalyn Baxandall, Linda Gordon, Susan Reverby, Joyce Kornbluh, Mary Frederickson, and Philip Foner have opened a place for women in labor history, and their works have been joined by dozens of other remarkable studies.

included in their own international union history. To integrate the heroines and their stories will be to rewrite the history and reshape the culture.

History, of course, is just one dimension of a union culture. Another revealing indicator is the "ideal" or model unionist. What behavior or work ethic does a union value or reward? For most unions, the ideal resembles a workaholic, eighteen-hour-a-day activist who always puts the union first. Most unions measure commitment by the number of hours worked, the willingness to give up weekends and nights. Unfortunately, this standard excludes more people than it includes, and certainly discourages women and single parents. Paradoxically few unions have adopted the kind of flexible work arrangements they advocate at the bargaining table: flextime, job sharing, or part-time work. Most of the women leaders I have spoken with about this issue rejected as unrealistic for practical, political, and financial reasons flexible job options for women in staff or leadership positions. Because unions are currently somewhat beleaguered—declining in membership and economically strapped—and because they embrace issues of economic and social justice, unions set high expectations for leadership and staff. Theirs is not an eight-hour job; the fight for justice is full-time.

How can more women—mothers, single parents, family people—combine personal life with union work and be viewed as committed to the union? It is not sufficient to allow individuals to limit their work hours, some women observed, if their peers continue to perceive them as less committed because they spend weekends at home. A number of the suggestions raised by women leaders focused on work method as a way around "work ethic." Different styles of leadership, including more work sharing and delegation, headed the list. If there is collective leadership in a local or in a campaign, I was told, no one person is essential around-the-clock. A leader can encourage the development of additional leaders and also find evenings for the family, if roles and responsibilities are divided, if decision-making is pushed further down in an organization. Too often leaders feel compelled to "be there": on the central labor council, at the press conference, at the banquet, at the testimonial, the political forum, the national conference, and so on. Often the same token or handful of women are sent everywhere. The UAW women's department, in contrast, requires that locals send new women each year to their women's educational conference. Many of the women interviewed stressed how they had begun to look at each engagement to determine who else could do it, and how it could serve as a learning and training experience. One woman noted that she now weighs each meeting or event against the time she has to spend with her children, and finds that she is spending more time with her family.

A number of women mentioned that national meetings and events for leaders are often scheduled over weekends and include social time, a custom that might have made sense when all leaders were men. Weekend meetings allowed the men to bring along spouses for whom a separate set of activities were arranged. Locations were distant and warm, perhaps adjacent to a golf course or gambling casino. Women, in contrast, rarely bring spouses (spouses rarely choose to attend), and since women still have primary child care and family responsibilities, weekends pose additional complications and costs. Weekend work may be part of the ethic, but some of the weekend scheduling is by tradition, not by necessity.

To reward the person who successfully combines union work with family, to measure commitment by the quality of the effort and not the quantity of the hours, to encourage the sharing of tasks and power, would open leadership and unions to more women and more workers. These standards are, however, in conflict with the ones set by the dominant culture.

There are many other ways in which union culture discourages female participation and leadership. Examples range from jokes and bumper stickers—"let a phone man put it in" (not union sanctioned)—to the unconscious but continual reliance on women to handle "women's work." The stereotypes and gender divisions of labor that pervade our society as a whole appear within unions as well. Community service work, for example, is often assigned to women; men dominate collective bargaining. Women seem to have a "knack" for fundraising activities; men project a stronger image and, therefore, handle public and employer relations. Women, as a result, labor behind the scenes or on the margins of what is considered key union activity.

The reward system reinforces and helps to perpetuate the low status of women's contributions: greater rewards and recognition go to the kind of work performed by men than women. Men, therefore, become more known and more "electable." Women shared stories of important meetings or conferences where all the unionists recognized for some achievement were men; probably only the women in the room were aware of their own exclusion. A bit of conscious planning could equalize the recognition, but unfortunately that happens only when women are in on the planning.

More female participation in planning tends to challenge a number of other aspects of once-accepted union culture. When women first raised the need for child care at national gatherings, the cost and liability seemed insurmountable obstacles. When compared, however, to the costs and liabilities of open bars, child care became more reasonable. Many unions now provide child care and children's activities at conferences and conventions.

The process of changing policies, practices, customs and expectations— changing the culture of the union—was set in motion by internal as well as external forces. The women's movement, the civil rights movement, the increasingly female, minority, and immigrant face of workers have all put pressure on unions to change. The alarming and continual decline in union membership has awakened in the current leadership a recognition that change is not only inevitable but preferable to further contraction or irrelevance. The old culture, the old boys' network, the old ways cannot be relied on to rebuild the labor movement in the 1990s.

Sharing Stories, Creating New Lives

Union women themselves have been and will have to continue creating new ways of leading union lives, opening the union to more workers. This process of change requires women to move beyond the more traditional behaviors of accommodation or resistance to the status quo. Union women need to invent a new culture of unionism, by dreaming alternatives collectively, modeling them, and then, by living them.

When interviewing women leaders for this commentary, I asked them to describe their vision of a union as it would be if they could shape policies and practices. What would the life of a local union or of a local union leader be like? Their responses revealed how difficult it was for them to imagine a union life not based on daily compromise, adjustment, or resistance. The kinds of changes in policies and practices they could identify were the incremental ones mentioned previously: more training, fewer meetings, more delegation, less weekend work.

Pressed to envision a woman-friendly union culture, they referred to their experiences at women's schools or conferences and to informal gatherings of women. Women role models, women in leadership, peer groups of women, they stressed, make a union friendlier and safer for women. Safe, one woman explained, is having people who look like you, have experiences like you, who can validate your experiences and feelings, share concerns, explore alternatives collectively, and then, strategize and act collectively as well.

The process of carving out a safe union space for women parallels in many ways the process that helped push the women's movement forward: small groups, women's groups, consciousness-raising groups.

"We must begin to tell the truth," wrote Carolyn Heilbrun in *Writing a Woman's Life,* "in groups, to each other." "Telling the truth" is, in fact, what initiated the most significant changes for women in unions: women sharing their stories and telling the truth about sexual harassment, pregnancy leave discrimination, child care. Carolyn Heilbrun describes as "painful" the lives of women writers who attempted to break with traditional roles or stereotypes.

"The price is high, the anxiety is intense," she added, "because there is no script to follow, no story portraying how one is to act, let alone any alternative stories" (1988:39). For the pioneer women who first assumed leadership positions, clearly there were no scripts. There was no one with whom to talk, no one to validate feelings, and therefore no way to move from individual pain to collective action.

Over the past decades, though, as women unionists met together, whether in the Coalition of Labor Union Women (CLUW) or in ad hoc gatherings, they began to share their stories. What began as a chorus of complaints was transformed through group validation into collective action and social change. What is needed, then, is more opportunities for women—for women of color, immigrant women, young and old, lesbian and heterosexual, otherwise abled—to tell their stories and imagine new ones for their lives. Only then will new narratives, new paths to leadership, new models of activism be created. No less is needed for many men. It is not just women who feel themselves outsiders in union culture. Men of color, immigrants, men of a younger generation do as well.

Collective storytelling has always played a role in union building; the Wobblies were among our greatest storytellers and song writers. Few could tell a story to open eyes and move workers like Woody Guthrie or Mother Jones. Sharing stories builds consciousness, empathy, solidarity, anger, and spirit; it helps women and workers to reject what is unjust and create new expectations and vision. The new feminist scholarship in history, sociology, and labor studies has contributed new stories and told the truth about our foremothers. Unions and union women owe them a great debt.

The more women tell the truth with each other, the greater will be their ability to know what in union culture is outdated or unfriendly. And the greater their capacity to invent alternatives and create a culture truly reflective of the diversity of the new work force.

Comments

Roberta Lynch

For more than a decade now, the American labor movement has been a deeply troubled institution. At the onset of the 1980s, unions found themselves confronted with a relentless employer offensive that sought to strip away gains at the bargaining table, while defaming the very notion of trade unionism in the public mind. Moreover, in tandem with the intensified internationalization of capital, U.S. corporations undertook a massive economic restructuring that resulted in the loss of millions of jobs, most of them in the industries that had formed the bedrock of organized labor.

This onslaught might have been weathered with less dire consequences had not much of the labor movement succumbed to a debilitating complacency, neglecting to organize new members, failing to adequately educate and motivate its own ranks, and even occasionally crossing the line into corrupt or illegal activities.

At precisely the moment that the full dimensions of labor's crisis began to emerge, another development was dramatically reshaping American society: women were entering the job market in record numbers, many of them in the new and growing service industries that had not been previously on the agenda of trade unions. Partly in reaction to pressures from the women's movement, and partly as a result of the labor movement's own urgent needs, unions of every stripe—even those that had a long tradition of ambivalence toward female participation—began to revise their ideas and their images to reach out to women workers. By the end of the decade, a number of labor unions were among the foremost champions of working women—leading the battles for pay equity, family leave, and child care, as well as for more traditional concerns such as decent wages, health insurance, and promotional opportunities.

In response, women have swelled the ranks of organized labor and now represent some one-third of all trade union members. Not surprisingly, this sudden influx has produced an array of reactions—from elation to dismay—within labor's house. Some unions have long had women in their ranks and have readily integrated them into organizational structures and programs. Others, largely those in male-dominated fields, have been slower to change and often resistant to creating an accessible environment for women members.

The essays by Lois Gray, and by Pamela Roby and Lynet Uttal ably describe the barriers that women have encountered as they seek to expand their roles within unions. Additionally, the authors identify the approaches that have most effectively aided in overcoming those barriers. But neither article sufficiently probes the concept of "feminizing" unions. To wit: How is the growing participation of women likely to alter the face of American trade unionism? Two somewhat divergent responses have emerged to this critical question.

In the first instance, feminization is seen largely as a matter of integration. This is the operational undergirding of the articles by Gray and by Roby and Uttal, and is in fact the basis on which many women function within the labor movement. Their aims are to bring more women into key leadership positions, to challenge sexist practices, and to supplement labor's traditional agenda with "women's" issues. This viewpoint essentially accepts labor's current structures and strategies, seeking only to modify them in ways such that women can be better accommodated within them.

The second version of feminization takes as its point of departure the need for a more profound metamorphosis, and asserts that women are possessed of characteristics so homogenous, of such cumulative weight, and so thoroughly congruent with labor's aspirations that increasing female participation will of itself be the catalyst for radical transformation. This strategy relies on the recruitment of women as its inherent design for change.

Although these two concepts may seem very different, even oppositional, in their most abstract forms, in reality they can lead to quite similar outcomes, for neither demands a thoroughgoing reconceptualization of organized labor's structures, strategies, or goals. In my view, without such a rethinking—and attendant changes—it will be next to impossible to construct a labor movement that can flourish once again and thus have meaning for the majority of women's lives.

Necessary but Not Sufficient

The tasks taken up by the "integrationists" are essential ones. In point of fact, no real progress will be possible unless the labor movement succeeds in assimilating women, their ideas, and their concerns. In recent years many unions have taken steps to prohibit all forms of discrimination, to discourage sexist behavior, and to foster women's involvement. The success of these initiatives varies greatly from union to union, and sometimes from local to local within a union. There are still too many instances in which a union closes its eyes to sexual harassment in the workplace, fails to alter cultural practices that exclude women, ignores the constraints of family responsibilities, or tolerates outright sexism in its own ranks. The efforts of women to transform these conditions and to shape a labor movement that is hospitable to their participation and their aspirations is one of the key variables in determining labor's fate.

But critical as this task may be, it will mean little if it is not coupled with a more probing analysis of labor's frailties. A critical point of departure is the enervation of the democratic impulse. Democracy has long been labor's hallmark. Labor unions were founded not just as the champion of working people, but as their voice, and unions remain among the most democratic institutions in American society. At their best, they offer working people one of the few venues in which it is possible to feel a sense of ownership. Measured against virtually every other major institution in our society, they are singularly open, flexible, and responsive. When measured against their own promise, however, too many unions are falling short.

In some instances, there has been a breakdown of all but the most nominal democratic procedures. The internal structure has calcified around a small clique of leaders whose sole goal is the perpetuation of their own power. This obsession with short-term power almost inevitably leads to the long-term weakening of the union because the most common tool for the maintenance of control is to discourage the involvement of the membership in the union. Meetings may be held infrequently and/or at inaccessible locations. Elections may be not just secret ballots, but secret events, barely publicized among the members. Constitutions or bylaws may be kept—almost literally—under lock and key. The union structure may be based on large, geographically disbursed locals in which thousands—even tens of thousands—of members don't even know who or where other members are. And, in a small minority of situations, there may be outright intimidation of those who dare to dissent.

Circumstances such as these would dissuade any but the most motivated; they pose a special challenge for women. Even in the best of situations, there is a large psychological barrier the average woman must overcome to enter into the political fray. Competing in an election requires a woman to publicly exhibit her ambition, to assertively argue her superiority, and to expose herself to public criticism—not behavior for which women in our society have been much applauded. Forming caucuses, engaging in political rivalries, electioneering for other candidates—even these activities can prove disconcerting for many women who are relative newcomers to the world of public conflict.

If in addition there is intimidation, fraud, even violence; if the local union is byzantine in its structure; if the election procedures are solidly stacked in favor of incumbents—how likely is it then that women will get involved in the internal life of the union?

Of course, there are many unions throughout the country that have managed to avoid this stagnation of the democratic tradition; they vigorously follow democratic procedures and strive to foster membership involvement. But even the most democratic of trade unions today must confront a daunting array of forces that propel members away from union activism.

Not the least of these is the change in family dynamics that has occurred as women have entered the work force. Men can no longer stop by the union hall for a drink or plan to attend a late-night meeting secure in the knowledge that a wife will be waiting at home with a warmed-up dinner and the kids safely tucked in bed. Now there is a growing expectation that even if men do not take on major family responsibilities, they will at least be present at home to lend a hand. Meanwhile women, who still bear overwhelming responsibility for family maintenance in addition to their jobs, may find it much more difficult to sandwich in union activities. Working women who are single heads of households carry an even heavier burden.

In another paradoxical development, one of the labor movement's prime achievements—improved social mobility—now provides an alternative to union activism. Enhanced possibilities for job advancement—combined with the growing lack of job security—drive more and more workers to devote their spare time to training or educational programs that can improve their situation on the job. Complementing such educational efforts are a growing menu of personal development activities, ranging from twelve-step recovery groups to physical fitness programs.

Employers have not hesitated to capitalize on these changing dynamics. An entire industry has developed around sophisticated new techniques to weaken allegiance to the union where one is present or undermine any potential attraction where it is not. These anti-union efforts were aided by the dominant culture of the Reagan-Bush years, which so relentlessly derided the possibilities of collective action while glamorizing individual initiative.

The strength of family responsibilities, the hope of job advancement, the lure of self-improvement, all of these stake powerful claims on union members' time—and on their identities as well. For many the union becomes something marginal to their lives, less meaningful than their bowling game or their weight-loss group.

When a local union is the province of a few, when it is manifestly disinterested in encouraging membership involvement, when it does not aggressively fight for its members' interests nor attempt to hear their concerns, the strength of these alternative forces becomes almost irresistible. The union not only loses the members' time, it loses their commitment, their belief in labor's legitimacy. It almost goes without saying that the will and ability of such a union to organize new members is seriously eroded.

This is why any strategy that concentrates its energies on substituting female leadership for male, on reducing sexist practices, and on adding women's issues to labor's agenda is laudable but far too limited. It would be the most Pyrrhic of victories if women succeed in attaining power in an institution that no longer has real power to effect change in the lives of the vast majority of working women.

Gender Is Not Destiny

For some, "feminizing" the labor movement means much more than ensuring women's access to leadership positions. It means that the unique character traits that women possess will enable them to reverse labor's flagging fortunes and restore its vitality. This view was set forth most straightforwardly in a March 1989 issue of *Labor Research Review* which asserted that women bring a fresh vision to the labor movement, "*one particularly skilled in and committed to solidarity among all workers* in bettering our lives" (emphasis added).

Although it is far too early to know what all the implications of women's entrance into the labor movement will be, thus far I have seen little in my own experience to convince me of the validity of this thesis. I work for a statewide council of AFSCME that represents some sixty-five thousand workers, more than half of whom are women and most of whom joined our union in just the past two decades. Our council is composed of more than two hundred local unions, many of which are led by women. While there are surely differences that could be identified (probably even quantified) in the leadership styles of the male and female officeholders, I can say with a good deal of certainty that those locals led by women are not as a group significantly fresher of vision or more solidaristic than those led by men.

The contention that women's singular characteristics can spawn dramatic change assumes far more homogeneity among women than actually exists. It may indeed be true that women are more likely to possess certain personality traits or share certain concerns, but there is also considerable diversity among women workers. In reality this diversity, as much as the commonalities, is likely to shape the nature of women's participation in the labor movement.

One difference of considerable consequence for labor strategy arises from the varied kinds of work that women do. There is ample evidence to suggest that work cultures influence which workers are most likely to be drawn to unionization, as well as the nature of participation for those who do unionize. For instance, of the forty-five thousand state of Illinois employees my union represents, the mental health workers—predominantly female—were among the earliest and most loyal union members. They remain some of our strongest activists to this day. But state clerical workers—also largely female—were among the last to join the union and even after years of union representation and major improvements in wages and working conditions, these employees remain (as a group) the least committed of our members.

Other differences that influence union participation are rooted in race, national origin, even regional geography. It is not that any of these differences are insurmountable. But such diversity is noteworthy because it challenges the notion of common female values or traits that can organically reshape labor strategy. In reality, it is generally easier to predict levels of militancy, commitment, or involvement by craft or profession than it is by gender. And women are far more likely to take action on problems or conditions that arise out of their own specific situations as workers than they are out of any more "natural" inclination toward solidarity.

The notion that female characteristics—invariably viewed as beneficial—will play a transformative role when brought to bear in the public arena is one side of a longstanding debate within the women's movement. Proponents have argued that these traits would remake all of society as more and more women entered public life. Such a transformation, however, has been slow in coming. In fact, there is growing evidence to suggest that as women have achieved higher positions in business, government, and politics, they have not proven to be significantly kinder or gentler than men. In my own experience, for example, we have encountered women employers who can be every bit as hostile to the union, as indifferent to the employees' concerns, and as mean-spirited as the men with whom we deal.

As a result of such developments, we now hear women exhorted to stop acting like men and return to their "natural" caring behavior. But these exhortations miss the point: If such behavior were indeed natural, then it would not be so easily cast aside. More likely, it is behavior born of circumstance, shaped by women's narrower sphere of activity. Once women enter any public institution—whether it be a labor union or a boardroom—they are going to find themselves altered by the demands of that situation. It is not that they are taking on the behavior of men, but rather that they are modifying their behavior to cope with the new realities that confront them, realities for which their previous experience and learned behaviors had not necessarily prepared them.

There are, to be sure, in our society today some character traits more common to women—not to all women, but to larger numbers of women than men. Some of these traits, though by no means all, may indeed be congruent with the requirements of a revitalized labor movement. Likewise, some of these traits may indeed over time—and I suspect it will be quite some time—facilitate changes in the overall character of the labor movement. Nonetheless, given the seriousness of the crisis confronting organized labor in this country, this set of possibilities seems to me to comprise far too thin a thread on which to hang the movement's future.

Shaping a Future

Neither of these versions of feminization offers the potential to transform the labor movement. If organized labor is to survive as more than a shell into the next century, it will need to define the role that it wants to play in American society, and then chart a conscious strategy to achieve that aim.

The overriding imperative is to change the culture of the labor movement, to make it an institution that plays a more vital role in the lives of those it represents and that has the capacity to alter the dynamics of the workplace in ways that can empower workers. If organized labor is to prevail against a culture that unconsciously undermines it by fostering individualism, cynicism, and apathy *and* against an employer community that consciously seeks to thwart it through legal, psychological, and even physical means, it will need a sophisticated, creative, and unceasing program of both internal and external organizing.

Some unions have already begun to chart a new course beginning with the AFL-CIO's surprisingly self-analytical report, "The Changing Situation of Workers and Their Unions," through such revitalizing and creative struggles as the Harvard clericals' organizing victory, the Pittston miners' strike, and the New York City hospital workers' contract victory; and ranging through one-on-one communication programs, literacy and other workplace-based educational programs, and union-crafted employee involvement programs.

The urgent task now is to open the doors to such changes on a massive scale: to shape a labor movement that has meaning for the changing lives of American workers and the changing workplace in which they labor. Such a transformation must balance anew one of the oldest dichotomies in the U.S. national character: individual initiative and communitarian impulses. On the one hand, it must respond to the growing emphasis on personal development and "job ownership" concepts; on the other, it must construct (or reconstruct) a web of social solidarity that can link workplace and community concerns, job and family responsibilities. Without a commitment to expanded democracy—both within unions and within workplaces—the labor movement will move farther and farther from being a force in the workplace of tomorrow.

To do so, however, labor will need a broader vision of its role and a more compelling and credible vision of what our society should be. The continued focus on the decline of organized labor has partially masked the more generalized crisis of the liberal vision of society. We have remained trapped in the backwater of industrial decline, educational stagnation, cultural divisiveness, and growing criminality because so few Americans have been convinced that there is an alternative. For all of the strains on its own legitimacy, organized labor remains one of the few institutions that might help to craft such an alternative vision.

The reality is that the labor movement will not be able to achieve such ambitious goals unless it includes women in its ranks and its leadership. First, because women now make up a significant portion of the labor force and the labor movement cannot grow if it does not reach out to women workers. Moreover, if women are not represented at every level of the trade union movement, then the labor movement will continue to be subjected—and deservedly so—to the criticisms that it is inhospitable to the aspirations of all working people and exists only to promote the well-being of a relative few. And finally, because women indubitably bring new zest and ideas that can help create the essential ferment for change.

The tasks that are critical to the revitalization of the labor movement cannot be accomplished without the active involvement of women, whose talents and energy must be drawn on to the fullest extent possible, but labor's aims are not assured merely by the presence of women. Change will only come when men and women together define what we truly value and then work to shape a labor movement that can embody that vision and effectively fight for its actualization.

References to Part VI

Acker, Joan. 1989a. "The Problem with Patriarchy." *Sociology* 23(2):235–40.

———. 1989b. *Doing Comparable Worth: Gender, Class and Pay Equity.* Philadelphia: Temple University Press.

Adams, Joyce Davis. 1986. "At the Bargaining Table." *Black Enterprise* (August):52–54.

AFL-CIO. Department of Organization and Field Services. 1989. *AFL-CIO Organizing Survey: 1986–87 NLRB Election.* Washington, D.C.: Minutes.

———. 1990. *AFL-CIO Organizing Survey.* Washington, D.C.

Andriappan, P., and Gary N. Chaisson. 1989. "The Emerging Role of Women in National Union Governance: The Results of a Canadian Study." International Industrial Relations Association, Sixth World Congress. March 28–31:1–44.

Apple, R. W., Jr. 1984. "In the Men's World of a British Union, She's the Boss." *New York Times* (April 2).

Baden, Naomi. 1986. "Developing an Agenda: Expanding the Role of Women in Unions." *Labor Studies Journal* (Winter):229–49.

Batstone, Erik, Ian Boraston, and Stephen Frenkel. 1977. *Shop Stewards in Action.* Oxford: Basil Blackwell.

Baxandall, Rosalyn, Linda Gordon, and Susan Reverby, eds. 1976. *America's Working Women: A Documentary History—1600 to the Present.* New York: Random House.

Bennis, Warren. 1990. "How to Be the Leader They'll Follow." *Working Women* (March):75–8.

Bergquist, V. A. 1974. "Women's Participation in Labor Unions." *Monthly Labor Review* 97(10):3–9.

Berheide, Catherine W. 1984. "Women's Work in the Home." *Marriage and Family Review* 7(3/4):37–55.

Bigler, Esta. 1990. "The Changing Work Force and Its Effect on Unions." In *Proceedings of the New York University 43rd Annual National Conference of Labor.* Boston: Little, Brown.

Blankertz, Laura E. 1980. "Perceptions of Discrimination among Women Labor Union Leaders." Conference paper, Pennsylvania Sociological Society.

BNA 1990a. "Working Women: Women Seen as a Source of Growth for American Labor Movement." *Labor Relations Weekly,* Feature Report, September 19(7):859–60.

———. 1990b. "Union Leadership: More Women Gaining Positions in Union Leadership Structure." *Labor Relations Weekly,* Special Report, September 19(7): 877–78.

Business Week. 1974. "Women Push for Union Power." March 30:102.

Catlett, Judith H. 1986. "After the Goodbyes: A Long-term Look at the Southern School for Union Women." *Labor Studies Journal* Winter(10):300–311.

Chaison, Gary N., and P. Andriappan. 1982. "A Study of Female Union Officers in Canada." Paper presented at the annual meeting of the Canadian Industrial Relations Association. Ottawa.

———. 1987. "Profiles of Local Union Officers—Males v. Females." *Industrial Relations* 26(3):281–83.

———. 1989. "An Analysis of the Barriers to Women Becoming Head Union Officers." *Journal of Labor Research* 10(2):149–62.

Clark, Paul, and Lois Gray. 1992. "The Management of Human Resources in National Unions." Paper presented at 44th Annual Meeting of the Industrial Relations Research Association.

CLUW. 1981. *Empowerment of Union Women: An 18-Month National Monitoring and Resource Project.* New York: CLUW.

———. 1990. *Bargaining for Our Families: A Union Member's Guide.* New York: CLUW and AFL-CIO.

Cockburn, Cynthia. 1991. *In the Way of Women: Men's Resistance to Sex Equality in Organizations.* Ithaca, N.Y.: ILR Press.

Cook, Alice H. 1962. "Dual Government in Unions: A Tool for Analysis." *Industrial and Labor Relations Review* 15:323–49.

———. 1968. "Women and American Trade Unions." *Annals of the American Academy of Political and Social Science* (January):124–32.

Cook, Alice H., Val R. Lorwin, and Arlene K. Daniels, eds. 1984. *Women and Trade Unions in Eleven Industrialized Countries.* Philadelphia: Temple University Press.

Dewey, Lucretia M. 1975. "Women in Labor Unions." *Monthly Labor Review* (February):42–48.

Eaton, Susan C. 1990. "Women in Trade Union Leadership: Our Time Has Come to Shine." Samuel Gompers Union Leadership Award paper, Center for Labor-Management Policy Studies, City University of New York. October 5.

Epstein, Cynthia F. 1983. *Women in Law.* Garden City, N.Y.: Anchor Press/ Doubleday.

Farber, M. A. 1991. "Molded in Schools: She Helps Mold Them." *New York Times* (March 7).

Fellner, Kim. 1990. "Women Still Have No Standing in Unions." *New York Times* (September 3).

Fiorito, Jack, and Charles R. Greer. 1986. "Gender Differences in Union Membership, Preferences, and Beliefs." *Journal of Labor Research* 7(2):145–64.

Foner, Philip S. 1979. *Women and the American Labor Movement: From Colonial Times to the End of World War I.* New York: Free Press.

———. 1980. *Women and the American Labor Movement: From World War I to the Present.* New York: Free Press.

Foner, Robin. 1991. "Women in Politics Gain But Road Is a Long One." *New York Times* (January 25).

Fonow, Mary Margaret. 1977. *Women in Steel: A Case Study of the Participation of Women in a Trade Union.* Ph.D. diss., Ohio State University.

Freeman, Richard B., and Jonathan S. Leonard. 1987. "Union Maids: Unions and the Female Work Force." In *Gender in the Workplace,* edited by Clair Brown and Joseph Pechman. Washington, D.C.: Brookings Institution.

Gifford, Courtney D. 1991. *Directory of United States Labor Organizations,* 1990–91 Edition. Washington, D.C.: Bureau of National Affairs.

Glassberg, Elyse, Naomi Baden, and Karin Gerstel. 1980. *Absent from the Agenda.* CLUW. New York: Center for Education and Research.

Gray, Lois. S. 1987. "Professional Careers for Women in Industrial Relations." In *Working Women: Past, Present and Future,* edited by K. Koziara, M. H. Moscow, and L. D. Tanner. Madison, Wis.: Industrial Relations Research Association.

———. 1988. "Women in Union Leadership Roles." *Interface.* August 17(3):7–9.

Gray, Lois S., and Joyce L. Kornbluh. 1990. "New Directions in Labor Education." In *New Developments in Worker Training: A Legacy for the 1990s,* edited by Louis A. Ferman, et al. Madison, Wis.: Industrial Relations Research Association.

Gustke, Constaquce. 1988. "Unions Move to Recruit Women." *Management Review* 77(2):52–53.

Harriford, Diane. 1989. "Leadership and Participation Styles of Black Union Activists: New York City CLUW." Unpublished paper, Vassar College. April 12.

Harrison, M. 1979. "Participation of Women in Trade Union Activities: Some Research Findings and Comments." *Industrial Relations Journal* 10(2):41–55.

Harvard Business Review. 1991. "Debate: Ways Men and Women Lead." January/February 69(1):150–60.

Heery, Edmund and John Kelly. 1988. "Do Female Representatives Make a Difference?: Women Full-Time Officials and Trade Union Work." *Work, Employment, and Society* (December) 2(4):487–505.

———. 1989. "A Cracking Job for a Woman—A Profile of Women Trade Union Officers." *Industrial Relations Journal* 26(3):192–201.

Heilbrun, Carolyn. 1988. *Writing a Woman's Life.* New York: W.W. Norton.

Helgesen, Sally. 1990. *The Female Advantage.* New York: Doubleday.

Hoyman, Michele. 1989. "Working Women: The Potential of Unionization and Collective Action in the United States." *Women's Studies Institute Forum* 12(1):51–58.

ILO Social and Labour Bulletin. 1978. "Sweden: Low Participation by Women among Trade Union Officials." (June):197.

———. 1986. "Women to Lead CLC." (December):3–4.

IMF News. 1989. "Women Call for Reserved Places at IMF Congress and Central Committee." (12):1–2.

Izraeli, Dafna N. 1982. "Avenues into Leadership for Women: The Case of Union Officers in Israel." *Economic and Social Democracy* (November): 212–21.

Jacobson, Beverly. 1985. "Women and Their Issues Gain Power in Unions." *World of Work Report* 10 (April):4–5.

Jacobson, Carolyn J. 1980. "New Challenges for Women Workers." *The AFL-CIO American Federationist* (April):1–8.

Josephs, Susan L., et al. 1988. "The Union as Help or Hindrance: The Experiences of Women Apprentices in the Construction Trades." *Labor Studies Journal* 13:3–18.

Kanter, Rosabeth Moss. 1977. *Men and Women of the Corporation.* New York: Basic Books.

Karlsson, G. 1983. "Women's Representation in Trade Unions: Review of the Situation in Western Europe." European Trade Union Institute, Brussels.

Karr, Albert R. 1988. "Labor Letter," *Wall Street Journal* (July 26).

Kates, Carol. 1989. "Working Class Feminism and Feminist Unions: Title VII, the UAW and NOW." *Labor Studies Journal* (Summer):28–45.

Kautzer, Kathy. 1985. "University of Hard Knocks: Lessons from the Yale Strike." *Dollars and Sense* (May):16–17.

Kenneally, James J. 1978. *Women and American Trade Unions.* St. Albans, Vt.: Eden Press.

Kessler-Harris, Alice. 1975. "Where Are the Organized Women Workers?" *Feminist Studies* 3 (Fall):92–160.

———. 1982. *Out to Work. A History of Wage-Earning Women in the United States.* New York: Oxford University Press.

Kornbluh, Joyce L., and Mary Frederickson, eds. 1984. *Sisterhood and Solidarity. Workers' Education for Women, 1914–1984.* Philadelphia: Temple University Press.

Koziara, Karen S., and Patricia J. Insley. 1982. "Organizations of Working Women Can Pave the Way for Unions." *Monthly Labor Review* 105(6):53–54.

Koziara, Karen S., and David A. Pierson. 1980. "Barriers to Women Becoming Union Leaders." Industrial Relations Research Association 33rd Annual Meeting. Proceedings:48–54.

———. 1981. "The Lack of Female Union Leaders: A Look at Some Reasons." *Monthly Labor Review* 104(5):30–32.

Larson, Peter E. 1986. "Fighting for Labor." *Canadian Business Review* (Winter):8–12.

LeGrande, Linda H. 1978. "Women in Labor Organizations: Their Ranks Are Increasing." *Monthly Labor Review* (August):8–14.

List, Wilfred. 1986. "Women Stake Their Claim at the Top." *Industrial Management* (April):20.

Lorber, Judith. 1984. *Women Physicians: Careers, Status, and Power.* New York: Tavistock.

Lublin, Joann S. 1974. "Getting Organized: More Women Enroll in Unions, Win Office and Push for Change." *Wall Street Journal* (January 15):1, 12.

Milkman Ruth, ed. 1985. *Women, Work and Protest: A Century of Women's Labor History.* Boston: Routledge & Kegan Paul.

———. Forthcoming. "Union Responses to Workforce Feminization in the U.S."

In *The Challenge of Restructuring: North American Labor Movements Respond,* edited by Jane Jenson and Rianne Mahon. Philadelphia: Temple University Press.

Mills, C. Wright. 1948. *The New Men of Power: America's Labor Leaders.* New York: Harcourt, Brace.

Naisbitt, John, and Patricia Aburdene. 1990. "The 1990s: Decade of Women in Leadership." In *Megatrends 2000: Ten New Directions for the 1990s.* New York: Avon Books.

Nash, Al. 1983. *The Union Steward: Duties, Rights, and Status.* Ithaca, N.Y.: ILR Press.

National Committee on Pay Equity. 1989. "Pay Equity Activity in the Public Sector, 1979–1989." Washington, D.C.

Needleman Ruth. 1988. "Women Workers: A Force for Rebuilding Unionism." *Labor Research Review* (Spring):2–13.

Needleman, Ruth, and Lucretia Dewey Tanner. 1987. "Women in Unions: Current Issues." In *Working Women: Past, Present and Future,* edited by K. Koziara, M. H. Moscow, L. D. Tanner, 205–18. Washington, D.C.: BNA.

New York Times. 1985. "Union Women at Work." *Washington Talk* (December 8):80.

Nielson, Georgia Painter. 1982. *From Sky Girl to Flight Attendant: Women and the Making of a Union.* Ithaca, N.Y.: ILR Press.

O'Cleireacain, Carol. 1986. "Women and the Future of the Labor Movement." *Social Policy* 16 (Winter):40–42.

O'Sullivan, Judith O., and Rosemary Gallick. 1975. *Workers and Allies: Female Participation in the American Trade Union Movement, 1824–1976.* Washington, D.C.: Smithsonian Institution.

Ortiz, Alta Garcia. 1990. "Ethnicity and Gender in a New York City Trade Union: Hispanic Female Garment Workers and ILGWU, 1945–1965." Unpublished paper.

Peck, Sidney M. 1963. *The Rank-and-File Leader.* New Haven: College and University Press.

Przybyla, Barbara Ann. 1980. *The Experience of Taking Responsibility in Leadership Roles among Selected Labor Union Women.* Ph.D. diss., University of Michigan: University Microfilms International.

Quaglieri, Philip L. 1988. "The New People of Power: The Backgrounds and Careers of Top Labor Leaders." *Journal of Labor Research* 9(3):271–84.

Raskin, A. H. 1977. "Women Are Still Absent from Labor's Top Ranks." *New York Times* (June 5):64.

Reed, Thomas F. 1990. "Profiles of Union Organizers from Manufacturing and Service Unions." *Journal of Labor Research* 11(1):73–80.

Robertson, Don, and Tom Schuller. 1982. *Stewards, Members and Trade Union Training.* Glasgow: Centre for Research in Industrial Democracy and Participation, Glasgow University.

Roby, Pamela Ann. 1985. "Women and Unions: The Experience of Rank-and-File Leadership." Conference paper, Society for the Study of Social Problems.

———. 1987. "Union Stewards and Women's Employment Conditions." In *Ingredients for Women's Employment Policy,* edited by Christine Bose and Glenna Spitze, 139–55. Albany, N.Y.: State University of New York Press.

Roby, Pamela, and Lynet Uttal. 1988. "Trade Union Stewards: Handling Union,

Family, and Employment Responsibilities." In *Women and Work: An Annual Review* 3:215–48.

Rohter, Larry. 1986. "New Teachers' Leader: Sandra Feldman." *New York Times* (January 10).

Rose, Margaret Eleanor. 1988. "Women in the United Farm Workers: A Study of Chicana and Mexicana Participation in a Labor Union, 1950–1980." Ph.D. diss., University of California, Los Angeles.

Rosener, Judy B. 1990. "Ways Women Lead." *Harvard Business Review* (November–December):119–25.

Rudolph, Barbara. 1990. "Why Can't a Woman Manage More Like . . . a Woman?" *Time* 136(19):53.

Sayles, Leonard, and George Strauss. 1967. *The Local Union*. Rev. ed. New York: Harcourt, Brace and World.

Schwartz, Arthur B., and Michele M. Hoyman. 1984. "The New American Labor Leader." *Annals of the American Academy of Political and Social Science* (May):64–75.

Sexton, Patricia Cayo. 1982. *The New Nightingales: Hospital Workers, Unions, and New Women's Issues*. New York: Enquiry Press.

Shostak, Arthur B. 1991. *Robust Unionism: Innovations in the Labor Movement*. Ithaca, N.Y.: ILR Press.

Simeone, Angela. 1987. *Academic Women: Working towards Equality*. South Hadley, Mass.: Bergin & Garvey.

Till-Retz, Roberta. 1986. "Unions in Europe: Increasing Women's Participation." *Labor Studies Journal* 10 (Winter):250–60.

Trust, Cathy. 1986. "More Family Issues Surface at Bargaining Table as Women Show Increasing Interest in Unions." *Wall Street Journal* (December 2).

UAW Solidarity. 1989. "A Woman's Work Is Never Done." (March):9–13.

U.S. Bureau of the Census. 1980. *1980 Census of Population, Detailed Population Characteristics*. Section A, United States Table 275. Washington, D.C.: GPO.

U.S. Bureau of Labor Statistics. 1990. "Presence and Age of Own Children of Civilian Women Sixteen Years and Over by Employment Status and Marital Status." *Current Population Survey*, unpublished table.

U.S. News and World Report. 1975. "Labor: Women in Unions Gaining Power but Little Room at the Top." (March 17):70–1.

———. 1984. "Women Flex Muscles in Union Movement." (October 29):76–77.

Uttal, Lynet. 1987. "I Took My Daughter to the Union Meeting: Gendered Domestic Responsibilities and Union Steward Activity." Master's essay, University of California, Santa Cruz.

Wertheimer, Barbara Mayer. 1977. *We Were There*. New York: Pantheon Books.

Wertheimer, Barbara Mayer, and Ann Nelson. 1975. *Trade Union Women: A Study of Their Participation in New York City Locals*. New York: Praeger.

White, Joyce. 1977. "Breaking Union Barriers." *Essence* (March):77–80.

Working Woman. 1990. "The New Breed of Leaders: Taking Charge in a Different Way." (March):73–78.

York, Carolyn. 1989. "The Labor Movement's Role in Parental Leave and Child Care." SEIU (February 24).

About the Contributors

Barbara R. Bergmann is distinguished professor of economics at American University, Washington, D.C. In 1991–92, she served as president of the American Association of University Professors. She has a doctorate in economics from Harvard University. She is the author of *The Economic Emergence of Women* (1986), which explores the reasons for the revolution in women's roles and outlines suggested reforms in the workplace, the marketplace, government policy, and the family.

Eileen Boris, associate professor of history at Howard University, holds a Ph.D. from Brown University (1981). She is the author of *Art and Labor: Ruskin, Morris, and the Craftsman Ideal in America* (1986) and coeditor of *Homework: Historical and Contemporary Perspectives on Paid Labor at Home* (1989) and *Major Problems in the History of American Workers* (1991). Her most recent book, *In Defense of Motherhood: The Politics of Industrial Homework in the United States,* is forthcoming from Cambridge University Press. She is part of an international network lobbying for an ILO convention to protect home-based workers. Currently Boris is coediting *Invisible No More: Global Perspectives on Homework.*

Gloria Busman's work in the labor movement includes thirteen years with the National AFL-CIO's Los Angeles/Orange Counties Organizing Committee. She joined the UCLA Center for Labor Research and Education in 1976, leaving in 1991 to again be involved in direct union advocacy. Her publications include *Union Representatives' Guide to the NLRB* (1977; rev. ed., 1981); and *Organizing for Empowerment* (1989). She was a founder of Coalition of Labor Union Women and served as cochair of its first organizing task force. She is former vice-president and national chair of the University and College Labor Education Association Professional Council.

Dennis Chamot is executive assistant to the president of the Department for Professional Employees of the AFL-CIO. He obtained a Ph.D. in chemistry from the University of Illinois and an M.B.A. from the Wharton School of the University of Pennsylvania. Dr. Chamot worked for several years as a research chemist with DuPont and has a particular concern with issues related to new workplace technologies. He has served on committees and advisory groups at the National Research Council, National Science Foundation, Congressional Office of Technology Assessment, Department of Labor, Department of Education, and a variety of other organizations.

Kathleen Christensen is a professor of environmental psychology and director of the Work Environments Research Group at the Graduate School, City University of New York. She received her doctorate in geography from Pennsylvania State University. She has studied work-at-home trends since 1983 and is the author or editor of numerous publications, including *Women and Home-based Work: The Unspoken Contract; The New Era of Home-based Work: Directions and Policies;* and *Flexible Workstyles: A Look at Contingent Labor.* She coauthored *Turbulence in the American Workforce.*

Dorothy Sue Cobble is an associate professor at Rutgers University where she teaches history, women's studies, and labor studies. She received her Ph.D. in history from Stanford University. Her book *Dishing It Out: Waitresses and Their Unions in the Twentieth Century* (1991) won the 1992 Herbert A. Gutman Award. She directed the Labor Studies Program at City College of San Francisco before moving to New Jersey and continues to coordinate and teach in educational programs for trade unionists.

Alice H. Cook, professor emerita, New York State School of Industrial and Labor Relations, Cornell University, is the author of articles in *Industrial and Labor Relations Review* and many other journals. Her most recent publications include: "Can Work Requirements Accommodate to Needs of Dual-Earner Families?," in *Cross-National Perspectives on Dual-Earner Families,* edited by Helen Hootsman, Suzan Lewis, and Daphne Izraeli (1992), and *The Most Difficult Revolution: Women and Trade Unions in Five Countries,* coauthored with Val Lorwin and Arlene Kaplan Daniels (1992). She is a former staff member of the Textile Workers Union and was assistant to the manager of the Joint Board, Philadelphia, Amalgamated Clothing Workers of America.

Susan Cowell, a vice-president of the International Ladies' Garment Workers' Union, has done extensive work in child care and family policy. She coordinated the creation of the Garment Industry Day Care Center of Chinatown, which opened in 1983; served on the New York State Commission on Child Care from 1985 to 1986; and was a member of the French-American Foundation's Child Care Study Panel of the French child care system in 1989. She received an M.Phil. in history from Yale University in 1979.

Carrie G. Donald, J.D., is assistant professor in the College of Business and Public Administration and director of the Labor-Management Center, University of Louisville. Professor Donald received her master's and law degrees from the University of Louisville. She has written numerous essays on labor and employment law and is a frequent speaker on these issues. One of her publications is "Comparable Worth: Litigation, Legislation, and Negotiation," in *Second Annual Labor and Employment Law Institute* (1986). She serves as cochair of the Subcommittee on Alternative Dispute Resolution for the American Bar Association Committee on Labor Arbitration and Collective Bargaining Agreements.

Virginia duRivage is a sociologist and writer living in Takoma Park, Maryland. She is completing a Ph.D. in sociology at Johns Hopkins University. She has written extensively about the problems of part-time workers, most notably in her reports on the subject for 9 to 5 and the Economic Policy Institute. Her articles have appeared in *Labor Law Journal, Business and Society Review,* and other journals.

Elizabeth Engberg is a research analyst for employee benefits at the Service Employees' International Union. Before coming to SEIU in 1989, she worked as assistant to the executive director of the New York State Industrial Cooperation Council. Ms. Engberg received her bachelor's degree in economics from the University of California at Berkeley and is currently enrolled in the M.B.A. program at George Washington University.

Kim Fellner, a union writer/organizer for eighteen years, started as a labor editor at Service Employees' International Union. Subsequently, she was public relations director for the Screen Actors Guild and a speechwriter for its president, Edward Asner. From 1986 through 1990, Fellner served as first executive director of the National Writers Union. She now freelances and coordinates the Committee for a National Organizers Association. Fellner holds an M.S. from the University of Pittsburgh and has published several articles on life in the labor movement.

Judith Gerson received her Ph.D. from Cornell University. Currently she is on the faculty of Rutgers University where she teaches sociology and women's studies. She is the author of *At Home and in the Office: A Comparison of Home- and Office-Based Clerical Workers* (forthcoming).

Jessica Govea has been a professional organizer since 1966. She was a founding organizer of the United Farm Workers of America, and during part of her sixteen-year tenure she served as an elected member of the UFW's nine-member national executive board and as the union's national director of organizing. In 1989, Ms. Govea was national associate director of social services and assistant director of civil rights for the Amalgamated Clothing and Textile Workers Union. She is currently on the faculty of the Labor Education Department at Rutgers University in New Brunswick, New Jersey.

Lois S. Gray is the Jean McKelvey-Alice Grant Professor of Labor-Management Relations in the New York State School of Industrial and Labor Relations, Cornell University, where she served as associate dean and director of the Division of Extension and Public Service from 1975 to 1987. Her published works deal with labor-management relations, women and minorities in the labor force, labor and adult education, labor economics, and union administration. She was awarded the Ph.D. degree in economics from Columbia University in 1965 and in 1991 she received an honorary doctor of laws degree from her alma mater, Park College, in Missouri.

Patricia A. Gwartney-Gibbs received her Ph.D. in sociology from the University of Michigan in 1981. She is currently associate professor of sociology and research associate, Center for the Study of Women in Society, both at the University of Oregon. Publications related to this chapter and coauthored with Denise H. Lach appear in *Sociological Practice* (1992), *Mediation Quarterly* (1992), *Negotiation Journal* (1991), *Journal of Peace Research* (1991), and *Dispute Resolution and Democracy in the 1990s* (1990). Other related publications appear in *Australian and New Zealand Journal of Sociology* (1988), *Women and Work: An Annual Review* (1988), *Sage: A Scholarly Journal of Black Women* (1986), and *Research in Social Stratification and Mobility* (1986).

Margaret Hallock is professor and director of the University of Oregon Labor Education and Research Center (LERC), which serves the research and educational needs of Oregon workers and their unions. Hallock has a Ph.D. in economics from Claremont Graduate School and a bachelor's degree from the University of Southern California. Hallock served as director of research for the Oregon Public Employees Union, SEIU 503, for five years and led their successful pay equity campaign for state employees. She has published papers on economics, pay equity, and tax reform.

Diane Harriford is an assistant professor of sociology at Vassar College. She received her Ph.D. from the State University of New York at Stony Brook. Dr. Harriford's research has focused on black women's work and their participation in labor union organizations. She is particularly interested in black women's styles of leadership and the meaning and relevance of feminism in their lives.

Heidi Hartmann is currently director of the Washington-based Institute for Women's Policy Research (IWPR). She holds an M.Ph. and a Ph.D. degree from Yale University in economics. Among her recent coauthored reports from IWPR are *Unnecessary Losses: Costs to Americans of the Lack of Family and Medical Leave* and *Low-Wage Jobs and Workers: New Findings on Race, Ethnicity and Gender*. Other publications include *Women, Work and Wages: Equal Pay for Jobs of Equal Value, Women's Work Men's Work: Sex Segregation on the Job,* and *Computer Chips and Paper Clips: Technology and Women's Employment.*

Shelley Herochik has an Ed.D. from Rutgers University Graduate School of Education in Labor Studies. As assistant education director and liaison to the legislative and political departments of the International Ladies' Garment Workers' Union, she served on the 1990 Industrial Homework Task Force, which developed and coordinated a series of seven Department of Labor hearings across the country on industrial homework in the garment industries. She is a contributor to *Labor Conflict in the United States,* edited by Ronald L. Filippelli, and has taught labor studies at Rutgers University and for several unions. She is currently district assistant to Congresswoman Jolene Unsoeld (D-Wash.).

Richard Hurd is professor and director of labor studies at the New York State School of Industrial and Labor Relations, Cornell University. He earned his doctor of philosophy degree in economics from Vanderbilt University in 1972. Professor Hurd has published numerous articles on union strategy, including several on the unionization of clerical workers. Among his publications on this topic are "Organizing Clerical Workers: Determinants of Success," with Adrienne McElwain, in *Industrial and Labor Relations Review* 41 (April 1988), and "Learning from Clerical Workers: Two Cases of Organizing Successes," in *Labor Studies Journal* 14 (Spring 1989).

David C. Jacobs is an associate professor of labor, business, and society at the American University in Washington, D.C. He received his Ph.D. in industrial and labor relations at Cornell University in 1983. He has published a number of essays exploring the potential of negotiations as an avenue of social reform, including "The Concept of Adversary Participation" and "Bargaining for Social Change: The Course of Solidarity," both appearing in *Negotiation Journal.* Jacobs is now at work on a book on "transformational unionism."

Gloria Tapscott Johnson received both her B.A. and M.A. degrees from Howard University. Prior to 1954, Mrs. Johnson taught at Howard University and served as an economist with the U.S. Department of Labor. Since 1954, Johnson has been with the International Union of Electronic, Electrical Salaried, Machine and Furniture Workers, AFL-CIO, and currently is director of the union's Department of Social Action. Chair of the IUE Women's Council and a member of the IUE national executive board, she helped found the Coalition of Labor Union Women in 1974, and she continues to serve CLUW as treasurer and on its national executive board.

Susan L. Josephs is the associate dean for educational and professional diversity in the College of Business at the Ohio State University. She is also an associate professor and was with the former Department of Labor Education and Research Service at the Ohio State University. Professor Josephs currently is working on a project funded through the Center for Labor Research at the Ohio State University that addresses the relationship between organizational commitment and labor-management administrative patterns. She holds degrees from the University of Keele, Staffordshire, England, and the University of Warwick, Coventry, England.

Marlene Kim, assistant professor of labor studies at Rutgers University, holds a Ph.D. in economics from the University of California, Berkeley. She served as an analyst for SEIU Local 1000 on the largest pay equity lawsuit in the nation and has published on wage discrimination. Her current research interests include discrimination, compensation, welfare, and the working poor. A long-time activist on women's and minority issues, she also teaches popular economics workshops and conducts research for labor, women's, religious, and other community organizations.

Denise H. Lach received her Ph.D. in sociology from the University of Oregon in 1992 and is a research scientist at Battelle Seattle Research Center. Publications related to this chapter and coauthored with Patricia A. Gwartney-Gibbs appear in *Sociological Practice* (1992), *Mediation Quarterly* (1992), *Negotiation Journal* (1991), *Journal of Peace Research* (1991), and *Dispute Resolution and Democracy in the 1990s* (1990). Her article coauthored with Jean Stockard on gender and conflict resolution appeared in the *1989 Annual Review of Conflict Resolution.*

Roberta Lynch is the director of public policy for the Illinois Council of the American Federation of State, County and Municipal Employees. She is the coauthor, with David Bensman, of *Rusted Dreams: Hard Times in a Steel Community,* and she writes frequently on contemporary social, political, and economic issues.

Maureen Martella received her Ph.D. in sociology from Temple University where she works in the Honors Program as an administrator, researcher, and teacher. She received a grant from the Women's Bureau of the U.S. Department of Labor to study temporary work, for which she authored the report, " 'Just a Temp': Expectations and Experiences of Women Clerical Temporary Workers."

Ruth Milkman is associate professor of sociology at the University of California, Los Angeles, and a research associate at the UCLA Institute of Industrial Relations. She holds a B.A. degree from Brown University and an M.A. and Ph.D. from the University of California, Berkeley. She writes extensively on workplace issues. Her most recent publication is the book *Japan's California Factories: Labor Relations and Economic Globalization* (1991). Her book *Gender at Work* was awarded the 1987 Joan Kelly Award by the American Historical Association. She is now at work on a study of automobile assembly workers.

Joyce D. Miller is the vice-president and director of social services of the Amalgamated Clothing and Textile Workers Union, AFL-CIO, CLC. She is also the national president of the Coalition of Labor Union Women and a member of the AFL-CIO Executive Council. She is a graduate of the University of Chicago, where she received her bachelor of philosophy degree in 1950 and her master of arts degree in 1951.

J. Suzanne Moore is a free-lance writer living in the Washington, D.C., area.

Ruth Needleman, former director of education for the Service Employees' International Union, is associate professor of labor studies at Indiana University. Needleman has chaired the Women's Committee of the University and College Labor Education Association, coordinated state and regional women's leadership schools, and published numerous articles on women workers and unions, including "Women in Unions: Current Issues," with Lucretia Tanner, in *Working Women: Past, Present, Future* (1987); "Women Workers: A Force for Rebuilding Unions," in *Labor Research Review* 7 (1): 1988; and "Women and Economic Change," in *Labor Studies Journal* 10 (3): 1986.

Leslie E. Nulty is assistant to the director of the United Food and Commercial Workers' public affairs department. She has held a wide variety of positions during the course of a twenty-year career in the U.S. labor movement. Mrs. Nulty is the author of numerous publications in the field of labor economics, the most recent being "Looking for Labor in All the Wrong Places," *Challenge Magazine* (September/October 1990), a study of part-time work and the use of child labor. Mrs. Nulty received her M.Sc. in economics from Cambridge University, Cambridge, England, in 1970.

Brigid O'Farrell is senior associate at the Center for Women's Policy Studies and former study director for the Committee on Women's Employment and Related Social Issues at the National Research Council. Her research focus is the implementation of equal employment opportunity policies for women in blue-collar and clerical occupations and labor unions, and related issues of child care and combining work and family responsibilities. She holds an Ed.M. in social policy from Harvard University. She most recently coedited the volume *Work and Family: Policies for a Changing Work Force.*

Anna Padia holds a bachelor of arts in speech communications from the University of Washington (1969). She is the human rights director for The Newspaper Guild, AFL-CIO, CLC. Ms. Padia currently serves on the Task Force on Minorities in the Newspaper Business, the board of directors of the National Committee on Pay Equity, Wider Opportunities for Women (vice-chairperson), and the Institute for Women's Policy Research (chairperson).

Patti R. Roberts is an attorney in private practice in Oakland, California, focusing on employment and labor law. She teaches in the labor studies and gay/lesbian studies departments at San Francisco Community College. Ms. Roberts is a contributor to "Recognizing Lesbian and Gay Families: Strategies for Extending Employment Benefits," published by the National Center for Lesbian Rights (a new edition was released in the fall of 1992) and the associate editor of "Sexual Orientation and the Law" (1985). She received her B.A. from Brooklyn College, CUNY, in 1967, and her J.D. from Boalt Hall School of Law, University of California at Berkeley, in 1970.

Pamela Roby is professor of sociology and graduate director at the University of California at Santa Cruz. She has authored *Women in the Workplace,* coauthored *The Future of Inequality* with S. M. Miller, and edited *Child Care—Who Cares? Foreign and Domestic Infant and Early Childhood Development Policies* and *The Poverty Establishment,* as well as having published extensively on education, prostitution laws, and income policies. She is past president of Sociologists for Women in Society and past chair of the American

Sociological Association's Section on Sex and Gender. She facilitates leadership development workshops for unions, community organizations, and student coalitions.

Jean Ross is currently the principal consultant to the Assembly Revenue and Taxation Committee of the California Legislature. She formerly served as the assistant research director of the Service Employees' International Union where she coordinated the union's pay equity research. Ms. Ross represented SEIU on the board of the National Committee on Pay Equity from 1985 through 1989 and chaired the committee's Research and Collective Bargaining Task Forces. She currently chairs the Human Rights Committee of the Human Rights and Fair Housing Commission of the city and county of Sacramento. She holds a master's degree in city and regional planning from the University of California, Berkeley.

Ronnie J. Steinberg is associate professor of sociology at Temple University. Her research has focused on discrimination in the labor market (particularly on pay equity), on barriers to career advancement, and on nontraditional job training. Dr. Steinberg is the author of *Wages and Hours: Labor and Reform in Twentieth Century America* and the editor, with Sharon Harlan, of *Equal Employment Policy for Women* and *Job Training for Women: The Promise and Limits of Public Policies.* She edits the book series "Women in the Political Economy" for Temple University Press. She is researching the design of gender-neutral compensation systems and the politics through which feminist reforms are contained.

Lynet Uttal is a Ph.D. candidate in sociology at the University of California, Santa Cruz. Her dissertation focuses on the social and economic relationship between employed mothers and child care providers. She examines how employed mothers shift parenting responsibilities to others and how these relationships, which frequently cross racial/ethnic and class boundaries, are negotiated. In 1983, she learned firsthand about unions when, as a union member, she filed a grievance.

Carolyn York is a labor economist in the research department of the American Federation of State, County and Municipal Employees in Washington, D.C., where she specializes in employee benefits, work and family issues, and pay equity. She recently published "The Labor Movement's Role in Parental Leave and Child Care," in *Parental Leave and Child Care: Setting a Research and Policy Agenda* (1991) and was a contributing author to *Bargaining for Pay Equity: A Strategy Manual* (1990). Ms. York holds a master of arts degree from Cornell University.

Index

Blue Cross/Blue Shield of South Carolina, 249
Blum, Linda, 4, 32, 33, 34n, 37
BNA. *See* Bureau of National Affairs
BNA Directory, 379
Board of Control of Labor Standards for Army
  Clothing, 213
Bok, Derek, 324, 325, 326, 329
Bond, James T., 130
Boraston, Ian, 365
Borchardt, Janis, 352
Boris, Eileen, 15, 154, 205, 226–27, 246, 260–
  62, 265, 268, 269, 428; trade unions and
  homework, 207–25
Boston City Council, 324
Brandeis, Elizabeth, 149
Brandt, Barbara, 15
Breitenbeck, Joseph T., 102
Brenner, Johanna, 34n
British Columbia: unions in, 40
British Columbia Federation of Labour: and
  narrowing gender wage gap, 40
Brody, David, 5
Bronfenbrenner, Kate, 10, 12, 244
Brown, Clair, 17
Brown, Clayola, 392
Brown, Jerry: and California farm workers, 344
Brown, Michael K., 189
building trades: discriminatory practices within,
  72
Bullock, David, 169
Bumpass, Larry L., 235
Bunch, Charlotte, 398
Bureau of Factory of Inspection, 211
Bureau of Labor Statistics, 63, 85, 94, 164, 165,
  175, 184, 246, 247, 316, 365
Bureau of National Affairs, 15, 152, 325, 326,
  327, 331, 333, 389. *See also Daily Labor
  Report*
Bush, George, 71, 152
Bush administration: and free trade agreement,
  267
Business Link, 154
Business Week, 13
Busman, Gloria, 280, 337, 428
Byrne, Marilyn, 322, 330, 331, 332

California farm workers: right to secret ballot, 344
California Western States Life Insurance
  Company, 251
"Campaign for Justice," 220
Canada, 267; The Newspaper Guild in, 64; pay
  equity movement in, 56; wage solidarity
  within, 28
Canadian Congress of Labour, 387, 391
Canadian Ministry of Labour, 154
Canadian Union of Public Employees: and
  "equal base rates," 40

capitalism, 46, 47
career development programs, 31, 50, 67, 68; in
  unions, 31, 50
career women: needs of, 4, 8. *See also* working
  women
Carlough family: and inherited union presidency,
  382
carpenters: percentage of women, 70
Carr, Irene, 133, 134, 135, 144
Carr, Shirley, 387, 388
Carter administration, 150
Cassei, Nedda, 379
Castells, Manuel, 177
Catalyst, 152
Cathcart, David A., 102
Catholic church, 398
CCL. *See* Canadian Congress of Labour
Census Bureau. *See* U.S. Bureau of the Census
central labor councils (AFL-CIO), 380
Chaison, Gary N., 384, 385
Chamot, Dennis, 206, 247, 268, 429
*Changing Situation of Workers and Their Unions,
  The,* 254, 420
Chavez, Cesar, 382
Chernow, Herneen, 354–55
Chicago Tribune, 323, 324
childbearing: timing of, 145
child care, 5, 8, 15, 48, 92, 113, 116, 119, 125,
  129, 131–37, 142–46, 155–56, 164, 193,
  262, 266; affordable, 164; and dependent care,
  118, 269; enacting federal laws for, 143; and
  homeworkers, 235–37, 242, 262, 266, 269;
  labor program for, 120, 121, 124, 131, 398;
  public support for, 115; tackling cost of, 143;
  worker tax breaks for, 77
child labor, 211, 227, 231
child labor laws, 116
Children's Lobby Day, 147
Children's Place, 134
Chinatown (New York), 281–84, 286, 291–93,
  342, 387; garment workers' day care center
  campaign in, 283, 288, 290; 1982 strike in,
  282, 283, 291–94; organizing immigrant
  women in, 281, 283–84, 286, 289–93, 342;
  wildcat strikes in, 293
Chinatown (San Francisco), 295, 298
Chinese Chorus of the ILGWU, 294
Chinese Committee of the CLUW, 294
Chodorow, Nancy, 6
Christensen, Kathleen, 14, 17, 205, 221, 246,
  247, 248, 250, 251, 252, 263, 264, 265,
  270, 271, 429
Chrysler: family benefits program within, 152
Cigar Makers' International Union, 209–10
CIO, 5, 280
Civil Rights Act, 47, 65, 74, 95, 102, 103,
  155